Off the Beaten Track

This collection of texts (originally published in German under the title *Holzwege*) is Heidegger's first post-war book and contains some of the major expositions of his later philosophy. Of particular note are "The Origin of the Work of Art," perhaps the most discussed of all of Heidegger's essays, and "Nietzsche's Word: 'God Is Dead,'" which sums up a decade of Nietzsche research. Although translations of the essays have appeared individually in a variety of places, this is the first English translation to bring them all together as Heidegger intended. The text is taken from the last edition of the work, which contains the author's final corrections together with important marginal annotations that provide considerable insight into the development of his thought. This fresh and accurate new translation will be an invaluable resource for all students of Heidegger, whether they work in philosophy, literary theory, religious studies, or intellectual history.

Julian Young is Honorary Research Associate at the University of Auckland. His publications include *Nietzsche's Philosophy of Art* (1992), *Heidegger, Philosophy, Nazism* (1997), *Heidegger's Philosophy of Art* (2001), and *Heidegger's Later Philosophy* (2002).

Kenneth Haynes is Assistant Professor of Classical Studies at Boston University, and writes on the classical tradition in modern European literature and philosophy. He is the author of a translation of Hamann's philosophical writings (forthcoming).

MARTIN HEIDEGGER

Off the Beaten Track

EDITED AND
TRANSLATED BY
JULIAN YOUNG
AND KENNETH HAYNES

PUBLISHED BY THE PRESS SYNDICATE OF THE UNIVERSITY OF CAMBRIDGE
The Pitt Building, Trumpington Street, Cambridge, United Kingdom

CAMBRIDGE UNIVERSITY PRESS
The Edinburgh Building, Cambridge CB2 2RU, UK
40 West 20th Street, New York, NY 10011-4211, USA
477 Williamstown Road, Port Melbourne, VIC 3207, Australia
Ruiz de Alarcón 13, 28014 Madrid, Spain
Dock House, The Waterfront, Cape Town 8001, South Africa

http://www.cambridge.org

The publication of this translation has benefited from the assistance of INTER NATIONES, Bonn.

Originally published as *Holzwege* by Vittorio Klostermann GmbH, Frankfurt am Main. © 1950.

First published 2002

Printed in the United Kingdom at the University Press, Cambridge

Typeface Janson 10/13 pt   *System* LaTeX 2ε   [TB]

A catalogue record for this book is available from the British Library

Library of Congress cataloguing in publication data

Heidegger, Martin, 1889–1976.
[Holzwege. English]
Off the beaten track/Martin Heidegger; edited and translated by Julian Young and Kenneth Haynes.
p. cm.
ISBN 0 521 80114 1 (hardback) ISBN 0 521 80507 4 (paperback)
1. Philosophy. I. Young, Julian. II. Haynes, Kenneth. III. Title.
B3279.H47 E5 2002
193–dc21

20020173887 CIP

ISBN 0 521 80114 1 hardback
ISBN 0 521 80507 4 paperback

"Wood" is an old name for forest. In the wood there are paths, mostly overgrown, that come to an abrupt stop where the wood is untrodden.

They are called *Holzwege.*

Each goes its separate way, though within the same forest. It often appears as if one is identical to another. But it only appears so.

Woodcutters and forest keepers know these paths. They know what it means to be on a *Holzweg.*

Contents

Translators' preface

Holzwege – here translated as *Off the Beaten Track* – is the title Heidegger gave to this collection of six essays and lectures which was first published in 1950. The essays and lectures themselves span a little more than a decade, from 1935 to 1946. The text used for this translation is taken from the seventh edition of *Holzwege*, which is itself based on volume V of the *Gesamtausgabe*. The notes at the foot of the page are Heidegger's own, generally marginalia or other notes in his working copies of the texts (see the "Editor's epilogue," translated below, for further bibliographical information). Where these notes refer to works that have been translated into English, references to the original texts have been replaced by references to these translations. Where no such translations exist, references to the German texts remain. The notes at the end of the volume are the translators' and are limited to identifying the sources of quotations and otherwise providing a minimum of information that seems helpful to readers of Heidegger in English.

In entitling his work *Holzwege*, literally, "Timber Tracks," or "Forest Paths," Heidegger chose a term that carefully balances positive and negative implications. On the one hand, a *Holzweg* is a timber track that leads to a clearing in the forest where timber is cut. On the other, it is a track that used to lead to such a place but is now overgrown and leads nowhere. Hence, in a popular German idiom, to be "on a *Holzweg*" is to be on the wrong track or in a cul-de-sac. A translation of Heidegger's note on the title appears at the beginning of the book, where it is found in most German editions. It is in order to capture something of Heidegger's dual meaning that we have adopted the title "Off the Beaten Track."

Each translator bears primary responsibility for three of the six essays: Julian Young translated "The Origin of the Work of Art," "The Age of the World Picture," and "Anaximander's Saying"; Kenneth Haynes translated the others. Each read the other's work closely, and translated in awareness of the other; nonetheless, in our collaboration we did not aim to eliminate all differences in style.

We have translated "*Sein*" as "being," preferring a lower-case "b" to a capital. This choice has not been made in order to take a stand in the controversy over the possible religious or quasi-religious implications of Heidegger's vocabulary. In fact, both translators agree with Julian Young's description of a fundamental ambiguity in Heidegger's use of the word *Sein*, which refers sometimes to presence, the ground of beings, the fundamental horizon of disclosure; and sometimes to this disclosure along with what is not disclosed or made intelligible (*Heidegger's Later Philosophy*, Cambridge University Press, 2002, chapter 1). That is, like the word "day," which may refer either to the period of daylight or to the period of both daylight and night, Heidegger's use of *Sein* must be read in context. However, it would have been unduly intrusive to translate sometimes with a capital "B" and sometimes without. Since some passages require the lower-case "b," we have translated *Sein* in this way throughout.

We have not generally attempted to reproduce Heidegger's word-play, since such attempts usually require very unidiomatic writing, which would give a false impression of the way Heidegger writes, in addition to obscuring his sense. However, rather than lose the word-play, we have often included the key German words in square brackets. The German has been included at other instances, when it seemed important to alert the reader to recurrences of crucial German words, when the German was particularly rich in meaning, or on the few occasions when we required some latitude in the English translation. The glossary has been kept short since the German has often been included in the main body of the translation; it is mainly concerned with words translated in several ways.

The Origin of the Work of Art[a]

Origin[b] means here that from where and through which a thing is what it is and how it is. That which something is, as it is, we call its nature [*Wesen*]. The origin of something is the source of its nature. The question of the origin of the artwork asks about the source of its nature. According to the usual view, the work arises out of and through the activity of the artist. But through and from what is the artist that[c] which he is? Through the work; for the German proverb "the work praises the master" means that the work first lets the artist emerge as a master of art. The artist is the origin of the work. The work is the origin of the artist. Neither is without the other. Nonetheless neither is the sole support of the other. Artist and work *are* each, in themselves and in their reciprocal relation, on account of a third thing, which is prior to both; on account, that is, of that from which both artist and artwork take their names, on account of art.

As the artist is the origin of the work in a necessarily different way from the way the work is the origin of the artist, so it is in yet another way, quite certainly, that art is the origin of both artist and work. But can, then, art really be an origin? Where and how does art exist? Art – that is just a word

[a] Reclam edition, 1960. The project [*Versuch*] (1935–37) inadequate on account of the inappropriate use of the name "truth" for the still-withheld clearing and the cleared. See "Hegel and the Greeks" in *Pathmarks*, ed. W. McNeill (Cambridge: Cambridge University Press, 1998), pp. 332ff.; "The End of Philosophy and the Task of Thinking" in *Time and Being*, trans. J. Stambaugh (New York: Harper and Row, 1972), p. 70 (footnote). – *Art* the use of the bringing-forth of the clearing of the self-concealing in the *Ereignis* – the hidden given form.
Bringing-forth and forming; see "*Sprache und Heimat*" in *Denkerfahrungen 1910–1976* (Frankfurt am Main: Klostermann, 1983), pp. 87–112.

[b] Reclam edition, 1960. Capable of being misunderstood this talk of "origin."

[c] Reclam edition, 1960: he who he is.

to which nothing real any longer corresponds. It may serve as a collective notion under which we bring what alone of art is real: works and artists. Even if the word art is to signify more than a collective notion, what is meant by the word could only be based on the reality of works and artists. Or are matters the other way round? Do work and artist exist only insofar[a] as art exists, exists, indeed, as their origin?

Whatever we decide, the question of the origin of the artwork turns into the question of the nature of art. But since it must remain open whether and how there is art at all, we will attempt to discover the nature of art where there is no doubt that art genuinely prevails. Art presences in the art-work [*Kunst-werk*]. But what and how is a work of art?

What art is we should be able to gather from the work. What the work is we can only find out from the nature of art. It is easy to see that we are moving in a circle. The usual understanding demands that this circle be avoided as an offense against logic. It is said that what art is may be gathered from a comparative study of available artworks. But how can we be certain that such a study is really based on artworks unless we know beforehand what art is? Yet the nature of art can as little be derived from higher concepts as from a collection of characteristics of existing artworks. For such a derivation, too, already has in view just those determinations which are sufficient to ensure that what we are offering as works of art are what we already take to be such. The collecting of characteristics from what exists, however, and the derivation from fundamental principles are impossible in exactly the same way and, where practiced, are a self-delusion.

So we must move in a circle. This is neither *ad hoc* nor deficient. To enter upon this path is the strength, and to remain on it the feast of thought – assuming that thinking is a craft. Not only is the main step from work to art, like the step from art to work, a circle, but every individual step that we attempt circles within this circle.

In order to discover the nature of art that really holds sway in the work let us approach the actual work and ask it what and how it is.

Everyone is familiar with artworks. One finds works of architecture and sculpture erected in public places, in churches, and in private homes. Artworks from the most diverse ages and peoples are housed in collections and exhibitions. If we regard works in their pristine reality and do not deceive ourselves, the following becomes evident: works are as naturally present as things. The picture hangs on the wall like a hunting weapon or

[a] Reclam edition, 1960. *It gives* art [***Es die Kunst gibt***].

a hat. A painting – for example van Gogh's portrayal of a pair of peasant shoes – travels from one exhibition to another. Works are shipped like coal from the Ruhr or logs from the Black Forest. During the war Hölderlin's hymns were packed in the soldier's knapsack along with cleaning equipment. Beethoven's quartets lie in the publisher's storeroom like potatoes in a cellar.

Every work has this thingly character. What would they be without it? But perhaps we find this very crude and external approach to the work offensive. It may be the conception of the artwork with which the freight-handler or the museum charlady operates, but we are required to take the works as they are encountered by those who experience and enjoy them. Yet even this much-vaunted "aesthetic experience" cannot evade the thingliness of the artwork. The stony is in the work of architecture, the wooden in the woodcarving, the colored in the painting, the vocal in the linguistic work, the sounding in the work of music. The thingly is so salient in the artwork that we ought rather to say the opposite: the architectural work is in the stone, the woodcarving in the wood, the painting in the color, the linguistic work in the sound, the work of music in the note. "Obviously," it will be replied. What, however, is this obvious thingliness in the artwork?

Given that the artwork is something over and above its thingliness, this inquiry will probably be found unnecessary and disconcerting. This something else in the work constitutes its artistic nature. The artwork is indeed a thing that is made, but it says something other than the mere thing itself is, ἄλλο ἀγορεύει. The work makes publicly known something other than itself, it manifests something other: it is an allegory. In the artwork something other is brought into conjunction with the thing that is made. The Greek for "to bring into conjunction with" is συμβάλλειν. The work is a symbol.

Allegory and symbol provide the conceptual framework from within whose perspective the artwork has long been characterized. Yet this one element that makes another manifest is the thingly element in the artwork. It seems almost as though the thingliness in the artwork is the substructure into and upon which the other, authentic, element is built. And is it not this thingly element which is actually produced by the artist's craft?

We wish to hit upon the immediate and complete reality of the artwork, for only then will we discover the real art within it. So what we must do, first of all, is to bring the thingliness of the work into view. For this we need to know, with sufficient clarity, what a thing is. Only then will we be able to say whether or not an artwork is a thing – albeit a thing to which something else adheres. Only then will we be able to decide whether the work is something fundamentally different and not a thing at all.

THE THING AND THE WORK

What, in truth, is a thing insofar as it is a thing? When we ask this question we wish to know the thing-being (the thingliness) of the thing. The point is to learn the thingliness of the thing. To this end we must become acquainted with the sphere within which are to be found all those beings which we have long called things.

The stone on the path is a thing, as is the clod of earth in the field. The jug is a thing, and the well beside the path. But what should we say about the milk in the jug and the water in the well? These, too, are things, if the cloud in the sky and the thistle in the field, if the leaf on the autumn wind and the hawk over the wood are properly called things. All these must indeed be called things, even though we also apply the term to that which, unlike the above, fails to show itself, fails to appear. One such thing which does not, itself, appear – a "thing in itself" in other words – is, according to Kant, the world as a totality. Another such example is God himself. Things in themselves and things that appear, every being that in any way exists, count, in the language of philosophy, as "things."

These days, airplanes and radios belong among the things that are closest to us. When, however, we refer to "last things," we think of something quite different. Death and judgment, these are the last things. In general, "thing" applies to anything that is not simply nothing. In this signification, the artwork counts as a thing, assuming it to be some kind of a being. Yet this conception of the thing, in the first instance at least, does not help us in our project of distinguishing between beings which have the being of things and beings which have the being of works. And besides, we hesitate to repeat the designation of God as a "thing." We are similarly reluctant to take the farmer in the field, the stoker before the boiler, the teacher in the school to be a "thing." A human being is not a thing. True, we say of a young girl who has a task to perform that is beyond her that she is "too young a thing." But this is only because, in a certain sense, we find human being to be missing here and think we have to do, rather, with what constitutes the thingliness of the thing. We are reluctant to call even the deer in the forest clearing, the beetle in the grass, or the blade of grass "things." Rather, the hammer, the shoe, the ax, and the clock are things. Even they, however, are not mere things. Only the stone, the clod of earth, or a piece of wood count as that: what is lifeless in nature and in human usage. It is the things of nature and usage that are normally called things.

We thus see ourselves returned from the broadest domain in which everything is a thing (thing = *res* = *ens* = a being) – including even the "first and last things" – to the narrow region of the mere thing. "Mere," here, means, first of all, the pure thing which is simply a thing and nothing more. But then it also means "nothing but a thing," in an almost disparaging sense. It is the mere thing – a category which excludes even the things that we use – which counts as the actual thing. In what, now, does the thingliness of things such as this consist? It is in reference to these that it must be possible to determine the thingliness of the thing. Such a determination puts us in a position to characterize thingliness as such. Thus equipped, we will be able to indicate that almost tangible reality of the work in which something other inheres.

Now it is a well-known fact that, since antiquity, as soon as the question was raised as to what beings as such are, it was the thing in its thingness which thrust itself forward as the paradigmatic being. It follows that we are bound to encounter the delineation of the thingness of the thing already present in the traditional interpretation of the being. Thus all we need to do, in order to be relieved of the tedious effort of making our own inquiry into the thingliness of the thing, is to grasp explicitly this traditional knowledge of the thing. So commonplace, in a way, are the answers to the question of what a thing is that one can no longer sense anything worthy of questioning lying behind them.

The interpretations of the thingness of the thing which predominate in the history of Western thought have long been self-evident and are now in everyday use. They may be reduced to three.

A mere thing is, to take an example, this block of granite. It is hard, heavy, extended, massive, unformed, rough, colored, partly dull, partly shiny. We can notice all these features in the stone. We take note of its characteristics. Yet such characteristics represent something proper to the stone. They are its properties. The thing has them. The thing? What are we thinking of if we now call the thing to mind? Obviously the thing is not merely a collection of characteristics, and neither is it the aggregate of those properties through which the collection arises. The thing, as everyone thinks he knows, is that around which the properties have gathered. One speaks, then, of the core of the thing. The Greeks, we are told, called it τὸ ὑποκείμενον. This core of the thing was its ground and was always there. But the characteristics are called τὰ συμβεβηκότα: that which always appears and comes forth along with the core.

These designations are by no means arbitrary. Within them speaks something which lies beyond the scope of this essay: the Greeks' fundamental experience of the being of beings in the sense of presence. It is through these determinations, however, that the interpretation of the thingness of the thing is grounded that will henceforth become standard and the Western interpretation of the being of beings established. The process begins with the appropriation of the Greek words by Roman-Latin thought; ὑποκείμενον becomes *subiectum*, ὑπόστασις *substantia*, and συμβεβηκός *accidens*. This translation of Greek names into Latin is by no means without consequences – as, even now, it is still held to be. Rather, what is concealed within the apparently literal, and hence faithful, translation is a *trans*lation [***Über****setzen*] of Greek experience into a different mode of thinking. *Roman thinking takes over the Greek words without the corresponding and equiprimordial experience of what they say, without the Greek word.* The rootlessness of Western thinking begins with this translation.

It is generally held that the definition of the thingness of the thing in terms of substance and accidents appears to capture our natural view of things. No wonder, then, that the way we comport ourselves to things – the way we address ourselves to, and talk about, them – has accommodated itself to this commonplace outlook on things. The simple declarative sentence consists of a subject – the Latin translation, and that means transformation, of ὑποκείμενον – and predicate, which expresses the thing's characteristics. Who would dare to threaten this simple and fundamental relationship between thing and sentence, between the structure of the sentence and the structure of the thing? Nonetheless, we must ask: is the structure of the simple declarative sentence (the nexus of subject and predicate) the mirror image of the structure of the thing (the union of substance and accidents)? Or is it merely that, so represented, the structure of the thing is a projection of the structure of the sentence?

What could be more obvious than that man transposes the way he comprehends things in statements into the structure of the thing itself? Yet this view, apparently critical but in reality overly hasty, has first to explain how the transposition of the sentence structure into the thing could be possible without the thing first becoming visible. The issue as to what comes first and provides the standard, the structure of the sentence or that of the thing, remains, to this day, undecided. It may even be doubted whether, in this form, it is capable of a decision.

In fact, it is the case neither that sentential structure provides the standard for projecting the structure of the thing nor that the latter is simply mirrored in the former. The structure of both sentence and thing derive, in their natures and the possibility of their mutual relatedness, from a common and more primordial source. In any case, this first of our interpretations of the thingness of the thing – thing as bearer of characteristics – is, in spite of its currency, not as natural as it seems. What presents itself to us as natural, one may suspect, is merely the familiarity of a long-established habit which has forgotten the unfamiliarity from which it arose. And yet this unfamiliar source once struck man as strange and caused him to think and wonder.

The reliance on the customary interpretation of the thing is only apparently well founded. Moreover, this conception of the thing (the bearer of characteristics) is applied not only to the mere, the actual, thing but to any being whatever. It can never help us, therefore, to distinguish beings which are things from those which are not. But prior to all reflection, to be attentively present in the domain of things tells us that this concept of the thing is inadequate to its thingliness, its self-sustaining and self-containing nature. From time to time one has the feeling that violence has long been done to the thingliness of the thing and that thinking has had something to do with it. Instead of taking the trouble to make thinking more thoughtful, this has led to the rejection of thinking. But when it comes to a definition of the thing, what is the use of a feeling, no matter how certain, if the word belongs to thought alone? Yet perhaps what, here and in similar cases, we call feeling or mood is more rational – more perceptive, that is – than we think; more rational, because more open to being than that "reason" which, having meanwhile become *ratio*, is misdescribed as rational. The furtive craving for the ir-rational – that abortive offspring of a rationality that has not been thought through – renders a strange service. To be sure, the familiar concept of the thing fits every thing. But it does not comprehend the essence of the thing; rather, it attacks it.

Can such an assault be avoided? How? Only if we grant to the thing, so to speak, a free field in which to display its thingness quite directly. Everything that, by way of conception and statement, might interpose itself between us and the thing must, first of all, be set aside. Only then do we allow ourselves the undistorted presence of the thing. But this allowing ourselves an immediate encounter with the thing is something we do not need either to demand or to arrange. It happens slowly. In what the senses of sight, hearing, and touch bring to us, in the sensations of color, sound, roughness, and hardness, things move us bodily, in a quite literal sense. The thing is the αἰσθητόν, that which, in the senses belonging to sensibility, is perceptible by means of sensations. Hence, the concept later became commonplace according to which the thing is nothing but the unity of a sensory manifold. Whether this unity is conceived as sum, totality, or as form changes nothing with respect to the standard-setting character of this concept of the thing.

Now this interpretation of the thingness of the thing is every bit as correct and verifiable as its predecessor. This is already sufficient to cast doubt on its truth. If we think through that for which we are searching, the thingness of the thing, then this concept of the thing again leaves us at a loss. In immediate perception, we never really perceive a throng of sensations, e.g. tones and noises. Rather, we hear the storm whistling in the chimney, the three-motored plane, the Mercedes which is immediately different from the Adler.[1] Much closer to us than any sensation are the things themselves. In the house we hear the door slam – never acoustic sensations or mere noises. To hear a bare sound we must listen away from the things, direct our ears from them, listen abstractly.

The concept of the thing under consideration represents, not so much an assault on the thing as an extravagant attempt to bring the thing to us in the greatest possible immediacy. But this can never be achieved as long as we take what is received by the senses to constitute its thingness. Whereas the first interpretation of the thing holds it, as it were, too far away from the body, the second brings it too close. In both interpretations the thing disappears. We must, therefore, avoid the exaggerations of both. The thing must be allowed to remain unmolested in its resting-within-itself itself. It must be accepted in its own steadfastness. This seems to be what the third interpretation does, an interpretation which is just as old as the first two.

That which gives to things their constancy and pith but is also, at the same time, the source of their mode of sensory pressure – color, sound, hardness, massiveness – is the materiality of the thing. In this definition of the thing as matter (ὕλη), form (μορφή) is posited at the same time. The permanence of a thing, its constancy, consists in matter remaining together with form. The thing is formed matter. This interpretation of the thing invokes the immediate sight with which the thing concerns us through its appearance (εἶδος). With this synthesis of matter and form we have finally found the concept of the thing which equally well fits the things of nature and the things of use.

This concept of the thing puts us in a position to answer the question of the thingly in the artwork. What is thingly in the work is obviously the matter of which it consists. The matter is the substructure and the field for artistic formation. But we could have proposed this plausible and well-known conclusion at the very beginning. Why did we make the detour through the other concepts of the thing? Because we also mistrust this concept of the thing, the representation of the thing as formed matter.

But is it not precisely this pair of concepts, matter and form, that are generally employed in the domain in which we are supposed to be moving? Of course. The distinction between matter and form is *the conceptual scheme deployed in the greatest variety of ways by all art theory and aesthetics*. This indisputable fact, however, proves neither that the matter–form distinction is adequately grounded, nor that it belongs, originally, to the sphere of art and the artwork. Moreover, the range of application of this conceptual pairing has long extended far beyond the field of aesthetics. Form and content are the commonplace concepts under which anything and everything can be subsumed. If one correlates form with the rational and matter with the ir-rational, if, moreover, one takes the rational to be the logical and the irrational the illogical, and if, finally, one couples the conceptual duality between form and matter into the subject–object relation, then one has at one's disposal a conceptual mechanism that nothing can resist.

If this is how it is, however, with the matter–form distinction, how can it help us comprehend the special region of the mere thing as distinct from other beings? But perhaps this characterization in terms of matter and form can regain its power of definition if we just reverse the process of the broadening and emptying of these concepts. Yet this, of course, presupposes that we know in which region of beings they exercise their real power of definition. That this might be the region of mere things is, so far, merely an assumption. Taking into account the extensive use of this conceptual framework in aesthetics might rather suggest that matter and form are determinations which have their origin in the nature of the artwork and have been transported from there back to the thing. Where does the origin of the matter–form schema have its origin; in the thingness of the thing or in the work-character of the artwork?

The granite block, resting in itself, is something material possessing a definite, if unstructured, form. "Form," here, means the distribution and arrangement of material parts in a spatial location which results in a particular contour, that of a block. But the jug, the ax, the shoes are also matter occurring in a form. Here, form as contour is not the result of a distribution of matter. On the contrary, the form determines the arrangement of the matter. And not just that; the form prescribes, in each case, the kind and selection of the matter – impermeability for the jug, adequate hardness for the ax, toughness combined with flexibility for the shoes. Moreover, the intermingling of form and matter that is operative in these cases is controlled beforehand by the purposes jug, ax, and shoes are to serve. Such serviceability is never assigned and added on afterwards to beings of this kind. But neither is it something which, as an end, hovers above them.

Serviceability is the basic trait from out of which these kinds of beings look at us – that is, flash at us and thereby presence and so be the beings they are. Both the design and the choice of material predetermined by that design – and, therefore, the dominance of the matter–form structure – are grounded in such serviceability. A being that falls under serviceability is always the product of a process of making. It is made as a piece of equipment for something. Accordingly, matter and form are determinations of beings which find their true home in the essential nature of equipment. This name designates what is manufactured expressly for use and usage. Matter and form are in no way original determinations belonging to the thingness of the mere thing.

A piece of equipment, for example, the shoe-equipment, when finished, rests in itself like the mere thing. Unlike the granite block, however, it lacks the character of having taken shape by itself. On the other hand, it displays an affinity with the artwork in that it is something brought forth by the human hand. The artwork, however, through its self-sufficient presence, resembles, rather, the mere thing which has taken shape by itself and is never forced into being. Nonetheless, we do not count such works as mere things. The nearest and authentic things are always the things of use that are all around us. So the piece of equipment is half thing since it is characterized by thingliness. Yet it is more, since, at the same time, it is half artwork. On the other hand, it is less, since it lacks the self-sufficiency of the artwork. Equipment occupies a curious position intermediate between thing and work – if we may be permitted such a calculated ordering.

The matter–form structure, however, by which the being of a piece of equipment is first determined, readily presents itself as the immediately comprehensible constitution of every being because, here, productive humanity is itself involved in the way in which a piece of equipment comes into being.[a] Because equipment occupies an intermediate position between mere thing and work, the suggestion arises of using equipment (the matter–form structure) as the key to understanding non-equipmental beings – things and works, and, ultimately, every kind of being.

[a] Reclam edition, 1960. (To its) into its presence.

The inclination to take the matter–form structure to be *the* constitution of every being receives, however, particular encouragement from the fact that, on the basis of religious – biblical – faith, the totality of beings is represented, in advance, as something created. And here, that means "made." The philosophy of this faith can, of course, assure us that God's creative work is to be thought of as different from the action of a craftsman. But when, at the same time or even beforehand, in accordance with a predetermination, taken on faith, of Thomistic philosophy for biblical interpretation, the *ens creatum* is thought out of the unity of *materia* and *forma*, then faith is interpreted by a philosophy whose truth is based on an unconcealment of beings that is of another kind than the world believed in by faith.[a]

Now it is indeed possible that the idea of creation which is grounded in faith can lose its power to guide our knowledge of beings as a whole. Yet, once in place, the theological interpretation of everything that is, the viewing of the world in terms of matter and form that was borrowed from an alien philosophy, can remain in force. This is what happened in the transition from the Middle Ages to the modern period. The metaphysics of modernity is based, too, on the matter–form structure, a structure devised in the Middle Ages but which itself, in its own words, merely recalls the buried essence of εἶδος and ὕλη. Thus the interpretation of the thing in terms of matter and form, whether it remains medieval or has become Kantian-transcendental, has become commonplace and self-evident. But for that reason, no less than the other interpretations of the thingness of the thing we have discussed, it represents an assault on the thing-being of the thing.

The situation reveals itself as soon as we call actual things "mere things." The "mere," after all, means the removal of the character of serviceability and of being made. The mere thing is a kind of equipment that has been denuded of its equipmental being. Its thing-being consists in what is then left over. But the kind of being possessed by this remainder is not actually determined. It remains questionable whether the process of stripping away everything equipmental will ever disclose the thingness of the thing. Thus the third interpretation of the thing, that which bases itself on the matter–form structure, also turns out to be an assault on the thing.

The three modes of defining the thing we have here discussed conceive it as, respectively, the bearer of traits, the unity of a sensory manifold, and as

[a] First edition, 1950. (1) The biblical faith in creation; (2) the causal-ontic explanation of Thomism; (3) the original, Aristotelian interpretation of the ὄν.

formed matter. In the course of the history of the truth about beings these interpretations have also combined with each other – a matter we may now pass over. This combination has intensified their tendency to expand in such a way as to apply in the same way to thing, equipment, and work. In this way they generate the mode of thinking according to which we think, not about thing, equipment, and work, in particular, but universally, about all beings. This long-familiar mode of thinking preconceives all our immediate experience of beings. The preconception shackles reflection on the being of particular beings. Thus it happens that the prevailing concepts of the thing block the way to the thingness of the thing, the equipmentality of equipment, and all the more to the workly character of the work.

This is the reason it is necessary to know about these concepts of the thing, in order, thereby, to pay heed to their limitless presumption as well as their semblance of self-evidence. This knowledge is all the more necessary when we venture the attempt to bring into view and to put into words the thingness of the thing, the equipmentality of equipment, and the workly character of the work. For this, however, just one condition is necessary: by keeping at a distance the preconceptions and assaults of the above modes of thinking, to allow, for example, the thing in its thing-being, to rest in itself. What could be easier than allowing a being to be just what it is? Or is it rather that this task brings us to what is the most difficult, particularly when such an intention – to allow a being to be as it is – is the opposite of that indifference which turns its back on beings in favour of an unexamined concept of being? We must return to the being and think about it itself in its being. At the same time, however, we must allow it to rest in its own nature.

This effort of thought seems to meet with its greatest resistance in attempting to define the thingness of the thing, for what else could be the reason for the failure of the above attempts? The inconspicuous thing withdraws itself from thought in the most stubborn of ways. Or is it rather that this self-refusal of the mere thing, this self-contained refusal to be pushed around, belongs precisely to the essential nature of the thing? Must not, then, this disconcerting and uncommunicative element in the essence of the thing become intimately familiar to a thinking which tries to think the thing? If so, we should not force our way into the thing's thingness.

The history of its interpretations outlined above, indicates beyond doubt that the thingness of the thing is particularly difficult and rarely capable of expression. This history coincides with the destiny in accordance with which Western thought has hitherto thought the being of beings. This, however, is not all we ascertain, for in this history we discover, at the same time, a clue. Is it mere chance that, in the interpretation of the thing, the interpretation which is carved out in terms of matter and form achieved a particular dominance? This definition of the thing is derived from an interpretation of the equipmentality of equipment. This being, the piece of equipment, is, in an especial way, close to human representation, since it achieves being through our own manufacture. This being, the piece of equipment, with whose being we are familiar, occupies a particular position intermediate between thing and work. Let us follow this clue and search, first of all, for the equipmentality of equipment. Perhaps we will learn from this something about the thingliness of the thing and the workly character of the work. We must, however, be careful to avoid turning thing and work into a subspecies of equipment. We will, on the other hand, ignore the possibility that, in the way that equipment is, historically essential distinctions are present.

But what is the path to the equipmentality of equipment? How are we to learn what equipment in truth is? Obviously the procedure we now need must keep itself apart from any attempt which carries within it the assault we have seen to be represented by the usual interpretations. The best guarantee of that is simply to describe a piece of equipment quite apart from any philosophical theory.

We will take as an example an everyday piece of equipment, a pair of peasant shoes. We do not need to exhibit actual examples of this sort of useful article in order to describe it. But since what concerns us here is direct description, it may be helpful to facilitate their visual realization. To this end, a pictorial presentation suffices. We will take a well-known painting by van Gogh, who painted such shoes several times. But is there a lot to be seen here? Everyone knows what shoes are like. If they are not wooden or bast shoes, there will be leather soles and uppers held together by stitching and nails. Equipment of this kind serves as footwear. Whether it is for work in the field or for dancing, material and form vary according to use.

Correct statements such as these only tell us what we already know: the equipmentality of equipment consists in its utility. But what about this utility itself? In understanding it do we already understand the equipmentality of equipment? In order for this to be so, must we not look out for the useful piece of equipment in its use? The peasant woman wears her shoes in the field. Only then do they become what they are. They are all the more genuinely so the less the peasant woman thinks of her shoes while she is working, or even looks at them, or is aware of them in any way at all. This is how the shoes actually serve. It must be in this process of usage that the equipmentality of the equipment actually confronts us.

But on the contrary, as long as we only imagine a pair of shoes in general, or merely look at the shoes as they stand there in the picture, empty and unused, we will never learn what the equipmental being of equipment in truth is. From van Gogh's painting we cannot even tell where these shoes are.[a] There is nothing surrounding this pair of peasant shoes to which and within which they could belong; only an undefined space. Not even clods of earth from the field or from the country path stick to them, which could at least point toward their use. A pair of peasant shoes and nothing more. And yet.

From out of the dark opening of the well-worn insides of the shoes the toil of the worker's tread stares forth. In the crudely solid heaviness of the shoes accumulates the tenacity of the slow trudge through the far-stretching and ever-uniform furrows of the field swept by a raw wind. On the leather lies the dampness and richness of the soil. Under the soles slides the loneliness of the field-path as evening falls. The shoes vibrate with the silent call of the earth, its silent gift of the ripening grain, its unexplained self-refusal in the wintry field. This equipment is pervaded by uncomplaining worry as to the certainty of bread, wordless joy at having once more withstood want, trembling before the impending birth, and shivering at the surrounding menace of death. This equipment belongs *to the earth* and finds protection in the *world* of the peasant woman. From out of this protected belonging the equipment itself rises to its resting-within-itself.

But perhaps it is only in the picture that we notice all this about the shoes. The peasant woman, by contrast, merely wears them. If only this simple wearing were that simple. Whenever in the late evening she takes off the shoes, in deep but healthy tiredness, and in the still dark dawn reaches for them once again, or passes them by on the holiday, she knows all this without observation or reflection. The equipmentality of equipment consists indeed in its usefulness. But this itself rests in the fullness of an essential being of the equipment. We call this reliability. In virtue of this reliability the peasant woman is admitted into the silent call of the earth; in virtue of the reliability of the equipment she is certain of her world. World and earth exist for her and those who share her mode of being only here[b] – in the equipment. We

[a] Reclam edition, 1960. Or to whom they belong.
[b] Reclam edition, 1960. "Exist ... here" = present.

say "only" but this is a mistake; for it is the reliability of the equipment which first gives the simple world its security and assures the earth the freedom of its steady pressure.

The equipmental being of the equipment, its reliability, keeps all things gathered within itself, each in its own manner and to its own extent. The usefulness of the equipment is, however, only the necessary consequence of reliability. The former vibrates in the latter and would be nothing without it. The individual piece of equipment becomes worn out and used up. But also, customary usage itself falls into disuse, becomes ground down and merely habitual. In this way equipmental being withers away, sinks to the level of mere equipment. Such dwindling of equipmental being is the disappearance of its reliability. Such dwindling, however, which gives things of use that boringly oppressive usualness, is only one more testament to the original nature of equipmental being. The worn-out usualness of the equipment then obtrudes as the sole kind of being that is (it seems) exclusively its own. Now nothing but sheer utility remains visible. It creates the appearance that the origin of equipment lies in a mere fabrication which gives form to some bit of matter. In fact, however, equipment acquires its equipmental being from a more distant source. Matter and form and the difference between them have a deeper origin.

The repose of equipment resting in itself consists in reliability. It is here that we first catch sight of what equipment, in truth, is. Yet we still know nothing of that for which we were originally looking: the thingness of the thing. And of that for which we are actually and solely looking – the workly character of the work in the sense of artwork – we know absolutely nothing.

Or have we now, rather, unexpectedly and, as it were, in passing, learnt something about the work-being of the work?

The equipmental being of equipment was discovered. But how? Not through the description and explanation of a pair of shoes actually present. Not through a report on the process of shoemaking. And not through the observation of the actual use of shoes as it occurs here and there. Rather, the equipmental being of equipment was only discovered by bringing ourselves before the van Gogh painting. It is this that spoke. In proximity to the work we were suddenly somewhere other than we are usually accustomed to be.

The artwork let us know what the shoes, in truth, are. To suppose that our description, as a subjective action, had first depicted everything thus and then projected into the painting would be the worst kind of self-delusion. If there is anything questionable here it is only this: that in the proximity of the work we have experienced too little, and what we have experienced has been described too crudely and hastily. Above all, however, the work did not serve, as might at first seem, merely to make it easier to visualize what a piece of equipment is. Rather, what comes to explicit appearance first and only through the work is the equipmental being of the equipment.

What is happening here? What is at work in the work? Van Gogh's painting is the disclosure of what the equipment, the pair of peasant shoes, in truth *is*. This being steps forward into the unconcealment of its being. The unconcealment of beings is what the Greeks called ἀλήθεια. We say "truth" and think little enough in using the word. In the work, when there is a disclosure of the being as what and how it is, there is a happening of truth at work.

In the work of art, the truth of the being has set itself to work. "Set" means here: to bring to stand. In the work, a being, a pair of peasant shoes, comes to stand in the light of its being. The being of the being comes into the constancy of its shining.

The essential nature of art would then be this: the setting-itself-to-work of the truth of beings. Yet until now art has had to do with the beautiful and with beauty – not with truth. Those arts which bring such works forth are called the beautiful or fine arts [*die schönen Künste*] in contrast to the crafts or industrial arts [*den Handwerklichen Künsten*] which manufacture equipment. In the fine arts, the art is not itself beautiful, but is, rather, called so because it brings forth the beautiful. Truth, by contrast, belongs to logic. But beauty is the preserve of aesthetics.

Yet perhaps the statement that art is truth's setting-itself-to-work seeks to revive the view, now fortunately abandoned, that art is the imitation and depiction of reality? The repetition of what is present at hand requires, to be sure, correspondence to beings, appropriateness to them: the Middle Ages spoke of *adaequatio*, Aristotle already spoke of ὁμοίωσις. Correspondence to beings has long been taken to be the essence of truth. But do we then mean that this painting by van Gogh depicts a pair of peasant shoes that are actually present and count, therefore, as a work because it does so successfully? Do we think that the painting takes a likeness from the real and transposes it into an artistic . . . production? By no means.

The work, then, is not concerned with the reproduction of a particular being that has at some time been actually present. Rather, it is concerned to reproduce the general essence of things. But where, then, is this general essence and how should it be for the artwork to correspond to or agree with it? With what essence of what thing should the Greek temple agree? Could anyone maintain the impossible position that the Idea of Temple is represented in the temple? And yet in this work, if it is a work, truth sets itself to work. Or take Hölderlin's hymn "The Rhine." What is given beforehand to the poet, and how is it given, so that it can be given once again in the poem? It may be that in the case of this hymn and similar poems, the idea of a copy-relation between a beautiful reality and the artwork clearly fails; yet the idea that the work is a copy seems to be confirmed in the best possible way by C. F. Meyer's[2] poem "The Roman Fountain"

The Roman fountain
The jet ascends, and falling fills
The marble basin round.
Veiling itself, this over-flows
Into a second basin's ground.
The second gives, it becomes too rich,
To a third its bubbling flood,
And each at once receives and gives
And streams and rests.

Der römische Brunnen
Aufsteigt der Strahl und fallend gießt
Er voll der Marmorschale Rund
Die, sich verschleiernd, überfließt
In einer zweiten Schale Grund;
Der dritten wallend ihre Flut,
Und jede nimmt und gibt zugleich
Und strömt und ruht.

This, however, is neither a poetic depiction of an actual fountain nor the reproduction of the general essence of a Roman fountain. Yet truth is set into the work. What is the truth that happens in the work? Can truth happen at all and be, therefore, historical? Yet truth, it is said, is something timeless and supratemporal.

We seek the reality of the artwork in order really to find, there, the art prevailing within it. The thingly substructure is what proved to be the most evident reality in the work. To grasp this thingly element the traditional concepts of the thing are inadequate; for these themselves fail to grasp the essence of the thingly. The dominant concept, thing as formed matter, is taken not from the essence of the thing but from the essence of equipment. What has also become clear is that for a long time the being of equipment has commanded a peculiar preeminence in the interpretation of beings. This – the not explicitly thought out preeminence of the being of equipment – indicated the need to pose the question of equipmentality anew while avoiding the familiar interpretations.

We allow a work to tell us what equipment is. By this means, it came to light what is at work in the work: the opening up of beings in their being, the happening of truth. If, however, the reality of the work is determined by nothing other than what is at work in the work, how do things stand with regard to our project of searching out the real artwork in its reality? As long as we supposed the reality of the work to lie primarily in its thingly substructure, we went astray. We now confront a remarkable result of our considerations – if "result" is what it can be called. Two points become clear.

First, the prevailing concepts of the thing represent an inadequate means of grasping the thingly element in the work.

Second, the thingly substructure, which we wanted to treat as the most evident reality of the work does not, in that way, belong to the work at all.

As soon as we become fixated on finding such an element in the work we have unwittingly taken the work as equipment to which we then ascribe a superstructure supposed to contain what is artistic about it. But the work is not a piece of equipment that is fitted out in addition with aesthetic worth adhering to it. The work is no more that than the mere thing is a piece of equipment minus the marks of authentic equipmentality – usefulness and being made.

Our posing the question of the work has been disturbed by the fact that we asked, not about the work but, rather, half about a thing and half about equipment. That, however, was not a way of raising the question first developed by us. This way of raising the question belongs, rather, to aesthetics. The way in which aesthetics is disposed, in advance, to view the artwork stands within the dominion of the traditional interpretation of beings in general. But to disturb this familiar mode of questioning is not what is essential. What really matters is that we open our eyes to the fact that the workliness of the work, the equipmentality of equipment, and the thingliness of the thing come nearer to us only when we think the being of beings. A condition of this is that the limits imposed by self-evidence first fall away and that current pseudo-concepts be set aside. This is why we had to take a roundabout route. But it brings us directly onto the path that may lead to a determination of the thingly aspect of the work. The thingly in the work should not be denied out of existence; rather, given that it belongs already to the work-being of the work, it must be thought out of that work-being. If this is so, then the path to the determination of the thingly reality of the work runs not from thing to work but from work to thing.

The artwork opens up, in its own way, the being of beings. This opening up, i.e., unconcealing, i.e., the truth of beings, happens in the work. In the artwork, the truth of beings has set itself to the work. Art is the setting-itself-to-work of truth. What is truth itself, that it happens,[a] at times, as art? What is this setting-itself-to-work?

THE WORK AND TRUTH

The origin of the artwork is art. But what is art? Art is real in the artwork. That is the reason we look, first of all, for the reality of the work. In what does it consist? Thingliness is exhibited by artworks universally, albeit in very different ways. The attempt to comprehend the thingly-character of the work *via* the usual concepts of the thing failed. It failed not only because these concepts of the thing failed to grasp the thingly, but also because, by asking about the work's thingly substructure, we forced it into a preconceived framework which obstructs access to the work-being of the work. Nothing can be discovered about the thingly aspect of the work until the pure standing-in-itself of the work has clearly shown itself.

But is the work in itself ever accessible? In order for this to happen it would be necessary to remove the work from all relation to anything other than itself in order to let it stand on its own and for itself alone. But that is already the innermost intention of the artist. Through him, the work is to be released into its purest standing-in-itself. Precisely in great art (which is all we are concerned with here) the artist remains something inconsequential in comparison with the work – almost like a passageway which, in the creative process, destroys itself for the sake of the coming forth of the work.

Well, then, the works themselves are located and hang in collections and exhibitions. But are they themselves, in this context, are they the works they are, or are they, rather, objects of the art business? The works are made available for the public and private enjoyment of art. Official agencies assume responsibility for the care and maintenance of the works. Art connoisseurs and critics busy themselves with them. The art dealer looks after the market. The art-historical researcher turns the works into the objects of a science. But in all this many-sided activity do we ever encounter the work itself?

The "Aegina" sculptures in the Munich collection and Sophocles' *Antigone* in the best critical edition are, as the works they are, torn out of

[a] Reclam edition, 1960. Truth from out of the Event.

their own essential space. However high their status and power to impress, however well-preserved and however certain their interpretation, their relocation in a collection has withdrawn them from their world. Yet even when we try to cancel or avoid such displacement of the work – by, for example, visiting the temple at its site in Paestum or Bamberg cathedral in its square – the world of the work that stands there has disintegrated.

World-withdrawal and world-decay can never be reversed. The works are no longer what they were. The works themselves, it is true, are what we encounter; yet they themselves are what has been. As what has been they confront us within the realm of tradition and conservation. Henceforth, they remain nothing but objects of this kind. That they stand there before us is indeed still a consequence of their former standing-in-themselves. But it is no longer the same as that. Their former self-sufficiency has deserted them. The whole of the art industry, even if taken to extremes and with everything carried out for the sake of the works themselves, reaches only as far as the object-being of the works. This, however, does not constitute their work-being.

But does the work remain a work when it stands outside all relations? Does it not belong to the work to stand in relations? Of course – except that it remains to be asked in which relations it stands.

Where does a work belong? As a work, it belongs uniquely within the region it itself opens up. For the work-being of the work presences in and only in such opening up. We said that in the work, the happening of truth is at work. The reference to van Gogh's picture tried to point to such a happening. The question arose, in this connection, as to what truth might be and how truth could happen.

We pose now the question about truth with the work in view. In order, however, to become more aware of what the question involves, it will be necessary to make the happening of truth in the work visible anew. For this attempt, let us choose a work that cannot be regarded as a work of representational art.

A building, a Greek temple, portrays nothing. It simply stands there in the middle of the rocky, fissured valley. The building encloses the figure of a god and within this concealment, allows it to stand forth through the columned hall within the holy precinct. Through the temple, the god is present in the temple. This presence of the god is, in itself, the extension and delimitation of the precinct as something holy. The temple and its precinct do not, however, float off into the indefinite. It is the temple work that first structures and simultaneously gathers around itself the unity of those paths and relations in which birth and death, disaster and blessing, victory and disgrace, endurance and decline acquire for the human being the shape of its destiny. The all-governing expanse of these open relations is the world of this historical people. From and within this expanse the people first returns to itself for the completion of its vocation.

Standing there, the building rests on the rocky ground. This resting of the work draws out of the rock the darkness of its unstructured yet unforced support. Standing there, the building holds its place against the storm raging above it and so first makes the storm visible in its violence. The gleam and luster of the stone, though apparently there only by the grace of the sun, in fact first brings forth the light of day, the breadth of the sky, the darkness of night. The temple's firm towering makes visible the invisible space of the air. The steadfastness of the work stands out against the surge of the tide and, in its own repose, brings out the raging of the surf. Tree, grass, eagle and bull, snake and cricket first enter their distinctive shapes and thus come to appearance as what they are. Early on, the Greeks called this coming forth and rising up in itself and in all things Φύσις. At the same time φύσις lights up that on which man bases his dwelling. We call this the *earth*. What this word means here is far removed from the idea of a mass of matter and from the merely astronomical idea of a planet. Earth is that in which the arising of everything that arises is brought back – as, indeed, the very thing that it is – and sheltered. In the things that arise the earth presences as the protecting one.

Standing there, the temple work opens up a world while, at the same time, setting this world back onto the earth which itself first comes forth as homeland [*heimatliche Grund*]. But men and animals, plants and things, are never present and familiar as unalterable things fortuitously constituting a suitable environment for the temple that, one day, is added to what is already present. We will get closer to what *is* if we think everything in reverse[a]– assuming, of course, that we have, in advance, an eye for how differently everything then faces us. A mere reversal, made for its own sake, reveals nothing.

Standing there, the temple first gives to things their look, and to men their outlook on themselves. This view remains open as long as the work is a work, as long as the god has not fled from it. So it is, too, with the sculpture of the god which the victor of the athletic games dedicates to him. The work is not a portrait intended to make it easier to recognize

[a] Reclam edition, 1960. Reversing – where to?

what the god looks like. It is, rather, a work which allows the god himself to presence and *is*, therefore, the god himself. The same is true of the linguistic work. In the tragedy, nothing is staged or displayed theatrically. Rather, the battle of the new gods against the old is being fought. In that the linguistic work arises from the speech of the people, it does not talk about this battle. Rather, it transforms that speech so that now every essential word fights the battle and puts up for decision what is holy and what unholy, what is great and what small, what is brave and what cowardly, what is noble and what fugitive, what is master and what slave (cf. Heraclitus, Fragment 53 in Diels, *Fragmente der Vorsokratiker*[3]).

In what, then, does the work-being of the work consist? Keeping in steady view what has just been – roughly enough – outlined, two essential features of the work may have become immediately clearer. With these we depart from the long-familiar foreground of the work's work-being, its thingliness, which underpins our usual relationship to the work.

When a work is brought into a collection or placed in an exhibition, we also say that it is "set up," but this setting up is essentially different from the construction of a building, the raising of a statue, the presentation of a tragedy in the holy festival. The setting up we refer to is an erecting in the sense of dedication and praise. Here, "setting up" no longer means merely putting in place. To dedicate means to consecrate [*heiligen*], in the sense that, in the workly construction, the holy [*Heilige*] is opened up as the holy and the god is called forth into the openness of its presence. Praise belongs to dedication as doing honor to the dignity and splendor of the god. Dignity and splendor are not properties beside and behind which there stands, additionally, the god. Rather, it is in the dignity, in the splendor, that the god comes to presence. In the reflected glory of this splendor there glows, i.e., illuminates itself, what we called "world." To erect [*Er-richten*] means: to open up the right in the sense of the measure which guides us along, in which form that which is essential gives its guidance. Why, however, is the setting up of the work an erecting that consecrates and praises? Because, in its work-being, the work demands it. How does the work come to demand such a setting up? Because it itself, in its own work-being, is something that sets up. What is it that the work, as work, sets up? Rising-up-within-itself the work opens up a *world* and keeps it abidingly in force.

To be a work means: to set up a world. But what is this item, a world? We gave some intimation of an answer in talking about the temple. On the path we must here follow, the nature of world can only be indicated. Even this indication is confined to warding off that which might initially distort our view into the essence of things.

World is not a mere collection of the things – countable and uncountable, known and unknown – that are present at hand. Neither is world a merely imaginary framework added by our representation to the sum of things that are present. *World worlds*, and is more fully in being than all those tangible and perceptible things in the midst of which we take ourselves to be at home. World is never an object that stands before us and can be looked at. World is that always-nonobjectual to which we are subject as long as the paths of birth and death, blessing and curse, keep us transported into being.[a] Wherever the essential decisions of our history are made, wherever we take them over or abandon them, wherever they go unrecognized or are brought once more into question, there the world worlds. The stone is world-less. Similarly, plants and animals have no world; they belong, rather, to the hidden throng of an environment into which they have been put. The peasant woman, by contrast, possesses a world, since she stays in the openness of beings. In its reliability, equipment imparts to this world a necessity and proximity of its own. By the opening of a world, all things gain their lingering and hastening, their distance and proximity, their breadth and their limits. In worlding there gathers that spaciousness from out of which the protective grace of the gods is gifted or is refused. Even the doom of the absence of the god is a way in which world worlds.

A work, by being a work, allows a space for that spaciousness. "To allow a space" here means, in particular: to make free the free of the open and to install this free place in its structure. This in-stalling [*Ein-richten*] presences as the erection [*Er-richten*] mentioned earlier. As a work, the work holds open the open of a world. Yet the setting up of a world is only the first of the essential traits of the work-being of the work that we need to discuss here. The second essential trait which belongs to it we shall attempt to make visible by starting, in the same manner as before, from the foreground of the work.

When a work is brought forth out of this or that work-material – stone, wood, metal, color, language, tone – we say that it is made, set forth [*hergestellt*] out of it. But just as the work required a setting up, in the sense of consecrating-praising erection (since the work-being of the work consisted in a setting up of world), so a setting forth [*Herstellung*] is also necessary, since the work-being of the work has itself the character of a

[a] Reclam edition, 1960. Being-there [*Da-sein*]. Third impression 1957: the Event.

setting forth. It belongs to the essence of a work, as a work, that it makes, sets forth. But what is it that the work sets forth? We will only discover this by investigating what, in a superficial and everyday sense, is referred to as the making or production of works.

To the work-being belongs the setting up of a world. Thinking of it from within this perspective, what is the nature of that which one usually calls the "work-material"? Because it is determined through usefulness and serviceability, equipment takes that of which it consists into its service. In the manufacture of equipment – for example, an ax – the stone is used and used up. It disappears into usefulness. The less resistance the material puts up to being submerged in the equipmental being of the equipment the more suitable and the better it is. On the other hand, the temple work, in setting up a world, does not let the material disappear; rather, it allows it to come forth for the very first time, to come forth, that is, into the open of the world of the work. The rock comes to bear and to rest and so first becomes rock; the metal comes to glitter and shimmer, the colors to shine, the sounds to ring, the word to speak.[a] All this comes forth as the work sets itself back into the massiveness and heaviness of the stone, into the firmness and flexibility of the wood, into the hardness and gleam of the ore, into the lightening and darkening of color, into the ringing of sound, and the naming power of the word.

That into which the work sets itself back, and thereby allows to come forth, is what we called "the earth." Earth is the coming-forth-concealing [*Hervorkommend-Bergende*]. Earth is that which cannot be forced, that which is effortless and untiring. On and in the earth, historical man founds his dwelling in the world. In setting up a world, the work sets forth the earth. "Setting forth [*Herstellen*]" is to be thought, here, in the strict sense of the word.[b] The work moves the earth into the open of a world and holds it there. *The work lets*[c] *the earth be an earth.*[d]

Why, however, must this setting forth of earth happen in such a way that the work sets itself back into it? What is the earth, that it reaches the unconcealed in just this manner? The stone presses downwards and manifests its heaviness. But while this heaviness weighs down on us, at the same time, it denies us any penetration into it. If we attempt such penetration by

[a] Reclam edition, 1960. Saying something [*verlauten*], speaking.

[b] Reclam edition, 1960. Inadequate.

[c] Reclam edition, 1960. This means? Compare "The Thing": the fourfold [*Ge-viert*].

[d] Reclam edition, 1960. The Event.

smashing the rock, then it shows us its pieces but never anything inward, anything that has been opened up. The stone has instantly withdrawn again into the same dull weight and mass of its fragments. If we try to grasp the stone's heaviness in another way, by placing it on a pair of scales, then we bring its heaviness into the calculable form of weight. This perhaps very precise determination of the stone is a number, but the heaviness of the weight has escaped us. Color shines and wants only to shine. If we try to make it comprehensible by analyzing it into numbers of oscillations it is gone. It shows itself only when it remains undisclosed and unexplained. Earth shatters every attempt to penetrate it. It turns every merely calculational intrusion into an act of destruction. Though such destruction may be accompanied by the appearance of mastery and progress in the form of the technological-scientific objectification of nature, this mastery remains, nonetheless, an impotence of the will. The earth is openly illuminated as itself only where it is apprehended and preserved as the essentially undisclosable, as that which withdraws from every disclosure, in other words, keeps itself constantly closed up. All the things of the earth, the earth itself in its entirety, flow together in reciprocal harmony. But this confluence is no blurring of outlines. What flows here is the self-sustaining stream of boundary-setting, a stream which bounds everything that presences into its presence. So in every self-secluding thing there is the same not-knowing-one-another. The earth is the essentially self-secluding. To set forth the earth means: to bring it into the open as the self-secluding.

This setting forth of the earth is what the work achieves by setting itself back into the earth. The self-seclusion of the earth is, however, no uniform, inflexible staying-in-the-dark [*Verhangenbleiben*], but unfolds, rather, into an inexhaustible richness of simple modes and shapes. To be sure, the sculptor uses stone just as, in his own way, the mason uses it. But he does not use it up. That can be, in a certain sense, said of the work only when it fails. To be sure, the painter, too, makes use of pigment; he uses it, however, in such a way that the colors are not used up but begin, rather, for the first time, to shine. To be sure, the poet, too, uses words, not, however, like ordinary speakers and writers who must use them up, but rather in such a way that only now does the word become and remain truly a word.

Nowhere in a work is there any trace of work-material. It is even doubtful whether, in the essential determination of equipment, that in which it consists is encountered in its equipmental essence when it is described as matter.

The setting up of a world and the setting forth of earth are two essential traits belonging to the work-being of the work. Within the unity of that work-being, however, they belong together.[a] This unity is what we seek when we reflect on the self-sufficiency of the work and try to express in words the closed, unitary repose of this resting-in-itself.

But, in the essential traits just mentioned, if our account is anywhere near the mark, what we have made visible in the work is by no means a repose but rather a happening: for what is rest if not the opposite of movement? It is, at any rate, not an opposite which excludes, but rather one which includes movement. Only what moves can rest. The mode of rest is determined by the mode of movement. In motion that is the mere change of place of a body, rest is, admittedly, only the limiting case of motion. When rest includes motion, there can be a rest which is an inner collection of motion. Such rest is, therefore, a state of extreme agitation – presupposing that the kind of motion in question requires such rest. The repose of the work that rests in itself is, however, of this sort. We will come, therefore, into the proximity of this repose if we can manage to grasp the movement of the happening in the work-being of the work as a unity. We ask: what relationship do the setting up of a world and the setting forth of the earth exhibit in the work itself?

The world is the self-opening openness of the broad paths of simple and essential decisions in the destiny of a historical people. The earth is the unforced coming forth of the continually self-closing, and in that way, self-sheltering. World and earth are essentially different and yet never separated from one another. World is grounded on earth, and earth rises up through world. But the relation between world and earth never atrophies into the empty unity of opposites unconcerned with one another. In its resting upon earth the world strives to surmount it. As the self-opening it will tolerate nothing closed. As the sheltering and concealing, however, earth tends always to draw the world into itself and to keep it there.

The opposition of world and earth is strife. We would, to be sure, all too easily falsify the essence of the strife were we to conflate that essence with discord and dispute, and to know it, therefore, only as disruption and destruction. In essential strife, however, the opponents raise each other into the self-assertion [*Selbstbehauptung*] of their essences. This self-assertion of essence is, however, never a rigid fixation on some condition that happens to be the case, but rather a surrendering into the hidden originality of the

[a] Fifth edition, 1957. Only here? Or here, rather, only in the mode of construction?

source of one's own being. In the struggle, each opponent carries the other beyond itself. As a consequence, the strife becomes ever more intense as striving, and ever more authentically what it is. The more intransigently the strife outdoes itself on its own part, the more uncompromisingly do the opponents admit themselves into the intimacy of their simple belonging to one another. The earth cannot do without the openness of world if it is to appear in the liberating surge of its self-closedness. World, on the other hand, cannot float away from the earth if, as the prevailing breadth and path of all essential destiny, it is to ground itself on something decisive.

In setting up world and setting forth earth the work instigates this strife. But this does not happen so that the work can simultaneously terminate and settle the conflict in an insipid agreement, but rather so that the strife remains a strife. By setting up a world and setting forth the earth, the work accomplishes this strife. The work-being of the work consists in fighting the fight between world and earth. It is because the strife reaches its peak in the simplicity of intimacy that the unity of the work happens in the fighting of the fight. The fighting of the fight is the continually self-surpassing gathering of the agitation of the work. The repose of the work that rests in itself thus has its essence in the intimacy of the struggle.

It is from out of this repose of the work that we are first able to see what is at work in the work. Until now the assertion that truth is set to work in the artwork has remained a merely provisional one. In what way does truth happen in the artwork, i.e., now, in what way does truth happen in the fighting of the fight between world and earth? What is truth?

How meager and truncated is our knowledge of the essence of truth is shown by the thoughtlessness with which we use this fundamental word. Mostly, we use "truth" to mean this or that particular truth. It means, in other words, something that is true. A piece of knowledge, articulated in a statement is an example of this kind of thing. It is not merely statements, however, but also things that we call "true" – true as opposed to fake gold. "True," here, is equivalent to "genuine" or "real" gold. What does this talk of "reality" mean? To us it means that which, in truth, is. That which is true is what corresponds to reality, and reality is that which, in truth, is. Once again the circle has closed.

What does "in truth" mean? Truth is the essence of what is true. What is it we are thinking of in speaking of "essence"? Usually, it is that common thing in which everything that is true agrees. An essence is discovered in generic and universal concepts which represent the one that holds indifferently for the many. This in-different essence (essentiality in the sense of *essentia*) is, however, only the inessential essence. In what does the essential essence of something consist? Presumably it lies in that which a being, in truth, *is*. The true essence of something is determined by its true being, by the truth of each being. At the moment, however, what we are looking for is not the truth of essence but rather the essence of truth. A curious entanglement reveals itself here. Is it a mere curiosity, is it the vacuous hair-splitting of a playing with concepts, or is it – an abyss?

Truth means the essence of what is true. We will think it from out of the memory of the word used by the Greeks. 'Αλήθεια means the unconcealment of beings. But is that really a definition of the essence of truth? Are we not passing off a mere change of words – "unconcealment" instead of "truth" – as a characterization of the fact of the matter? Certainly we do not get beyond a change of names so long as we fail to experience what must happen for us to be compelled to speak the *essence* of truth in the word "unconcealment."

Does this require a revival of Greek philosophy? Not at all. A revival, even were such an impossibility possible, would not help us. For the hidden history of Greek philosophy consists from its beginning in this: that it does not measure up to the essence of truth that lit up in the word ἀλήθεια, and so, of necessity, has misdirected its knowing and saying about the essence of truth more and more into the discussion of the derivative essence of truth. In the thought of the Greeks and all the more completely so in the philosophy that followed, the essence of truth as ἀλήθεια remained unthought. Unconcealment is, for thought, what is most concealed in Greek existence. At the same time, however, it is that which, from early times, has determined the presence of everything present.

But why can we not be satisfied with the essence of truth that has, by now, been familiar to us for centuries? Truth means, today, as it has done for a long time, agreement of knowledge with the facts. In order, however, for knowledge, and for the sentence that forms and expresses it, to correspond to the facts it is necessary, first of all, that the fact which is to be binding on the sentence show itself to be such. And how is it to show itself if it is unable to stand out of concealment, unable to stand in the unconcealed? A statement is true by conforming to the unconcealed, i.e., to that which is true. The truth of statements is always, and is nothing but, such correctness. The critical concepts of truth which, since Descartes start out from truth as certainty, are mere variations on the definition of truth as correctness. This familiar essence of truth, truth as the correctness of representation, stands and falls with truth as the unconcealment of beings.

When, here and elsewhere, we conceive of truth as unconcealment, we are not merely taking refuge in a more literal formulation of the Greek word. We are reflecting upon that which, unexperienced and unthought, underlies our familiar and therefore worn out essence of truth in the sense of correctness. From time to time we bring ourselves to concede that, of course, in order to verify and grasp the correctness (truth) of an assertion we must return to something that is already manifest. This presupposition, we concede, is unavoidable. But as long as we talk and think in this way, we understand truth merely as correctness. This requires, of course, a still further presupposition, one that we just make, heaven knows how or why.

But it is not we who presuppose the unconcealment of beings. Rather, the unconcealment of beings (being[a]) puts us into such an essence that all our representing remains set into, and in accordance with, unconcealment. It is not only the case that that *in conformity with which* a cognition orders itself must already be somehow unconcealed. Rather, the whole *region* in which this "conformity with something" occurs must already have happened as a whole within the undisclosed; and this holds equally of that *for* which a particular correspondence of a statement to the facts becomes manifest. With all our correct representations we would be nothing – we could never make the presupposition of there being something manifest to which we conform ourselves – if the unconcealment of beings had not already set us forth into that illuminated realm[b] in which every being stands for us and from which it withdraws.

But how does this happen? How does truth happen as this unconcealment? First, however, we must make it clearer what this unconcealment itself is.

Things are, and human beings, gifts, and sacrifices are, animals and plants are, equipment and work are. The being stands in being. Through being passes a covert fate ordained between the godly and what goes against the godly. There is much in beings man cannot master. But little comes to be known. The known remains an approximation, what is mastered insecure. Never is a being – as it might, all too easily, appear – something of our making or merely our representation. When we contemplate this whole in its unity we grasp, it seems, all that is – though we grasp it crudely enough.

[a] Reclam edition, 1960: i.e., the Event.

[b] Reclam edition, 1960. If the clearing were not to happen, i.e., the appropriating [*Er-eignen*].

And yet: beyond beings – though before rather than apart from them – there is still something other that happens.[a] In the midst of beings as a whole an open place comes to presence. There is a clearing. Thought from out of beings, it is more in being than is the being. This open center is, therefore, not surrounded by beings. Rather, this illuminating center itself encircles all beings – like the nothing that we scarcely know.

The being can only be, as a being, if it stands within, and stands out within, what is illuminated in this clearing. Only this clearing grants us human beings access to those beings that we ourselves are not and admittance to the being that we ourselves are. Thanks to this clearing, beings are unconcealed in certain and changing degrees. But even to be *concealed* is something the being can only do within the scope of the illuminated. Each being which we encounter and which encounters us maintains this strange opposition of presence in that at the same time it always holds itself back in a concealment. Concealment, however, reigns in the midst of beings, in a twofold manner.

Beings refuse themselves to us down to that one and seemingly most trivial feature which we meet most immediately when all we can say of a being is that it is. Concealment as refusal is not primarily or only the limit of knowledge in each particular case; it is, rather, the beginning of the clearing of what is illuminated. But concealment, though of course of another sort, also occurs within the illuminated. Beings push themselves in front of others, the one hides the other, this casts that into shadow, a few obstruct many, on occasion one denies all. Concealment, here, is not simple refusal. Rather, a being indeed appears but presents itself as other than it is.

This concealment is an obstructing [*Verstellen*]. If beings did not obstruct one another we could not err in seeing and doing, we could not go astray and transgress, and, in particular, could not overreach ourselves. That, as appearance, the being can deceive us is the condition of the possibility of our deceiving ourselves rather than the other way round.

Concealment can be either a refusal or merely an obstructing. We are never really certain whether it is the one or the other. Concealment conceals and obstructs itself. This means: the open place in the midst of beings, the clearing, is never a fixed stage with a permanently raised curtain on which the play of beings enacts itself. Rather, the clearing happens only as this twofold concealment. The unconcealment of beings – this is never a state

[a] Third edition, 1957. The Event.

that is merely present but rather a happening[a]. Unconcealment (truth) is a property neither of the facts, in the sense of beings, nor of statements.

In the immediate circle of beings we believe ourselves to be at home. The being is familiar, reliable, ordinary. Nonetheless, the clearing is pervaded by a constant concealment in the twofold form of refusal and obstructing. Fundamentally, the ordinary is not ordinary; it is extra-ordinary, uncanny [*un-geheuer*]. The essence of truth, i.e., unconcealment, is ruled throughout by a denial. This denial is, however, neither a defect nor a fault – as if truth were a pure unconcealment that has rid itself of everything concealed. If truth could accomplish this it would no longer be itself. *Denial, by way of the twofold concealing, belongs to the essence of truth as unconcealment.* Truth, in its essence, is un-truth. We put it this way emphatically to indicate, with a perhaps off-putting directness, that refusal in the mode of concealing is intrinsic to unconcealment as clearing. On the other hand, the sentence "the essence of truth is un-truth" should not be taken to claim that truth, fundamentally, is falsehood. Equally little does it mean that truth is never itself but, dialectically represented, is always its opposite as well.

Truth presences as itself only because the concealing denial, as refusal, is the continuing origin of all clearing but yet, as obstructing, metes out to all clearing the rigorous severity of error. "Concealing denial" is intended to denote that opposition which exists within the essence of truth between clearing and concealment. It is the conflict of the primal strife. The essence of truth is in itself the ur-strife [*Urstreit*][b] in which is won that open center within which beings stand, and from out of which they withdraw into themselves.

This open happens in the midst of beings. It displays an essential trait we have already mentioned. To the open belongs a world and the earth. But world is not simply the open which corresponds to the clearing, earth is not simply the closed that corresponds to concealment. World, rather, is the clearing of the paths of the essential directives with which every decision complies. Every decision, however, is grounded in something that cannot be mastered, something concealed, something disconcerting. Otherwise it would never be a decision. Earth is not simply the closed but that which rises up as self-closing. World and earth are essentially in conflict, intrinsically belligerent. Only as such do they enter the strife of clearing and concealing.

[a] First edition, 1950. The Event.

[b] Reclam edition, 1960. The Event.

Earth rises up through world and world grounds itself on the earth only insofar as truth happens as the ur-strife between clearing and concealment. But how does truth happen? We answer: it happens in a few essential ways.[a] One of these ways in which truth happens is the work-being of the work. Setting up a world and setting forth the earth, the work is the fighting of that fight in which the disclosure of beings as a whole – truth – is won.

Truth happens in the temple's standing there. This does not mean that something is correctly portrayed and reproduced here but rather that that which is as a whole is brought into unconcealment and held there. "To hold" originally means "to watch over [*hüten*]." Truth happens in van Gogh's painting. That does not mean that something present is correctly portrayed; it means, rather, that in the manifestation of the equipmental being of the shoe-equipment, that which is as a whole – world and earth in their counterplay – achieves unconcealment.

In the work truth is at work – not, that is to say, merely something that is true. The picture which shows the peasant shoes, the poem that says the Roman fountain, does not merely show what these isolated beings as such are – if, indeed, they show anything at all. Rather, they allow unconcealment with regard to beings as a whole to happen.[b] The more simply and essentially the shoe-equipment is absorbed in its essence, the more plainly and purely the fountain is absorbed in essence, the more immediately and engagingly do all beings become, along with them, more in being. In this way self-concealing being becomes illuminated. Light of this kind sets its shining into the work. The shining that is set into the work is the beautiful. *Beauty is one way in which truth as unconcealment comes to presence.*

In certain respects, we have, now, certainly grasped the essence of truth more clearly. What is at work in the work may, therefore, have become clearer. Yet the work-being of the work that has now become visible still tells us nothing at all about the most immediate and salient reality of the work, its thingliness. It even seems as if, in pursuing the all-consuming aim of comprehending the self-subsistence of the work itself as purely as possible, we have completely overlooked one crucial point: a work is always a work, which is to say, something worked or produced [*ein Gewirktes*]. If anything distinguishes the work as a work it is the fact that it has been created. Since the work is created, and since creation requires a medium

[a] Reclam edition, 1960. Not an answer since the question remains: what is it which happens in these ways?

[b] Reclam edition, 1960. The Event.

out of and in which the work is created, thingliness, too, must be part of the work. So much is indisputable. The question remains, however: how does being created belong to the work? This issue can only be elucidated when two points have been clarified:

(1) What is meant, here, by being-created and by creation as distinct from making and being-made?
(2) What is the innermost essence of the work itself, from which it can be gauged to what extent being created belongs to it, and to what degree being-created determines the work-being of the work?

Creation, here, is always thought with reference to the work. To the essence of the work there belongs the happening of truth. The nature of creation we define in advance in terms of its relation to the essence of truth as the unconcealment of beings. The belonging of being-created to the work can only come to light through a still more primordial clarification of the essence of truth. The question of truth and its essence returns.

If the statement that truth is at work in the work is to be something more than a mere assertion, we must raise this question once again.

First of all, we must now ask, in a more essential way: to what extent is an impulse to something like a work contained in the essence of truth? What is the essence of truth, that it can be set into the work – even, under certain conditions, must be set into the work – in order to have its being as truth? The setting-of-truth-into-the-work is, however, how we defined the essence of art. Hence, the question just posed becomes:

What is truth, that it can happen as art, or even must so happen? To what extent *is there* [*gibt es*] such a thing as art?

TRUTH AND ART

Art is the origin of both the artwork and the artist. An origin is the source of the essence in which the being of a being presences. What is art? We seek to discover its essential nature in the actual work. The reality of the work was defined in terms of what is at work in the work, in terms, that is, of the happening of truth. This happening we think of as the contesting of the strife between world and earth. In the intense agitation of this conflict presences repose [*Ruhe*]. It is here that the self-subsistence, the resting-in-itself [*insichruhen*] of the work finds its ground.

In the work, the happening of truth is at work. But what is thus at work is at work *in* the work. This means that the actual work is already presupposed, here, as the bearer of this happening. Straight away we confront again the question concerning the thingliness of the work before us. One thing thus finally becomes clear: however diligently we inquire into the self-subsistence of the work, we will fail to discover its actual reality as long as we fail to understand that the work is to be taken as something worked. To take it thus rests on what is closest at hand; for in the word "work [*Werk*]" we hear "worked [*Gewirkte*]." The workly character of the work consists in its being created by the artist. It may appear strange that this most obvious and all-clarifying determination of the work is mentioned for the first time only now.

The work's createdness, however, can obviously be grasped only in terms of the process of creation. Hence, we are constrained by the facts to agree to investigate the activity of the artist in order to discover the origin of the artwork. The project of determining the work-being[a] of the work purely from the work itself proves to be incapable of completion.

Turning away now from the work to investigate instead the nature of the creative process, it will be as well, nonetheless, to keep in mind what was said initially about the peasant shoes and the Greek temple.

We think of creation as a bringing forth. But the making of equipment, too, is a bringing forth. Admittedly, handicraft [*Handwerk*] – a significant turn of phrase – creates no work [*Werk*], even when we contrast the hand-made with the factory product. But what is it that distinguishes bringing forth as creation from bringing forth in the mode of making? It is as easy to make a verbal distinction between the creation of works and the making of equipment as it is difficult to track down the essential traits of the two modes of bringing forth. Going by first appearances, we find the same kind of behaviour in the activity of the potter, the sculptor, the carpenter, and the painter. The creation of works requires the activity of handicraft. Great artists prize craftsmanly ability above all else. Before everything else they demand its careful cultivation based on complete command. More than any-one else they are at pains constantly to renew their grounding in a thorough craftsmanship. It has often enough been pointed out that the Greeks (who understood a thing or two about works of art) used the same word, τέχνη, for both handicraft and art, and used the same term, τεχνίτης, to refer to both the craftsman and the artist.

It seems advisable, therefore, to determine the nature of creation in terms of its aspect as craft. The reference, however, to the linguistic usage of the

[a] Reclam edition, 1960. What does "work-being" mean? Ambiguous.

Greeks – which indicates their experience of the facts – must give pause for thought. Thus, however usual and plausible the reference to the Greek practice of using the same word,τέχνη, to designate both craft and art may be, it remains, nonetheless, off-target and superficial; for τέχνη means neither craft nor art, and absolutely not the technical in the modern sense. It never means any kind of practical accomplishment.

Rather, τέχνη designates a way of knowing. "Knowing" means: having seen, in the broad sense of seeing which means the apprehension of something present as something present. For Greek thought, the essence of knowing is based on ἀλήθεια, on, that is, the unconcealment of beings. Unconcealment supports and guides all comportment toward beings. As knowledge experienced in the Greek manner, τέχνη is a bringing forth of beings in that it brings *forth* what is present, as such, *out of* concealment, specifically *into* the unconcealment of their appearance. τέχνη never designates the activity of making.

The artist is not a τεχνίτης because he is also a craftsman but rather because both the setting-forth [*Her-stellen*] of works and the setting-forth of equipment happen in that bringing forth which allows beings, by assuming an appearance, to come forth into their presence. All this happens, however, in the midst of beings which arise of their own accord, in the midst of φύσις. The designation of art as τέχνη does not at all mean that the activity of the artist can be discovered *via* handicraft. What looks like craft in the creation of the work is a different kind of thing. Such activity is determined and pervaded by the essential nature of creation, and remains, as well, contained within it.

If not handicraft, what is to guide our thinking about the essential nature of creation? How could it be anything other than having in view the to-be-created, the work? Though the work first becomes an actual thing through the completion of creative activity and is, therefore, dependent on such activity for its reality, the essence of creation is determined by the essence of the work. And now it can no longer seem strange that, first of all and for a long time, we spoke only about the work and brought its createdness into view only at the end. If its being-created is as essential to the work as the word "work" makes it sound, then we must try to understand still more essentially what up to now has been identified as the work-being of the work.

In the light of the delineation of the essence of the work we have reached, according to which the happening of truth is at work in the work, we can characterize creation as the allowing of something to come forth in what has been brought forth. The work's becoming a work is a mode of the becoming and happening of truth. Everything depends on the essence of truth. What, however, is truth for it to be the case that it has to happen in something like a creation? To what extent does truth, on the basis of its essence, have an impulse towards the work? Can we understand this from the essence of truth as it has been clarified to date?

Truth is un-truth in that there belongs to it the originating region [*Herkunftsbereich*] of the not-yet- (the un-)disclosed in the sense of concealment. In un-concealment as truth is present, too, the other "un-" of the twofold refusal. Truth as such is present in the opposition between clearing and the twofold concealment. Truth is the ur-strife in which, always in some particular way, the open is won; that open within which everything stands and out of which everything withholds itself – everything which, as a being, both shows and withdraws itself. Whenever and however the strife breaks out and happens, it is through it that the contesting parties, clearing and concealing, separate from one another. In this way the open of the field of combat is won. The openness of this open, i.e., truth, can only be what it is, namely *this* open, when and as long as it establishes itself in its open. In this open, therefore, there must be a being in which the openness takes its stand and achieves constancy. In taking possession of the open, the openness holds it open and supports it. Setting and taking possession [*Setzen und Besetzen*] are here always thought in the sense of the Greek θέσις, which means a setting up in the unconcealed.

With reference to the self-establishment of openness in the open,[a] our thinking touches on an area which cannot here be elucidated. Only this should be noted; that if, in some manner, the essence of unconcealment belongs to being itself (compare *Being and Time*, section 44), then it is being which, in virtue of its essence, allows the freeplay of openness (the clearing of the "there") to happen, and introduces it as *a place of the sort* in which, in its own manner, each being arises.

Truth happens only by establishing itself in the strife and space it itself opens up. Since truth is the opposition of clearing and concealment, there belongs to it what may here be called "establishment." But truth is not present in itself beforehand, somewhere among the stars, so as then, later on, to find accommodation among beings. This is impossible since it is the openness of beings which first affords the possibility of a somewhere and

[a] Reclam edition, 1960. In this connection, the "ontological difference"; see *Identity and Difference*, trans. J. Stambaugh (New York: Harper and Row, 1969), pp. 47ff.

a place filled by the things that presence. Clearing of the openness and establishment in the open belong together. They are the same thing, an essence of the happening of truth. This happening is, in many different ways, historical.

One essential way in which truth establishes itself in the beings it has opened up is its setting-itself-into-the-work. Another way in which truth comes to presence is through the act which founds a state. Again, another way in which truth comes to shine is the proximity of that which is not simply a being but rather the being which is most in being. Yet another way in which truth grounds itself is the essential sacrifice. A still further way in which truth comes to be is in the thinker's questioning, which, as the thinking of being, names being in its question-worthiness [*Frag-würdigkeit*]. Science, by contrast, is not an original happening of truth but always the cultivation of a domain of truth that has already been opened. It does this through the apprehension and confirmation of that which shows itself to be possible and necessarily correct within this sphere. If, and to the extent that, a science transcends correctness and arrives at a truth – i.e., an essential disclosure of beings as such – it is philosophy.

Since it belongs to the essence of truth to establish itself within beings in order first to become truth, an *impulse to the work* belongs to the essence of truth as one of truth's distinctive possibilities for achieving being in the midst of beings.

The establishment of truth in the work is the bringing forth of a being of a kind which never was before and never will be again. The bringing forth places this being in the open in such a way that what is to be brought forth first clears the openness of the open into which it comes forth. When this bringing forth brings with it specifically the openness of beings, that is, truth, that which is brought forth, is a work. Bringing forth of this kind is creation. As such a bringing it is, better expressed, a receiving and taking over that occurs within the pull [*Bezug*] toward unconcealment. In what, then, does createdness consist? It may be elucidated through two essential determinations.

Truth establishes itself in the work. Truth is present only as the strife between clearing and concealing in the opposition between world and earth. As this strife of world and earth, truth wills its establishment in the work. The strife is not resolved in something brought forth specifically for that purpose, but neither is it merely housed there. The strife is, rather, opened up by the work. This being must, therefore, contain within itself the essential traits of the strife. In the strife the unity of world and earth is won. As a world opens itself up, it puts up for decision, by a historical humanity, the question of victory or defeat, blessing and curse, lordship and slavery. The dawning world brings to the fore that which is still undecided and without measure and decisiveness.

As a world opens itself up, however, the earth rises up. It shows itself as that which bears all, as that which is secure in its law and which constantly closes itself up. World demands its decisiveness and measure and allows beings to attain to the openness of its paths. Earth, bearing and rising up, strives to preserve its closedness and to entrust everything to its law. The strife is not rift [*Riss*], in the sense of a tearing open of a mere cleft; rather, it is the intimacy of the mutual dependence of the contestants. The rift carries the contestants into the source of their unity, their common ground. It is the fundamental design [*Grundriss*]. It is the outline sketch [*Auf-riss*] that marks out the fundamental features of the rising up of the clearing of beings. This design [*Riss*] does not allow the contestants to break apart. It brings the contest between measure and limit into a shared outline [*Umriss*].

Truth establishes itself as strife in a being that is to be brought forth only in such a way that the strife opens up in this being; the being itself, in other words, is brought into the rift-design [*Riss*]. The rift-design is the drawing together into a unity of sketch and fundamental design rupture and outline. Truth establishes itself in a being in such a way, indeed, that this being itself occupies the open of truth. This occupying, however, can only happen in such a way that what is to be brought forth, the rift, entrusts itself to the self-closing that rises up in the open. The rift must set itself back into the pull of the weight of the stone, into the dumb hardness of the wood, into the dark glow of the colors. As the earth takes the rift back into itself, the rift is for the first time set forth into the open and therefore placed, i.e., set, into that which rises up in the open as the self-closing and as the protecting.

This strife which is brought into the rift-design, and so set back into the earth and fixed in place, is the *figure* [***Gestalt***]. The createdness of the work means: the fixing in place of truth in the figure. Figure is the structure of the rift in its self-establishment. The structured rift is the jointure [*Fuge*] of the shining of truth. What we here call "figure" is always to be thought out of *that particular* placing [*stellen*] and placement [*Ge-stell*] as which the *work* comes to presence when it sets itself up and sets itself forth.

In the creation of the work, the strife, as rift, must be set back into the earth; the earth itself must be set forth and made use of as the self-closing. This making use of, however, does not use up and misuse the earth as mere matter; rather, it frees it to be, for the first time, itself. Such using of the earth is a working with it that indeed looks like the employment of matter in handicraft. This is what created the appearance that the creation of a work is also craft activity. It never is. But it remains always a using of earth in the fixing in place of truth in the figure. By contrast, the making of equipment is never, in the first instance, an effecting of the happening of truth. The production of equipment is finished when the material has been so formed as to be ready for use. The equipment's readiness for use means that it is released beyond itself to disappear into usefulness.

Not so the createdness of the work. This will become clear through a consideration of the second characteristic, which may be introduced at this point.

The readiness of equipment and the createdness of the work have in common that each is something that has been brought forth. But what makes the createdness of the work different from every other bringing forth is that it is also created into the created work. But is this not true of everything that has been brought forth or in any other way has come into being? Everything that is brought forth, if endowed with anything at all, is endowed, surely, with its having-been-brought-forth. Certainly. But in the work createdness is expressly created into what is created, with the result that it expressly rises up out of the work. If this is how things are, then it must be possible to experience createdness in the work itself.

That createdness stands forth out of the work does not mean that it should be a salient feature of the work that it is made by a great artist. The point is not that the created work be certified as a product of ability so as thereby to raise the public profile of the producer. What is announced is not "*N.N. fecit.*" Rather, "*factum est*" is what is to be held forth into the open by the work: in other words this, that an unconcealment of beings has happened here and, as this happening, happens here for the first time; or this, that this work *is* rather than is not. The thrust that the work, as this work, is and the unceasingness of this inconspicuous thrust constitute the constancy of the self-subsistence of the work. Precisely where the artist and the process and circumstances of the work's coming into being remain unknown, this thrust, this "that [*dass*]" of createdness, steps into view at its purest from out of the work.

To be sure, "that" it is made also belongs to every piece of equipment that is available for, and in, use. This "that," however, is not salient in the equipment; it disappears into usefulness. The handier a piece of equipment, the more inconspicuous is the fact that, for example, a hammer of a certain kind is, that is, exists; the handier a piece of equipment, the more completely it preserves itself in its equipmentality. We are capable, in general, of noticing of anything present that such a thing is; but as soon as this is noted it falls, just as quickly, into the oblivion of the commonplace. What, however, is more commonplace than that a being is? In the work, on the other hand, the fact that it *is* as such a thing, is what is unusual. The happening of its createdness does not simply reverberate through the work; rather, the work casts before itself the eventful fact that, as a work, this work is, and exhibits this fact constantly. The more essentially the work opens itself, the more luminous becomes the uniqueness of the fact that it is rather than is not. The more essentially this thrust comes into the open, the stranger and more solitary the work becomes. In the bringing forth of the work there lies the offering forth of the "that it is."

The question of the createdness of the work should have brought us closer to the work-character of the work and thereby to its reality. Createdness has revealed itself to be the strife's being fixed in place through the rift in the figure. By this means, createdness itself is specifically created into the work and stands as the silent thrust into the open of the "that." But even createdness fails to exhaust the reality of the work. However, this view of the essence of the createdness of the work puts us into a position to take the step to which everything that has been said up to now leads.

The more solitary the work, fixed in the figure, stands within itself, the more purely it seems to sever all ties to human beings, then the more simply does the thrust that such a work *is* step into the open, and the more essentially the extraordinary is thrust to the surface and the long-familiar thrust down. Yet there is nothing violent about this multidirectional thrust, for the more purely is the work itself transported into the openness of beings it itself opens up, then the more simply does it carry us into this openness and, at the same time, out of the realm of the usual. To submit to this displacement means: to transform all familiar relations to world and to earth, and henceforth to restrain all usual doing and prizing, knowing and looking, in order to dwell within the truth that is happening in the work. The restraint of this dwelling allows what is created to become, for the first time, the work that it is. This allowing the work to be a work is what we call its preservation. It is in such preservation that, in its createdness, the work first gives itself as the real which now means, is present in its work-character.

Just as a work cannot be without being created, just as it stands in essential need of creators, so what is created cannot come into being without preservers.

If, however, a work does not – or does not immediately – find preservers who respond to the truth happening in the work, that does not mean that a work can be a work without preservers. If it is in other respects a work, it always remains tied to preservers even, and precisely, when it only waits for preservers and only solicits and awaits their entry into its truth. Even the oblivion into which the work can fall is not nothing: it is still a preserving. It lives off the work. Preservation of the work means: standing within the openness of beings that happens in the work. This urgent standing-withinness [*Inständigkeit*] of preservation is, however, a knowing. Yet knowing does not consist in mere acquaintance with and ideas about something. Whoever truly knows what is knows what he wills in the midst of what is.

The willing referred to here, which neither merely applies knowledge nor decides in advance of it, is thought out of the foundational experience of the thinking of *Being and Time*. The knowing that is a willing, and the willing that is a knowing, is the existing [*existierenden*] human being's allowing himself ecstatic [*ekstatische*] entrance into the unconcealment of beings. The resoluteness[4] which is thought in *Being and Time* is not the decisive action of a subject, but rather the human being's [*Daseins*] opening up from out of its captivity by beings into the openness of being. In his existence, however, man does not move from something inward to something outer. Rather, the essence of existence is the out-standing standing-within the essential separation belonging to the clearing of beings. Neither the creating discussed earlier nor the willing that is our current topic is thought of as the achievement or action of a subject who sets himself a goal that he strives to achieve.

Willing is the sober resoluteness [*Ent-schlossenheit*] of that existential [*existierenden*] self-transcendence which exposes itself to the openness of beings as it is set into the work. In this way, the urgent standing-within is brought into law. As knowing, preservation of the work is the sober standing-within the awesomeness of the truth that happens in the work.

This knowing which, as willing, makes its home in the truth of the work – and only thus remains a knowing – does not take the work out of its self-subsistence, does not drag it into the sphere of mere experience [*Erlebens*] and does not degrade it to the role of a mere stimulant to experience. Preservation of the work does not individualize human beings down to their experiences but rather, brings them into a belonging to the truth that happens in the work. By so doing it founds their being-with-one-another [*Miteinander-sein*] as the historical standing out of human existence [*Da-seins*] from out of the relation to unconcealment. Most particularly, knowing in the mode of preservation is far removed from that merely cultivated connoisseurship of the formal features of the work, its qualities and intrinsic charms. Knowing as having seen is a being-decided; it is a standing-within the strife that the work has fixed into the design [*Riss*].

The manner of the proper preservation of the work is created and prefigured for us only and exclusively by the work itself. Preservation happens at different levels of knowledge, always with differing degrees of scope, constancy, and lucidity. If works are presented to be enjoyed merely as art, it is not yet established that they stand in preservation as works.

As soon as the thrust into the extra-ordinary [*Un-geheure*] is captured by familiarity and connoisseurship, the art business has already begun to take over the works. Even the careful handing down of works to posterity and the scientific attempt to recover them no longer reach to their work-being itself, but only to a memory of it. But even this can still offer a place to the work from out of which it can contribute to the shaping of history. The ownmost reality of the work, however, comes to bear only where the work is preserved in the truth that happens through it itself.

The reality of the work is determined, in its fundamental features, from out of the essence of its work-being. We are now in a position to return to our opening question: how do matters stand with that thingliness of the work which guarantees the work's immediate reality? They stand in such a way that we no longer ask the question about the work's thingliness. For as long as we pose that question we take it as a foregone conclusion that the work is present to us as an object. In this way, our questioning proceeds not from the work, but from ourselves. From ourselves – we who do not allow the work to be a work but represent it, rather, as an object that is supposed to bring about certain conditions within us.

That element within the work, however, which looks like its thingliness when the work is taken as an object (according to the usual concepts of the thing), experienced from out of the work, is its character as earth. Earth rises up within the work because the work is present as something in which truth is at work, and because truth only presences where it establishes itself in a being. In the earth, however, as the essentially self-closing, the openness of the open encounters the highest form of resistance and through this finds the site of its steady stand in which the figure must be fixed in place.

Was it, then, superfluous to go into the question of the thingliness of the thing? By no means. It is true that the work's thingliness cannot be defined in terms of its work-character, but, on the other hand, knowing the work-character of the work can point the question of the thingliness of the thing in the right direction. This is no mean achievement, when we recollect that those modes of thinking familiar from ancient times are an attack upon the thingliness of the thing, and all the more when we recollect that they submit beings as a whole to an interpretation which is incapable of grasping the essence of equipment and of work, and makes us blind to the primordial essence of truth.

To determine the thingliness of the thing, neither reference to the bearer of properties nor to the unity of the manifold of the sensorily given is adequate. Least adequate of all is the matter–form structure, taken by itself, which is taken from the realm of equipment. To provide an authoritative and deep interpretation of the thingliness of the thing we must turn to the belonging of the thing to earth. The essential nature of earth, of the unmasterable and self-closing bearer, reveals itself, however, only in its rising up into a world, in the opposition between world and earth. This strife is fixed in place within the work's figure and becomes manifest through this figure. What is true of equipment, that we experience its equipmentality proper only through the work is true, also, of the thingliness of the thing. That we never know of the thingliness of the thing directly, and if we know it at all do so only in an indefinite kind of way – in other words, that we need the work – this fact shows indirectly that in the work-being of the work the happening of truth, the disclosure of beings, is at work.

But, we might finally object, if the work is indeed to bring thingliness into the open in a striking way, must not the work, for its part – before, and for the sake of its createdness – have been brought into relation to the things of the earth, to nature? Someone who must have known about it, Albrecht Dürer, made, after all, the well-known remark: "For in truth, art is found in nature; whoever can wrest it from her has it." "Wrest [*reißen*]" means here, to bring forth the rift [*Riss*] and to seize [*reißen*] it with drawing pen and drawing board. Immediately, however, we raise the counter-question: how can the rift be wrested forth except as the rift, and that means if it has not first been brought into the open, through the creative sketch, as the strife between measure and unmeasure? Certainly, there is found in nature a rift, measure, and limit, and bound to them the potentiality for a bringing forth, art. But it is just as certain that this art which is in nature is made manifest only by the work, made manifest because it is found in the work in a primordial way.

Our efforts concerning the reality of the work should have prepared the ground for discovering, in the reality of the work, art and its essential nature. The question of the nature of art, and of the path to knowing it, needs first to be placed on firm ground again. The answer to the question is only the final result of the last step of a long sequence of questioning steps. Each answer remains in force as an answer only as long as it is rooted in questioning.

In the light of its work-being, the reality of the work has become not only clearer but, at the same time, essentially richer. To the createdness of the work the preservers belong just as essentially as the creators. But it is the work which makes the creators possible in their essence and which, in virtue of its essence, needs the preservers. If art is the origin of the work this means that it lets originate, in its essence, the essential belonging together at work of creator and preserver. What, however, is art itself that justifies us in calling it an "origin"?

In the work, the happening of truth is at work; at work, indeed, in the manner of a work. Accordingly, the essential nature of art was specified, in advance, as the setting-itself-to-work of truth. But this definition is intentionally ambiguous. On the one hand, it says: art is the fixing in place of self-establishing truth in the figure. This happens in creation, understood as the bringing forth of the unconcealment of beings. At the same time, however, setting-to-work also means: bringing the work-character of the work into motion and happening. This happens as preservation. Thus art is: the creative preservation of the truth in the work. *Art is, then, a becoming and happening of truth*. Does truth, then, arise out of nothing? It does indeed, if by nothing is meant the mere not of beings, and if we represent the being as that which is present in the ordinary way – that which later comes to light through the standing there of the work as what is merely presumed to be a true being, that which is brought into question. Truth will never be gathered from what is present and ordinary. The disclosure of the open and the clearing of beings happen, rather, only insofar as the approaching openness is projected within thrownness.

Truth, as the clearing and concealing of that which is, happens through being poeticized.[a] *All art*, as the letting happen of the advent of the truth of beings, is, *in essence*, *poetry*. The essence of art, on which both the artwork and the artist depend, is truth's setting-itself-into-work. From out of the poeticizing essence of truth it happens that an open place is thrown open, a place in which everything is other than it was. In virtue of the projection

[a] Reclam edition, 1960. Questionability of "poetry" – as the use of the saying [*als Brauch der Sage*]. The relationship between clearing and concealing inadequately portrayed.

of the unconcealedness of beings which is set into the work and casts itself toward us, everything ordinary and hitherto existing becomes an unbeing. This unbeing has lost the capacity to give and to preserve being as measure. What is curious here is that the work in no way affects hitherto existing beings through causal connection. The effecting [*Wirkung*] of the work does not consist in a taking effect [*wirken*]. It lies in a transformation of the unconcealment of beings which happens from out of the work, a transformation, that is to say, of being.[a]

Poetry, however, is no aimless imagining of whimsicalities, and no flight of mere representations and fancies into the unreal. What poetry, as clearing projection, unfolds of unconcealment and projects into the rift within the figure is the open; poetry allows this open to happen in such a way, indeed, that now, for the first time, in the midst of beings, it brings them to shine and sound. If we fix our gaze on the essence of the work and its relation to the happening of the truth of beings, it becomes questionable whether the essence of poetry, of that is to say, projection, can be adequately thought in terms of imagination and the power of imagining.

It may here be emphasized that the essence of poetry, of which we have now learned in its full breadth (but not, on that account, in a vague kind of way) is something worthy of questioning, is something that remains to be thought through.[b]

If the essence of all art is poetry, then architecture, the visual arts, and music must all be referred back to poesy. That is completely arbitrary. Certainly it is, if we mean that these arts are branches of the art of language – if we may be allowed to designate poesy with a title easily capable of misunderstanding. But poesy is only a mode of the illuminating projection of truth, of, that is to say, poeticizing in this broader sense. Nonetheless, the linguistic work, poetry in the narrower sense, has a privileged position among the arts as a whole.

To see this all we need is the right concept of language. According to the usual account, language is a kind of communication. It serves as a means of discussion and agreement, in general for achieving understanding. But language is neither merely nor primarily the aural and written expression of what needs to be communicated. The conveying of overt and covert

[a] Reclam edition, 1960. Inadequate – relationship between unconcealment and "Being"; Being = presence, compare *Time and Being*.

[b] Reclam edition, 1960. Also worthy of questioning is that which is unique to art.

meanings is not what language, in the first instance, does. Rather, it brings beings as beings, for the first time, into the open. Where language is not present, as in the being of stones, plants, or animals, there is also no openness of beings, and consequently no openness either of that which is not a being [*des Nichtseienden*] or of emptiness.

Language, by naming beings for the first time, first brings beings to word and to appearance. This naming nominates beings *to* their being and *from out of* that being. Such saying is a projection of the clearing in which announcement is made as to what beings will come into the open as. Projecting [*Entwerfen*][a] is the releasing of a throw [*Wurf*] as which unconcealment sends itself into beings as such. This projective announcement immediately becomes a renunciation of all dim confusion within which beings veil and withdraw themselves.[b]

Projective saying is poetry: the saying of world and earth, the saying of the arena of their strife and, thereby, of all nearness and distance of the gods. Poetry is the saying of the unconcealment of beings. The prevailing language is the happening of that saying in which its world rises up historically for a people and the earth is preserved as that which remains closed. Projective saying is that in which the preparation of the sayable at the same time brings the unsayable as such to the world. In such saying, the concepts of its essence – its belonging to world-history, in other words – are formed, in advance, for a historical people.

Poetry is here thought in such a broad sense, and at the same time in such an intimate and essential unity with language and the word, that it must remain open whether art, in all its modes from architecture to poesy, exhausts the nature of poetry.

Language itself is poetry in the essential sense. But since language is that happening in which, each time, beings are first disclosed as beings, poesy, poetry in the narrower sense, is the most primordial form of poetry in the essential sense. Language is not poetry because it is ur-poesy; rather, poesy happens in language because the latter preserves the primordial essence of poetry. Building and plastic creation, on the other hand, happen, always and only, in the open of saying and naming. It is this open which permeates and guides them. For this reason, they remain their own particular ways and manners in which truth orders itself into the work. They are an

[a] Reclam edition, 1960. Projecting – not the clearing as such, for it is only in this that the projection is located. Rather, projecting of rift-designs [*Risse*].

[b] Reclam edition, 1960. Only thus? Or as destiny? Compare the set-up [*das Ge-stell*].

always unique poeticizing within the clearing of beings which has already happened, unnoticed, in the language.[a]

As the setting-into-work of truth, art is poetry. It is not only the creation of the work that is poetic; equally poetic, though in its own way, is the preservation of the work. For a work only actually is as a work when we transport ourselves out of the habitual and into what is opened up by the work so as to bring our essence itself to take a stand within the truth of beings.[b]

The essence of art is poetry. The essence of poetry, however, is the founding [*Stiftung*] of truth. "Founding" is understood, here, in a threefold sense: as bestowing, as grounding, and as beginning. But it only becomes actual in preserving. Thus to each mode of founding there corresponds a mode of preserving. All we can do at present is to make this essential structure visible in a few strokes, and even that only to the extent that the earlier characterization of the essential nature of the work provides an initial clue.

The setting-into-work of truth thrusts up the extra-ordinary [*Ungeheure*] while thrusting down the ordinary, and what one takes to be such. The truth that opens itself in the work can never be verified or derived from what went before. In its exclusive reality, what went before is refuted by the work. What art founds, therefore, can never be compensated and made good in terms of what is present and available for use. The founding is an overflowing, a bestowal.

The poeticizing projection of truth, which sets itself into the work as figure, is never carried out in the direction of emptiness and indeterminacy. In the work, rather, truth is cast toward the coming preservers, that is to say, a historical humanity. What is cast forth, however, is never an arbitrary demand. The truly poeticizing projection is the opening up of that in which human existence [*Dasein*], as historical, is already thrown [*geworfen*]. This is the earth (and, for a historical people, its earth), the self-closing ground on which it rests, along with everything which – though hidden from itself – it already is. It is, however, its world which prevails from out of the relationship of existence to the unconcealment of being. For this reason, everything with which man is endowed must, in the projection, be fetched forth from out of the closed ground and explicitly set upon this ground. In this way, the ground is first founded as a ground that bears.

[a] Reclam edition, 1960. What does this mean? Does clearing happen through language or is it the Event of clearing [*das ereignende Lichtung*] which first grants saying and renouncing [*Entsagen*], and therefore language. Language and body (sound and script).

[b] Reclam edition, 1960. In the sense of an urgent standing-within our practice [*Brauch*].

Because it is such a fetching-forth, all creation is a fetching, as in fetching water from a spring. Modern subjectivism, of course, misinterprets creation as the product of the genius of the self-sovereign subject. The founding of truth is a founding, not merely in the sense of a free bestowal, but in the sense, too, of this ground-laying grounding. The poeticizing projection comes out of nothing in the sense that it never derives its gift from what is familiar and already here. In another sense, however, it does not come out of nothing; for what it projects is but the withheld determination of man's historical existence itself.

Bestowal and grounding have in themselves the abruptness of what we call a beginning. But this suddenness of the beginning, the uniqueness of what is unique to the leap[a] from out of this suddenness, does not exclude – rather it includes – the fact that the beginning has inconspicuously prepared itself over the longest time. As a leap, the genuine beginning is always a leaping-ahead, a leaping-ahead in which everything to come is already leapt over, even if as something veiled. Concealed within itself, the beginning[b] contains already the end. A genuine beginning, of course, is not a beginning in the sense of being primitive. The primitive, because it lacks the bestowing, grounding leap and the leap-ahead, has no future. It cannot release anything more from itself since it contains nothing save that in which it is caught.

A beginning, by contrast, always contains the undisclosed fullness of the extraordinary, and that means the strife with the ordinary. Art as poetry is founding in the third sense of the instigation of the strife of truth; it is founding as beginning. Whenever what is as a whole, as what is, itself demands a grounding in openness, then art, as founding, accedes to its historical essence. In the West, this first happened in Greece. What would, in the future, be called being was set into the work in a standard-setting way. The thus-opened totality of beings was then transformed into beings in the sense of God's creation. This happened in the Middle Ages. This kind of being was again transformed at the beginning, and during the course, of the modern age. Beings became transparent objects capable of being mastered by calculation. Each time, the openness of beings had to be established in beings themselves, through the fixing in place of truth in the figure. Each time, the unconcealment of beings happened. It set itself into the work, a setting which is accomplished by art.

[a] Reclam edition, 1960. Concerning "the leap" see *Identity and Difference*, the lecture about identity.

[b] Reclam edition, 1960. To think the beginning as the beginning in terms of the Event.

Whenever art happens, whenever, that is, there is a beginning, a thrust enters history and history either begins or resumes. History, here, does not mean a sequence of events in time, no matter how important. History is the transporting of a people into its appointed task [*Aufgegebenes*] as the entry into its endowment [*Mitgegebenes*].

Art is the setting-itself-to-work of truth. An essential ambiguity is concealed in this sentence, present because "truth" functions as both subject and object. Yet "subject" and "object" are inappropriate terms, here. They prevent our thinking this ambiguous essence – a task that no longer belongs to our reflections. Art is historical and, as historical, is the creative preservation of truth in the work. Art happens as poetry. This is founding in the threefold sense of bestowing, grounding, and beginning. As founding, art is essentially historical. This does not just mean that art has a history, a history in the external sense that, in the passage of time, art appears together with many other things, and in the process changes and passes away, and offers changing aspects to the study of history. Art is history in the essential sense: it is the ground of history.

Art allows truth to arise [*entspringen*]. Art arises as the founding preservation of the truth of beings in the work. To allow something to arise, to bring something into being from out of the essential source in the founding leap [*Sprung*] is what is meant by the word "origin [*Ursprung*]."

The origin of the artwork – of, that is, creators and preservers, which is to say, the historical existence of a people – is art. This is so because, in its essence, art is an origin: a distinctive way in which truth comes into being, becomes, that is, historical.

We are inquiring into the essential nature of art. Why do we thus inquire? We do so in order to be able to ask properly whether or not, in our historical existence, art is an origin, whether, and under what conditions, it can and must become one.

Such reflections cannot compel art and its coming-to-be. But this reflective knowledge is the preliminary and therefore indispensable preparation for the coming-to-be of art. Only such knowledge prepares, for art, the space,[a] for creators, the path, and for preservers the location.

In such knowledge, which can only grow slowly, it is decided whether art can be an origin – and therefore must be a leap ahead – or whether it should remain a mere postscript, in which case it can only be carried along as a cultural phenomenon that has become routine.

[a] Reclam edition, 1960. The place of its staying.

Are we, in our existence, historically at the origin? Or do we, rather, in our relationship with art, appeal, merely, to a cultured knowledge of the past?

For this either-or and its decision there is a certain sign. Hölderlin, the poet whose work still stands before the Germans as a test, put it into words when he said:

> Reluctant to leave the place
> Is that which dwells near the origin.
>
> Schwer verlässt
> Was nahe dem Ursprung wohnet, den Ort.
> ("The Journey," ed. Hellingrath, vol. IV, p. 167)

AFTERWORD

The foregoing considerations are concerned with the enigma [*Rätsel*] of art, the enigma that art itself is. They are far from claiming to solve the enigma. The task is to see the enigma.

Almost as soon as specialized thinking about art and the artist began, such reflections were referred to as "aesthetic." Aesthetics treated the artwork as an object, as indeed an object of αἴσθησις, of sensory apprehension in a broad sense. These days, such apprehension is called an "experience." The way in which man experiences art is supposed to inform us about its essential nature. Experience is the standard-giving source not only for the appreciation and enjoyment of art but also for its creation.[a] Everything is experience. But perhaps experience is the element in which art dies.[b] This dying proceeds so slowly that it takes several centuries.

One speaks, of course, of the immortal works of art and of art as an eternal value. One speaks this language which, in all essential matters, deals with nothing precisely because one fears that dealing with things precisely calls, in the end, for – thinking. What fear is today greater than the fear of thinking?

[a] Reclam edition, 1960. Has modern art moved out of the realm of experience? Or is it only *what* is experienced that has changed, so that, of course, what is experienced has become even more subjective than before: the object of experience is now "the technology of the creative drive" itself – the how of making and invention. "Art without form [*informel*]" and the corresponding indefiniteness and emptiness of the "symbolic," that itself still remains metaphysics. The experience of the self as "society."

[b] Reclam edition, 1960. This statement does not, however, say that art is absolutely at an end. That would only be the case if experience remained the absolute element for art. Everything depends on getting out of experience and into being-there [*Da-sein*], which means achieving an element for the "becoming" of art quite other than experience.

Does this talk of the immortal works and eternal values of art have any content or substance? Or are these merely the half-thought clichés of an age in which great art, together with its essence, has departed from among men?

The most comprehensive reflections on the nature of art possessed by the West – comprehensive because thought out of metaphysics – are Hegel's *Lectures on Aesthetics*. Here one finds the following statements:

> Art no longer counts as the highest way in which truth finds existence for itself.[a]
>
> (*Werke*, vol. X, I, p. 134)

> One may well hope that art will continue to advance and perfect itself, but its form has ceased to be the highest need of spirit.
>
> (*ibid.*, p. 135)

> In all these connections art is, and remains, with regard to its highest vocation, a thing of the past.
>
> (*ibid.*, p. 16)

The judgment made in these sentences cannot be evaded by pointing out that since the last time Hegel lectured on his aesthetics, the winter of 1828–9, we have seen the advent of many new artworks and art movements. This possibility was one Hegel never wanted to deny. Yet the question remains: is art still an essential and necessary way in which that truth happens which is decisive for our historical existence, or is this something that art no longer is? But if art is that no longer, the question remains as to why this is so. A decision concerning Hegel's judgment has not yet been made; for behind the judgment there stands Western thinking since the Greeks, a thinking which corresponds to a truth of beings that has already happened. The decision about the judgment will be made, when it is made, from and about this truth of beings. Until then, the judgment remains in force [*in Geltung*]. But for this very reason we need to ask whether the truth it expresses is final and conclusive, and what then follows if it is.

Questions such as these which touch us, sometimes quite clearly, sometimes only in a vague kind of way, can only be asked if we give thought to the essence of art. We attempt to take a few steps in this direction by posing the question of the origin of the work of art. What is needed is to bring into view the work-character of the work. What we mean, here, by the word "origin" is thought out of the essence of truth.

The truth of which we have spoken does not coincide with what is generally recognized under this name – that which is assigned to knowledge

[a] Reclam edition, 1960. Art as mode of truth (here, the certainty of the absolute).

and science as a quality to be distinguished from the beautiful and the good, terms which function as the values of non-theoretical activities. Truth is the unconcealment of beings as beings.[a] Truth is the truth of beings. Beauty does not occur alongside this truth. It appears when truth sets itself into the work. This appearing (as this being of truth in the work and as the work) is beauty. Thus beauty belongs to the advent of truth. It does not exist merely relative to pleasure, and purely as its object. Beauty does, however, consist in form, but only because the *forma* once took its light from being and the being of beings. At that time, being made its advent as εἶδος. The ἰδέα fits itself into the μορφή. The σύνολον, the unitary whole of μορφή and ὕλη, in other words, the ἔργον, *is* in the manner of ἐνέργεια. This mode of presence became the *actualitas* of the *ens actu*. This *actualitas* became actuality, reality. Reality becomes objectivity. Objectivity becomes experience. In the manner in which, for the world determined in the Western way, beings exist as the real, there lies concealed a particular convergence of beauty and truth. To the transformation of the essence of truth there corresponds the essential history of Western art. This can no more be grasped by taking beauty by itself than it can in terms of experience – supposing that the metaphysical concept of art is adequate to the essence of art.

APPENDIX

On pages 38 and 44, the attentive reader will be forced to take note of a real difficulty: it looks as though the remarks about the "fixing in place of truth" and about the "letting happen of the advent of truth" can never be made consistent with each other. For in "fixing in place [*Feststellen*]" there is implied a willing which blocks and prevents truth's advent. In "*letting* happen," on the other hand, what is presented is a submitting – and, therefore, so to speak, a not-willing – as that which clears a space for the advent of truth.

The difficulty is resolved if we think "fixing in place" in the sense in which it is intended throughout the entire text of the essay, above all, in the key specification "*setting*-to-work."[b] Together with "to place [*stellen*]" and "to set" belongs "to lay"; all three meanings are contained as a unity within the Latin "*ponere*."

[a] Third edition, 1957. Truth is the self-illuminating being of beings. Truth is the clearing of the difference [*Unter-schied*] (settlement) through which clearing determines itself out of the difference.

[b] Reclam edition, 1960. Better "bringing into work"; bringing forth; bringing as allowing; ποίησις.

"To place" must be thought in the sense of θέσις. So one reads on p. 36: "Setting and taking possession [*Setzen und Besetzen*] are here always (!) thought in the sense of the Greek θέσις, which means a setting up in the unconcealed." The Greek "setting" means: placing as allowing to arise, for example, a statue. It means: laying, laying down a sacred offering. "Placing" and "laying" have the sense of bringing *hither*[a] into unconcealment, bringing *forth* among what is present, that is, allowing to lie forth. "Setting" and "placing" here never mean the summoning of things to be placed over and against the self (the "I" as subject) as conceived in the modern fashion. The standing of the statue (i.e., the presence of the radiance that faces us) is different from the standing of what stands over and against us [*Gegenstand*] in the sense of an object [*Objekt*]. "Standing" (cf. p. 16 above) is the constancy of the radiance. In the dialectic of Kantian and German idealism, on the other hand, thesis, antithesis, and synthesis refer to a placing within the sphere of the subjectivity of consciousness. Accordingly, Hegel – correctly in terms of his own position – interpreted the Greek θέσις as the immediate positing [*Setzen*] of the object. This positing is for him, therefore, untrue since it is not yet mediated by antithesis and thesis (compare "Hegel and the Greeks" in *Pathmarks*[5]).

But if, in the context of the artwork-essay, we keep in mind the Greek sense of θέσις – to let lie forth in its radiance and presence – then the "fixed" corresponding to "fix in place" can never mean the stiff, motionless, and secure.

"Fixed" means: outlined, admitted into the boundary (πέρας), brought into the outline (compare pp. 38ff. above). The boundary, in the Greek sense, does not block off but, rather, as itself something brought forth, first brings what is present to radiance. The boundary sets free into unconcealment: by means of its outline, the mountain stands in the Greek light in its towering and repose. The boundary which fixes and consolidates is what reposes, reposes in the fullness of movement. All this is true of the work in the sense of the Greek ἔργον. The work's "being" is ἐνέργεια, a term which gathers into itself infinitely more movement than the modern "energies."

It follows, then, that, properly thought, the "fixing in place" of truth can never run counter to "allowing to happen." In the first place, this "allowing" is nothing passive; rather, it is the highest form of action (see *Vorträge und Aufsätze*, 1954, p. 49) in the sense of θέσις, an "effecting" and "willing" which, in the present essay, is characterized as "the existing human being's

[a] Reclam edition, 1960. "Hither": from out of the clearing.

allowing himself ecstatic entrance into the unconcealment of beings" (p. 41 above). In the second place, the "happen" in the "letting happen of truth" is the prevailing movement in clearing *and* concealment or, more precisely, in their union; in other words, it is the movement of the clearing of self-concealment as such, from which, in turn, all self-illumination arises. This "movement" even requires a fixing in place in the sense of a bringing forth, where this "bringing" is to be understood in the sense indicated on p. 37, in that the creating (creative) bringing forth "(is) a receiving and taking over that occurs within the pull [*Bezug*] toward unconcealment."

The meaning of the word "*Ge-stell* [placement]" used on p. 38, is to be understood in accordance with the above elucidation: the gathering together of the bringing forth, the allowing to come forth into the rift as bounding design (πέρας). The Greek meaning of μορφή as figure is clarified by "*Ge-stell*" understood in this way. Now, in fact, the use of "*Ge-stell*" in later writings specifically as the key word for designating the essence of modern technology[6] is thought out of this use of the word – *not* from bookcase [*Büchergestell*] or installation. This derivation is the more essential one since it corresponds to the destiny of being. *Ge-stell*, as the essence of modern technology, comes from letting-lie-before experienced in the Greek manner, λόγος, from the Greek ποίησις and θέσις. In the putting in place of *Ge-stell* – which now means the summoning of everything into assured availability – there speaks the claim of *ratio reddenda*, i.e., of λόγον διδόναι. It speaks, of course, in such a way that, today, this claim that is made by *Ge-stell* assumes dominion over the absolute. And placing-before, representation [*Vor-stellen*], gathered out of the Greek notion of apprehension, becomes making fast and fixing in place.

When we hear the words "fix in place" and "*Ge-stell*" in "The Origin of the Artwork" we must, on the one hand, forget the modern meaning of placing and enframing. Yet on the other, we must not overlook the fact that, and extent to which, being as *Ge-stell*, definitive of modernity, comes forth from out of the Western destiny of being and is nothing thought up by philosophers; rather, it is something which is thought to the thoughtful (compare *Vorträge und Aufsätze*, p. 28 and p. 49).

There remains the difficult task of discussing the definitions given on pp. 36ff. for the "establishing" and "self-establishing of truth in beings." Here again, we must avoid understanding "establishing" in the modern sense, avoid understanding it as "organizing" and "making ready" in the manner of a lecture on technology. Rather, "establishing" thinks toward the "impulse of truth toward the work" referred to on p. 37, the impulse that, in the midst of beings, truth itself should be as a work, should come to be in being (p. 37 above).

If we recollect how truth as the unconcealment of beings means nothing other than the presence of beings as such – that is, of *being* (see p. 45) – then the talk of the self-establishment of truth (i.e., of being) in beings touches on the questionableness [*das Fragwürdige*] of the ontological difference (compare *Identity and Difference*, pp. 47ff.). For this reason p. 36 of "The Origin of the Work of Art" sounds a note of caution: "With reference to the self-establishment of openness in the open our thinking touches on an area which cannot here be elucidated." The entire essay moves knowingly yet implicitly, along the path of the question of the essence of being. Reflection on what *art* may be is completely and decisively directed solely toward the question of *being*. Art is accorded neither an area of cultural achievement nor an appearance of spirit; it belongs, rather, to the Event out of which the "meaning of being" (compare *Being and Time*) is first determined. What art may be is one of the questions to which the essay offers no answer. What may give the impression of such an answer are directions for questioning (compare the first sentences of the Afterword).

Among these directions are two *important hints* (on p. 44 and p. 49). At both places there is talk of "ambiguity." On p. 49 an "essential ambiguity" is mentioned with respect to the definition of art as the "setting-to-work of truth." On the one hand, "truth" is the "subject," on the other the "object." *Both* characterizations remain "inappropriate." If truth is subject, then the definition "setting-to-work of truth" means the setting-*itself*-to-work of truth (compare p. 44 and p. 16). In this manner art is thought out of the Event. Being, however, is a call to man and cannot be without him. Accordingly, art is at the same time defined as the setting-to-work of truth, where truth *now* is "object" and art is human creating and preserving.

Within the *human* relation lies the other ambiguity in the setting-to-work which, on p. 44, is identified as that between creation and preservation. According to pages 44 and 33, it is the art*work* and art*ist* that have a "special" relationship to the coming into being of art. In the label "setting-to-work of truth," in which it remains undetermined (though determin*able*) who or what does the "setting," and in what manner, lies concealed *the relationship of being to human being*. This relationship is inadequately thought even in this presentation – a distressing difficulty that has been clear to me since *Being and Time*, and has since come under discussion in many presentations (see, finally, "On the Question of Being" and the present essay p. 36 "Only this should be noted; that . . . ").

The problematic issue that prevails here, then, comes to a head at the very place in the discussion where the essence of language and of poetry is touched upon, all this, again, only in reference to the belonging together of being and saying.

It remains an unavoidable necessity that the reader, who naturally comes to the essay from without, at first and for a long time thereafter, represent and interpret the facts of the case from out of the silent domain that is the source of what has been thought. But for the author himself there remains the necessity to speak each time in the language that is, in each case, appropriate to the various stations on his way.

The Age of the World Picture

In metaphysics, reflection on the essence of beings and a decision concerning the essence of truth is accomplished. Metaphysics grounds an age in that, through a particular interpretation of beings and through a particular comprehension of truth, it provides that age with the ground of its essential shape. This ground comprehensively governs all decisions distinctive of the age. Conversely, in order for there to be adequate reflection on these phenomena [*Erscheinungen*], their metaphysical ground must allow itself to be recognized in them. Reflection is the courage to put up for question the truth of one's own presuppositions and the space of one's own goals (Appendix 1).[1]

One of the essential phenomena of modernity is its science. Of equal importance is machine technology. One should not, however, misconstrue this as the mere application of modern mathematical science to praxis. Machine technology is itself an autonomous transformation of praxis, a transformation which first demands the employment of mathematical science. Machine technology still remains the most visible outgrowth of the essence of modern technology, an essence which is identical with the essence of modern metaphysics.

A third, equally essential phenomenon of modernity lies in the process of art's moving into the purview of aesthetics. This means the artwork becomes an object of experience [*Erlebens*] and consequently is considered to be an expression of human life.

A fourth modern phenomenon announces itself in the fact that human action is understood and practiced as culture. Culture then becomes the realization of the highest values through the care and cultivation of man's highest goods. It belongs to the essence of culture, as such care, that it, in turn, takes itself into care and then becomes the politics of culture.

A fifth phenomenon of modernity is the loss of the gods [*Entgötterung*]. This expression does not mean the mere elimination of the gods, crude atheism. The loss of the gods is a twofold process. On the one hand, the world picture Christianizes itself inasmuch as the ground of the world is posited as infinite and unconditioned, as the absolute. On the other hand, Christendom reinterprets its Christianity as a world view (the Christian world view) and thus makes itself modern and up to date. The loss of the gods is the condition of indecision about God and the gods. Christianity is chiefly responsible for bringing it about. But loss of the gods is far from excluding religiosity. Rather, it is on its account that the relation to the gods is transformed into religious experience [*Erleben*]. When this happens, the gods have fled. The resulting void is filled by the historical and psychological investigation of myth.

What conception of beings and what interpretation of truth lies at the basis of these phenomena?

We confine the question to the first of the phenomena mentioned above, natural science.

In what is the essence of modern science to be found?

What conception of beings and of truth grounds this essence? If we can manage to come upon the metaphysical ground which provides the foundation of science as a modern phenomenon, then it must be possible to recognize from out of that ground the essence of modernity in general.

As we use the word science these days, it means something essentially different from the *doctrina* and *scientia* of the Middle Ages, different, too, from the Greek ἐπιστήμη. Greek science was never exact precisely because, according to its essence, it neither could be, nor needed to be, exact. Hence, it makes no sense at all to assert that contemporary science is more exact than the science of antiquity. Neither can one say that Galileo's doctrine of free-falling bodies is true while Aristotle's teaching that light bodies strive upwards is false. For the Greek understanding of the nature of body and place and of the relation between them rests on a different interpretation of beings. It determines, therefore, a correspondingly different way of seeing and questioning natural occurrences. No one would presume to say that Shakespeare's poetry is more advanced than that of Aeschylus. It is even more impossible to say that the contemporary understanding of beings is more correct than that of the Greeks. If, then, we wish to grasp the essence of contemporary science we must first free ourselves of the habit of comparing modern with older science – from the perspective of progress – merely in terms of degree.

The essence of what is today called science is research. In what does the essence of research consist?

It consists in the fact that knowing establishes itself as a procedure within some realm of beings in nature or history. Procedure, here, does not just mean methodology, how things are done. For every procedure requires, in advance, an open region within which it operates. But precisely the opening up of such a region constitutes the fundamental occurrence in research. This is accomplished through the projection, within some region of (for example, natural) beings, of a ground-plan [*Grundriss*] of natural processes. Such a projection maps out in advance the way in which the procedure of knowing is to bind itself to the region that is opened up. This commitment [*Bindung*] is the rigor of research. Through the projection of the ground-plan and the prescribing of rigor, procedure secures for itself, within the realm of being, its sphere of objects. A glance at mathematical physics – the earliest of modern sciences which is, at the same time, normative for the rest – will make clear what we mean. Insofar as modern atomic physics still remains physics, what is essential – which is all that concerns us here – will be true of it as well.

Modern physics is called "mathematical" because it makes use, in a remarkable way, of a quite specific kind of mathematics. But it is only able to proceed mathematically because, in a deeper sense, it is already mathematical. Τὰ μαθήματα means, in Greek, that which, in his observation of beings and interaction with things, man knows in advance: the corporeality of bodies, the vegetable character of plants, the animality of animals, the humanness of human beings. Along with these, belonging to the already-known, i.e., "mathematical," are the numbers. When we discover three apples on the table we recognize that there are three of them. But the number three, threeness, we know already. That is to say: the number is something "mathematical." Only because numbers represent, so to speak, the most striking of the always-already-known, and therefore the best-known instances of the mathematical, is "the mathematical" directly reserved as a name for the numerical. The essence of the mathematical, however, is in no way defined in terms of the numerical. Physics is, in general, knowledge of nature. In particular, it is knowledge of material corporeality in motion; for corporeality manifests itself immediately and universally – albeit in different ways – in all natural things. When, therefore, physics assumes an explicitly "mathematical" form, what this means is the following: that through and for it, in an emphatic way, something is specified in advance as that which is already known. This specification concerns nothing less than what, for the sought-after knowledge of nature, is henceforth to count as "nature": the closed system of spatio-temporally related units of mass. Pertaining to this ground-plan, in accordance with its prior specification, are to be found, among others, the following definitions. Motion is change of place. No motion or direction of motion takes precedence over any other. Every place is equal to every other. No point in time has precedence over any other. Every force is defined as – is, that is, nothing but – its consequences as motion within the unity of time; and that means, again, change of place. Every natural event must be viewed in such a way that it fits into this ground-plan of nature. Only within the perspective of this ground-plan does a natural event become visible as such. The ground-plan of nature is secured in place in that physical research, in each step of investigation, is obligated to it in advance. This obligation [*Bindung*], the rigor of research, has, at a given time, its own character in keeping with the ground-plan. The rigor of mathematical science is exactitude. Every event, if it enters at all into representation as a natural event, is determined, in advance, as a magnitude of spatio-temporal motion. Such determination is achieved by means of numbers and calculation. Mathematical research into nature is not, however, exact because it calculates precisely; rather, it must calculate precisely because the way it is bound to its domain of objects has the character of exactness. The human sciences, by contrast, indeed all the sciences that deal with living things, precisely in order to remain disciplined and rigorous, are necessarily inexact. One can, indeed, view living things, too, as magnitudes of spatio-temporal motion, but what one apprehends is then no longer living. The inexactness of the historical human sciences is not a deficiency but rather the fulfillment of an essential requirement of this type of research. It is true, also, that the projecting and the securing of the domain of objects is, in the historical sciences, not only different, but far more difficult to achieve than is the rigor of the exact sciences.

Science becomes research through the projected plan and through the securing of the plan in the rigor of procedure. Projection and rigor, however, first develop into what they are in method. Method constitutes the second essential characteristic of research. If the projected region is to become objectified, then it must be brought to encounter us in the full multiplicity of its levels and interweavings. Procedure must therefore be free to view the changeableness in what it encounters. Only from within the perspective of the ever-otherness of change does the plenitude of the particular, of the facts, reveal itself. The facts, however, are to become objective. Procedure must, therefore, represent the changeable in its changing; it must bring it to stand and yet allow the motion to remain a motion. The fixedness of the facts and the constancy of their change as such is the rule. The constancy of change in the necessity of its course is the law. Only from the perspective of rule and law do facts become clear as what they are. Research into the facts in the realm of nature is the setting up and confirmation of rule and law. The method by means of which a domain of objects is represented has the character of a clarification [*Klärung*] from out of the clear, of explanation [*Erklärung*]. Explanation always has two sides to it. It accounts for something unknown through something known, and at the same time confirms the known through that unknown. Explanation takes place in investigation. In the natural sciences this happens in the experiment, always according to the nature of the field of investigation and the kind of explanation aimed at. However, natural science does not first become research through experiment. It is rather the other way round: experiment is only possible where knowledge of nature has already transformed itself into research. It is only because contemporary physics is a physics that is essentially mathematical that it is capable of being experimental. Since neither the medieval *doctrina* nor the Greek ἐπιστήμη were science in the sense of research, there was, for them, no question of experiment. To be sure, Aristotle was the first to grasp the meaning of ἐμπειρία (*experientia*): the observation of the things themselves, their characteristics and alterations under changing conditions, resulting in knowledge of the way in which they behave as a rule. But observation directed toward knowledge of this kind, the *experimentum*, is essentially different from that which belongs to science as research, the research-experiment. It remains essentially different even where ancient and medieval observation also works with number and measure, and even where it makes use of specific apparatus and instruments. For what is completely absent here is what is decisive about the experiment. This begins with the fundamental postulation of a law. To set up an experiment is to represent a condition according to which a specific nexus of motions can become capable of being followed in its necessary course, which is to say that it can be mastered, in advance, by calculation. The setting up of the law, however, is accomplished with reference to the ground-plan of the sphere of objects. This provides the standard and constrains the anticipatory representation of the condition. Such representing with and within which the experiment begins is no arbitrary invention. This is why Newton says *hypotheses non fingo*; the fundamental postulations are not arbitrarily thought up. They are, rather, developed out of the ground-plan of nature and are sketched into it. Experiment is that method which, in its planning and execution, is supported and guided by what is postulated as a fundamental law, in order to bring forth the facts which either confirm the law or deny it such confirmation. The more exact the projection of the ground-plan of nature the more exact is the possibility of experiment. The often mentioned medieval scholastic, Roger Bacon, can, therefore, never be the forerunner of the contemporary experimental researcher but remains, rather, merely the successor of Aristotle. For in the meantime, genuine possession of the truth has, through Christianity, been transferred to faith – to the truth preserved in the written word and in church doctrine. The highest knowledge and teaching is theology considered as interpretation of the divine word of revelation that is recorded in scripture and proclaimed by the Church. Here, knowledge is not research but rather right understanding of the normative word and of the authorities who proclaim it. For this reason, discussion of the words and doctrinal opinions of the various authorities takes precedence in the process of knowledge-acquisition in the Middle Ages. The *componere scripta et sermones*, the *argumentum ex verbo*, is decisive and, at the same time, the reason why the Platonic and Aristotelian philosophy that had been adopted, had to become scholastic dialectic. If, then, Roger Bacon demands the *experimentum* – as he did – what he means is not the experiment of science as research. Rather he demands, in place of the *argumentum ex verbo*, the *argumentum ex re*;[2] instead of the discussion of doctrinal opinions, observations of the things themselves, in other words, Aristotelian ἐμπειρία.

The modern research-experiment is, however, not merely an observation that is more precise in degree and scope. It is, rather, an essentially different kind of methodology for the verification of law within the framework and in the service of an exact projection of nature. In the historical human sciences "source criticism" corresponds to the experiment of physical research. This name covers, here, the whole range of discovery, examination, verification, evaluation, preservation, and interpretation. It is indeed true that the historical explanation based on source-criticism does not subsume the facts under laws and rules. Yet it is not reduced to a mere reporting of the facts. As in the natural sciences, method in the historical sciences is aimed at presenting the constant and at making history an object. History can only be objectified when it is something past. The constancy of the past, that on the basis of which historical explanation takes into account the unique and diverse in history, is the having-always-already-been-there, that which can be compared. Through the constant comparisons of everything with everything else the intelligible is worked out and, as the ground-plan of history, certified and secured. The sphere of historical research extends only as far as the reach of historical explanation. The unique, the rare, the simple – in short, greatness in history – is never self-evident and hence remains incapable of explanation. It is not that historical research denies greatness in history; rather, it explains it as the exception. In such explanation the great is measured against the ordinary and average. There is no other kind of historical explanation as long as explanation means subsuming under the intelligible, and as long as historical science remains research, i.e., explanation. Because, as research, history projects and objectifies the past as an explicable and surveyable nexus of effects, it demands source-criticism as the instrument of objectification. The standards of such criticism alter to the degree that historical science approaches journalism.

As research, every science is based on the projection of a bounded object domain and necessarily possesses, therefore, an individualized character. In developing its projection through its methodology, moreover, every individual science must focus on a particular field of investigation. This focusing (specialization) is, however, by no means merely the dire side effect of the increasing unsurveyability of the results of research. It is not a necessary evil, but rather the essential necessity of science as research. Specialization is not the consequence but rather the ground of the progress of all research. Research does not, through its methodology, become dispersed into random investigations so as to lose itself in them. For the character of modern science is determined by a third fundamental occurrence: constant activity [*Betrieb*] (Appendix 2).

By this term is to be understood, first of all, that phenomenon whereby a science, whether natural or humanistic, in order to achieve proper recognition today as a science is required to be capable of being institutionalized. Research is not, however, constant activity because its work is carried out in institutions; rather, institutions are necessary because science, as, intrinsically, research, has the character of constant activity. The methodology through which individual object domains are conquered does not simply amass results. Rather, it uses its results to direct itself toward a new procedure. In the mechanical installation that enables physics to smash the atom we have the whole of physics up to now. Similarly, in historical research, the stock of sources only becomes usable when the sources themselves are verified by historical explanation. In these processes the methodology of a science is circumscribed by its own results. More and more, methodology adapts itself to the possibilities of procedure it itself opens up. This having-to-be-based on its own results as the ways and means of a progressing methodology, is the essence of the character of research as constant activity. That character, however, is the inner ground for the necessity of its institutional character.

It is in constant activity that the projection of the object domain is, for the first time, built into beings. All arrangements that facilitate the planned amalgamation of different types of methodology, promote the reciprocal checking and communication of results, and regulate the exchange of labor are measures which are by no means merely the external consequence of the fact that research work is expanding and diversifying. Rather, they are the distant and still by no means comprehended sign that modern science begins to enter the decisive phase of its history. Only now does it take possession of its own complete essence.

What is going on in the spread and entrenchment of the institutional character of the sciences? Nothing less than the establishment of the precedence of methodology over the beings (of nature and history) which, at a particular time, are objectified in research. On the basis of their character as constant activity, the sciences create for themselves the appropriate coherence and unity. For this reason, historical or archeological research that has become institutionally active is essentially nearer to research in physics that is organized in a similar way than it is to a discipline in its own faculty of humanities which has remained within mere scholarship. The decisive unfolding of the character of modern science as constant activity produces, therefore, a human being of another stamp. The scholar disappears and is replaced by the researcher engaged in research programs. These, and not the cultivation of scholarship, are what places his work at the cutting edge [*geben seiner Arbeit die scharfe Luft*]. The researcher no longer needs a library at home. He is, moreover, constantly on the move. He negotiates at conferences and collects information at congresses. He commits himself to publishers' commissions. It is publishers who now determine which books need to be written (Appendix 3).

From an inner compulsion, the researcher presses forward into the sphere occupied by the figure of, in the essential sense, the technologist. Only in this way can he remain capable of being effective, and only then, in the eyes of his age, is he real. Alongside him, an increasingly thinner and emptier romanticism of scholarship and the university will still be able to survive for some time at certain places. The effective unity and therefore the reality of the university, however, does not lie in the spiritual-intellectual [*geistige*] power of the primordial unity of the sciences, a power emanating from the university because nourished and preserved by it. The reality of the university is that it is an establishment which still, in a unique way, on account of its administratively self-contained form, makes possible and visible both the fragmentation of the sciences into the specialities and the peculiar unity of constant activity. Because it is in constant activity that the essential forces of modern science become immediately and unambiguously effective, it is only self-directed research activities which, proceeding from themselves, can prefigure and establish an inner unity with other appropriate research activities.

The real system of science consists in the coherence of procedure and stance with respect to the objectification of beings, in conformity, at any given time, with planning. The advantage this system is required to promote is no contrived and rigid unification of the contents of the object domains. Rather, it is the greatest possible free, though regulated, flexibility in the changing around and initiation of research with respect to whatever are the principle tasks of the moment. The more exclusively a science becomes focused on the complete carrying out and mastery of its process of working, the more these activities are – without illusion – shifted into research institutes and professional schools for research, then the more irresistibly do the sciences achieve the completion of their modern essence. The more unconditionally, however, science and research take seriously the modern shape of their essence, the more unequivocally and immediately are they themselves able to stand ready to serve the common good; and the more unreservedly, too, will they have to withdraw into the public anonymity of all socially useful work.

Modern science simultaneously founds and differentiates itself in the projection of particular object domains. These projections are developed by the appropriate methodologies which are made secure by means of rigor. Method establishes itself at any given time in constant activity. Projection and rigor, method and constant activity, each demanding the other, make up the essence of modern science, make it into research.

We are reflecting on the essence of modern science in order to discover its metaphysical ground. What understanding of beings and what concept of truth is it that underlies the transformation of science into research?

Knowledge as research calls beings to account with regard to the way in which, and the extent to which, they can be placed at the disposal of representation. Research has beings at its disposal when it can, through calculation, either predict their future or retrodict their past. In the prediction of nature and retrodiction of history, nature and history are set in place in the same way. They become objects of explanatory representation. Such representation counts on nature and takes account of history. Only what becomes, in this way, an object *is* – counts as in being. We first arrive at science as research when the being of beings is sought in such objectness.

This objectification of beings is accomplished in a setting-before, a representing [*Vor-stellen*], aimed at bringing each being before it in such a way that the man who calculates can be sure – and that means certain – of the being. Science as research first arrives when, and only when, truth has transformed itself into the certainty of representation. It is in the metaphysics of Descartes that, for the first time, the being is defined as the objectness of representation, and truth as the certainty of representation. The title of his main work reads *Meditationes de prima philosophia*, *Meditations on First Philosophy*. Πρώτη φιλοσοφία is the term coined by Aristotle for that which was later called "metaphysics." The whole of modern metaphysics, Nietzsche included, maintains itself within the interpretation of the being and of truth opened up by Descartes (Appendix 4).

If, now, science as research is an essential phenomenon of modernity, it must follow that what constitutes the metaphysical ground of research determines, first, and long in advance, the essence of modernity in general. The essence of modernity can be seen in humanity's freeing itself from the bonds of the Middle Ages in that it frees itself to itself. But this characterization, though correct, is merely the foreground. And it leads to those mistakes which prevent one from grasping the essential ground of modernity and, proceeding from there, judging the breadth of that essence. Certainly the modern age has, as a consequence of the liberation of humanity, introduced subjectivism and individualism. But it remains just as certain that no age before this one has produced a comparable objectivism, and that in no age before this has the non-individual, in the shape of the collective, been accorded prestige. Of the essence here is the necessary interplay between subjectivism and objectivism. But precisely this reciprocal conditioning of the one by the other refers us back to deeper processes.

What is decisive is not that humanity frees itself from previous bonds but, rather, that the essence of humanity altogether transforms itself in that man becomes the subject. To be sure, this word "subject" must be understood as the translation of the Greek ὑποκείμενον. The word names that-which-lies-before, that which, as ground, gathers everything onto itself. This metaphysical meaning of the concept of the subject has, in the first instance, no special relationship to man, and none at all to the I.

When, however, man becomes the primary and genuine *subiectum*, this means that he becomes that being upon which every being, in its way of being and its truth, is founded. Man becomes the referential center of beings as such. But this is only possible when there is a transformation in the understanding of beings as a whole. In what does this transformation manifest itself? What, in accordance with it, is the essence of modernity?

When we reflect on the modern age, we inquire after the modern world picture. We characterize this by contrasting it with the world picture of the Middle Ages and of antiquity. But why is it that, in interpreting a historical age, we inquire into its world picture? Does every historical epoch have its world picture – have it in such a way, indeed, so as, from time to time, to concern itself about that picture? Or is it only a modern kind of representing that inquires into a world picture?

What is it – a "world picture"? Obviously, a picture of the world. But what is a world? What does "picture" mean here? "World" serves, here, as a name for beings in their entirety. The term is not confined to the cosmos, to nature. History, too, belongs to world. But even nature and history – interpenetrating in their suffusion and exceeding of each other – do not exhaust world. Under this term we also include the world-ground, no matter how its relation to world is thought (Appendix 5).

Initially, the word "picture" makes one think of a copy of something. This would make the world picture, as it were, a painting of beings as a whole. But "world picture" means more than this. We mean by it the world itself; the totality of beings taken, as it is for us, as standard-giving and obligating. "Picture" means, here, not a mere imitation, but rather that which sounds in the colloquial expression to be "in the picture" about something. This means: the matter itself stands in the way it stands to us, before us. To "put oneself in the picture" about something means: to place the being itself before one just as things are with it, and, as so placed, to keep it permanently before one. But a decisive condition in the essence of the picture is still missing. That we are "in the picture" about something means not just that the being is placed before, represented by, us. It means, rather, that it stands before us together with what belongs to and stands together with it as a system. To be "in the picture" resonates with: being well informed, being equipped and prepared. Where the world becomes picture, beings as a whole are set in place as that for which man is prepared; that which, therefore, he correspondingly intends to bring before him, have before him, and, thereby, in a decisive sense, place before him (Appendix 6). Understood in an essential way, "world picture" does not mean "picture of the world" but, rather, the world grasped as picture. Beings as a whole are now taken in such a way that a being is first and only in being insofar as it is set in place by representing-producing [*vorstellend-herstellenden*] humanity. Whenever we have a world picture, an essential decision occurs concerning beings as a whole. The being of beings is sought and found in the representedness of beings. Where, however, beings are *not* interpreted in this way, the world, too, cannot come into the picture – there can be no world picture. That beings acquire being in and through representedness makes the age in which this occurs a new age, distinct from its predecessors. The familiar phrases "world picture of modernity" and "modern world picture" say the same thing twice. And they presuppose something that could never before have existed, namely, a medieval and ancient world picture. The world picture does not change from an earlier medieval to a modern one; rather, that the world becomes picture at all is what distinguishes the essence of modernity. For the Middle Ages, by contrast, the being is the *ens creatum*, that which is created by the personal creator-God who is considered to be the highest cause. Here, to be a being means: to belong to a particular rank in the order of created things, and, as thus created, to correspond to the cause of creation (*analogia entis*) (Appendix 7). But never does the being's being consist in its being brought before man as the objective. Never does it consist in being placed in the realm of man's information and disposal so that, in this way alone, is it in being.

The modern interpretation of beings is still further removed from that of the Greeks. One of the oldest expressions of Greek thinking about the being of beings reads: Τὸ γὰρ αὐτὸ νοεῖν ἐστίν τε καὶ εἶναι.[3] This statement of Parmenides means: the apprehension of beings belongs to being since it is from being that it is demanded and determined. The being is that which rises up and opens itself; that which, as what is present, comes upon man, i.e., upon him who opens himself to what is present in that he apprehends it. The being does not acquire being in that man first looks upon it in the sense of representation that has the character of subjective perception. Rather, man is the one who is looked upon by beings, the one who is gathered by self-opening beings into presencing with them. To be looked at by beings,[a] to be included and maintained and so supported by their openness, to be driven about by their conflict and marked by their dividedness, that is the essence of humanity in the great age of Greece. In order to fulfill his essence, therefore, man has to gather (λέγειν) and save (σώζειν), catch up and preserve, the self-opening in its openness; and he must remain exposed to all of its divisive confusion. Greek humanity *is* the receiver [*Vernehmer*] of beings,

[a] First edition, 1950: by being as presencing *taken as* εἶδος.

which is the reason that, in the age of the Greeks, the world can never become picture. On the other hand, however, is the fact that the beingness of beings is defined, for Plato, as εἶδος (appearance, view). This is the presupposition which – long prevailing only mediately, in concealment and long in advance – predestined the world's having to become picture (Appendix 8).

In distinction from the Greek apprehension, modern representing, whose signification is first expressed by the word *repraesentatio*, means something quite different. Representation [*Vor-stellen*] here means: to bring the present-at-hand before one as something standing over-and-against, to relate it to oneself, the representer, and, in this relation, to force it back to oneself as the norm-giving domain. Where this happens man "puts himself in the picture" concerning beings. When, however, in this way, he does this, he places himself in the scene; in, that is, the sphere of what is generally and publicly represented. And what goes along with this is that man sets himself forth as the scene in which, henceforth, beings must set-themselves-before, present themselves – be, that is to say, in the picture. Man becomes the representative [*Repräsentant*] of beings in the sense of the objective.

What is new, however, in this occurrence does not at all consist in the fact, merely, that the position of man in the midst of beings is other than it was for ancient of medieval man. What is decisive is that man specifically takes up this position as one constituted by himself, intentionally maintains it as that taken up by himself, and secures it in place as the basis for a possible development of humanity. Now for the first time there exists such a thing as the "position" of man. Man makes depend on himself the way he is to stand to beings as the objective. What begins is that mode of human being which occupies the realm of human capacity as the domain of measuring and execution for the purpose of the mastery of beings as a whole. The age that is determined by this event is not only new in retrospective comparison with what had preceded it. It is new, rather, in that it explicitly sets itself up as the new. To be "new" belongs to a world that has become picture.

If, then, we wish to clarify the pictorial character of the world as the representedness of beings, then in order fully to grasp the modern essence of representedness we must scent out the original naming power of that worn-out word and concept "to represent": to put forth and relate to oneself. It is through this that the being comes to stand as an object and so first receives the seal of being. That the world becomes picture is one and the same process whereby, in the midst of beings, man becomes subject (Appendix 9).

Only because and insofar as man, altogether and essentially, has become subject is it necessary for him to confront, as a consequence, this explicit question: is it as an "I" that is reduced to its random desires and abandoned to an arbitrary free-will or as the "we" of society; is it as individual or as community; is it as a personal being within the community or as a mere member of the body corporate; is it as a state, nation, or people or as the indifferent humanity of modern man, that man wills and must be that subject which, *as* the essence of modernity, he *already is*? Only where, in essence, man has become subject does there exist the possibility of sliding into the unbeing of subjectivism in the sense of individualism. But it is also the case that only where man *remains* subject does it make any sense to struggle explicitly against individualism and for the community as the goal and arena of all achievement and utility.

The interweaving of these two processes – that the world becomes picture and man the subject – which is decisive for the essence of modernity illuminates the founding process of modern history, a process that, at first sight, seems almost nonsensical. The process, namely, whereby the more completely and comprehensively the world, as conquered, stands at man's disposal, and the more objectively the object appears, all the more subjectively (i.e., peremptorily) does the *subiectum* rise up, and all the more inexorably, too, do observations and teachings about the world transform themselves into a doctrine of man, into an anthropology. No wonder that humanism first arises where the world becomes picture. In the great age of the Greeks, however, it was as impossible for a humanism to gain currency as it was for there to be anything like a world picture. Humanism, therefore, in the narrower, historical sense, is nothing but a moral-aesthetic anthropology. The name "anthropology," here, does not refer to an investigation of humanity by natural science. Neither does it mean the doctrine established within Christian theology concerning created, fallen, and redeemed humanity. It designates, rather, that philosophical interpretation of man which explains and evaluates beings as a whole from the standpoint of, and in relation to, man (Appendix 10).

The ever more exclusive rooting of the interpretation of the world in anthropology which has set in since the end of the eighteenth century finds expression in the fact that man's fundamental relation to beings as a whole is defined as a world view [*Weltanschauung*]. It is since then that this term has entered common usage. As soon as the world becomes picture the position of man is conceived as world view. It is, to be sure, easy to misunderstand the term "world view," to suppose it to have to do merely with a disengaged contemplation of the world. For this reason, already in the nineteenth century, it was rightly emphasized that "world view" also means, and even means primarily, "view of life." The fact that, nonetheless, "world view" has asserted itself as the name for the position of man in the midst of beings proves how decisively the world becomes picture as soon as man makes his life as subject the primary center of reference. This means: the being counts as in being only to the degree and extent that it is taken into, and referred back to, this life, i.e., is lived out [*er-lebt*], and becomes life-experience [*Er-lebnis*]. As every humanism had to remain something unsuited to Greece, so a "medieval world view" was an impossibility; and a "Catholic world view" is an absurdity. Just as, for modern man, the more unbounded the way in which he takes charge of the shaping of his essence, everything must, by both necessity and right, become "experience," just as certainly, the Greeks at the Olympic festivals could never have had "experiences."

The fundamental event of modernity is the conquest of the world as picture. From now on the word "picture" means: the collective image of representing production [*das Gebild des vorstellenden Herstellens*]. Within this, man fights for the position in which he can be that being who gives to every being the measure and draws up the guidelines. Because this position secures, organizes, and articulates itself as world view, the decisive unfolding of the modern relationship to beings becomes a confrontation of world views; not, indeed, any old set of world views, but only those which have already taken hold of man's most fundamental stance with the utmost decisiveness. For the sake of this battle of world views, and according to its meaning, humanity sets in motion, with respect to everything, the unlimited process of calculation, planning, and breeding. Science as research is the indispensable form taken by this self-establishment in the world; it is one of the pathways along which, with a speed unrecognized by those who are involved, modernity races towards the fulfillment of its essence. With this battle of world views modernity first enters the decisive period of its history, and probably the one most capable of enduring (Appendix 11).

A sign of this event is the appearance everywhere, and in the most varied forms and disguises, of the gigantic. At the same time, the huge announces itself in the direction of the ever smaller. We have only to think of the numbers of atomic physics. The gigantic presses forward in a form which seems to make it disappear: in destruction of great distances by the airplane, in the representations of foreign and remote worlds in their everydayness produced at will by the flick of a switch. One thinks too superficially, however, if one takes the gigantic to be merely an endlessly extended emptiness of the purely quantitative. One thinks too briefly if one finds the gigantic, in the form of the continual never-having-been-here-before, to spring merely from a blind impulse to exaggerate and excel. One thinks not at all if one takes oneself to have explained this appearance of the gigantic with the slogan "Americanism" (Appendix 12).

The gigantic is, rather, that through which the quantitative acquires its own kind of quality, becoming thereby, a remarkable form of the great. A historical age is not only great in a different way from others; it also has, in every case, its own concept of greatness. As soon, however, as the gigantic, in planning, calculating, establishing, and securing, changes from the quantitative and becomes its own special quality, then the gigantic and the seemingly completely calculable become, through this shift, incalculable. This incalculability becomes the invisible shadow cast over all things when man has become the *subiectum* and world has become picture (Appendix 13).

Through this shadow the modern world withdraws into a space beyond representation and so lends to the incalculable its own determinateness and historical uniqueness. This shadow, however, points to something else, knowledge of which, to us moderns, is refused (Appendix 14). Yet man will never be able to experience and think this refusal as long as he goes around merely negating the age. The flight into tradition, out of a combination of humility and presumption, achieves, in itself, nothing, is merely a closing the eyes and blindness towards the historical moment [*Augenblick*].

Man will know the incalculable – that is, safeguard it in its truth – only in creative questioning and forming from out of the power of genuine reflection. Reflection transports the man of the future into that "in-between" in which he belongs to being and yet, amidst beings, remains a stranger (Appendix 15). Hölderlin knew about this. His poem, above which is written "To the Germans," closes:[4]

True, narrowly bounded is our lifetime,
We see and count the number of our years
But the years of the peoples,
Have they been seen by mortal eye?

Even if your soul soars in longing
beyond its own time, mourning
You linger on the cold shore
Among your own, and know them not.

Wohl ist enge begränzt unsere Lebenszeit,
Unserer Jahre Zahl sehen und zählen wir,
Doch die Jahre der Völker
sah ein sterbliches Auge sie?

Wenn die Seele dir auch über die eigne Zeit
Sich die sehnende schwingt, trauernd verweilest du
Dann am kalten Gestade
Bei den Deinen und kennst sie nie.

APPENDICES

(1) Such reflection is neither necessary for all nor is it to be accomplished, or even found bearable, by everyone. On the contrary, absence of reflection belongs, to a very great extent, to the particular stages of accomplishing and being constantly active. The questioning that belongs to reflection, however, does not fall into that which is groundless and beyond questioning because, in advance, it asks after being. This remains that which is most worthy of question [*Fragewürdigste*]. Reflection finds in being the utmost resistance, which constrains it to deal seriously with beings as they are drawn into the light of their being. Reflection on the essence of modernity places thought and decision within the sphere of effectiveness belonging to the authentically essential forces of the age. These forces work, as they work, beyond the reach of everyday evaluation. With respect to such forces there is only preparedness for the resolution or else the evasive turning to the ahistorical. In this connection, however, it is not sufficient, for example, to affirm technology or, out of a stance incomparably more essential, to set up "total mobilization" as an absolute, once it is recognized as being at hand.[5] It is a matter of, in advance and continually, grasping the essence of the age from out of the truth of being that prevails in it; for only thus is that which is most-worthy-of-questioning simultaneously experienced – that which bears and constrains a creating into the future which takes us beyond what is at hand, and lets the transformation of humanity become one that springs from the necessity of being itself.[a] No age lets itself be done away with by a negating decree. Negation merely throws the negator off the track. Modernity requires, however, in order, in the future, for it to be resisted in its essence and on the strength of that essence, an originality and breadth of reflection for which, perhaps, we moderns can prepare somewhat, but over which we can certainly never gain mastery.

(2) The phrase "constant activity" [*Betrieb*] is not intended here in a pejorative sense. Yet because the essence of research is constant activity, the

[a] First edition, 1950: usage [*Brauch*].

industrious activity of mere busyness [*Betriebsamkeit des bloßen Betriebs*] which is always a possibility, creates the appearance of a higher reality behind which the excavations of research-work are accomplished. Constant activity becomes mere busyness when its methodology no longer holds itself open on the basis of an ever new completion of its projection, but rather leaves this behind as something simply given and no longer ever requiring confirmation; instead, all it does is to chase after results piling on top of each other and their calculation. Mere busyness must, at all times, be resisted – precisely because, in its essence, research is constant activity. If one seeks to discover the scientific in science merely in serene erudition, then it indeed seems as though the repudiation of constant activity would also be the denial of the essential character of research as constant activity. What, however, is certainly true is that the more completely research becomes constant activity and in this way becomes fruitful, the more steadily there grows within it the danger of becoming mere busyness. In the end we reach a situation where the difference between constant activity and busyness [*Betrieb und Betrieb*] is not only unrecognizable, but has become unreal. Precisely the leveling out of its essence and non-essence in the averageness of the taken-for-granted, makes research – as the shape of science and so of modernity in general – capable of enduring. But where, within constant activity, is research to discover a counter-balance to mere busyness?

(3) The growing importance of the publishing business is not merely based on the fact that the publishers (through, for example, the book trade) have a better eye for the needs of the public, or that they understand business better than do authors. Rather, their distinctive work takes the form of a process of planning and organizing aimed, through the planned and limited publication of books and periodicals, at bringing the world into the picture the public has of it and securing it there. The predominance of collected works, sets of books, journal series, and pocket editions is already the result of this work on the part of the publishers. This work coincides, in turn, with the aims of researchers, since these not only become more easily and rapidly known and respected through series and collections, but also, along a wider front, immediately achieve their intended effect.

(4) The metaphysical foundation of Descartes' position is taken over historically from Platonic-Aristotelian metaphysics. Despite its new beginning, it attends to the very same question: what is the being? That this question is not explicitly posed in Descartes' *Meditations* only goes to prove how

essentially the fundamental position determines a transformation in the answer to it. It is Descartes' interpretation of beings and of truth which first creates the preconditions for the possibility of a theory or metaphysics of knowledge. Through Descartes, realism is for the first time put in the position of having to prove the reality of the external world, of having to rescue the being as such.

The essential modifications of Descartes' fundamental position which have been achieved by German thinking since Leibniz in no way overcome this fundamental position. They only expand its metaphysical scope and establish the preconditions of the nineteenth century – still the most obscure of all the centuries up to now. They indirectly reinforce Descartes' fundamental position in a form that is scarcely recognizable, yet not, on that account, any the less real. By contrast, mere Cartesian scholasticism, together with its rationalism, has lost all power for the further shaping of the character of modernity. With Descartes, there begins the completion of Western metaphysics. Since, however, such a completion is only possible as metaphysics, modern thinking has its own kind of greatness.

With the interpretation of man as *subiectum*, Descartes created the metaphysical presupposition for future anthropology of every kind and tendency. In the rise of anthropologies he celebrates his greatest triumph. Through anthropology, the transition of metaphysics into the event of the simple cessation and suspension of all philosophy is inaugurated. That Dilthey disavowed metaphysics – that, at bottom, he no longer understood its question and stood helpless before metaphysical logic – is the inner consequence of the anthropological character of his fundamental position. His "philosophy of philosophy" is a leading example of anthropology's doing away with – as opposed to overcoming – philosophy. This is why every anthropology that makes use of philosophy as the occasion arises, yet simultaneously declares it to be, as philosophy, superfluous, has the advantage of seeing clearly what is demanded by the affirmation of anthropology. Through this, the intellectual situation is somewhat clarified. The laborious fabrication of such absurd entities as "National Socialist philosophies," on the other hand, merely creates confusion. The world view indeed needs and makes use of philosophical erudition, but it needs no philosophy since, as world view, it has already adopted its own interpretation and structuring of what is. But one thing, surely, even anthropology cannot do. It cannot overcome Descartes, nor even resist him. For how could the consequence ever attack the ground on which it stands?

Descartes can only be overcome through the overcoming of that which he himself founded, through the overcoming, namely, of modern (and that means, at the same time, Western) metaphysics. "Overcoming" means here, however, the primal asking of the question of the meaning of being; of, that is, the sphere of projection and with it the truth of being. This question unveils itself as, at the same time, the question of the being of truth.

(5) The conception of the world as developed in *Being and Time* is to be understood only within the perspective of the question about "being-there [*Da-sein*]." This question remains, for its part, closely connected with the fundamental question concerning the meaning of being (not of beings).

(6) To the essence of the picture belongs standing-together, system. By this, however, we do not mean the artificial, external simplification and collecting together of the given but, rather, the unfolding, developing unity of structure within that which is set-before, represented as such, which arises from the projection of the objectness of beings. In the Middle Ages a system is impossible. For there, all that is essential is the order of correspondences or, more precisely, the order of beings in the sense of what is created and, as his creation, watched over by God. System is still more foreign to Greece – even though, these days, one speaks, in a quite unjustified way, of the Platonic and Aristotelian "systems." The constant activity of research is a particular embodiment and ordering of the systematic, in which, at the same time, the latter reciprocally determines the ordering. When the world becomes picture, system achieves dominion – and not only in thought. Where system takes the lead, however, there always exists the possibility of its degeneration into the externality of a system that is merely fabricated and pieced together. This is what happens when the original power of the projection remains absent. The uniqueness of the systematic of Leibniz, Kant, Fichte, Hegel, and Schelling – a systematic that is inherently diverse – has still not been understood. The greatness of the systematic of these thinkers consists in the fact that it does not unfold, as with Descartes, out of the *subiectum* as *ego* and *substantia finita*. Rather, it unfolds either, as with Leibniz, out of the monad or, as with Kant, out of the transcendental essence of finite reason rooted in the imagination, or, as with Fichte, out of the infinite "I," or, as with Hegel, out of the spirit of absolute knowledge, or, finally, as with Schelling, from out of freedom as the necessity of every particular being which, as such a being, remains determined through the distinction between ground and existence.

No less essential to the modern interpretation of beings is the representation of value. Where beings have become objects of representation, there, for the first time, in a certain sense, a loss of being occurs. This loss – vaguely and uncertainly enough perceived – is correspondingly quickly made up for through the fact that we attribute to the object and the thus-interpreted being a value; in general, we assess beings according to values and make them the goal of all action and activity. Since this latter conceives itself as culture, values become "cultural values" and these become the general expression of the highest goals of creation devoted to the self-establishment of man as *subiectum*. From here it is only a short step to making values into objects in themselves. Values become the objectification of needs as goals brought about by a representing self-establishment within the world as picture. Values appear to be the expression of the fact that, in relation to them, man strives to promote precisely what is most valuable. In fact, however, it is precisely "values" that are the powerless and threadbare mask of the objectification of beings, an objectification that has become flat and devoid of background. No one dies for mere values. For the sake of illuminating the nineteenth century, we should note, here, the intermediate position of Hermann Lotze. At the same time as he was interpreting Plato's ideas as values, Lotze undertook, under the title *Microcosmos*, that *Attempt at an Anthropology* (1856) which, while still drawing on the spirit of German idealism for the nobility and simplicity of its mode of thinking, at the same time also opened that thinking to positivism. Because Nietzsche's thought remains imprisoned in value-representation, he has to express what is essential to him in a retrospective form as the revaluation of all values. Only when we succeed in grasping Nietzsche's thought independently of value-representation, do we achieve a standpoint from which the work of the last thinker of metaphysics can be comprehended as an exercise in questioning, and his antagonism to Wagner as a necessity of our history.

(7) Correspondence, thought as the fundamental feature of the being of beings, provides the pattern for the very definite possibilities and ways in which the truth of this being of beings, within beings, sets itself into the work. The artwork of the Middle Ages and the absence of a world picture during this age belong together.

(8) But did not a Sophist at about the time of Socrates venture to say that "Man is the measure of all things, of what are, that they are, of what are not, that they are not"? Does not this statement of Protagoras sound as

though it were Descartes speaking? Is it not through Plato that the being of beings is fully grasped as the visible, the ἰδέα? Is not the relation to beings as such, for Aristotle, pure looking? And yet it is no more the case that Protagoras' Sophistic statement is subjectivism than it is the case that Descartes had the capacity to bring about the overturning of Greek thought. Through Plato's thinking and Aristotle's questioning there occurred, to be sure, a decisive transformation of the interpretation of beings and of man. But this transformation always remained within the Greeks' fundamental experience of beings. Precisely as a struggle against the Sophistic, and so as dependent on it, this transformed interpretation proves so decisive as to become the ending of the Greek world, an ending which indirectly helps to prepare the possibility of the modern age. This is the reason that, later on, not just in the Middle Ages but right through the modern age and up to the present, Platonic and Aristotelian thought was able to be taken as Greek thought *per se*, and why all pre-Platonic thought could be considered to be merely a preparation for Plato. Because we have long been accustomed to understand Greece in terms of a modern humanistic interpretation, it remains denied to us to think being as it opened itself to Greek antiquity, to think it in a way that allows it its ownness and strangeness.

Protagoras' statement reads:

πάντων χρημάτων μέτρον ἐστὶν ἄνθρωπος, τῶν μὲν ὄντων ὡς ἔστι, τῶν δὲ μὴ ὄντων ὡς οὐκ ἔστιν.

(cf. Plato's *Theaetetus* 152a)

Of all things (those, namely, that man has around him in use and usage, χρήματα χρῆσθαι) man is (in each case) the measure, of what presences, that it so presences, of that, however, to which presencing is denied, that it does not presence.

The being whose being is up for decision is understood, here, as that which is present in the sphere of man, arriving in this region, of itself. Who, however, is "man"? Plato tells us in the same passage by having Socrates say:

Does he (Protagoras) not understand this somewhat as follows? Whatever, at a given time, something shows itself to me as, of such an aspect is it (also) for me; but whatever it shows itself to you as, is it not such in turn for you? But you are a man just as much as I.

Man is here, accordingly, the man in each particular case (I and you, he and she). And should not this ἐγώ coincide with Descartes' *ego cogito*?

Never. For in every essential respect, what determines the two fundamental metaphysical positions with equal necessity is different. What is essential to a fundamental metaphysical position embraces:

(1) The manner and way in which man is man, that is, himself: the essential nature of selfhood which by no means coincides with I-ness, but is rather determined by the relationship to being as such.
(2) The essential interpretation of the being of beings.
(3) The essential projection of truth.
(4) The sense in which, in any given instance, "man is the measure."

None of the essential moments of the fundamental metaphysical position can be understood apart from the others. Each, by itself, indicates the totality of a fundamental metaphysical position. For what reason, and to what extent, just these four moments bear and structure a fundamental metaphysical position in advance is a question which can no longer be asked or answered out of or through metaphysics. To ask it is already to speak out of the overcoming of metaphysics.

For Protagoras, to be sure, beings remain related to man as ἐγώ. Of what kind is this relation to the I? The ἐγώ stays, in the sphere of that which is apportioned to it as this particular unconcealment. Accordingly, it apprehends everything that presences within this sphere as in being. The apprehending of what presences is grounded in this staying within the sphere of unconcealment. The belonging of the I to what presences *is* through this staying alongside what presences. This belonging to what presences in the open draws the boundary between what is present and what absent. From out of this boundary man receives and preserves the measure of that which presences and that which absences. In his restriction to that which is unconcealed at a particular time, man gives himself the measure which confines a self in each case to this and that. Man does not set the measure to which all beings in their being here have to accommodate themselves, out of a detached I-ness. One who stands in the Greeks' fundamental relationship to beings and their unconcealment is μέτρον (measure) insofar as he accepts restriction to the sphere of unconcealment limited after the manner of the I; and, as a consequence, acknowledges the concealment of beings and that their presence or absence, together with the visible appearance of what is present, lies beyond his power of decision. This is why Protagoras says (Fragment 4 in Diels, *Fragmente der Vorsokratiker*) περὶ μὲν θεῶν οὐκ ἔχω εἰδέναι, οὔθ' ὡς εἰσίν, οὔθ' ὡς οὐκ εἰσίν, οὔθ' ὁποῖοί τινες ἰδέαν. "Concerning the gods, I am, admittedly, not in the position to know (i.e., for the

Greeks, to have something in "sight") either that they are, or that they are not, nor how they are in their visible aspect (ἰδέα)."

πολλὰ γὰρ τὰ κωλύοντα εἰδέναι, ἥ τ' ἀδηλότης καὶ βραχὺς ὢν ὁ βίος τοῦ ἀνθρώπου. "Many, that is, are the things that prevent the apprehending of the being as what it is: both the un-openness (concealment) of beings and the brevity of man's course in history.

In view of this thoughtful circumspection on Protagoras' part, it is no wonder that Socrates says of him (Plato, *Theaetetus* 152 b) εἰκὸς μέντοι σοφὸν ἄνδρα μὴ ληρεῖν. "We may suppose that he (Protagoras), as a sensible person, was not (in his statement about man as the μέτρον) simply babbling."

The fundamental metaphysical position of Protagoras is merely a narrowing down – which means, nonetheless, a preserving – of the fundamental position of Heraclitus and Parmenides. Sophism is only possible on the basis of σοφία, i.e., on the basis of the Greek interpretation of being as presence and truth as unconcealment – an unconcealment which remains itself an essential determination of being, which is why that which presences is determined out of unconcealment, and presencing out of the unconcealed as such. But how far removed is Descartes from this beginning of Greek thought, how different is the interpretation of man which represents him as subject? In the concept of the *subiectum*, there still lingers on the sound of the Greek essence of being (the ὑποκεῖσθαι of the ὑποκείμενον) in the form of a presencing that has become unrecognizable and unquestioned (namely, that which lies permanently at hand). Precisely because of this, we can recognize in this concept of presencing the transformation of the fundamental metaphysical position.

It is one thing to preserve the always limited sphere of unconcealment through the apprehension of what presences (man as μέτρον). It is something different to proceed into the unlimited region of possible objectification through the calculating of the representable of which everyone is capable and which is binding on all.

Every subjectivism is impossible within Greek Sophism since man can never, here, become *subiectum*. This cannot happen because, in Sophism, being is presencing and truth is unconcealment.

In unconcealment, φαντασία happens: the coming to appearance, as a particular something, of that which presences – for man, who himself presences to what appears. Man as the representing subject fantasizes, however: he moves in *imaginatio* in that his representation imagines the being as object into the world as picture.

(9) How does it happen at all that that which is sets itself forth, in an emphatic way, as *subiectum*, with the result that the subjective achieves dominance? For up to Descartes, and still within his metaphysics, the being, insofar as it is a being, is a *sub-iectum* (ὑπο-κείμενον); something which lies before us from out of itself and which, as such, lies at the foundation of both its own permanent characteristics and its changing circumstances. The preference given to a *sub-iectum* (that which lies at the basis as ground) which is preeminent in that it is, in an essential respect, unconditioned, stems from man's demand for a *fundamentum absolutum inconcussum veritatis*; for an unshakable ground of truth, in the sense of certainty, which rests in itself. Why and how does this demand come to have decisive validity? The demand springs from the liberation of humanity from the bonds of the truth of Christian revelation and the doctrines of the Church, a liberation which frees itself for a self-legislation that is grounded in itself. Through this liberation the essence of freedom – being bound to something that binds – is posited anew. Because, however, in accordance with this freedom, self-liberating man himself posits what is obligatory, this can henceforth be defined in different ways. The obligatory may be human reason and its law; it may be beings, set up and ordered as objects by such a reason; or it may be that chaos – not yet ordered and only to be mastered through objectification – which, in a certain age, comes to demand mastery.

This liberation, however, without knowing it, is still freeing itself from the bonds of the truth of revelation in which the salvation of man's soul is made certain and guaranteed. Hence this liberation *from* the certainty of salvation disclosed by revelation has to be, in itself, a liberation *to* a certainty in which man secures for himself the true as that which is known through his own knowing. That was only possible in that self-liberating man himself guaranteed the certainty of the knowable. This, however, could only happen through man's deciding, from and for himself, what was knowable for him, and what the knowing and securing of the known, i.e., certainty, should mean. Descartes' metaphysical task became the following: to create the metaphysical ground for the freeing of man to freedom considered as self-determination that is certain of itself. This ground, however, not only had to be one that was certain. Since every measure taken from other domains was forbidden, it had, at the same time, also to be of such a nature that, through it, the essence of the freedom demanded was posited as a self-certainty. Everything that is certain from itself must, at the same time, however, certify as certain that being from which such knowledge is certain and through which everything knowable is made secure. The *fundamentum*, the foundation at the basis of this freedom, the *subiectum*, must be something certain which satisfies the aforementioned essential requirements. A *subiectum* distinguished in all these respects becomes necessary. What is this certainty which forms and provides the ground? It is the *ego cogito* (*ergo*) *sum*. This certainty is a principle which says that, simultaneously with man's thinking (at the same time and lasting an equal length of time), he himself is indubitably co-present; is, that is, given to himself. Thinking is representation, setting-before, a representative relation to the represented (*idea* as *perceptio*).

To represent means here: of oneself, to set something before one and to make what has been set in place [*das Gestellte*] secure as thus set in place. This placing-in-securedness must be a calculating, since only calculation guarantees being certain, in advance and always, of that which is to be presented. Representing is no longer the apprehending of what presences within whose unconcealment the apprehending itself belongs, belongs, indeed, as its own kind of presence to the things that are unconcealedly present. Representation is no longer the self-disclosure for . . . but rather the laying hold and grasping of . . . . That which presences does not hold sway; rather, setting-upon rules. According to the new freedom, representation is now something that proceeds from itself into the region of the secured, a region which has first to be made secure. The being is no longer that which presences. Rather, it is that which, in representation, is first set over and against [*entgegen Gestellte*], with the character of an object [*Gegen-ständige*]. Representation, setting-before, is a making everything stand over and against as object [*Ver-gegen-ständlichung*] which masters and proceeds against. In this way, representation drives everything into the unity of the thus-objectified. Representation is *coagitatio*.

Every relationship to something – will, point of view, sensibility – is already representing. It is *cogitans*, which one translates as "thinking." This is why Descartes is able to label all forms of the *voluntas* and *affectus*, all *actiones* and *passiones* with the at first strange-sounding name "*cogitatio*." In the *ergo cogito sum*, the *cogitare* is understood in this essential and new sense. The *subiectum*, the fundamental certainty, is that always secured entity which representing man always co-represents along with human or non-human beings, along, that is, with the objectified. The fundamental certainty is the *me-cogitare* = *me esse* which is, at all times, indubitably representable and represented. This is the fundamental equation of all calculating belonging to self-securing representing. In this fundamental certainty, man becomes certain that, as the representer of all representation, the setter-before of all setting-before, and therewith the realm of all representedness and hence of all certainty and truth, he is securely established – which means, now, that he *is*. Only because, in the fundamental certainty (in the *fundamentum absolutum inconcussum* of the *me cogitare = me esse*), man is necessarily co-represented; only because man who has been liberated to himself belongs, of necessity, within the *subiectum* of this freedom – only for this reason can and must this man himself become the preeminent being, a *subiectum* which, in respect of the primary [*erste*] true (i.e., certain) beings, takes precedence over all other *subiecta*. That is the fundamental equation of certainty. The fact, therefore, that in the authentic *subiectum*, the ego is named, does not mean that man now becomes an I-ness and is egoistically defined. It means only this: to be the subject now becomes the distinctiveness of man, of man as the being that thinks and represents. The human "I" is placed in the service of this *subiectum*. The certainty lying at the foundation of this *subiectum* is, as such, indeed subjective i.e., holding sway in the essence of the *subiectum*, but is not egoistic. In the same way, everything that is to be secured by means of representing objectification, and is established thereby as in being, is binding for everyone. From this objectification, however, which is at the same time the decision as to what may count as an object, nothing can escape. To the essence of the subjectivity of the *subiectum*, and of man as subject, belongs the unconditional delimiting forth [*Entschränkung*] of the sphere of possible objectification and the right to determine this objectification.

We have now explained the sense in which man is, and must be, the subject, measure, and center of beings: of, that is, objects [*Objekte*], things which stand over and against [*Gegenstände*]. Man is no longer the μέτρον in the sense of restraining his apprehension to the sphere of the unconcealment of what presences at his time – the sphere toward which man then presences. As *subiectum* man is the *co-agitatio* of the *ego*. Man establishes himself as the measure of all measures with which whatever can count as certain, i.e., true, i.e., in being, is measured off and measured out. Freedom is new as the freedom of the *subiectum*. In the *Meditationes de prima philosophia* the liberation of man to his new freedom is brought to that which grounds it. The liberation of modern humanity does not first begin with the *ego cogito ergo sum*, and neither is the metaphysics of Descartes merely supplied later on as something built on externally, a metaphysics in the sense of an ideology. In the *co-agitatio* representation gathers everything that is an object in the gatheredness of representedness. The *ego* of the *cogitare* now discovers, in the self-securing togetherness of representedness, in the *con-scientia*, its essence. *Conscientia* is the representing gathering of the objectual together with the representing man within the sphere of representedness which he preserves. Everything that presences receives from out of this representedness the meaning and mode of its presence [*Anwesenheit*]; the meaning and mode, that is, of presence [*Praesenz*] in *repraesentatio*. The *con-scientia* of the *ego* as the *subiectum* of the *coagitatio*, the subjectivity of the *subiectum* marked out in the above way, determines the being of beings.

The *Meditationes de prima philosophia* provide the pattern for the ontology of the *subiectum* constructed from the perspective of a subjectivity defined as *conscientia*. Man has become the *subiectum*. He can, therefore, determine and realize the essence of subjectivity – always according to how he conceives and wills himself. Man as the rational being of the Enlightenment is no less subject than man who grasps himself as nation, wills himself as people [*Volk*], nurtures himself as race and, finally, empowers himself as lord of the earth. Now in all these fundamental positions of subjectivism, too, different kinds of I-ness and egoism are possible; for man is always defined as I and thou, we and you. Subjective egoism for which – usually without knowing it – the I is pre-determined as subject can be beaten down through the insertion of the I into the we. Through this, subjectivity only gains in power. In the planetary imperialism of technically organized man the subjectivism of man reaches its highest point from which it will descend to the flatness of organized uniformity and there establish itself. This uniformity becomes the surest instrument of the total, i.e., technological, dominion over the earth. The modern freedom of subjectivity is completely absorbed into the corresponding objectivity. By himself, man cannot abandon this destining of his modern essence; he cannot abolish it by fiat. But he can, in thoughtful anticipation, ponder this: that mankind's being a subject is not the only possibility of the primal essence of historical humanity there has ever been or ever will be. The shadow of a passing cloud over a hidden land – that is the darkening which truth as the certainty of subjectivity (a truth prepared for by the certainty of salvation of Christianity) lays over an Event [*Ereignis*] that it remains denied to subjectivity to experience.

(10) Anthropology is that interpretation of humanity which already knows, fundamentally, who man is and can, therefore, never ask who he might be. For with this question it would have to confess itself shaken and overcome. But how is this to be expected of anthropology when the task is specifically to achieve nothing but the securing that follows from the self-security of the *subiectum*?

(11) For what is happening now is the melting down of the self-completing essence of modernity into the obvious. Only when this is secured as a world view will the possibility arise of a fertile ground for being to become capable of a primal questioning – a question-worthiness which opens the leeway for the decision as to whether being will once more be capable of a god, as to whether the essence of the truth of being will make a more primordial claim upon the essence of man. Only when the completion of the modern age affirms the ruthlessness of its own greatness is future history being prepared.

(12) Americanism is something European. It is that still uncomprehended species of the gigantic – the gigantic that is still not properly assembled and still fails to arise from the complete and collected essence of modernity. The American interpretation of Americanism in terms of pragmatism still remains outside the realm of metaphysics.

(13) Everyday opinion sees in the shadow merely the absence of light, if not its complete denial. But, in truth, the shadow is the manifest, though impenetrable, testimony of hidden illumination. Conceiving of the shadow this way, we experience the incalculable as that which escapes representation, yet is manifest in beings and points to the hidden being [*Sein*].

(14) But what if the refusal itself had to become the highest and hardest disclosure of being? Conceived from out of metaphysics (i.e., from the question of being in the form "What is the being?") the hidden essence of being, the refusal, reveals itself first of all as the absolute non-being, as the nothing. But the nothing, as the nothing of beings is the keenest opponent of mere negating. The nothing is never nothing, and neither is it a something in the sense of an object; it is being itself whose truth will be given over to man when he has overcome himself as subject, when, that is, he no longer represents beings as objects.

(15) This open in-between is the being-there [*Da-sein*], understanding the word in the sense of the ecstatic region of the disclosure and concealment of being.

Hegel's Concept of Experience[a]

"Science of the *Experience* of Consciousness" – this is the title which Hegel put at the head of *The Phenomenology of Spirit* when it was published in 1807. The word "experience" is printed in boldface midway between the two other terms. "Experience" identifies what "phenomenology" is. What is Hegel thinking by stressing the word "experience" in this way? The answer is provided by the passage which, following after the "Preface" to the *System of Science*, inaugurates the work. The text in the original edition runs:[1]

[1] It is natural to suppose that, before philosophy enters upon the matter proper to it – namely, the real knowledge of what truly is – it is necessary to come first to an understanding concerning knowledge, which is looked upon as the instrument by which to take possession of the absolute, or as the means through which to get a sight of it. The precaution seems legitimate, partly because there are various kinds of knowledge, among which one might be better adapted than another for the attainment of our purpose, – and thus a wrong choice is possible; and partly because knowing is a faculty of a definite kind and with a determinate range, and so without the more precise determination of its nature and limits we might take hold on clouds of error instead of the heaven of truth. This apprehensiveness is sure to pass even into the conviction that the whole enterprise, which sets out to secure for consciousness by means of knowledge the in-itself, is in its very nature absurd; and that between knowledge and the absolute there lies a boundary which completely cuts off the one from the other. For if knowledge is the instrument by which to get possession of absolute essence, the suggestion immediately occurs that the application of an instrument to anything does

[a] First edition, 1950: implicitly thought from the Event.

not leave it as it is for itself, but rather entails in the process and has in view a molding and alteration of it. Or, again, if knowledge is not an instrument which we actively employ, but a kind of passive medium through which the light of the truth reaches us, then here, too, we do not receive it as it is in itself, but as it is through and in this medium. In either case we employ a means which immediately brings about the very opposite of its own end; or, rather, the absurdity lies in making use of any means at all. It seems indeed open to us to find in the knowledge of the way in which the *instrument* operates, a remedy for this parlous state of affairs; for thereby it becomes possible to remove from the result the part which, in our idea of the absolute received through that instrument, belongs to the instrument, and thus to get the truth in its purity. But this improvement would, as a matter of fact, only bring us back to the point where we were before. If we take away again from a definitely formed thing that which the instrument has done in the shaping of it, then the thing (in this case the absolute) stands before us once more just as it was previous to all this trouble, which, as we now see, was superfluous. If the absolute were only to be brought on the whole nearer to us by this agency, without any change being wrought in it, like a bird caught by a limestick, it would certainly scorn a trick of that sort, if it were not, and did not intend to be, in and for itself with us from the start. For a trick is what knowledge in such a case would be, since by all its busy toil and trouble it gives itself the air of doing something quite different from bringing about a relation that is merely immediate and so a waste of time to establish. Or, again, if the examination of knowledge, which we represent as a *medium*, makes us acquainted with the law of its refraction, it is likewise useless to eliminate this refraction from the result. For knowledge is not the divergence of the ray, but the ray itself by which the truth comes in contact with us; and if this be removed, the bare direction or the empty place would alone be indicated.

[2] Meanwhile, if the fear of falling into error introduces an element of distrust into science, which without any scruples of that sort goes to work and really does know, it is not easy to understand why, conversely, a distrust should not be placed in this very distrust, and why we should not take care lest the fear of error is not just the initial error. As a matter of fact, this fear presupposes something, indeed a great deal, as truth, and supports its scruples and consequences on what should itself be examined beforehand to see whether it is truth. It starts with *ideas* of *knowledge* as an *instrument*, and as a *medium*; and presupposes a *distinction of ourselves from this knowledge*.

More especially it takes for granted that the absolute stands *on one side*, and that *knowledge on the other side*, for itself and cut off from the absolute, is still something real; in other words, that knowledge, which, by being outside the absolute, is certainly also outside truth, is nevertheless true – a position which, while calling itself fear of error, makes itself known rather as fear of the truth.

[3] This conclusion comes from the fact that the absolute alone is true or that the true is alone absolute. It may be set aside by making the distinction that a knowledge which does not indeed know the absolute as science wants to know it, is none the less true too; and that knowledge in general, though it may possibly be incapable of grasping the absolute, can still be capable of truth of another kind. But we shall see as we proceed that random talk like this leads in the long run to a confused distinction between the absolute truth and a truth of some other sort, and that "absolute," "knowledge," and so on, are words which presuppose a meaning that has first to be got at.

[4] With suchlike useless ideas and expressions about knowledge, as an instrument to take hold of the absolute, or as a medium through which we have a glimpse of truth, and so on (relations to which all these ideas of a knowledge which is divided from the absolute and an absolute divided from knowledge in the last resort lead), we need not concern ourselves. Nor need we trouble about the evasive pretexts which the incapacity of "science" creates out of the presupposition of such relations, in order at once to be rid of the toil of science, and to assume the air of serious and zealous effort about it. Instead of being troubled with giving answers to all these, they may be straightway rejected as adventitious and arbitrary ideas; and the use which is here made of words like "absolute," "knowledge," as also "objective" and "subjective," and innumerable others, whose meaning is assumed to be familiar to everyone, might well be regarded as so much deception. For to pretend that their significance is universally familiar and that everyone indeed possesses their concept, rather looks like an attempt to dispense with the only important matter, which is just to give this concept. With better right, on the contrary, we might spare ourselves the trouble of taking any notice at all of such ideas and ways of talking which would have the effect of warding off science altogether; for they make a mere empty show of knowledge which at once vanishes when science comes on the scene. But science, in the very fact that it comes on the scene, is itself a phenomenon; its "coming on the scene" is not yet *itself* carried out in all the length and breadth of its truth. In this regard, it is a matter of indifference

whether we consider that it (science) is the phenomenon because it makes its appearance *alongside another kind of knowledge*, or call that other untrue knowledge its process of appearing. Science, however, must liberate itself from this phenomenality, this seeming, and it can only do so by turning against it. For science cannot simply reject a form of knowledge which is not true, and treat this as a common view of things, and then assure us that itself is an entirely different kind of knowledge, and that it holds the other to be of no account at all; nor can it appeal to the fact that in this other there are presages of a better. By giving that "assurance" it would declare its force and value to lie in its bare *existence*; but the untrue knowledge appeals likewise to the fact that it is, and "assures" us that to it science is nothing. One barren assurance, however, is of just as much value as another. Still less can science appeal to the presages of a better, which are to be found present in untrue knowledge and are there pointing the way toward science; for, on the one hand, it would be appealing again in the same way to a merely existent fact; and, on the other, it would be appealing to itself, to the way in which it exists in untrue knowledge, i.e., to a bad form of its own existence, to its appearance, rather than to how it is in and for itself. For this reason we shall here undertake the presentation of knowledge as a phenomenon.

[5] Now because this presentation has for its object only phenomenal knowledge, the presentation itself seems not to be science, free, self-moving in the shape proper to itself, but may, from this point of view, be taken as the pathway of natural consciousness which is pressing forward to true knowledge. Or it can be regarded as the path of the soul, which is traversing the series of its own forms of embodiment, like stages appointed for it by its own nature, that it may possess the clearness of spirit when, through the complete experience of its own self, it arrives at the knowledge of what it is in itself.

[6] Natural consciousness will prove itself to be only the concept of knowledge and not real knowledge. Since, however, it immediately takes itself to be the real and genuine knowledge, this pathway has a negative significance for it; what is a realization of the concept of knowledge means for it rather the ruin and overthrow of itself; for on this road it loses its own truth. Because of that, the road can be looked on as the path of *doubt*, or more properly a highway of despair. For what happens there is not what is usually understood by doubting, a jostling against this or that supposed truth, the outcome of which is again a disappearance in due course of the doubt and a return to the former truth, so that at the end the matter is taken as it

was before. On the contrary, that pathway is the conscious insight into the untruth of phenomenal knowledge, for which that is the most real which is after all only the unrealized concept. On that account, too, this thoroughgoing skepticism is not what doubtless earnest zeal for truth and science fancies it has equipped itself with in order to be ready to deal with them – viz. the *resolve*, in science, not to deliver itself over to the thoughts of others on their mere authority, but to examine everything for itself, and only follow its own conviction, or, still better, to produce everything itself and hold only its own act for true. The series of shapes, which consciousness traverses on this road, is rather the detailed history of the *formation* of consciousness itself up to the level of science. That resolve represents this mental development in the simple form of an intended purpose, as immediately finished and complete, as having taken place; this pathway, on the other hand, is, as opposed to this abstract intention, or untruth, the actual carrying out of that process of development. To follow one's own conviction is certainly more than to hand oneself over to authority; but by the conversion of opinion held on authority into opinion held out of personal conviction, the content of what is held is not necessarily altered, and truth has not thereby taken the place of error. If we stick to a system of opinion and prejudice resting on the authority of others, or upon personal conviction, the one differs from the other merely in the conceit which animates the latter. Skepticism, directed to the whole compass of phenomenal consciousness, on the contrary, makes spirit for the first time qualified to test what truth is; since it brings about a despair regarding what are called natural views, thoughts, and opinions, which it is a matter of indifference to call personal or belonging to others, and with which the consciousness that proceeds *immediately* to criticize and test is still filled and hampered, thus being, as a matter of fact, incapable of what it wants to undertake.

[7] The *completeness* of the forms of unreal consciousness will be brought about precisely through the necessity of the advance and the necessity of their connection with one another. To make this comprehensible we may remark, by way of preliminary, that the presentation of untrue consciousness in its untruth is not a merely negative process. Such a one-sided view of it is what the natural consciousness generally adopts; and a knowledge, which makes this one-sidedness its essence, is one of those shapes assumed by incomplete consciousness which falls into the course of the inquiry itself and will come before us there. For this view is skepticism, which always sees in the result only *pure nothingness*, and it abstracts away the fact that

this nothing is specifically the nothing of *that out of which it comes as a result*. Nothing, however, is only, in fact, the true result, when taken as the nothing of what it comes from; it is thus itself a *determinate* nothing, and has a *content*. The skepticism which ends with the abstraction "nothing" or "emptiness" can advance from this not a step farther, but must wait and see whether there is possibly anything new offered, and what that is, – in order to cast it into the same abysmal void. When once, on the other hand, the result is apprehended, as it truly is, as *determinate* negation, a new form has thereby immediately arisen; and in the negation the transition is made by which the progress through the complete succession of shapes comes about of itself.

[8] The *goal*, however, is fixed for knowledge just as necessarily as the succession in the process. The terminus is at that point where knowledge is no longer compelled to go beyond itself, where it finds its own self, and the concept corresponds to the object and the object to the concept. The progress toward this goal consequently is without a halt, and at no earlier stage is satisfaction to be found. That which is confined to a life of nature is unable of itself to go beyond its immediate existence; but by something other than itself it is forced beyond that; and to be thus wrenched out of its setting is its death. Consciousness, however, is for itself its own *concept*; thereby it immediately transcends what is limited, and, since this latter belongs to it, consciousness transcends its own self. Along with the particular there is at the same time set up the "beyond," even if this were only, as in spatial intuition, *beside* what is limited. Consciousness, therefore, suffers this violence at its own hands; it destroys its own limited satisfaction. At the feeling of this violence, anxiety for the truth may well withdraw, and struggle to preserve for itself that which is in danger of being lost. But it can find no rest. Should that anxious fearfulness wish to remain always in unthinking indolence, thought will agitate the thoughtlessness, its restlessness will disturb that indolence. Or let it take its stand as a form of sentimentality which assures us it finds everything good in its own kind, and this assurance likewise will suffer violence at the hands of reason, which finds something *not* good just because and in so far as it is a *kind*. Or, again, fear of the truth may conceal itself from itself and others behind the pretext that it is precisely burning zeal for the very truth which makes it so difficult, nay impossible, to find any other truth except that of which alone vanity is capable – that of being ever so much cleverer than any ideas, which one gets from oneself or others, could make possible. This sort of conceit which understands how to belittle every truth and turn away from it back into itself,

and gloats over this its own private understanding which always knows how to dissipate every possible thought, and to find, instead of all the content, merely the barren ego – this is a satisfaction which must be left to itself; for it flees the universal and seeks only an isolated existence on its own account [*Fürsichseyn*].

[9] As the foregoing has been stated, provisionally and in general, concerning the manner and the necessity of the process of the inquiry, it may also be of further service to make some observations regarding the *method of carrying this out*. This presentation, viewed as a *process* of relating *science* to *phenomenal* knowledge, and as an *inquiry* and *critical examination into the reality of knowing*, does not seem able to be effected without some presupposition which is laid down as an ultimate *criterion*. For an examination consists in applying an accepted criterion, and, on the final agreement or disagreement therewith of what is tested, deciding whether the latter is right or wrong; and the criterion in general, and science as well (if science were to be the criterion) is thereby accepted as the *essence* or the *in-itself*. But, here, where science first appears on the scene, neither science nor any sort of criterion has justified itself as the essence or the in-itself; and without this no examination seems able to be instituted.

[10] This contradiction and the removal of it will become more definite if, to begin with, we call to mind the abstract determinations of knowledge and of truth as they are found in consciousness. Consciousness, we find, *distinguishes* from itself something, to which at the same time it *relates* itself; or, to use the current expression, there is something *for* consciousness; and the determinate form of this *process of relating*, or of there *being* something *for a consciousness*, is *knowledge*. But from this being for another we distinguish *being in-itself*; what is related to knowledge is likewise distinguished from it, and posited as also *existing* outside this relation; the aspect of this in-itself is called *truth*. What really lies in these determinations does not further concern us here; for since the object of our inquiry is phenomenal knowledge, its determinations are also taken up, in the first instance, as they present themselves immediately to us. And they present themselves to us very much in the way we have just stated.

[11] If now our inquiry deals with the truth of knowledge, it appears that we are inquiring what knowledge is *in itself*. But in this inquiry knowledge is *our* object, it is *for us*; and the in-itself of knowledge, were this to come to light, would be rather its being *for us*: what we should assert to be its essence

would rather be not the truth of knowledge but only our knowledge of it. The essence or the criterion would lie in us; and what was to be compared with this criterion, and decided upon as a result of this comparison, would not necessarily have to recognize that criterion.

[12] But the nature of the object which we are examining surmounts this separation, or semblance of separation, and presupposition. Consciousness furnishes its own criterion in it itself, and the inquiry will thereby be a comparison of itself with its own self; for the distinction, just made, falls inside itself. In consciousness there is one element *for* an other, or, in general, consciousness implicates the specific character of the moment of knowledge. At the same time this "other" is to consciousness not merely *for it*, but also outside this relation, or has a being in itself, i.e., there is the moment of truth. Thus in what consciousness inside itself declares to be the *in-itself* or *true* we have the criterion which it itself sets up, and by which we are to measure its knowledge. Suppose we call *knowledge* "the concept," and the essence or the *true* "the being that is" or "the *object*," then the examination consists in seeing whether the concept corresponds with the object. But if we call the *essence*, or the in-itself, of the object "the concept," and, on the other side, understand by "object" the concept *as* object, i.e., the way the concept is *for* an other, then the examination consists in our seeing whether the object corresponds to its own concept. It is clear, of course, that both of these processes are the same. The essential fact, however, to be borne in mind throughout the whole inquiry is that both these moments, *concept* and *object*, "being for another" and "being in itself," themselves fall within that knowledge which we are examining. Consequently we do not require to bring criteria with us, nor to apply *our* fancies and thoughts in the inquiry; and just by our leaving these aside we are enabled to consider the matter as it actually is *in itself* and *for itself*.

[13] But not only in this respect, that concept and object, the criterion and what is to be critically examined, are ready to hand in consciousness itself, is any contribution of ours superfluous, but we are also spared the trouble of comparing these two and of making an *examination* in the strict sense of the term; so that in this respect, too, since consciousness critically examines itself, all we are left to do is purely to watch, to look on. For consciousness is, on the one hand, consciousness of the object, on the other, consciousness of itself; consciousness of what to it is true, and consciousness of its knowledge of that truth. Since both are *for the same consciousness*, it is itself their comparison; it is for *the same consciousness* to decide and know

whether its knowledge of the object corresponds with this object or not. The object, it is true, appears only to be in such wise for consciousness as consciousness knows it. Consciousness does not seem able to get, so to say, behind it as it is, not *for consciousness*, but *in itself*, and consequently seems also unable to test knowledge by it. But just because consciousness has, in general, knowledge of an object, there is already present the distinction that what the object is *in itself*, is one thing *to consciousness*, while knowledge, or the being of the object *for* consciousness, is another moment. Upon this distinction, which is present as a fact, the examination turns. Should both, when thus compared, not correspond, consciousness seems bound to alter its knowledge, in order to make it fit the object. But in the alteration of the knowledge, the object itself also, in point of fact, is altered; for the knowledge which existed was essentially a knowledge of the object; with change in the knowledge, the object also becomes different, since it belonged essentially to this knowledge. Hence consciousness comes to find that what formerly to it was the *in-itself* is not in itself, or rather that it was *in itself* only *for consciousness*. Since, then, in the case of its object consciousness finds its knowledge not corresponding with this object, the object likewise fails to hold out; or more precisely, the criterion for examining is altered when the intended object of the criterion does not hold its ground in the course of the examination; and the examination is not only an examination of knowledge, but also of the criterion used in the process.

[14] This *dialectical* movement which consciousness executes on itself – on its knowledge as well as on its object – *in the sense that* out of it *the new and true object arises*, is precisely what is termed *experience*. In this connection, there is a moment in the process just mentioned which should be brought into more decided prominence, and by which a new light is cast on the scientific aspect of the following presentation. Consciousness knows *something*; this something, the object, is the essence or the *in-itself*. This object, however, is also the in-itself *for consciousness*. Hence comes the ambiguity of this truth. Consciousness, as we see, has now two objects: one is the first *in-itself*, the second is the *being-for-consciousness* of this *in-itself*. The last object appears at first sight to be merely the reflection of consciousness into itself, i.e., an idea not of an object, but solely of its knowledge of that first object. But, as was already indicated, by that very process the first object is altered; it ceases to be the in-itself, and becomes something which is *in itself* only *for consciousness*. Consequently, then, *this being-for-consciousness of the in-itself* is the true – which, however, means that this true is the *essence*, or the *object*

which consciousness has. This new object contains the nothingness of the first; the new object is the experience concerning that first object.

[15] In this presentation of the course of experience, there is a moment in virtue of which it does not seem to be in agreement with what is ordinarily understood by experience. The transition from the first object and the knowledge of it to the other object, in regard to which we say we have had experience, was so stated that the knowledge of the first object (the *for*-consciousness of the first in-itself) is itself to become the second object. But it usually seems that we learn by experience the untruth of our first concept by appealing to *some other* object which we may happen to find casually and externally; so that, in general, what we have is merely the bare and simple *apprehension* of what is in and for itself. On the view above given, however, the new object is seen to have come about by a *reversal of consciousness* itself. This way of looking at the matter is our doing, what we contribute; by its means the series of experiences through which consciousness passes is lifted into a scientific route, but this does not exist for the consciousness we contemplate. We have here, however, the same sort of circumstance, again, of which we spoke a short time ago when dealing with the relation of this presentation to skepticism, viz. that the result which at any time comes about in the case of an untrue mode of knowledge cannot possibly collapse into an empty nothing, but must necessarily be taken as the negation *of that of which it is a result* – a result which contains what truth the preceding mode of knowledge has in it. What we have here is presented to us in this form: since what at first appeared as object is reduced, when it passes into consciousness, to a knowledge of the object, and since the *in-itself* becomes a *being-for-consciousness* of the *in-itself*, then as a result this latter is the new object, whereupon there appears also a new shape or embodiment of consciousness, the essence of which is something other than that of the preceding shape. It is this circumstance which carries forward the whole succession of the shapes of consciousness in their necessity. It is only this necessity, or this *origination* of the new object (which offers itself to consciousness without consciousness knowing how it comes by it), that takes place for us, so to say, behind its back. In this way there enters into the movement of consciousness a moment of the *being in itself or being for us*, which does not specifically present itself to consciousness which is in the grip of experience itself. The *content*, however, of what we see arising exists *for consciousness*, and we lay hold of and comprehend merely its formal character, i.e., its bare origination; *for consciousness*, what has thus arisen has

merely the character of object, while, *for us*, it appears at the same time as movement and becoming.

In virtue of that necessity this pathway to *science* is itself already *science*, and is, moreover, as regards its content, science of the *experience of consciousness*.

[16] The experience which consciousness has concerning itself can, by its own concept, conceive within itself nothing less than the entire system of consciousness, the whole realm of the truth of spirit, and in such wise that the moments of truth present themselves in the specific and peculiar character they here possess – i.e., not as abstract pure moments, but as they are for consciousness, or as consciousness itself appears in its relation to them, and in virtue of which the moments of the whole are *shapes or configurations of consciousness*. In pressing forward to its true existence, consciousness will come to a point at which it lays aside its semblance of being hampered with what is foreign to it, with what is only for it and exists as an other; it will reach a position where appearance becomes identified with essence, where, in consequence, its presentation coincides with just this very point, this very stage of the genuine science of spirit. And, finally, when it grasps this its own essence, it will indicate the nature of absolute knowledge itself.

The first paragraph gives the subject matter of philosophy. "It contemplates what is present as that which is present and (contemplates) therefore what is already predominant in it (in what is present) on its own," θεωρεῖ τὸ ὂν ᾗ ὂν καὶ τὰ τούτῳ ὑπάρχοντα καθ' αὑτό (Aristotle, *Metaphysics* Γ 1, 1003a21). Predominance concerns coming-to-light in unconcealedness. Philosophy contemplates what is present in its presencing. Contemplation observes [*betrachtet*] what is present. It strives [*trachtet*] toward it so that it looks at what is present only as such. Philosophy looks at [*sieht an*] what is present in regard to its looks [*Ansehen*]. No hidden depth is simmering in the vision [*Schau*] of this contemplation [*Beschauens*]. θεωρία makes all knowledge sober. Philosophy, Hegel says in the language of his thought, is "the real knowledge of what truly is." In the meantime, the beings that truly are have proved to be beings that are real, beings whose reality is spirit. The essence of spirit, however, is based in self-consciousness.

In his lectures on the history of modern philosophy (*Werke*, vol. XV, p. 328[2]), after discussing Bacon and Jakob Böhme, Hegel says:

It is only now that we do in fact arrive at the philosophy of the modern world, and we begin it with Descartes. With him we actually enter upon an autonomous philosophy, one that knows that its autonomy comes from reason and that self-consciousness is the essential moment of truth. Here, we can say, we are at home, and like the mariner after a long voyage on stormy seas, we can shout, "Land ho!"... The principle in this new period is thinking, thinking which proceeds from itself.

Thinking seeks in the unshakeable certainty of what it has thought the *fundamentum absolutum* for itself. The land in which philosophy has subsequently made itself at home is the unconditional self-certainty of knowing. The land has been conquered and fully surveyed only gradually. Full possession is attained only when the *fundamentum absolutum* is thought as the absolute itself. For Hegel, the absolute is spirit: that which is present to itself [*bei sich*] in the certainty of unconditional self-knowing. Real knowledge of beings as beings now becomes the absolute knowledge of the absolute in its absoluteness.

However, this philosophy of the modern age, dweller in the land of self-consciousness, demands of itself (in keeping with the climate of this land) that it have a prior certainty of its principle. It intends to come to a prior understanding about the mode of knowing in which it knows absolutely. Unexpectedly, knowledge thus appears as a means about whose proper employment knowledge must be apprehensive. It is essential, on the one hand, to recognize and to select among the diverse modes of representation that mode which alone is suitable for absolute knowledge. This was Descartes' task. On the other hand, once the suitable knowledge of the absolute has been selected, it must be gauged with respect to its nature and its limits. This was Kant's task. Yet as soon as knowledge – as a means to take possession of the absolute – is taken to task, the conviction immediately arises that, in relation to the absolute, every means (which, as a means, is relative) is unsuited to the absolute and necessarily fails before it. If knowledge is a means, then every intention to know the absolute is an absurd project, whether the means assumes in this case the character of an instrument or a medium. In the one case we actively busy ourselves with knowledge as an instrument, in the other we passively suffer knowledge as the medium through which the light of truth is supposed to reach us.

We could still try to remedy this unfortunate state of affairs (in which the means is precisely *not* mediating) through an examination of the means, distinguishing what it alters about the absolute and what it leaves unaltered, when it grasps the absolute or lets it pass. However, when we subtract the alteration that was caused by the means, and therefore do not apply the means, it also does not mediate to us the remainder of the unaltered absolute. Fundamentally, the examination of the means does not know what it is doing. It must judge [*messen*] knowledge, as regards its appropriateness [*Angemessenheit*] to the absolute, by means of the absolute. It must have known the absolute all along, and in fact known it as the absolute, or else all critical demarcations of limits turn out to be empty. Moreover, something else comes to light: the fact that discussing the instrument matters more to the examination than knowing the absolute. However, even if the instrument mattered to knowledge as the only means to bring the absolute any closer to us, the project would still be bound to fail risibly in the face of the absolute. What is the point of all this critical activity regarding knowledge if right from the start knowledge is going to wriggle free from the immediate relationship of the absolute to the knower, on the grounds that it must first clear up the business of criticism? Contrary to its better immediate knowledge, the critical examination of the instrument does not turn its attention to the absolute. The absolute, moreover, does not scorn critical toiling; for to do this it would have to share with criticism the assumption that knowledge is a means and that it itself, the absolute, is far enough removed from knowledge to oblige it to exert itself before capturing the absolute. But in this case the absolute would not be the absolute.

It is only in passing, however, and by relegating it to a subordinate clause, that Hegel makes this remark: the absolute is from the start in and for itself with us and intends to be with us. This being-with-us (παρουσία) is in itself already the mode in which the light of truth, the absolute itself, beams [*anstrahlt*] upon us. To know the absolute is to stand in the ray [*Strahl*] of light, to give it back, to radiate [*strahlt*] it back, and thus to be itself in its essence the ray, no mere medium through which the ray must first find its way. The first step which knowledge of the absolute must take is simply to accept and to take [*hin- und aufzunehmen*] the absolute in its absoluteness, i.e., in its being-with-us. This presencing-with-us, parousia, is characteristic of the absolute in and for itself. When philosophy as knowledge of the absolute takes seriously what it is as such knowledge, then it is by that fact alone the real knowledge that represents what real beings themselves are in their truth. In the beginning and in the course of the first paragraph it appears as though Hegel were trying to meet the critical demands by natural representation for a test of knowledge. In truth, what matters to him is to indicate the absolute in its parousia among us. All that happens as a result is that we are directed specifically into that relationship with the absolute in which we already are. In this way Hegel seems to surrender all the critical achievements of modern philosophy. So is he not dismissing, in general, all of critical examination in favor of backsliding into arbitrary assertions and assumptions? Not at all. Hegel is the first to prepare a critical examination. The first step in its preparation consists in our abandoning the usual idea of knowledge. However, if knowledge is not a means, then examination also can no longer consist in appraising knowledge first of all on the basis of its suitability to mediate. Perhaps it is already a sufficient examination for us to observe what knowledge is when it cannot be a means a priori. Not only what is to be examined, but the examination itself, shows a different nature.

The second paragraph touches on the core of the criticism to which science has subjected all previous philosophical critiques of knowledge. In all his following paragraphs, Hegel no longer uses the word "philosophy." He speaks of science. For in the meantime, modern philosophy has attained to the perfection of its nature; the terra firma on which it set foot for the first time has now been fully taken into its possession. The land is the self-certainty of representation in respect to itself and what it represents. To take this land fully into possession means: to know the self-certainty of self-consciousness in its unconditional essence and to be in this knowledge as in knowledge par excellence.[a] Philosophy is now unconditional knowledge within the knowledge of self-certainty. In knowledge as such, philosophy has made itself fully at home. The whole essence of philosophy is constituted by the unconditional self-knowing of knowledge. Philosophy is *the* science. This term does not imply that philosophy adopted a model from the other sciences that were available and fully realized it in an ideal. When, within an absolute metaphysics, the term "science" takes the place of the term "philosophy," it takes its meaning from the essence of the subject's self-certainty which knows itself unconditionally. This subject is now that which truly (which now means "certainly") lies before us, the *subiectum*, the ὑποκείμενον, which philosophy since antiquity has had to recognize as that which presences. Philosophy has become science because it has remained philosophy. Its responsibility is to contemplate beings as beings. Since Leibniz, however, beings have appeared for thinking in such a manner that *every ens qua ens* is a *res cogitans* and in this sense is a subject. That this is so is not because of some thinker's opinion but is due to the being of beings. The subject, needless to say, is not subjective in the sense of an egotism intent on itself. The subject has its essence in a representational relation to the object. However, as this relation, it is already a relation of

[a] First edition, 1950: i.e., to know.

representation to itself. Representation [*Vorstellen*] presents [*präsentiert*] the object by representing [*repräsentiert*] it to a subject; in this representation [*Repräsentation*], the subject itself presents itself [*präsentiert*] as such. Presentation [*Präsentation*] is the fundamental trait of knowledge in the sense of the self-consciousness of the subject. Presentation [*Präsentation*] is an essential mode of presence [*Präsenz*] (παρούσια). As such a mode, i.e., as presencing [*das Anwesen*], it is the being of beings that have the nature of a subject. As self-knowing that sets its own conditions (i.e., is unconditional), self-certainty is the beingness (οὐσία) of the subject. The subjectity of the subject is constituted by the subject being a subject, i.e., by the subject being in a subject–object relation. Subjectity consists in unconditional self-knowing. The essence of the subject is composed [*beschaffen*] in the mode of self-knowing, so that the subject, in order to be as a subject, has to do [*sich zu schaffen macht*] with this single composition [*Beschaffenheit*], with knowing. As absolute self-certainty, the subjectity of the subject is "science." Beings (τὸ ὄν) are in the way that beings are [*als das Seiende*] (ᾗ ὄν) to the extent that they are in the mode of the unconditional self-knowing of knowledge. For this reason, the presentation that represents these beings as beings, philosophy, is itself science.

As the subjectity of the subject, unconditional self-knowing is the absoluteness of the absolute. Philosophy is absolute knowledge. Philosophy is science because it wills the will of the absolute, i.e., the absolute in its absoluteness. Thus willing, it intends to contemplate beings as beings. Thus willing, philosophy wills its essence. Philosophy is science, the science. In the last sentence, "is" does not mean that philosophy bears along with itself, as a predicate, some definite quality of being scientific; rather it means: philosophy *is* as absolute knowledge and is only as it is that it may belong with the absoluteness of the absolute, achieving absoluteness in its own way. Philosophy as absolute knowledge is science, but this is by no means a consequence of striving to make its procedure exact and its results conclusive – thereby making itself equal to that which, in essence and rank, is beneath it: scientific research.

Philosophy is science because, knowing absolutely, it remains at its work. To it "scruples of that sort" – scruples which critical reductions have brought to bear on knowledge in the past – are foreign. Hegel carefully [*mit Bedacht*] says "scruples [*Bedenklichkeiten*] of that sort." He is not maintaining that philosophy may go to work unscrupulously [*bedenkenlos*] and throw critical examination to the winds. Absolute knowledge is, on the contrary, more thoughtful [*bedenkender*] about knowing the absolute than the apprehensive [*bedenkliche*] kind of criticism has hitherto ever been able to be. The current critical fear about knowing the absolute indeed dreads error. However, only within a particular relation could it even commit error, a relation that had unhesitatingly [*bedenkenlos*] been presupposed to be true, a relation within which knowledge, taken as a means, becomes error itself. This fear of error, which looked like critical examination, is itself error. In what way?

As soon as knowledge is taken as a means (instrument or means) – how long has it been taken in this way, and why? – it is considered to be something that comes forth on its own [*für sich*] between the absolute and those who know it. Knowledge exists cut off from the absolute, but also from us who handle knowledge. Totally cut off from each other in this way, the absolute stands on the one side and those who know it stand on the other side. Yet what is an absolute that stands on one side? What kind of absolute stands on any side at all? Whatever it is it is not the absolute.

At the same time, reductive criticism takes knowledge to be something real, or even what is primarily and normatively real. Therefore it appeals to something true, which means something that is certain even for criticism, something whose certainty, however, is supposed still to exist though cut off from the unconditional self-certainty of everything that is certain. This *ens creatum* in the sense of the *ego cogito* is supposed to be certain without the absolute, as the *ens certum*; however, its certainty is retrospectively secured through the backdoor, by means of a proof of God's existence; this was already the case in Descartes. Critical concern, it is true, intends to arrive at something absolute, but it would like to manage it without the absolute. It even seems that this concern may be thinking in a way suited to the absolute when it provisionally banishes the absolute to the realm of the inaccessible, thereby seemingly putting it as high as possible. Criticism, however, though supposedly apprehensive about the high esteem of the absolute, underestimates the absolute. It drags the absolute down into the narrowness of its doubts and its means. Criticism tries to drive the absolute out of its parousia, as though the absoluteness of the absolute could be introduced at some subsequent moment. The apparently critical fear of making an overhasty error is the uncritical evasion of the truth which has already begun its stay. When, on the other hand, science carries out and specifically accepts its own essence, then it has already examined itself. Part of this examination is to know that science as absolute knowledge stands in the parousia of the absolute. But all this is based on the content of the next paragraph.

The third paragraph states: the absolute, uniquely, is true. The true, uniquely, is absolute. The propositions are posited without grounds. They cannot be grounded because no grounding reaches into their ground. No grounding ever reaches their ground because grounding, as the will to ground, constantly moves away from their ground. The propositions are ungrounded but not arbitrary in the sense of a gratuitous assertion. The propositions are ungroundable. They have posited that which grounds in the first place. In them, there speaks the will of the absolute, which in and for itself wills to be already with us.

Since modern philosophy set foot on its terra firma, truth has prevailed as certainty. The true is that which is known in the unconditional self-knowledge of the self. Previously, truth was taken as the correspondence of representation with beings. It is one property of representation. As certainty [*Gewissheit*], however, truth now becomes representation [*Vorstellen*] itself since it hands [*zustellt*] itself over to itself and makes itself certain of itself as representation. Knownness [*Gewussheit*], which has made itself certain of its knowledge (and, in fact, has done so before itself and with itself), has thereby also withdrawn itself from any particularized representation of objects. It no longer fastens to objects in order to have what is true by means of this fastening to them. Knowledge becomes uncoupled from the relation to objects. The representation that knows itself as a handing over detaches itself (*absolvere*) from the search to find its sufficient certainty within a one-sided representation of objects. The detachment permits this representation to continue to exist in such a way that it no longer clings exclusively to its object. This self-uncoupling of self-certainty from an objective relation is its absolvence. It is characteristic of absolvence to affect any relation that applies only in a direct way to the object. Absolvence is only absolvence to the extent that it is completed in every respect, i.e., entirely absolved. In the absolving of its absolvence, the self-certainty of representation attains to certainty, which, for it, means that it attains to the free space of its essence. It acquits itself of its one-sided connection to objects and of its mere representation of them. Unconditional self-certainty is, therefore, its own self-absolution. The unity of absolvence (uncoupling from relation), absolving (completeness of uncoupling), and absolution (acquittal on the basis of that completeness) characterize the absoluteness of the absolute. All these moments of absoluteness have the character of representation. In them there essences the parousia of the absolute. The true in the sense of unconditional self-certainty is, uniquely, the absolute. The absoluteness of self-representation, as we have characterized it here, is, uniquely, the true.

And yet, despite any explanation, however extended, these propositions remain empty. Explanations even promote misunderstanding; for what those sentences give is the phenomenology of spirit – which *is* in its presentation. That is why Hegel is content to offer the propositions *tout court* and risk every appearance of willfulness. However, the reason he states them is to make us ready for what science as absolute knowledge wills. In its own manner, science wills only what the absolute wills. The will of the absolute is, in and for itself, to be already with us. Now that means: since the absolute is willing in this way, only the absolutely true is with us, when we are the ones who know the absolute. Therefore, anyone who is still claiming that besides absolute knowledge (which philosophy arrogates to itself in its uncritical way) other truths also exist does not know what he is talking about. As soon as he adduces something true, he has already represented the absolute. As long as the seemingly cautious and prudent distinction is maintained between an absolute truth and some other truth, we are loitering in a confused distinction. In fact, we have already turned this confusion into the principle of criticism and the decisive norm for science. And yet it is the responsibility of science alone to get at what these words mean: absolute, knowledge, true, objective, subjective. This requires, however, that with its first step science already reaches into the parousia of the absolute, i.e., is with the absoluteness of the absolute. Otherwise it would not be science. If this is the case, it is an offense against its nature for science to engage at all with considerations that are outside the realm of truth and beneath its own level. However, even if science keeps itself clear of critical considerations unsuited to it, it will still remain under the suspicion that though it indeed asserts itself absolutely as absolute knowledge, it does not prove itself to be such. It therefore offends most bitterly against the claim of certainty, the pure fulfillment of which it claims to be. Science must, therefore, be brought before the forum which alone is competent to decide how it is to be examined. This forum can only be the parousia of the absolute. Therefore, it is of renewed importance to clarify the absoluteness of the absolute.

The fourth paragraph indicates what is required of us, as those who know, by the will prevailing in the parousia of the absolute, the will to be, in and of itself, with us. Current criticism of philosophical knowledge unquestioningly takes such knowledge to be a means. It thereby gives proof that it neither knows absolute knowledge nor is capable of achieving it. The incapacity to perceive and to accept the parousia of the absolute before all else is the incapacity for science. The overzealous efforts related to doubts and examinations evade the toils which science exerts to be engaged with this acceptance. The absolute does not grant us the step into the parousia of the absolute in our sleep. That this step is strangely difficult is not at all because we first have to arrive at the parousia from somewhere outside it, as people think; rather, it is a matter, from within the parousia and therefore from out of the parousia, of bringing forth our relationship to it before it. That is why the toil of science is not limited to the labor which the knower, doggedly persisting, expends on that step. The toil of science stems rather from its relation to the parousia.

The absoluteness of the absolute, the absolution that absolves itself absolvently, is the labor of self-comprehension by unconditional self-certainty. It is the painful strain to endure being torn to pieces; this is how the infinite relation *is* in which the essence of the absolute is fulfilled. Once, early in his career, Hegel made this note: "A mended sock is better than a torn one, but not so for self-consciousness."[3] When Hegel speaks of the labor of the concept, he does not mean the sweat of cerebral exertions by scholars, but the self-wresting by the absolute itself into the absoluteness of its self-comprehending on the basis of unconditional self-certainty. The effortlessness that characterizes the parousia (as the relation of being present among us) can nonetheless be reconciled with efforts of this kind by the absolute. The absolute, simply as the absolute, is involved in this relationship. The toil within the absolute to bring about the presence of the absolute and to make it appear in this presence corresponds to the toil of science. On the basis of the straining of the one, the exertions of the other are determined. In comparison, the zealous bustle of critical examination neglects the most difficult aspect of science's toil: to bear in mind that the knowledge that is to be critically examined is absolute knowledge, i.e., philosophy. The normal activities of the usual criticisms in regard to philosophical knowledge are equivalent to the procedure of someone who intends to represent an oak but takes no notice that it is a tree.

It might be tempting, therefore, to consider this critical conduct – which pretends to examine something without even having first presented it to itself for examination – to be a deception. It gives the impression of already having the essential concepts while actually everything depends on giving the concepts of the absolute, knowledge, the true, the objective and subjective, in the first place. The concern of criticism is not at all focused on the subject which it is continually talking about. This kind of examining is an "empty show of knowledge." What would it be like if science spared itself the trouble of a confrontation with such criticism, seeing that it needs all its efforts in order to maintain itself in its essence? What would it be like if science were content simply to come on the scene without any critical preliminaries? Yet it is here, in the middle of the paragraph, that Hegel inserts his decisive "But":

"But science, in the very fact that it comes on the scene, is itself a phenomenon." Science emerges, as other knowledges also do. Of course it can assure us that it is the absolute knowledge before which all other ideas must vanish. However, by putting on such airs, it makes itself every bit as common as the empty shows of knowledge. Those empty shows can aver that they too are present. One assurance is as barren as the other. Mere assurance will never get the living sap of real knowing to flow. However, science might possibly be contrasted in other ways with mere shows of knowledge. It might allude to the fact that it itself is that knowledge which untrue knowledge, without knowing it, is seeking in itself. Science could come on the scene as that truth which is presaged in the untrue. Yet in so doing science would again lapse into mere assurances. Besides, it would then be appealing to a mode of arrival that would ill become it as absolute knowledge. The merely presaged truth is far removed from being the truth in and for itself.

What happens when science comes on the scene? It must make its appearance when it comes on. However, the question will be raised about what that appearing is in which science alone can appear. To appear means in the first place: to emerge alongside others in the mode of self-assertion. Furthermore, to appear means: to happen, to come about and in this coming about to point to something else that does not yet come forth. To appear means: to be the light in which something comes to light, something which itself neither appeared in the past nor will ever appear in the future. These modes of appearance remain unsuited to how science comes onto the scene; for within those modes it can never extend itself as itself and therefore cannot fully set itself up. On the other hand, neither can science arrive all at once as absolute knowledge. It must bring itself forth into its truth, but it must also bring its truth forth along with itself. In every phase in which science comes forth, *it* is what issues forth as the absolute; and it issues forth absolutely. The sort of appearing that is suited to science can therefore only consist in its presenting itself [*darstellt*] in the way it brings itself about and thus sets itself up [*aufstellt*] as knowledge that is a phenomenon. Science may come on the scene only by accomplishing the presentation of knowledge as phenomenon. In this way there must arise – as here only it can arise – what that appearance is in which science truly comes on the scene as itself.

In its appearance science represents itself in the fullness of its essence. The empty shows of knowledge do not disappear by being rejected or just ignored. The knowledge that only appears, that is only a phenomenon, is not supposed to disappear at all, but rather to enter into its appearance. In this way it appears as untrue knowledge, i.e., the not yet true knowledge within the truth of absolute knowledge. In the appearance by which science brings itself forth, the presentation of knowledge as phenomenon must turn against the semblance [*Anschein*] of knowledge; but it must do so in a conciliatory manner, which even in mere seeming [*Schein*] makes the pure shining [*Scheinen*] of the ray of light to gleam. If, however, we dismiss mere seeming simply as falsehood, then we have not yet perceived it even in its seeming. At any rate, the unfolding entrance of science is never based on its merely overcoming seeming. If that were the case, the true would be acknowledging the suzerainty of the untrue. The phenomenon of science has its necessity in that shining which even semblance requires in order to be mere seeming.

Hegel's sentence "But science, in the very fact that it comes on the scene, is itself a phenomenon" is ambiguously expressed, deliberately and with a lofty intention. Science is not only a phenomenon in the sense that the empty shows of untrue knowledge are also a phenomenon – by showing themselves at all. Science, rather, is in itself already a phenomenon in the single sense that it, as absolute knowledge, is the ray of light as which the absolute, the light of truth itself, shines upon us. To appear by means of this shining ray signifies: presencing in the full gleam of self-presenting representation. Appearance is genuine presencing itself: the parousia of the absolute. In keeping with its absoluteness, the absolute is with us on its own. In its will to be with us, the absolute is presencing, becoming-present. By thus bringing itself within itself to itself, it is for itself. It is for the sake of the parousia alone that the presentation of knowledge as phenomenon is necessary. The presentation is compelled to remain turned toward the will of the absolute. The presentation is itself a willing, i.e., not a wishing and a striving, but activity itself as it collects itself into its essence. The moment that we recognize this necessity, we must reflect on what this presentation is in order to know in what way it is, that we may be capable of being in the way that it is, i.e., of carrying it out.

The fifth paragraph launches this reflection. In presenting phenomenal knowledge, science must itself – through this presentation and throughout the course of it – come fully to appearance. That is, it does not come crashing somewhere onto the scene. It makes its entry by proving itself at every step to be what it is. On what stage does this proving take place? Where else but before the eyes of natural representation? At every step this representation follows the appearance of knowledge across the diversity of its phenomena and so is in pursuit from waystation to waystation as merely phenomenal knowledge puts aside its seeming and finally presents itself as true knowledge. The presentation of merely phenomenal knowledge escorts natural representation through the outer court of knowledge up to the door leading to absolute knowledge. The presentation of merely phenomenal knowledge is the path of natural consciousness to science. Since the appearances belonging to untruth have increasingly dropped away *en route*, the path is the path of the soul toward possessing clearness of spirit. The presentation of merely phenomenal knowledge is an *itinerarium mentis in Deum*.[4]

What can be more welcome to natural consciousness and more useful for philosophy than the description of the journey on this path? Because the path to be described runs along the phenomena, it is a path of experience. All kinds of knowledge ought to prefer an empiricism that follows data to mere construction and deduction. The presentation of phenomenal knowledge, phenomenology, keeps to the phenomena. It goes the way of experience. Step by step, it escorts natural representation into the realm of the science of philosophy.

These are indeed the circumstances of the presentation of phenomenal knowledge if we observe the presentation with the eyes of natural representation, which always remains occupied with what, in its opinion, it has before itself at a given time. But can a relative opinion ever catch sight of absolute knowledge. No. What represents itself to natural consciousness under the name of merely phenomenal knowledge and claiming to be the first knowledge that leads to the true is a mere semblance. However, in the opinion of philosophy even today, the phenomenology of spirit is an *itinerarium*, a description of a journey, which is escorted by everyday consciousness toward the scientific knowledge of philosophy. Yet what the phenomenology of spirit, conceived of in this way, appears to be is not what it is in its essence. This appearance, however, is not deceptive by chance. It is a consequence of the essence of the phenomenology of spirit; it forces itself before that essence and conceals it. The appearance, taken in itself, leads us astray. Natural representation, which has here insinuated itself into philosophy, takes phenomenal knowledge only as phenomenal; behind it a non-phenomenal, a non-appearing, knowledge keeps itself hidden. However, this presentation is not at all the presentation of merely phenomenal knowledge as distinct from a true knowledge to which this presentation is supposed to be the first to lead us. On the contrary, the presentation is only the presentation of phenomenal knowledge in its appearing. This "only" does not say that the presentation is not yet science, but it does say that it is not yet science in every respect. The appearing of phenomenal knowledge is the truth of knowledge. The presentation of phenomenal knowledge in its appearing is itself science. The moment the presentation begins it is already science. Hegel writes: "Now because this presentation has for its object only phenomenal knowledge, the presentation itself seems not to be science . . . but may . . . be taken . . . " Hegel neither speaks of a knowledge that is merely phenomenal, nor says that the presentation is only in the process of evolving into science, nor claims that the presentation may only be understood as an *itinerarium* if it is to be grasped in its essence.

The presentation, however, is by no means the guide of natural representation through the museum of the shapes of consciousness, so that at the end of the tour it is to be admitted through a special door into absolute knowledge. On the contrary, with its first step if not before, the presentation dismisses natural consciousness as constitutionally incapable of following the presentation. The presentation of phenomenal knowledge is not a route which natural consciousness can take. Nor, however, is it a path that at each step gains distance from natural consciousness in order to meet up with absolute knowledge somewhere in its subsequent course. Nonetheless, the presentation is a path. Nonetheless, it moves back and forth constantly in the interstice that obtains between natural consciousness and science.

The sixth paragraph begins to mark out the path of the presentation and to clarify the interstice within which the presentation necessarily moves in making phenomenal knowledge appear as a phenomenon. Accordingly, the paragraph begins with a distinction that will resurface from paragraph to paragraph in diverse aspects, though all the while it will remain hidden to what extent those aspects belong together and what constitutes the ground of their unity. We must first of all focus our attention on the distinction between natural consciousness and real knowledge.

Hegel uses the words "consciousness [*Bewusstsein*]" and "knowledge [*Wissen*]" for the same thing. The one explains the other. Consciousness, being-conscious [*Bewusst-sein*] means: to be in a state of knowledge. Knowledge itself delivers, presents, and determines in this way the mode of the "being" in "being-conscious." In such a state there are, above all, that which is known (i.e., that which the knower represents directly) and the representer, along with representing as how he behaves. To know, however, means *vidi*, I have seen, I have taken a view [*Ansicht*] of something, a look [*Einsicht*] into something. The perfect tense "I have seen" is the present tense "I know," in the presence of which that which has been seen is present.[5] Seeing is thought of here as having something before oneself in representation. Representation presents, no matter whether what is present is perceived by the senses or is something thought, or willed, or felt, apart from the senses. To represent is to catch sight of in advance, to hold in sight what has been seen; it is *idea*, but in the sense of the *perceptio*. *Perceptio* occupies itself [*nimmt sich vor*] with each thing that is present as such a thing, deals with [*nimmt durch*] it, scrutinizes and secures it. Representing prevails in all the modes of consciousness. It is neither a mere sensory apprehension nor yet a thought in the sense of a conceptual judgment. Representing gathers together (*co-agitat*) in advance into a have-seen. In the gathering, what has been caught sight of presences. *Conscientia* is the gathering into that presence which is present through representation. As the mode of having caught sight of something, representing brings the sight, the image, into presence. Representing is the in-bringing [*Einbringen*] of the image [*Bild*], an in-bringing that prevails in knowledge as having-seen: imagination [*Einbildung*]. Consciousness, to be conscious, means: to come to presence in bringing-to-pass [*Zubringen*] out of representedness. Such is the mode in which what has already been represented and the representer along with his representing exist and exist together as closely related.

Consciousness, being-conscious, refers to a kind of being. However, this "being-" must not remain a mere empty sound for us. It says: presencing in the mode of the gathering of what has been caught sight of. And yet, in accordance with a usage that has long been customary, the "being-" we have just used means at the same time the beings themselves that are in this mode. The other name for beings that are in the mode of knowledge is "subject": that which everywhere is already lying before us, presencing, and hence accompanies all consciousness: the representer himself in his representing which delivers [*zustellt*] what it has represented [*sein Vor-gestelltes*] to itself and so puts it back [*zurückstellt*]. Representation [*Vorstellen*] – putting before – presents [*präsentiert*] in the mode of representation [*Repräsentation*]. The being that belongs to what precedes all that has been represented, the being of the subject taken as the subject–object relation reflected in itself, is called subjectity. It *is* presence in the mode of representation. To come to presence in the condition of being represented means: to present itself within knowledge as knowledge: to appear in the immediate sense of coming out into an unconcealedness: to come to presence, to be present, there. Consciousness as such is that which appears in itself. To be immediately present through consciousness or knowledge is to appear, and to appear in such a way that the place where something appears is formed as the stage on which it appears *within*, and by means of, appearance. It may now be more evident what the rubric "the presentation of phenomenal knowledge" means. It does not mean the presentation of that which only emerges at first in mere semblance. It has one meaning alone: to represent, in its appearing, the knowledge that in its immediacy is nothing other than that which appears. In addition to representing phenomenal knowledge, the presentation represents the consciousness that is as it is, i.e., it represents it as the effective, real knowledge.

The reality of this real knowledge, the subjectity of the subject, is appearance itself. The being of this being (i.e., appearance), however, like all the being of all beings in all metaphysics, enters into representation only when beings present themselves as beings (ὂν ᾗ ὄν). But now the ὄν is the *ens qua ens perceptum*. It presences in presentation through the *cogitationes*, which are as the *conscientia*. It is now the subject as subject that is to be presented, and the phenomenal as the phenomenal. The presentation of phenomenal knowledge is the ontology of real consciousness as real.

Presentation is a path, but it does not traverse the distance from prephilosophical representation to philosophy. Philosophy itself is this path, as the course of representation that presents. The movement of this representation must be determined on the basis of that which presentation follows: on the basis of phenomenal consciousness as such, i.e., of the real knowledge which is the truth of natural knowledge.

Hence Hegel must begin his characterization of the essence of presentation with a sentence that throws into relief real knowledge as such. "Natural consciousness will prove itself to be only the concept of knowledge and not real knowledge."

Natural knowledge is contrasted with real. Therefore, the natural is not the real and the real not natural. One might think that both are the same. The natural is what comes from nature, belongs to it, and corresponds to it. Nature is the being that is itself without effort. Yet this effortless being is supposed not to be what is real, by which is understood the effectively real, which is nothing but beings themselves, nature? Hegel employs the distinction between natural and real in relation to that knowledge or consciousness which, in itself, is what appears. The subject presences in the mode of appearance; with it, simultaneously and in its reference to the subject, the object presences. The phenomenal subject (i.e., the subject that appears) is the knowledge that presences, is natural consciousness. However, according to Hegel's sentence, natural consciousness proves itself to be something that is not real knowledge. Natural consciousness even proves itself to be "only the concept of knowledge." One might think that Hegel thinks that nature is a mere concept and so not at all real. One might think that, confronted with this evaporation of nature into a mere abstraction, it would be essential to invest nature with its rights as the real. Hegel, however, does not deny that nature is something real, yet he demonstrates that it cannot be reality, the being of beings. In no way does he claim that nature is only a concept. He does say: natural consciousness will prove itself to be "only the concept of knowledge and not real knowledge." What "only the concept of knowledge" means here will be determined only on the basis of what Hegel is thinking with the expression "real knowledge."

The real is that which truly is. Since Descartes, the true, the *ens verum*, is the *ens certum*: that which knows itself in certainty, which presences in knowledge. However, the *ens certum* is truly known only when it is known *qua ens*. This occurs when the *esse* of the *ens* is specifically represented, and a being in its being, the real in its reality, is known. Real knowledge is the knowledge that represents, always and everywhere, beings in their beingness (reality), phenomena in their appearing. The knowledge of the reality of the real is therefore known as real knowledge. When natural knowledge proves itself not to be real knowledge, this means: it turns out to be [*stellt sich heraus*] that knowledge which everywhere fails to represent [*vorstellt*] beings as such but rather in its representation only fastens on beings. As it seeks beings in their truth, it always attempts to explain beings on the basis of beings. The beings in which consciousness is engrossed [*aufgeht*] are all that it is cognizant of [*aufgeht*] and therefore all that it takes to be natural. Such representation itself becomes engrossed in the beings it is cognizant of and thus remains surrounded by them; that is why this knowledge is natural knowledge. Yet this representation itself can become absorbed in beings themselves and take everything everywhere to be beings only if it already has, unknowingly, a representation in general of the beingness of beings. Intrinsically and necessarily, the natural representation of beings is this general representation of the beingness of beings – a representation, however, that has no specific knowledge of the beingness of beings, the reality of the real. In its representation of beings, natural consciousness does not attend to being; nonetheless, it must do so. It cannot help but participate in the representation of the being of beings in general because without the light of being it cannot even be lost *amidst* beings. In this respect, natural consciousness is only the representation of beingness generally and indeterminately: "only the concept of knowledge," not the knowledge that is certain of the reality of the real.

In this passage, Hegel uses the word "concept" in its traditional meaning in accordance with the precepts of logic that define the forms and rules of natural thinking. A concept is the representation of something in general; "only the concept" means that this representation does not even specifically grasp what it represents. It is characteristic of natural consciousness, however, not only to be constantly engrossed in the beings it represents but also to take these beings as uniquely true and therefore to take its knowledge as the real knowledge. This is why Hegel continues as follows: "Since, however, it (natural consciousness) immediately takes itself to be the real and genuine knowledge, this pathway (that is, the path of presenting phenomenal knowledge in its appearance) has a negative significance for it . . . " Whenever real knowledge places the being of beings in full light, natural knowledge pays no attention to it because its own truth is thereby contested. Natural knowledge holds to its own. Everything that occurs to it can be expressed as follows: it is and remains mine [*das Meine*] and is a being as this thing that I meant [*als dieses Ge-meinte*]. In understanding representation as opinion [*Meinen*], Hegel detects in "opinion [*meinen*]" several related meanings: "*meinen*" as being directed, without mediation, toward . . . ; "*meinen*" as the trusting acceptance of what is given; and "*meinen*" in the sense of keeping and claiming something as one's own. This *meinen*, opinion, is the fundamental state of all representing in which natural consciousness moves. For this reason, Hegel is able to say in the paragraph that natural consciousness "sticks to a system of opinion."

What Hegel calls natural consciousness is by no means the same as sensory consciousness. Natural consciousness is alive in all shapes of the spirit; it lives each spiritual shape in its own way, including (and especially) that shape of absolute knowledge which occurs as absolute metaphysics and is at times visible to a few thinkers only. This metaphysics is far from having collapsed when it was confronted by the positivism of the nineteenth and twentieth centuries; on the contrary, the modern technological world in its unlimited entitlement is nothing other than natural consciousness which (in accordance with the manner of its opinion) has at last made feasible the unlimited, self-securing production of all beings through the inexorable objectification of each and every thing. Nonetheless, absolute metaphysics is not the cause of what is established in its way as the confirmation of what takes place in the essence of technology. The naturalness of consciousness is not based on the senses and what can be perceived by the senses, but rather on what consciousness is cognizant of [*aufgeht*] without mediation and as such is received [*eingeht*] by consciousness without mediation. In this way natural consciousness also accepts all that is not sensory, whether the non-sensory (reason and logic) or supra-sensory (the spiritual).

On the other hand, as soon as the appearing of phenomenal knowledge comes to light, this seeming is what matters in knowledge. Natural consciousness sees itself placed in another light without, however, ever being able to glimpse this light as such. In this light, natural knowledge loses *its* truth, since this truth now turns out to be the not-yet-true; for the appearance of the phenomenon which is itself is its own truth and reality. The presentation of the appearance realizes what had been "only the concept of knowledge." It produces the real in its reality; it empowers reality within the real. In the process, phenomena are neither eliminated nor cut off from real knowledge. They are safeguarded [*verwahrt*] in the real knowledge that in truth [*Wahrheit*] is their own, i.e., their own reality and truth. In fact, natural consciousness and real knowledge are the same since the former as not-yet-true necessarily belongs with the latter as its truth. However, for that very reason the two are not identical [*das Gleiche*].

From the perspective of natural consciousness, the presentation of phenomenal knowledge in its appearance continually disturbs what natural consciousness takes to be true. Such disturbance about truth can be regarded as doubt. However, the path of sheer doubt, like the course Descartes traverses in his *Meditations*, is of another sort. Although it calls many different modes of representation into question, it does so only in order to remain at the point from which the examination set out: to learn to doubt, which itself is not doubted at all. The path of doubt only makes clear that doubting has already brought itself to safety, certainty, which is taken as the *fundamentum absolutum*. But the absoluteness of this absolute is neither doubted, nor questioned, nor even just cited in its essence. As Hegel is aware that absolute knowledge can only exist when it begins (however else it begins) with absoluteness, his path is different. For Hegel's thinking, therefore, natural consciousness appears for the first time in the land proper to it; though Descartes sets foot on the land of modern philosophy (the *subiectum* as the *ego cogito*), fundamentally he does not see the country at all.

In the absolute presentation of phenomenal knowledge, there is no way for natural consciousness to return to its truth. The path of the presentation of phenomena in their appearing is "the conscious insight into the untruth of the phenomenal knowledge, for which that is the most real which is after all only the unrealized concept." *En route* natural consciousness loses definitively that which had been its truth, but it never loses its own self in the process. Instead, it establishes itself in its old way in the new truth. From the point of view of the science of phenomenal knowledge, the way of presentation is the way of despair for natural consciousness, though such consciousness does not know it. Natural consciousness itself, however, never despairs. Doubt [*Zweifeln*] in the sense of despair [*Verzweiflung*] is the matter for the presentation, i.e., for absolute knowledge. However, the presentation also despairs on this path, not of itself, but of natural consciousness, because such consciousness has no intention of realizing what it is, constantly – the mere concept of knowledge; and yet it never ceases to claim for itself the truth of knowledge and to pretend to be the only norm for knowledge. The more fully the presentation goes the way of despair, the sooner science completes its own phenomenon.

The presentation of phenomenal knowledge brings [*bringt*] itself fully [*völlig*] into the constancy of despair. It brings [*Vollbringen*] despair to fulfillment. Hegel writes that it is "the thoroughgoing [*sich vollbringende*] skepticism." We thus restore to the word "skepsis" its original meaning: σκέψις signifies the seeing [*Sehen*], watching [*Zusehen*], inspecting [*Besehen*], that oversees [*nachsieht*] what and how beings are as beings. Skepsis understood like this follows the being of beings with its eyes open. Its watching has seen the being of beings in advance. This is the perspective from which it inspects the matter itself. Thinkers are intrinsically skeptics about beings because of the skepsis into being.

Skepsis moves and stands within the light of the ray by which the absoluteness of the absolute – the absoluteness that in and for itself is with us – has already touched us. The having-seen of skepsis is the *vidi* (I have seen and I see now) which has the reality of the real in view. If, however, reality is the appearance of phenomenal knowledge, then appearance attains its presentation only if the presentation follows appearance and moves as its wake. In this movement, the appearance of phenomena comes to be attached to the presentation. In this coming, the phenomena themselves, taking themselves to be the real, go away. This intrinsically united coming and going is the movement as which consciousness itself *is*. Consciousness is in the unity of natural and real knowledge, a unity by which consciousness places itself in relation to itself in accordance with the knowledge it has of itself in each case, and by which it appears in the condition of having so been placed [*Gestelltheit*]. Thus consciousness is always a shape [*Gestalt*].

Skepsis drops into consciousness, which develops into skepticism, which in the appearance of phenomena produces and transforms one shape of consciousness into the other. Consciousness is consciousness in the mode of thoroughgoing skepticism. Skepticism is the history of consciousness itself, which is neither natural consciousness merely in itself, nor real knowledge merely for itself, but rather the originary unity of both of them, in and for itself. That movement of the coming of appearance and of the going of phenomena is the happening which, from shape to shape, brings consciousness into the sight – that is, the image – of its essence. This history is the "the history of the *process of training and educating* consciousness itself up to the level of science." Hegel does not say: "the history of the *process of training and educating* natural consciousness up to the level of the philosophical;" he is thinking only of the appearance of phenomenal consciousness in view of its complete coming forth. As this coming forth, consciousness is already science itself.

Thoroughgoing skepticism is the historicity of history. It is as this history that consciousness develops into the phenomenon of absolute knowledge. Skepticism is no longer taken here as an attitude of the isolated human subject. If that were the case, it would remain the mere subjective resolution never to rely on a foreign authority but rather to test everything oneself, i.e., according to the sense of this subject. Although this skepticism invokes the unique understanding of a self-representing ego, it is not a skepsis into the being of beings. Skepsis is not confined in the narrow horizon of what is restricted to the self-evident. In looking out upon the appearance of phenomenal knowledge, it looks into the whole scope of phenomenal knowledge. The isolated, self-representing *ego cogito* remains trapped within this scope. But perhaps even this scope, thought more essentially than Hegel was able to think it, is still only a recollection of the *esse* of the *ens certum* of the *ego cogito*, a recollection in the shape of its extension into the reality of absolute knowledge. Admittedly, this extension requires the antecedent [*vorgängige*] skepsis into the breadth of the self-appearing unconditional subjectity. However, this action [*Vorgehen*] is at the same time the decisive and complete retreat into that truth of beings which, as absolute certainty, takes itself to be being itself.

At this point, it is no longer possible to avoid a clarification of the language we have been using and which is now in need of clarification. Once he settled on his terminology, Hegel identifies as "beings" that which becomes objective in immediate representation. These objects [*Gegenständliche*] are that which is represented one-sidedly and exclusively from the side of standing-against [*Gegenstehen*] without taking either representation or that which represents into consideration. "Being," the term used by Hegel for beings, is the name for that which actually is not yet truly the true and the real. Hegel uses "being" to designate the reality which in his sense is still untrue. It is in this way that he interprets ancient philosophy. Because ancient philosophy had not yet set foot in that land of philosophy (self-consciousness) where represented objects first exist as such, it thinks the real only as beings. For Hegel, "being" is always taken in the reduction "only being," for true beings are the *ens actu*, the effectively real, whose *actualitas*, effective reality, consists in the knowledge of self-knowing certainty. Only this certainty can truly – which now means out of the constant certainty of absolute knowledge – claim to "be" all reality, *the* reality. Of course it is right here, where being was supposed to disappear, that it recurs. However, the absolute knowledge of science takes no notice of it.

In contrast to Hegel's language, we use the word "being" both for what Hegel (with Kant) calls "objectiveness [*Gegenständlichkeit*]" and "objectivity [*Objektivität*]" and for what he represents as the truly real and the reality of spirit. We do not, as Hegel does from his perspective, interpret εἶναι, being for the Greeks, as the objectivity of immediate representation by a subjectivity that has not yet arrived at itself. Not from this perspective, that is, but from the perspective of the Greek Ἀλήθεια as the presencing out of and into unhiddenness. However, the presence that happens in the representation by the skepsis of consciousness is a mode of presentness that essences as much as the οὐσία of the Greeks out of the yet unthought essence of a concealed time. The beingness of beings – which from the beginning of Greek thinking to Nietzsche's theory of the eternal return of the same has happened as the truth of beings – is for us only one mode (even if a decisive one) of being which by no means must necessarily appear exclusively as the presence of what presences.[a] In the way Hegel uses the word "being," he should not, strictly speaking, have continued to designate that which for him is the true reality of the real, spirit, with a word still containing "being." And yet he does so everywhere, since the essence of spirit is self-consciousness, literally being-self-conscious. The usage is not, of course, the consequence

[a] First edition, 1950. Because being is the being *of* beings (cf. p. 274), being is part of the ontological difference and thereby it itself refers toward an originary essence. It thus becomes clear that this, *in the way* it knows metaphysics (beingness), is only *one* mode of being [*Seyn*]. Being [*Sein*] – the name taken over from metaphysics – as being [*Seyn*] for the *difference*.

of an imprecise and inconsistent terminology but rather is a result of the concealed manner in which being itself discloses and hides itself.

However, if our reading of Hegel's text imposes the word "being" on the appearance of phenomenal knowledge, as well as on the absoluteness of the absolute, then this may very well appear at first to be arbitrary. Yet it is neither arbitrary, nor an instance of mere terminology (assuming it is at all licit to bring the language of thinking together with a terminology, which in accordance with its essence is an instrument of the sciences). Rather, the language of thinking, which has grown on the basis of its destiny, calls what has been thought in other thinking into the clarity of its own thinking, in order to release the former into its own essence.

What happens when the skepsis of consciousness anticipates the appearance of phenomenal knowledge and presents it? To what extent does the presentation thereby make its appearance in such a way that it ceases to be a mere entry on the stage? The presentation escapes this only when it is certain that there appears in it the entire history of the formation of consciousness. It is in the structures of consciousness that natural consciousness is able to find the truth of all its shapes.

The seventh paragraph develops the question concerning "the completeness of the forms of unreal consciousness." These are the shapes of phenomenal knowledge, because this knowledge has not yet appeared in its appearance and so been placed into its reality. The complete coming forth of the shapes can only result from the route of its arrival. This route [*Gang*] is the progress [*Fortgang*] of appearance. It must be a necessary progress. For it is only in this way that a tight cohesiveness prevents any accidental gaps. What is it that makes the progress in the route of the presentation necessary? In what does the essence of the progress consist?

In order to answer in the right way, we must not continue to hold the view which natural consciousness generally adopts of the presentation of phenomenal knowledge. Out of principle this view is one-sided, for natural representation always sees only one side (which for it is not even a side, but rather the entirety), the side of things that meet it outright. Natural consciousness never looks on the other side, never looks to the being of beings. This essential one-sidedness of natural consciousness can even come on the scene as a proper shape of consciousness. It must expose itself to us within the history of its formation. It shows itself to be that skepticism which comes to an end in all knowledge and behavior by finding that there is nothing to the knowledge that was supposed to have been acquired. As the sheer addiction to doubt possessed by an unconditional sophistry, this skepticism has a constant result: empty nothingness.

To what extent, within this shape of the consciousness, has the one-sidedness of natural knowledge been elevated into a known principle? To the extent that natural consciousness finds everywhere and always only beings, only phenomena, and judges all that meets it in accordance with the results of its findings. Whatever is not of the nature of its finding falls victim to the decree that there is no such thing. Natural consciousness only finds beings, and being is not of the nature of what it finds. For this reason the appearance of phenomena, the reality of the real, are taken as something void from within the perspective of natural consciousness. In the judgment of natural consciousness, every step taken by the presentation of phenomenal knowledge leads to nothing. The presentation never gets beyond the first step, which has already led it to nothing. How is the presentation to go further from there, and where is it to go? Any progress will remain denied to it unless it continually permits another shape of phenomenal knowledge to come to it from somewhere, in order to find in this other shape the intended appearance and with it to fall again into nothingness.

The view to which natural consciousness must be devoted whenever it makes judgments about the presentation of phenomenal knowledge, however, is expressed often enough in the objections, supposedly philosophical, that have been advanced against Hegel's philosophy. In defense, Hegel in the paragraph under discussion only says that the nothingness to which the presentation of knowledge that is appearing in its appearance leads is not empty, but rather "the nothing of that out of which it comes as a result." Now appearance comes as a result of the phenomena, that is, of those things that appear. Consequently, if what results from the progress for the presentation is a result of where its course has come from and not as a result of where its next step has yet to go, then it is no wonder that the natural consciousness finds the course of the presentation strange. It is all the more essential to prevent from the start the one-sided view which natural consciousness adopts about the progress of the presentation; it is a view which causes total confusion.

The eighth paragraph sketches the characteristic movement of the historical route of the historical formations of consciousness. The progress through the complete succession of shapes is supposed to ensue of its own accord. "Of its own accord" can only mean here: on the basis of the way that consciousness in itself is a route. That is why consciousness has to come into consideration at this point. Accordingly, this paragraph leads up to the first of the three statements about consciousness which Hegel expresses in our text. "Formation of consciousness" means: consciousness puts itself in the picture concerning its own essence, which is to be science in the sense of absolute knowledge. Two things follow: consciousness appears to itself in its appearance and at the same time establishes itself in the light of its own essence in accordance with the essential aspects of its seeming, and it thus organizes itself as the realm of its own shapes. Consciousness itself is neither only natural consciousness nor only real consciousness. Nor is it just the coupling of the two. Consciousness itself is the originary unity of the two. Real and natural knowledge do not lie in consciousness like lifeless bits of inventory. Consciousness *is* both of them since it appears to itself in the originary unity of both of them and as this unity.[a] The two are distinguished in consciousness. How? The distinction prevails as the restlessness of the natural against the real and the real against the natural. Consciousness itself is intrinsically this restlessness of the self-distinguishing between natural and real knowledge. The movement of the course of history is based on this restlessness of consciousness itself and has even already taken its direction from it. Consciousness is not set in motion only after the fact, nor only then pointed in its direction.

In the historical route of its formation, natural consciousness proves itself "to be only the concept of knowledge." Still, this "only" is already sufficient. That is, since natural consciousness, in representing beings, inevitably though not explicitly co-represents the beingness of beings, natural consciousness is in itself beyond and yet not outside itself. Not only does natural consciousness take no notice of the "concept" which it is all along, it even thinks that it can manage without it – though in truth that realm of beings in which natural consciousness is resident is determined, in its scope and in how to dominate it, uniquely on the basis of what consciousness itself is as the knowledge of the beingness of beings. However, natural consciousness conceals from itself the restlessness of the beyond-itself which prevails in it. It flees before that restlessness and so, in its own way, binds itself to it. Natural consciousness takes its opinion as the true, and thus enlists truth for itself, which shows that what it takes to be its own is not its own. Its own opinion constantly betrays its restlessness at being torn inexorably into the beyond-itself. The presentation of phenomenal knowledge

[a] First edition, 1950. Its equally complete appearing-to-itself; "absolute idea" presence in and for itself – as the complete presencing-to-itself.

has only to be drawn into this restlessness in order to find itself already in the route of its progress. The inexorableness of the movement, however, can only be determined on the basis of that to which restlessness in itself is held. Restlessness holds itself to that which tears it away. What tears it away is the reality of the real, which *is* only in that it appears to itself in its truth. The reality of the real, seen from the direction of the progress, is the goal of the route. Thought on the basis of the restlessness of consciousness, the route begins with the goal. The route is a movement out away from the goal, but in such a way that the goal is not left behind but rather arrives, with the movement itself, precisely at its own development. The goal of the route of consciousness is fixed for knowledge in its essence as this very knowledge. In its very restlessness, consciousness is the goal's fixing-itself-before. This is the reason that the eighth paragraph begins its characterization of the motion of consciousness with the sentence "The *goal*, however, is fixed for knowledge just as necessarily as the succession in the process." The paragraph, however, does not discuss the goal, or at least not in the form in which it is usually represented, by taking it to be that toward which something is driven. Were it permissible here to adopt a locution from mechanics, we could say: progress in the historical route of the historical formations of consciousness is not pushed forward by the shape that consciousness has taken at a given time into what has not yet been determined; rather, it is pulled by the goal that has already been fixed. In its attraction, the attractive goal brings itself forth into its appearance, and it brings the route of consciousness, in advance, into the plenty of its plentifulness.

Through its skepsis, thoroughgoing skepticism has already brought this goal into sight and thereby brought it into the center of the restlessness of consciousness itself. Because this center is constantly beginning the movement, the skepsis that prevails in the essence of knowledge has therefore already encompassed all possible forms of consciousness. In keeping with this encompassment, the compass of the forms of unreal knowledge is complete. The way that the presentation represents all phenomenal knowledge in its appearance is nothing but the co-accomplishing of the skepsis that prevails in the essence of consciousness. Skepsis endures in advance the inexorable tearing of consciousness out beyond itself, i.e., the tearing of natural out into real knowledge. In this tearing, natural consciousness loses what it takes as its truth and its life. This tearing is thus the death of natural consciousness. In this constant death, consciousness offers up its own death as a sacrifice to gain its resurrection to itself out of the sacrifice. In this tearing, natural consciousness suffers violence. However, this violence comes from consciousness itself. Violence is the prevailing of restlessness in consciousness itself. This prevailing is the will of the absolute that wants to be in its absoluteness in and for itself among us, with us, we who reside constantly in the mode of natural consciousness in the midst of beings.

Now perhaps the sentence which we have called the first statement about consciousness may have become clearer: "Consciousness, however, is for itself its own *concept*..." This means something different from what the reference at the beginning of the sixth paragraph means: "Natural consciousness will prove itself to be only the concept of knowledge..." The discussion is now concerned not with natural consciousness but rather with consciousness itself as such. The word "concept" is now specifically emphasized. "Concept" now means: the appearing-to-itself of consciousness in its truth. The essence of this truth is based on unconditional certainty. In keeping with this certainty, something known has not yet been grasped conceptually if it has only been represented in general. It must rather be referred back, in being known, to the knowledge that belongs to it, and it must be represented in this relation with that very knowledge. The known, only in this way, is totally within knowledge; as a result, knowledge becomes a general representation (a conceiving) in an encompassing and also unconditional sense. In relation to this concept, in which consciousness itself conceives of itself, natural consciousness is always "only the concept." For insofar as it is consciousness, it has an idea of what it is to be known generally. It is only because consciousness is for itself its own concept that natural consciousness (as something that belongs to consciousness itself) can persist in being only the concept of knowledge. However, we will not understand the first statement about consciousness until we not only pay attention to the distinction which Hegel stresses between "*concept*" and "only the concept" but also reconsider our reflections in the last paragraphs. In the sentence "Consciousness, however, is for itself its own *concept*" the stress actually falls on the "is." The "is" has this significance: consciousness brings about its own appearing-to-itself, and as it does so it forms for itself, in its appearing-to-itself, the site of appearance; this site is part of its essence. In this way consciousness finds itself in its concept.

Since Hegel has demonstrated the truth of consciousness in the first statement about consciousness, he is now able to clarify natural consciousness in respect to its being unreal knowledge. He also calls it untrue consciousness. However, in no way does this mean that natural consciousness is merely the overburden of the false, deceptive, and erroneous. Rather, it means: natural consciousness is always the not-yet-true, which is overmastered by the violence which tears it forth into its truth. Natural consciousness feels this violence and falls into anxiety about its own continued existence. Hegel, whose rationalism cannot be sufficiently praised or reviled, speaks in the decisive passage (where he identifies the relation of natural knowledge to the being of beings) of the "feeling of violence." This feeling of will's violence – the will that is how the absolute *is* – describes the way in which natural consciousness is "only the concept of knowledge." Still it would be foolish to think that Hegel is of the opinion that the natural anxiety which makes consciousness evade the being of beings is also the mode in which, or indeed the organ through which, philosophy thinks the being of beings, simply because it is the natural relation to being. This would mean that when thinking has to refer back to feeling, philosophy too would at once be handed over to sheer feeling instead of being grounded in science. However, this superficial opinion (which has its adherents today as ever) is itself part of the vanity of an understanding that gloats over the indolence of its thoughtlessness and which dissipates everything into its thoughtlessness. It is at the end of this paragraph, the same paragraph which with that first statement about consciousness looks out into the truth of knowledge, that the untruth of knowledge appears in the shape of the "barren ego." In restricting itself to the beings that encounter it, the barren ego finds its only satisfaction.

The "barren ego" is the name for the imperious behavior of ordinary opinion within philosophy. Nonetheless, the term does not identify an "I" isolated in itself in distinction to a community of the "We." The "barren ego," rather, is precisely the subject of the many in their common opinion. The "barren ego" lives in the egoism of the "they" [*man*], who escape from their anxiety at thoroughgoing skepticism into the dogmatism of opinion. The dogmatic principle is to close one's eyes at the presentation of phenomenal knowledge and to refuse to go along with the advance of that presentation. For this reason, the dogmatism of customary opinions must be left to its own devices. With this decision, philosophy does not reject natural consciousness. How could it, seeing that science is the truth of the not-yet-true, and so it *is* the not-yet-true, though in the truth of the not-yet-true. Philosophy is the first to discover natural consciousness in its naturalness and to recognize it. On the other hand, philosophy does indeed move past natural consciousness when this consciousness puts on philosophical airs in order to erase the boundary separating it from philosophy and to turn its back on philosophy as the knowledge of the being of beings. However, in this case philosophy only moves past what had already turned its back on philosophy, what had already turned away from it; philosophy, however, in moving past natural consciousness, nonetheless does not neglect it but rather concerns itself exclusively with it in order to be the route through which the truth of consciousness appears.

The presentation of phenomenal knowledge is thoroughgoing skepticism. In going thoroughly, it works itself out fully [*führt sich aus*]. The presentation brings itself forward [*führt sich vor*], instead of merely entering upon the stage. The path of the presentation does not go from natural to real consciousness, but rather consciousness itself, which exists as this distinction between natural and real in every shape of consciousness, progresses from one shape to another. This progress is a route whose movement is determined out of the goal, i.e., out of the violence of the will of the absolute. The presentation, which the appearance of phenomenal knowledge comes to meet, follows that appearance. The natural representation of absolute knowledge – that it is a means – has now disappeared. Nor does knowledge now let itself be put any longer to the test, at least not as a means that is applied to an object. Moreover, since the presentation itself presents itself, testing seems to have become quite superfluous. Therefore, after this clarification, the presentation could begin immediately. But it does not begin, assuming that it has not already begun. New sections of reflection follow. This betrays that the essence of the presentation of phenomenal knowledge has not yet been brought sufficiently near us and that a relation of our own to the presentation has not yet been gained. The way that the presentation and what is to be presented belong together, whether and to what extent the two are even the same though without being confounded indifferently, is still obscure. If the absolute in and for itself is already with us, how is absolute knowledge supposed to be a path to the absolute? If here we may still speak at all of a path, then we may do so only of the path along which the absolute itself goes because it *is* this path. Could the presentation of phenomenal knowledge be this path and route? The essence of the presentation has grown still more enigmatic. All that remains clear is that the presentation does not come from somewhere else, cut off from the absolute, in order to face the absolute, as natural consciousness represents knowledge.

The ninth paragraph, all the same, takes up again just this natural representation of knowledge. Of course it does so only in order to pose once again the question of the critical examination of absolute knowledge. That knowledge is not a means is far from invalidating the critical examination of knowledge;

on the contrary, it is only now, in fact, that the examination can be made worthy of investigation. When the presentation brings phenomenal knowledge forth into its appearance, it places the not-yet-true consciousness into its truth. It measures the phenomena appearing as such phenomena according to their appearance. Appearance is the criterion. From where does the presentation take this criterion? In taking over the critical examination of phenomenal knowledge, science itself comes onto the scene as the court and thus as the criterion of the examination. Science's entry onto the scene may very well be the carrying out of the presentation; nonetheless, with its first step, science must bring with it the criterion of critical examination as an already proven criterion. On the one hand, science, in order to be carried out, needs the criterion; on the other hand, the criterion can only be given in the course of carrying it out, assuming, that is, that absolute knowledge is not able to adopt a criterion from just anywhere. Whenever the presentation must measure untrue knowledge by its truth, it is obliged to reconcile the irreconcilable. The impossible stands in its way. How is this obstacle to be removed?

The tenth paragraph continues this reflection and shows that Hegel is not glossing over or eliminating the contradiction in the essence of the presentation by means of logical arguments. The apparently irreconcilable does not lie in the essence of the presentation. It is the fault of the inadequate way in which we see the presentation, we who continue to be dominated by the representational mode of natural consciousness. The presentation approaches the appearance of knowledge. The presentation, too, is a knowledge. They both fall within consciousness itself. If the question about the criterion and the critical examination has any validity, then it can find its answer only in and from consciousness. Is consciousness itself, as consciousness, in itself something like a measure or a criterion? Is consciousness as such of its own accord a critical examination? Consciousness itself is now moving more clearly into the light in which it may be essentially seen. Nonetheless, the fundamental trait in the essence of consciousness at which reflection is aiming is not coming to light.

As though he had said nothing at all in the previous paragraphs about consciousness, Hegel begins by referring to two determinations "as they are found in consciousness." He calls them knowledge and truth. They are called "abstract determinations" because they are a product of an inspection of consciousness that has lost sight of the full essence of the condition of consciousness and the unity of that condition. Here consciousness is understood as presenting itself immediately (i.e., ever one-sidedly) to natural representation.

Consciousness [*Bewusst-sein*] states that something is in the state of being known [*Gewussten*]. What is known, however, exists in knowledge and as a knowledge. This known is that to which consciousness, in the mode of knowledge, relates itself. What stands in this relation is the known. It exists, in that it is "for" consciousness. Such beings are in the mode of "being for . . . " However, "being for" is a mode of knowledge. In this mode something is "for consciousness," but it is also something else for consciousness, namely something that is known. In knowledge as "being for," the one thing and the other are "for consciousness." However, it is not simply that the known is represented in general, but rather that this representation thinks of the known as a being that exists in itself (i.e., truthfully). This being-in-itself of the known is called truth. Truth, too, is both one thing (something represented) and another (a being-in-itself) "for consciousness." The two determinations of consciousness, knowledge and truth, are distinguished as "being for" and "being-in-itself." Hegel simply turns our attention to these two determinations without going into "what really lies in them." Nonetheless, Hegel has imperceptibly, though intentionally, indicated a fundamental and distinguishing trait of consciousness. The first sentences of the paragraph even name it in passing.

In consciousness something is distinguished from[a] consciousness by consciousness. As itself, and through itself, it is one thing in relation to another. What is made distinct in this distinction (the object for the subject in the subject), however, remains related by the distinction precisely to what distinguishes it. In representing, consciousness cuts something off from itself, but what has been cut off it adds to itself. Consciousness is a differentiation that does not differentiate. As this difference that is not different, consciousness in its essence is ambiguous. This ambiguity is the essence of representation. The ambiguity is the reason that the two determinations, knowledge and truth, "being for" and "being-in-itself," are immediately found everywhere in consciousness, and in fact are themselves ambiguous.

What is the presentation now that it, as representation, itself remains a mode of consciousness, seen from the perspective of the two determinations? It represents the phenomena in their appearance. It inquires into knowledge about its truth. It examines knowledge for its truth. It moves within the differentiation of the difference as which consciousness itself *is*.

[a] First edition, 1950: against consciousness.

So with a glance toward this difference, a prospect is opened onto the essential possibility that the presentation gets its criterion and its character of critical examination from that in which it moves. The prospect will become clearer as soon as there emerges that toward which – seen from the perspective of consciousness itself – the measuring examination is approaching.

The eleventh paragraph asks directly what is the object of the inquiry by the presentation of phenomenal knowledge. However, the question is not raised directly until it asks not only what is being inquired into but also who is inquiring. This is because the object of our inquiry, if it is something that is known, will be in our knowledge for us who are inquiring. With this characterization of a science that presents phenomenal knowledge in its appearance, we unexpectedly come into the play of the presentation. It proves to be the case that we are already in the play, in that what the presentation presents is "for us." Therefore the question cannot be evaded concerning the role that falls to the "for us" in science. The repercussions of that question reach into a dimension which we now scarcely imagine.

What are we inquiring into when we examine knowledge for its truth? Truth is being-in-itself. Knowledge is being for a consciousness. When we inquire into [*untersuchen*] the truth of knowledge, we are seeking [*suchen*] knowledge in itself. However, through our inquiry knowledge becomes our object. If we were to place it in its being-in-itself before us, if we were to represent it, it would have become a being for us. We would not be grasping the truth of knowledge but only our knowledge of knowledge. Being for us would remain the criterion with which we would measure the being-in-itself of knowledge. Yet how would knowledge have arrived at such a point where it conforms to a criterion that changes what is supposed to be measured into the measure? If the presentation of phenomenal knowledge is to be conducted by the results of considering the two determinations of consciousness, knowledge and truth, then all that the presentation can do is continually change its behavior into the opposite.

The twelfth paragraph frees the presentation from this new difficulty. The presentation is freed as a result of the straightforward reference to the nature of the object which it presents. The object is consciousness itself. Its nature is that which comes forth on its own into appearance. Does consciousness have the character of a criterion from within its own nature? If it does, then consciousness on its own must present the possibility of being at once the measure and the measured. It must be intrinsically differentiated in this respect but at the same time not different. Something like this came to light in the tenth paragraph. The essential ambiguity of consciousness – to be the difference of representation, which representation is at the same time not a difference – points to a duality in the nature of consciousness. In it there is the possibility to be in essence at once both the one and the other: measure and measured. Let us take the ambiguity not as a lack of clarity but rather as the mark of its essential unity. Then consciousness in its ambiguity shows how those determinations, knowledge and truth, which at first had been represented as divided, belong together. The possibility of measuring and measure results from the nature of consciousness.

Hegel characterizes the nature of the object of the presentation that represents phenomenal knowledge in his second statement about consciousness. The first, pronounced in the eighth paragraph, runs: "Consciousness, however, is for itself its own *concept*." Now the second statement follows it: "Consciousness furnishes its own criterion in it itself." The statement is conspicuous in its language. Hegel, however, is intimately acquainted with this language that is strange to us; his intimacy is a result of what has proved to be the nature of the object. Why does Hegel say "in it itself [*an ihm selbst*]" rather than "in itself [*an sich selbst*]"? Because one essential aspect of consciousness is that there is a criterion for it. The criterion is not fetched from somewhere in order for consciousness to take it in itself and so to have it for itself. Nor is the criterion something that is first applied to consciousness. The criterion is part of consciousness itself, and this is the case because criterionness is already a product of consciousness since consciousness is dually measure and measured. But in that case would it not be just as well or better to say that consciousness furnishes its criterion in itself? Yet what is consciousness in itself? Consciousness is in itself when it is by itself, and it is by itself when it is specifically for itself and thus in and for itself. If consciousness furnished its criterion in itself, the implication, rigorously thought, would be: consciousness furnishes itself a criterion for itself. Yet ordinarily the question of what consciousness truly is is just what consciousness pays no attention to. On the other hand, truth does not fall to consciousness out of nowhere. Consciousness itself is already for itself its concept. Therefore it has its criterion in it. Therefore it itself puts the criterion at the disposal of it itself. The "in it itself" signifies the duality: consciousness bears [*hat liegen*] the criterion in its essence. However, what belongs [*liegt*] to consciousness and not to anything else is not something given directly by consciousness to itself. It furnishes the criterion in it itself. It gives, and yet at the same time it does not give.

Inasmuch as natural consciousness represents beings in themselves, what has been represented is therefore true and moreover true "for it," that is, for the consciousness that represents immediately. Hegel uses this "for it" (which usage corresponds to the "in it itself") to mean that consciousness holds to be true that which it has directly represented. In directly representing, consciousness is absorbed within what it represents and does not specifically refer this back to itself as the representer. It is true that consciousness does have what it represents within its representation, but not for itself, only "for it." However, along with its true representation for it, consciousness in it itself has also given "for us" (we who attend to the truth of the true) the truth of the true, i.e., the criterion. By presenting phenomenal knowledge as such, we take appearance as the criterion in order thereby to measure the knowledge which takes these phenomena as true. In phenomenal knowledge, the true is that which knowledge knows. If we call this particular truth the object and this knowledge the concept, then the critically examining presentation of phenomena in respect to their appearance consists in our watching whether knowledge (i.e., that which natural consciousness takes to be its knowledge) corresponds to what this particular truth is. Or conversely, if we call the knowledge that we are critically examining the object and the in-itself of the known the concept, then the critical examination consists in watching whether the object corresponds to the concept. What is decisive, what is crucial to grasp about this point, is the following: each time that we represent the phenomena in their appearance, that which we measure and that with which we measure fall within consciousness itself. Consciousness in it itself supplies the two essential moments of the critical examination. For us, the presenters, the result is the maxim which directs all representation of phenomena in their appearance. It runs: leave all your notions and opinions about phenomena aside. Accordingly, the fundamental attitude of absolute knowledge does not consist in bombarding phenomenal consciousness with an array of knowledges and arguments but rather in leaving these aside. By leaving them aside we attain to the pure watching which enables us to see appearance. In watching we are enabled to "consider the matter as it actually is *in itself* and *for itself*." The matter, however, is phenomenal knowledge as phenomenal. The state of the matter, the reality of the real, is appearance itself.

Phenomenal consciousness is in it itself what is to be measured and the criterion of measure. Hegel's way of making clear that both fall within consciousness itself merely gives the impression of a dubious wordplay that invites suspicion. Knowledge, and the true that is known in knowledge, belong to consciousness. It appears to come to the same thing whether we call knowledge the concept and the true the object or, conversely, the true the concept and knowledge the object. In fact it does come to the same thing. However, that does not imply that there is no difference – and that therefore it is a matter of indifference – in the way we use the terms concept and object. If the true that has been represented in natural consciousness is called the object, then this is the object "for it," for natural consciousness. If, however, knowledge is called the object, then knowledge as phenomenal knowledge is the object "for us," who are considering phenomena in regard to their appearance. If the knowledge by which natural consciousness represents the known is called the concept, then conceiving is the representation of something as something. In this case, the word "concept" is taken in the sense of traditional logic. If on the other hand the true that has been represented in consciousness is called the concept by which knowledge as object for us has been measured, then the concept is the truth of the true, the appearance, in which phenomenal knowledge is brought to itself.

This use of the terms object and concept seems at first sight to be willful, but it is in no way arbitrary. It has been tied in advance to the nature of consciousness, a nature which is expressed in the first statement about consciousness: "Consciousness, however, is for itself its own *concept*." In what consciousness holds to be true, a shape of its truth is made real. The true is the object "for it." Truth is the object "for us." Hegel expresses this in the sentence which we may now, with the help of our own emphasis, understand more clearly: "Thus in what consciousness inside itself declares to be the "in-itself" or "true," we (that is, we who know absolutely) *have* the criterion which *it* itself sets up, and by which we are to measure *its* knowledge."

Because the criterion for critical examination has been placed at our disposal out of consciousness itself, the examination in this respect needs no addition from us. However, the fact that this is at our disposal insofar as we ourselves are consciousness does not mean that it is yet explicitly at our disposal. The presentation may be placed under the maxim of pure watching, but it still remains obscure how we are to receive anything through merely leaving our views aside and how it is that we already have the criterion as such. Let us admit that the knowledge that is to be measured and the criterion fall within consciousness in such a way that all we have to do is accept them; even so, measuring and achieving the measurement do not go on their own without our addition. In the end, is not what is essential in the presentation still left to our own activity? And what about the critical examination itself, without which neither the measured nor the criterion is what it is?

The thirteenth paragraph answers this question by giving, and explaining, the third statement about consciousness. The statement is inconspicuously relegated to a subordinate clause. In the form of a main clause, it runs: "Consciousness critically examines itself." This means: consciousness, insofar as it is consciousness, is critical examination. The fundamental word of modern metaphysics, consciousness or being-conscious, has not been thought until we also think, within this "being-," that characteristic of critical examination which is determined by the consciousness of knowledge.

In critical examination, both the measure and what is to be measured are together. Therefore, the fact that they are found together in consciousness is never the result of an additional action whereby one of them is applied to the other. The nature of consciousness consists of the cohesion of both. This nature has been demonstrated in multiple respects. Natural consciousness is the immediate knowledge of an object which it holds to be true. At the same time, natural consciousness is a knowledge of its knowledge of the object, even if it does not explicitly refer itself back to this knowledge. The consciousness of the object and the consciousness of knowledge is the same, and for that same both of them, object and knowledge, are known. Object and knowledge are "for the same." The one and the other are at once for the same, for consciousness itself. For it, consciousness is the differentiation of the two against each other. In accordance with its nature, consciousness is the comparison of the one with the other. This comparison *is* the critical examination. "Consciousness critically examines itself."

However, consciousness is actually critical examination all the while only in the sense that the question becomes for it in the first place the question whether knowledge corresponds to the object of knowledge and so is truly the object, whether the object corresponds to that which knowledge fundamentally knows. The critical examination exists only through the occurrence of such a process of becoming. This becoming comes over consciousness when it finds out what that is in truth which it had immediately taken to be true, when it finds out [*dahinter kommt*] what it then knows with certainty once it represents the object in its objectivity. For consciousness, accordingly, there must still be something behind the object as well as behind its immediate representation of the object, something for it to approach [*dahin kommen*], to which it must first have opened itself [*sich aufmachen*] and for which it must first have set out [*sich aufmachen*].

In the commentary on the first of the statements about consciousness it became evident that natural consciousness is "only the concept of knowledge." Admittedly, it has a general representation of its object as object, and similarly of its knowledge as knowledge. Nonetheless, natural consciousness ignores this "as," because it only accepts as valid what has been immediately represented – even though it does so with the help, always, of this "as." Because, in keeping with its own sense, it does not admit this "as," natural consciousness stubbornly never goes back of its own accord to that which, in a strange way, it has before itself as its own background. Thus consciousness is comparison and then, again, it is not. By its own nature, when consciousness represents an object, it is the differentiation between "being in itself" and "being for itself," between truth and knowledge. Consciousness is not only this differentiation which at the same time is not a differentiation; it is also, thereby, a comparison of the object with its objectivity and of knowledge with its knownness. Consciousness itself is the comparison, which, admittedly, natural consciousness never explicitly carries out.

In the nature of consciousness knowledge and object are sundered, and yet they can never be separate. Similarly, in the nature of consciousness object and concept are sundered in that "as," and yet they can never be separate. In the nature of consciousness the "both" is itself sundered and yet cannot be separate. Hegel differentiates all this, but yet he levels out the differences into a general differentiation, preventing them from coming into their own. The concealed reason for this is found in the essence of metaphysics, not in the fundamental metaphysical position of Hegel's philosophy. The concealed essence of metaphysics is also the reason that the level at which the differences have been leveled off is determined on the basis of the discreteness of the one and the other; this discreteness is introduced in the distinctions of *ratio*. Hegel grasps distinction as the negation of negation.

With due caution and with the requisite caveats, a difference may be adduced regarding the differentiations established by Hegel, a difference that was mentioned elsewhere earlier. Because natural consciousness goes directly to the object as a being, as well as to its knowledge of the object as a being, and because it remains constantly with them, natural consciousness may be called ontic consciousness. The term "ontic" is derived from the Greek τὸ ὄν, the being that is; it means that which concerns beings. However, the Greek ὄν, a being, shelters within itself a particular essence of beingness (οὐσία), which has by no means remained the same in the course of its history. In the thoughtful use of the terms ὄν and "a being," the first thing that has been presupposed is that we are in fact thinking, that is, that we are attentive to the way that the meaning is changing at any particular time and to how the meaning in history becomes fixed at any particular time. When beings appear as objects (since beingness has been illuminated as objectivity) and when, consequently, being is received as non-objective, all this is already based on an ontology by which the ὄν has been determined as the ὑποκείμενον, and the ὑποκείμενον as the *subiectum*, but the being of the *subiectum*, in contrast, on the basis of the subjectity of consciousness. Because ὄν means both "that which is [*Seiendes*]" as well as "being [*Seiend*]," the ὄν as that which is can be gathered together (λέγειν) with regard to the fact of its being. In fact, in keeping with its ambiguity, the ὄν as that which is is already gathered together with regard to its beingness. It is ontological. However, this gathering, the λόγος, changes at any time as the essence of the ὄν changes, and on the basis of it; and as the λόγος changes, so does the ontology. From the time the ὄν, that which presences, emerged as φύσις, the presence of what presences has been based, for Greek thinkers, in φαίνεσθαι, in the self-displaying appearance of the unconcealed. Correspondingly, the multiplicity of what presences, τὰ ὄντα, has been thought as that which in its appearance is simply received as what presences. To receive means here: to accept it without more ado and to content oneself with it in its presencing. Receiving (δέχεσθαι) has nothing further to do. That is, it does not think further about the presencing of what presences. It remains in δόξα. In contrast, νοεῖν is that perception which examines [*vernimmt*] explicitly what is present in its presencing and thereupon undertakes it [*vornimmt*].

The ambiguity of the ὄν identifies what presences as well as the presencing. It identifies both at once but neither as such. To this essential ambiguity of the ὄν there corresponds the fact that the νοεῖν of the εἶναι, of the ἐόν, belongs together with the δόξα of the δοκοῦντα, i.e., of the ἐόντα. What the νοεῖν perceives is not that which truly is in contrast to mere seeming. Rather, the δόξα perceives immediately that which itself presences, rather than the presencing of what presences, which presencing the νοεῖν perceives.

If we think – as it will be necessary to think from now on – of the essence of metaphysics as the emergence of the twofoldness of presencing and what presences out of the self-concealing ambiguity of the ὄν, then the beginning of metaphysics coincides with the beginning of Western thinking. On the other hand, if we take as the essence of metaphysics the separation of a supersensory from a sensory world and if the supersensory is taken as what truly is in contrast to the sensory as what merely appears to be, then metaphysics begins with Plato and Socrates. Even so, what began with their thinking is only an explicitly oriented interpretation of the earlier twofoldness in ὄν. With this interpretation, the direness [*Unwesen*] of metaphysics begins. Because of this direness, subsequent thinking till our own day has mistaken the essential beginning of metaphysics. However, the direness that we must think now is not a negative if we bear in mind that even in the essential beginning of metaphysics the difference prevailing in the ambiguity of the ὄν remains unthought; in fact, this remaining-unthought constitutes the essence of metaphysics. As it remains unthought, the λόγος of the ὄν remains ungrounded. However, it is this ungroundedness that gives to onto-logy the force of its essence.

Behind the rubric "ontology," the history of being conceals itself from us. Ontological means: to carry out the gathering of beings in respect to their beingness. That creature is ontological which, in accordance with its nature, stands within this history by enduring it each time in accordance with the unconcealedness of beings. Thus we can say: in its immediate representation of beings, consciousness is ontic consciousness. For ontic consciousness, a being is an object. However, the representation of the object represents, though unthinkingly, the object as object. It has already gathered the object into its objectivity and is therefore ontological consciousness. However, because natural consciousness fails to think objectivity as such, while nonetheless representing it, natural consciousness both is ontological and yet is not. We say that ontic consciousness is pre-ontological. As such, natural ontic-preontological consciousness *is*, latently, the distinction between the ontically true and the ontological truth. Consciousness, *being*-conscious, means *being* this distinction; that is the reason that consciousness, on the basis of its own nature, is the comparison of what has been represented ontically and what ontologically. As this comparison, it exists in critical examination. Intrinsically, representation by consciousness is a natural putting-itself-to-the-test.

This is the reason that consciousness itself is never natural consciousness solely in the mode of remaining cordoned off, as it were, from what its object truly is and from what its knowledge is with certainty. Natural consciousness rests in its own nature. It exists in accordance with one of the modes of its nature. However, it is not itself its own nature. Rather, what it finds natural is never to arrive at its own nature on its own, never, therefore, to arrive at what is constantly going on behind its back. Nonetheless, as naturally pre-ontological consciousness, it is already underway toward its truth. Yet while underway, it already constantly turns back and remains for it. Ordinary opinion is not concerned to watch what is [*steckt*] actually behind and what hides [*sich versteckt*] behind what it holds to be true. It balks at this watching, which is how skepsis has a look at what, as truth, is truly behind the true. One day skepsis may even succeed in seeing that what philosophy had thought of as "behind it" is in truth "in front of it." Natural consciousness never discovers its truth, as its truth is its background. Its truth is itself, i.e., it is in truth the foreground of the light within which every sort of knowledge and consciousness already exists as a have-seen.

However, philosophy itself fights against skepsis at times. It prefers the ordinary opinion of natural consciousness. It does admit that objectivity must indeed belong to the object as object, but to philosophy objectivity is only the non-objective. Philosophy likes ordinary opinion and even persuades it that it is actually right, on the grounds that the non-objective can be represented only in the representations of natural consciousness, which are as a result inadequate and so are a mere playing with symbols. These assurances natural consciousness finds quite agreeable, and it even takes from them the impression that these assurances constitute critical philosophy because of their skeptical attitude toward ontology. However, this sort of skepsis is only the semblance of skepsis; it is the flight from thinking into a system of opinions.

On the other hand, when skepsis is achieved as thoroughgoing skepticism, then thinking is *en route* within metaphysics as the comparison, explicitly carried out by ontological consciousness, of ontic and pre-ontological consciousness. Ontological consciousness is not cut off from natural consciousness, but rather returns into the nature of consciousness as the unity of ontic and pre-ontological representation. When that comparison occurs, the critical examination is underway. In that occurrence, consciousness is its own appearing-to-itself in appearance. It is presencing to itself. It is. Consciousness is, in that it comes into its truth, becomes to itself in its truth.

Becoming is, in that the critical examination, which is a comparison, is taking place [*vor sich geht*]. The critical examination can only proceed [*geht*] at all by preceding itself [*vor sich her geht*]. Skepsis looks ahead of itself [*sieht vor sich*] and takes care [*sieht sich vor*]. Skepsis looks ahead at what knowledge and the object of knowledge are, truly. The sixth paragraph has already made it clear that natural consciousness loses its truth on the path of the examination. When that which natural consciousness presumes to be true is considered with respect to truth, it turns out that knowledge does not correspond to its object since knowledge is not concerned with the objectivity of its object. In order to be fit for the truth of the object, consciousness must alter the previous knowledge. However, in altering its knowledge of the object, the object has also been altered.

Objectivity is now the object, and what is now called the object can no longer be settled on the basis of the former opinion about objects. Those opinions, however, are still at play or at work where objectivity is claimed on the basis of the previous object and where it is passed off, in an ever more negative way, as non-objective. Philosophy, that is, is concerned to glorify the thoughtless incapacity of ordinary opinion.

The comparison that is a critical examination looks ahead into the appearance of phenomenal knowledge; in this comparison, not only does the natural knowledge of the object (a knowledge presumed to be uniquely and genuinely true) fail to stand firm, but also the object itself relinquishes its standing as the criterion for critically examining. In the critical examination which is as consciousness itself, neither the examined nor the criterion passes the examination. Neither stands up before what has arisen in the meantime in the examination itself.

The fourteenth paragraph begins with the sentence: "This *dialectical* movement which consciousness executes on itself – on its knowledge as well as on its object – in the sense that out of it the new and true object arises, is precisely what is termed experience." What is Hegel naming with the word "experience"? He is naming the being of beings. Beings, meanwhile, have become subjects and, along with subjects, have become objects and the objective. Since antiquity, being has meant: presencing. The mode in which consciousness (that which *is* out of being known) comes to presence is appearance. As the being that it is, consciousness is phenomenal knowledge. With the term "experience" Hegel names phenomena as phenomena, the ὄν ᾗ ὄν. In the word "experience," that ᾗ is thought. It is on the basis of the ᾗ (*qua*, as) that beings are thought in their beingness. Experience is now no longer the name of a kind of knowledge. Experience is now the word of being, of being that is perceived by beings as beings. Experience gives a name to the subjectity of the subject. Experience says what the "being-" in "being-conscious," in consciousness, means; in fact, only on the basis of this "being-" does it become clear and binding what remains to be thought in the word "-conscious."

The strange word "experience" as the name for the being of beings falls [*fällt ein*] into our consideration because it has come due [*fällig*]. Its use here, admittedly falls outside [*fällt heraus*] the ordinary as well as the philosophical usage. But it drops [*fällt*] like the fruit of the very thing in whose presence Hegel's thinking has persevered. The justification of this usage, which is essentially different from a mere manner of speaking, lies in what Hegel has brought into view in the previous paragraphs about the nature of consciousness. The three statements about consciousness outline the basic structure of this nature.

> "Consciousness, however, is for itself its own *concept*."
> "Consciousness furnishes its own criterion in it itself."
> "Consciousness critically examines itself."

In one respect, the second statement is an explication of the first: it says that "its own concept," in which consciousness conceives of itself in its truth, is the measure on the route of self-conceiving and that this measure falls, along with what is measured, within consciousness. The third statement points in the direction of the originary unity of measure and what is measured: consciousness essences as this unity in that it itself *is* the comparison that critically examines, a comparing out of which the two come forth along with the appearance of phenomena. The essence of appearance is experience. "Experience" must now retain the meaning which it gained from this reference to the nature of consciousness.

In the preceding comments, however, something emerged from those three statements that has needed to be made explicit all along, since it is in its own way unavoidable. It is not until the paragraph in which the decisive word "experience" comes that Hegel expresses it explicitly. The verbs in all three sentences are ambiguous: the "is" in the first statement, the "furnishes" in the second, and the "critically examines" in the third.

Consciousness is for itself its own concept, and at the same time it is not. It is its own concept in such a way that the concept comes to be for consciousness and that consciousness finds itself in the concept.

Consciousness furnishes its own criterion in it itself, and at the same time it does not. It does, in that the truth of consciousness comes out of consciousness itself, which arrives in its appearance as absolute certainty. It does not, in that it repeatedly withholds the criterion, which (as the object that at any particular moment is not true) never stands firm; as a result consciousness, as it were, hushes it up.

Consciousness critically examines itself, and then again it does not. It does examine itself critically in that it is what it is as a result of the comparison of objectivity and object. It does not, in that natural consciousness insists on its own opinion and passes off, unexamined, what is true for it as the absolutely true.

In this ambiguity, consciousness betrays the fundamental trait of its essence: at the same time, to be already that which it is not yet. Being in the sense of being-conscious, consciousness, means: to reside in the not-yet of the already, and to do this in such a way that this already presences in the not-yet. This presence is in itself a self-referral into the already. It sets off on the path to the already. It makes itself a path [*Weg*]. The being of consciousness consists in the fact that it moves on a path [*sich be-wegt*]. The being which Hegel thinks as experience has the fundamental trait of movement. Hegel starts that sentence which expresses the essence of experience with the words: "This *dialectical* movement . . . is precisely what is termed experience" – experience, that is, taken here as reflecting on what the science of phenomenal knowledge presents. It would be the grossest misreading of the text if we thought that Hegel described the presentation as a sort of experience only in order to emphasize that it must keep to the phenomena and be on its guard lest it degenerate into a construction. The experience that we must think here is not part of the presentation as a description of its nature; rather, the presentation is part of the essence of experience. Experience is the appearance of phenomena which appear as such. The presentation of appearance is part of appearance; it is part of appearance as it is part of the movement in which consciousness realizes its reality.

Hegel stresses his word for this movement: "dialectical." However, he uses the term only here, offering no comment on it in the preceding or subsequent paragraphs of the piece. Accordingly, we will attempt to understand the dialectical on the basis of what emerged from our previous reflections on the nature of consciousness. One might have thought of explaining the dialectical on the basis of the unity of thesis, antithesis, and synthesis, or on the basis of the negation of negation. However, everything that is in any way thetic has its essence in consciousness, in which negativity, too, has its ground, if negativity is understood on the basis of negation. However, the essence of consciousness ought to be determined only by how its nature unfolds. Likewise, we can leave aside whether the dialectic is only a method of knowledge or whether it belongs in the objectively real as itself something real. That problem is just a sham-problem so long as it remains undetermined what the reality of the real consists in, to what extent this reality is based in the being of consciousness, and what is going on with this being. Discussions about dialectic are like trying to explain a rushing fountain in terms of the stagnant water in a sewer. Probably the way to the fountain is still quite far. Nonetheless, we are going to try to point in its direction by enlisting Hegel's help.

Consciousness, as consciousness, is the movement of consciousness, for it is the comparison between ontic/pre-ontological knowledge and ontological knowledge. The former exerts its claim on the latter. The latter claims that it is the truth of the former. Between (δια) the one and the other is the articulation of these claims, a λέγειν. In this dialogue, consciousness ascribes truth to itself. The διαλέγειν is a διαλέγεσθαι. However, the dialogue does not stand still in *one* shape of consciousness. As the dialogue that it is, it goes through (δια) the entire realm of the shapes of consciousness. In this movement of going-through, it gathers itself into the truth of its essence. διαλέγειν, thoroughgoing gathering, is a self-gathering (διαλέγεσθαι).

Consciousness is consciousness in that it is the dialogue[a] between natural and real knowledge, a dialogue that accomplishes the gathering of its essence through its shapes. Since the formation of consciousness takes place *at once* as both the self-gathering dialogue *and* the self-expressing gathering, the movement of consciousness is dialectical.

It is only on the basis of the dialogical character of ontic-ontological consciousness that the thetic character of representation-by-consciousness is brought out; for this reason, characterizing the dialectic by the unity of thesis, antithesis, and synthesis is still correct but still only derivative. The same is true of the interpretation of the dialectic as in-finite negativity. This negativity is grounded upon the self-gathering through the dialogue shapes of consciousness, a self-gathering unto the absolute concept, which is what consciousness in its accomplished truth *is*. Both the quality of being thetic (that is, positional) and the negating negativity presuppose the originary dialectical appearance of consciousness, but they never constitute the structure of the nature of consciousness. The dialectical cannot be explained logically, in terms of positing or negating by representation, nor can it be established ontically as a special activity and form of movement within real consciousness. As the mode of appearance, the dialectical is part of being which unfolds out of presence as the beingness of beings. Hegel does not conceive of experience dialectically; rather, he thinks the dialectical on the basis of the essence of experience. Experience is the beingness of beings, which is determined as *subiectum* on the basis of subjectity.

The decisive moment in the essence of experience is when the new, true object arises in it for consciousness. The crucial matter is that the new object arises as truth arises; it is not crucial that notice is taken of an object [*Gegenstand*] as something that confronts [*ein Gegenüber*]. The object is now no

[a] First edition, 1950. In what respect is this also true for "logic"? The dialogue between?

longer to be thought as something that confronts representation, but rather as what arises as the truth of consciousness, as opposed to the old object in the sense of the not yet true. Experience is the mode in which consciousness, in that it is, departs for its concept, which is what it is in truth. This sufficiency [*das Auslangen*] that departs for its concept gains [*erlangt*], within the true that appears, the appearance of truth. Gaining it [*erlangend*], it arrives [*gelangt*] into the appearing-to-itself of appearance itself. The "*fahren* [go, guide, drive]" in *Erfahren* [experience], has the original meaning of going, of drawing or being drawn somewhere. The carpenter, in constructing a house, is guided [*fährt*] along the direction of the main beam. "*Fahren*" is to reach for . . . : one man flies [*fährt*] into the face of another. "*Fahren*" is to accompany in arriving [*Gelangen*] at . . . : the shepherd departs [*fährt aus*] with his flock and drives [*fährt zu*] them to the mountain. Experience, *Erfahren*, is what suffices to gain its attainment [*das auslangend-erlangende Gelangen*]. *Experience is a mode of presence, i.e., of being*. Through experience, phenomenal consciousness presences as phenomenal into its own presence with itself. Experience gathers consciousness into the gathering of its own essence.

Experience is the mode of the presentness of the presences which essences in self-re-presentation. This new object that arises for consciousness at whatever point in the history of the formation of consciousness is not just any true thing, any being, but rather the truth of the true, the being of beings, the appearance of phenomena, experience. According to the concluding sentence of the fourteenth paragraph, the new object is nothing other than experience itself.

The *essentia* of the *ens* in its *esse* is presence. Presence, however, essences in the mode of presentation. However, since in the meantime the *ens*, the *subiectum*, has become the *res cogitans*, presentation is also intrinsically representing, i.e., representation. It is not until Hegel thinks into the word "experience" that what the *res cogitans* is, as the *subiectum co-agitans*, finds expression. Experience is the presentation of the absolute subject that essences in representation and so is the self-absolving absolute subject. Experience is the subjectity of the absolute subject. As the presentation of absolute representation, experience is the parousia of the absolute. Experience is the absoluteness of the absolute; it appears in the absolving appearing-to-itself. Everything depends on thinking experience, as it is given here, as the being of consciousness. However, being means presence. Presence manifests itself as appearance. Appearance is now the appearance of knowledge. In being (and it is as being that experience is essentially present) there is, as the character of appearance, representation in the sense of presentation. Even when he uses the word "experience" in the conventional sense of empiricism, Hegel is above all attentive to the moment of presence in it. He, then, understands by experience "attentiveness to the immediately present as such" (see the "Preface" to *The Phenomenology*). Hegel is very careful not to say merely that experience is paying attention to the immediately present, but rather that it is paying attention to the immediately present in its presence.

Experience is concerned with what presences in its presence. However, since consciousness exists by critically examining itself, it departs for its presence in order to arrive at it. It is part of the appearance of phenomenal knowledge that such knowledge represents itself in its presence, i.e., presents itself. The presentation is part of experience, in fact it is an essential part of experience. It is not merely a counterpart to experience which might perhaps be absent. This is the reason that experience is not thought in its full essence as the beingness of beings in the sense of the absolute subject until the mode comes to light in which the presentation of phenomenal knowledge belongs to appearance as such. The penultimate paragraph of the introduction takes this last step into the essence of experience as the existence of the absolute.

The fifteenth paragraph takes as its starting point the representation which natural consciousness has of what is called experience. This representation runs contrary to experience as Hegel thinks it. This means: experience, thought metaphysically, remains inaccessible to natural consciousness. It is the beingness of beings, which is to say that it is not found anywhere among beings as an extant resource. When we are having a good experience with an object, for example in using a tool, we have the experience in connection with another object to which the first object (the one with which we are having the experience) is applied. When we are having a bad experience with a person, we have the experience on specific occasions, in a situation, and in relationships in which that person was to have proved himself or herself. Our experience with an object is not something we have with it, but rather with some other object which we produce and become involved with. In ordinary experience (*experiri*), we see the object to be critically examined under the conditions that obtain when it has been placed by other objects. What is going on with the object is a result of these other objects. When it is necessary to change the representations that we had previously had of the object to be examined, the difference the change requires comes to us from the newly introduced objects. The untruth of the old object is demonstrated by the new object which we at once represent in order to set it, just as we have represented it, into a comparative relation with the already known object with which we are planning to have the experience. However, it is exactly the other way round within the experience as which consciousness itself is.

If we represent the objectivity of an object, the truth of something true, this experience is had in connection with the old object, and it is had in such a way that the new object, objectivity, arises precisely because of its connection with the old object. In connection with the old object and out of it, the new object is lifted into its status. The important thing is not merely not to move away [*wegzugehen*] toward some other object immediately at hand, but rather to be responsive [*einzugehen*], for the first time, specifically to the old object. Natural consciousness represents what it represents and also its representation immediately and as beings, but without paying attention to being, which it will also have represented in the process. If, therefore, it is to become aware of the being of beings, it must not remain merely among beings, but rather engage [*eingehen*] with them in such a way that it goes back [*zurückgeht*] explicitly to that which, in the representation of beings, was already implicit for it in representedness. If the appearance of phenomena comes to light, then consciousness in certain respects has already abandoned ordinary representation and has returned itself, and thus turned itself around, from phenomena to appearance.

In the appearing-to-itself of appearance, there prevails a "reversal of consciousness itself." The fundamental trait of the experience of consciousness is this reversal. It is even "our doing, what we contribute." What presents itself, at this reversal, to consciousness is not "for consciousness," not, that is, for natural consciousness. What presents itself in the reversal is not "for consciousness" which "we contemplate" but rather "for us," we who are contemplating. Who is this "we"?

"We" are the ones who, in the reversing of natural consciousness, leave that consciousness to its opinions, but at the same time explicitly look at [*sehen auf*] the appearance of the phenomena. This seeing [*Sehen*] that specifically watches appearance is the watching [*Zusehen*] which is how skepsis takes place – skepsis which had in mind [*vorgesehen auf*] the absoluteness of the absolute and equipped itself [*sich versehen*] in advance with it. What comes to appearance in thoroughgoing skepticism shows itself "for us," i.e., for those who, thinking of the beingness of beings, are already provided with being. The reversal of consciousness that prevails in skepsis is the viatical journey [*Versehgang*] along which consciousness provides itself [*sich versieht*] with appearance itself. That which shows itself to those who have been thus equipped, is indeed part of consciousness itself, as regards its content, and is "for consciousness." However, the mode in which phenomena show themselves (namely as appearance) is the mien, the look, of phenomena, their εἶδος, which forms all phenomena, places them in view, and shapes them; it is the μορφή, the *forma*. Hegel calls this the "formal character." This is never "for consciousness," that is, for natural consciousness which represents immediately. Insofar as the formal character is for consciousness, it is always for it as an object only, never as objectivity. The formal character, the beingness of beings, is "for us," we who in the reversal do not see right to the phenomena, but rather to the appearance of the phenomena. The reversal of consciousness, which is a reversal of representation, does not turn off from this rash representation onto a byway, but rather from within natural representation it engages with that which alone entitles rash representation to what it perceives as presencing.

In the reversal of consciousness we are engaged with something which natural consciousness does not discover. We look at what "takes place, as it were, behind its back." The reversal is also part of this. Through it the appearance of phenomena comes to be presented. The reversal alone turns experience around and puts it into the presentation. The experience of consciousness "is lifted into a scientific route" through the reversal. The presentation represents the being of beings. It is the science of the ὄν ᾗ ὄν. The reversal, in which watching turns itself toward the phenomena as phenomenal, brings seeing onto the route which science goes. Skepsis at the being of beings restores beings to themselves, so that they show themselves as beings in that "as." The reversal specifically permits the ᾗ to occur in relation to the ὄν. Thus, what is decisive in the experience through which consciousness appears to itself in its appearance lies with the reversal. This, however, is "our doing, what we contribute."

However, did not Hegel use all his reflecting in the preceding paragraphs (cf., in particular, the twelfth) to show that in the presentation of phenomenal knowledge we should leave aside precisely all our fancies and thoughts, so that what remained to us was "purely to watch"? Does he not explicitly say in the thirteenth paragraph that consciousness critically examines itself and that therefore any "addition of ours" would be superfluous? By leaving aside all our contributions we are supposed to reach the point where the phenomena, of their own accord, show themselves in their appearance. But this relinquishing, this letting-go, does not look after itself. If letting is ever an activity, then this is, this letting-go. This activity is necessarily the activity that we contribute. For it is only if the skepsis of thoroughgoing skepticism has in mind the being of beings that beings can freely appear of their own accord and let their appearance appear. The contribution of the reversal of consciousness is to let phenomena appear as such. The contribution does not force something upon experience which is foreign to it. Rather, it explicitly brings forth from it only what lies in it as the being of consciousness, which (according to the first statement of consciousness) is for itself its own concept. Hence the contribution can also never sublate [*aufheben*] the pure watching that is necessary for the presentation. Rather, in the contribution and through it, pure watching begins [*hebt an*]. Therefore, watching continues in the contribution.

In the previous paragraph, Hegel states that experience is the movement which consciousness itself executes on itself. This execution is the prevailing of the force [*Walten der Gewalt*] which, as the will of the absolute, wills that the absolute come to presence in its absoluteness with us. The will as which the absolute is prevails in the mode of experience. This is what suffices to gain its attainment [*das auslangend-erlangende Gelangen*], which, as appearance, appears to itself. As this attainment (presence), experience characterizes the essence of the will, whose essence conceals itself with the essence of experience in the essence of being. The experience to be thought here is neither a mode of knowledge nor a mode of willing as it is usually represented. The will of the absolute to be with us, i.e., to appear for us as phenomena, prevails as experience. For us, the phenomena present themselves in their appearance, if we make the contribution of our reversal. Accordingly, the contribution wills the will of the absolute. The contribution itself is what the absoluteness of the absolute wills. There is nothing selfish on our part that is added to the absolute by the reversal of consciousness. The reversal restores us into our essence, which is to presence in the parousia of the absolute. This means, for us: to present the parousia. The presentation of experience is willed out of the essence of experience as something belonging to experience. When we watch, our contribution brings to light that we are, and how we are, kin to the absoluteness of the absolute.

Experience is the being of beings. Beings, meanwhile, have appeared in the character of consciousness; in representation, they *are* as phenomena. But if the presentation is part of the essence of experience; if the presentation is grounded in the reversal; and if the reversal, as our contribution, is the carrying out of our essential relationship to the absoluteness of the absolute; *then our essence itself is part of the parousia of the absolute.* The reversal is the skepsis into absoluteness. It reverses all phenomena in their appearance. By providing itself in advance with appearance, it overtakes all phenomena as such, envelops [*umfängt*] them, and opens the expanse [*Umfang*] of the site in which appearance appears to itself. Within this site, and through it, the presentation takes its route by constantly, skeptically, preceding itself. In the reversal, the presentation has the absoluteness of the absolute before itself and so it has the absolute with itself. The reversal opens and encloses the site of the historical formation of consciousness. In this way it secures the completeness and the progress of the experience of consciousness. Experience proceeds by preceding itself, by returning to itself in this preceding, by unfolding itself into the presence of consciousness in this return to itself, by becoming *constant* as this presence. The absolved, constant presence of consciousness is the being of the absolute. Through the reversal, phenomenal consciousness shows itself in its appearance, and only in its appearance. The phenomena externalize themselves in their appearance. In this self-externalizing [*Entäußerung*], consciousness goes out into the farthest reaches [*Äußerste*] of its being. However, it goes away neither from itself nor from its essence; nor does the absolute, in the externalization, sink into a void of its own debility. Externalization, rather, is the self-maintaining of the fullness of appearance out of the strength of the will, which is the mode in which the parousia of the absolute prevails. The externalization of the absolute is its internalization, its recollection, into the route of the appearance of its absoluteness. Externalization is far from being an alienation into abstraction; in fact, it is precisely through externalization that appearance comes to be at home in phenomena as such.

Of course it is an entirely different question whether and to what extent subjectity is a destiny proper to the essence of being, within which the unconcealedness of being – not the truth of beings – *withdraws* and thereby determines an appropriate epoch. Within subjectity, every being as such becomes an object. All beings are beings from out of and within steadfast reliability. In the age of subjectity, in which the essence of technology is grounded, if nature as being is put in opposition to consciousness, then this nature is only another name for beings as the objects of modern technological objectification which indiscriminately attacks the continued existence of things and men.

The first thing the reversal of consciousness does is to open, specifically and in advance, the interstice or the between (δια) within which the dialogue between natural consciousness and absolute knowledge is articulated in its own language. As skepsis at the absoluteness of the absolute, the reversal also opens the complete realm across (δια) which consciousness gathers its history into the achieved truth and forms it itself in this way. The reversal of consciousness illuminates the twofold δια of the twofold λέγεσθαι. Beforehand and in the first place, the reversal forms the essential free space for the dialectical character of that movement as which experience achieves itself as the being of consciousness.

The reversal of consciousness is the carrying out of the seeing of skepsis, which sees since it has already provided itself with absoluteness and is provided with it by absoluteness. The having-seen of skepsis (*vidi*) is the knowledge of absoluteness. The reversal of consciousness is the essential center of that knowledge as which the presentation of phenomenal knowledge unfolds itself. Thus, the presentation is the route of consciousness itself to the appearing-to-itself within appearance. It is "the pathway to science." The presentation, when it is so conceived as the pathway to science, is itself science, for the path [*Weg*] into which it moves [*be-wegt*] is movement in the sense of experience. The force prevailing within and as this experience is the will of the absolute that wills itself in its parousia. It is within this will that the path has its necessity.

Hegel summarizes the results of his reflection, in the fourteenth and fifteenth paragraphs, on the essence of experience in one sentence, which he separates from the continuous text of the paragraph into its own paragraph. Thus the sentence pulls together in one place all the previous paragraphs of the piece into the decisive thought. It runs:

> In virtue of that necessity this pathway to science is itself already *science*, and is, moreover, as regards its content, science of the *experience of consciousness*.

If we put the emphasized words together, they give the title which Hegel originally gave to *The Phenomenology of Spirit*: "Science of the Experience of Consciousness." The previous paragraphs contain the exegesis (as the literary term is) of this title. Experience is the appearance of phenomenal knowledge as phenomenal. The science of the experience of consciousness presents the phenomena as phenomena. The phenomena are the ὄν, beings in the sense of consciousness. The skepsis of the presentation θεωρεῖ τὸ ὂν ᾗ ὂν καὶ τὰ τούτῳ ὑπάρχοντα καθ' αὑτό; it contemplates what is present (in appearance) as that which is (in this way) present and (contemplates) therefore what is already predominant in it (in phenomena in their appearance) on its own.

The presentation provides itself with the force of the will as which the absolute wills its presentness (parousia). Aristotle characterizes the contemplation of beings as beings as ἐπιστήμη τις, a way in which our seeing and perceiving stands by, that is, stands by what is present as such. As a way of standing by what is constantly present, the ἐπιστήμη is itself a kind of human presencing among unconcealed presences. We commit an error when we translate ἐπιστήμη as "science" and make it hostage to whatever happens to be known by that term at a given time. When we translate ἐπιστήμη here as science, the only justification for this interpretation is that we understand knowledge as having-seen and think having-seen on the basis of that seeing which stands before the look of what presences as such and looks at presentness itself. When knowledge is thought in this way, then the ἐπιστήμη τις of Aristotle retains – and not coincidentally – an essential relation to what Hegel calls "science," the knowledge of which, however, has changed with the change in the presence of what presences. If we understand the word "science" in this sense alone, then what are usually called the sciences are science only secondarily. The sciences are fundamentally philosophy, but they are a philosophy in which they abandon their own ground and establish themselves, in their own way, in that which philosophy has made open to them. This is the realm of τέχνη.

Aristotle calls this science he characterized (the science which inspects beings as beings) "first philosophy." However, not only does it observe beings in their beingness, but it also, at the same time, observes that being which corresponds purely to beingness, the highest being. This particular being, τὸ θεῖον, the divine, is also called – in a strange ambiguity – "being" itself. As ontology, first philosophy is also the theology of true beings. It would be more accurate to call it theiology. The science of beings as such is intrinsically onto-theological.

Accordingly, Hegel calls the presentation of phenomenal knowledge not the science of the experience of consciousness, but rather "science." That presentation is only a part of science. That is why "Part One" explicitly comes above the title "Science of the Experience of Consciousness." The science of the experience of consciousness points within itself to the other part of science. In the hierarchy, the second part is no more subordinate to the first than theology is to ontology within first philosophy. But neither does it take precedence. Nor are the two ranked equal to each other. The two, each in its own way, are the same. Talking about a first and a second part remains extrinsic, but not accidental, since from Plato and Aristotle to Nietzsche the ground of the unity of the onto-theological essence of metaphysics has remained so hidden that it has not even been inquired into. Instead, the ranks of ontology and theology fluctuate reciprocally depending on whether one or the other is seen as the very first and genuine science within first philosophy. For Hegel, the science of the experience of consciousness, i.e., the ontology of true beings in their existence, points to the other part of science as "genuine science."

The sixteenth paragraph, with which the piece comes to an end, opens a prospect onto this connection between the two parts of science. However, that connection shows itself only if we keep it in view that experience is the beingness of beings, which come to presence as consciousness in the shapes of consciousness. Already for Greek thinkers, ever since the ὄν arose as φύσις, the presentness of presences, the οὐσία of the ὄν, is φαίνεσθαι: appearance that shows itself. Accordingly, the manifoldness of what presences (τὰ ὄντα) is thought as that which is simply taken and accepted [*auf- und angenommen*] in its appearance: τὰ δοκοῦντα. The δόξα takes and accepts immediately that which presences. νοεῖν, on the other hand, is a perceiving [*Vernehmen*] which accepts [*annimmt*] what presences as such and undertakes [*vornimmt*] it in regard to its presence. Since the ὄν, that which presences, has a double signification as both that which itself presences as well as the presencing, the ὄν stands in an essentially necessary and equiprimordial relation to νοεῖν and δόξα.

The being of what is known in certainty also has the essential trait of presence. It essences as appearance. However, in the presencing of knowledge, i.e., of the *subiectum* in the sense of the *res cogitans*, appearance is no longer the *idea* showing itself as εἶδος, but rather as *perceptio*. Appearance is now presence in the mode of the presentation within the realm of representation. The appearance of phenomenal knowledge is the immediate presencing of consciousness. However, this presencing essences in the mode of experience. With experience, the absolute, spirit, arrives into the "whole realm of the truth of spirit." Yet the moments of its truth are the shapes of consciousness which along the route of experience have laid aside all the things which seemed to be true at a given time exclusively for natural consciousness because they, at that point in its history, were exclusively for it. But when experience is achieved, then the appearance of phenomena will have arrived into that pure seeming as which the absolute absolutely presences with itself and is its essence itself. On the basis of this pure seeming, the force prevails which forces consciousness into the movement of experience. The force of the absolute, the force that prevails in experience, "is pressing consciousness forward to its true existence." Existence means here presencing in the mode of appearing-to-itself. At this point, the pure appearance of the absolute coincides with its essence.

The parousia is the presentness in which the absolute is with us and at the same time is by itself as the absolute. Accordingly, at this point the presentation of appearance also coincides with "the genuine science of spirit." The science of phenomenal knowledge leads and comes into genuine science. Genuine science makes the presentation of how the absolute presences to itself in its absoluteness. Genuine science is the "science of logic." The word is taken from tradition. Logic is taken to be the knowledge of the concept. The concept, however, by which consciousness is for itself its own concept, now refers to the absolute self-conceiving of the absolute in its being seized absolutely by itself. The logic of the concept is the ontological theiology of the absolute. It does not, like the science of the experience of consciousness, present the parousia of the absolute, but rather the absoluteness in its parousia to itself.

In the title "Science of the *Experience* of Consciousness," the word "experience" is emphasized in the center. It mediates between consciousness and science. In this respect, what is said by the title corresponds to the subject matter. As the being of consciousness, experience is in itself the reversal through which consciousness presents itself in its appearance. Which means: experience, in presenting, is science. Yet natural representation understands the mediating title immediately, and only in the sense that science has as its object experience, which in its turn is the experience of consciousness. But this title heads a work that performs the reversal of consciousness by presenting it. The reversal reverses natural consciousness. For this reason, the title has not been understood while it is read according to the habit of natural consciousness. The two genitives "of the experience" and "of consciousness" are not objective genitives but subjective genitives. Consciousness, not science, is the subject that is in the mode of experience. And experience is really the subject of science. On the other hand, it is not to be denied that the objective genitives retain their sense, though they do so only because the subjective genitive is true. Thought rigorously, neither takes precedence over the other. They both refer to the subject–object relationship of the absolute subject in its subjectity. In view of that relationship, which has its essence in experience, we must always think the title at once both backwards and forwards through that mediating word.

In both their meanings, the genitives identify the relation which the reversal makes use of, without ever explicitly thinking it: the relation of being to beings as the relation of beings to being. The dialectical movement establishes itself in the site which, though it is opened by the reversal, is concealed precisely as the openness of that relation. The skeptical dialogue between natural and absolute consciousness looks through [*durchblickt*] this site in previewing [*im Vorblick*] the absoluteness of the absolute. The dialectical skepsis is the essence of philosophy. The genitives that enter into the title are neither exclusively subjective nor exclusively objective, and certainly no mere coupling of the two. They are the dialectical-speculative genitive. This genitive shows itself in the title only because it has already dominated from the start the language in which the experience of consciousness is articulated as it achieves its presentation.

The title Hegel chose at first – "Science of the *Experience* of Consciousness" – was dropped during the printing of the work, but the piece that explains it remains. The title was replaced by another one: "Science of the Phenomenology of Spirit." As a result, only the remaining piece – which nowhere mentions a phenomenology of spirit – correctly interprets the new title. This new title appeared as part of the complete title of the work as it was published in 1807: "System of Science Part I, The Phenomenology of Spirit." When the work was reprinted shortly after Hegel's death as the second volume of the *Collected Works* (1832), the title was merely: "Phenomenology of Spirit." Behind this subtle dropping of the article there is hidden a decisive change in Hegel's thinking and in the way he communicates his thinking. As regards content, the change affects the system; as regards time, it begins shortly after the publication of the *Science of the Phenomenology of Spirit*. Presumably, it was motivated and confirmed by his switch to teaching in the Nuremberg Gymnasium. The school lessons he delivered here also influenced his teaching at the university, which he resumed later.

At the time of the initial publication of *The Phenomenology of Spirit*, the complete title "System of Science" has a dialectical-speculative ambiguity. It does not mean: the sciences classified according to a carefully reasoned order. Neither does it mean: philosophy presented as a coherent science. "System of Science" means: science is intrinsically the absolute organization of the absoluteness of the absolute. The subjectity of the subject essences in such a way that it knows itself and arranges itself into the completeness of its structure. This self-arranging is the mode of being in which subjectity is. "System" is the assembly of the absolute which gathers itself into its absoluteness and by this gathered stance is made steadfast into its own presence. Science is the subject of the system, not its object. However, it is the subject in such a way that science, part of subjectity, participates in constituting the absoluteness of the absolute. For Hegel around the time of the first publication of *The Phenomenology of Spirit*, science is the onto-theiological knowledge of true beings as beings. Science unfolds in its entirety in a twofold way, into the "science of the phenomenology of spirit," and into the "science of logic." Hegel's "science of logic" at this time is absolute theiology and not ontology. On the contrary, ontology unfolds as the "science of the experience of consciousness." Phenomenology is the "first science," and logic is the genuine science within first philosophy as the truth of beings as such. This truth is the essence of metaphysics. However, no more than Kant before him and the later Schelling after him is Hegel able to master the power long-entrenched in the didactic systematizing of academic metaphysics. Nietzsche rails against this systematizing only because his thinking must remain in the essential, onto-theiological system of metaphysics.

Why did Hegel abandon the title he had chosen at first, "Science of the *Experience* of Consciousness"? We do not know. We may, however, conjecture. Did he shrink from the word "experience" which he himself emphasized and put at the center? Now this term names the being of beings. For Kant, it is the term that designates the only possible theoretical knowledge of beings. Did it seem too daring to make the original meaning of the word "experience," which we may presume was echoing in his thoughtful ear, resound again: experience as the sufficing toward attainment [*auslangendes Gelangen*], and attainment, in its turn, as the mode of presence, of εἶναι, of being? Did it seem too daring to raise this ancient sound as the keynote of the language in which the work speaks, even when the word "experience" does not occur? At all the essential passages *en route*, in the transitions, it does occur. It does, admittedly, recede in the last main section, which presents the appearance of consciousness as spirit. On the other hand, the preface, written after the completion of the work, still speaks of the "system of the experience of spirit."

Nonetheless, the heading "Science of the *Experience* of Consciousness" disappears. The word "consciousness," too, disappears along with it from the title of the work, even though consciousness as self-consciousness constitutes the essential realm of the absoluteness of the absolute, even though consciousness is the new land of modern metaphysics, a land which has now been taken possession of as the "system of science" and has been fully surveyed.

The heading "Science of the *Experience* of Consciousness" disappears in favor of the new heading: "Science of the Phenomenology of Spirit." The new one is constructed in a rigorous correspondence to the old. We must think its genitive likewise as dialectical-speculative. The word "phenomenology," which was already commonly used in academic philosophy at the time, takes the place of the word "experience." *The essence of experience is the essence of phenomenology*. The φαίνεσθαι, the appearing-to-itself of the absolute subject, which is called "spirit," gathers itself in the mode of a dialogue between ontic and ontological consciousness. The "-logy" in "phenomenology" is the λέγεσθαι in the sense of the ambiguous διαλέγεσθαι, which characterizes the movement by which the experience of consciousness is the being of being-conscious, consciousness. Phenomenology is the self-gathering of the talk of the dialogue of spirit with its parousia. Phenomenology, here, is the term for the existence of spirit. Spirit is the subject of phenomenology, not its object. The word, here, neither means a discipline of philosophy, nor is it a designation for a specialized kind of research whose concern is to describe what is given. However, because the self-gathering of the absolute into its parousia demands (in keeping with its essence) to be presented, it has already been determined from within the essence of phenomenology that phenomenology be science; not, however, because it is a representation of spirit, but rather because it is the existence, the presentness of spirit. Thus the abridged title "The Phenomenology of Spirit," thought correctly, does not fall away into vague indeterminacy. It compels thinking into the last possible recollection. "The Phenomenology of Spirit" means: the parousia of the absolute in its prevailing. A decade after the publication of *The Phenomenology of Spirit*, "phenomenology" has declined into a narrowly circumscribed part of the philosophy of spirit within the academic system of the *Encyclopedia* (1817). As it was in the eighteenth century, the name "phenomenology" again becomes the name for a discipline. It is found between anthropology and psychology.

But what is the phenomenology of spirit, if it is the experience of consciousness? It is thoroughgoing skepticism. Experience is the dialogue between natural consciousness and absolute knowledge. Natural consciousness is the historically existing spirit extant in its time. This spirit, however, is not ideology. As subjectity, it is the reality of the real. At each time, a historical spirit is always internalized, recollected, in itself to itself. Absolute knowledge, however, is the presentation of the appearance of the existing spirit. It achieves the "organization" of the structure of the being of the spiritual realm. The route of the dialogue is gathered into the site which the dialogue enacts (reaches) in its route only in order that, in passing through the site, it establishes itself in it, and, arriving there, comes to presence. The route of arrival of the talk is the path of despair, along which consciousness each time loses its not-yet-true, sacrificing it for truth to appear. At the consummation of the dialogue by thoroughgoing skepticism, the utterance comes: it is finished. It comes at that place along the path where consciousness itself dies the death into which it has been torn by the power of the absolute. At the conclusion of his work, Hegel calls the phenomenology of the spirit "the Golgotha of absolute spirit."

The science of the phenomenology of spirit is the theology of the absolute as regards its parousia within a dialectical-speculative Good Friday. The absolute dies here. God is dead. This means everything except that there is no god. The "science of logic," in contrast, is the science of the absolute which comes to presence originally with itself in its self-knowledge as the absolute concept. It is the theology of the absoluteness of the absolute before creation. Both theologies are ontologies, are secular [*weltlich*]. They think the worldliness [*Weltlichkeit*] of the world, if we take "world" to mean here: beings in their entirety, beings that have the fundamental trait of subjectity. The world, understood in this way, determines its beings so that they are present in the representation that represents the absolute. However, the reason that the science of absolute knowledge is the secular theology of the world is not that it secularizes Christian and ecclesiastical theology but rather that it is part of the essence of ontology. Ontology is older than every Christian theology, which for its part must have been effectively real before a process of secularization could start on it. The theology of the absolute is the knowledge of beings as beings, which, for Greek thinkers, brings to light and follows its onto-theiological essence, without ever being able to follow that essence into its ground. Within the language of absolute science, it comes to light that Christian theology is – in what it knows and how it knows what it knows – metaphysics.

The proposition "The experience of consciousness is thoroughgoing skepticism" and the proposition "Phenomenology is the Golgotha of absolute spirit" join the completion of the work to its beginning. However, what is essential about *The Phenomenology of Spirit* is not the work as the accomplishment of a thinker, but the work as the reality of consciousness itself. Because phenomenology is experience, the beingness of beings, it is therefore the gathering of the appearing-to-itself upon the appearance out of the seeming of the absolute.

The gathering self-recollection, however, is the implicit essence of the will. The will wills itself in the parousia of the absolute with us. Phenomenology is itself being, in the mode of which the absolute in and for itself is with us. This being wills, since will is its essence. It remains to consider how being has arrived at its essence.

"To be with us" is part of the absoluteness of the absolute. Without this "with us," the absolute would be the solitary one; it would not be able to appear to itself among phenomena. It could not rise into its unconcealedness. With this rise (φύσις), it would not be with life (ζωή). Experience is the movement of the dialogue between natural and absolute knowledge. It is both of them, as the uniting unity by which it gathers. It is the nature of natural consciousness, which is historical in the accident of the shapes in which it appears. It is the self-comprehending of these shapes in the organization of their appearance. The book, therefore, reaches its conclusion in the sentence: "Both together – history (intellectually) comprehended – form at once the recollection and the Golgotha of absolute spirit, the reality, the truth, the certainty of its throne, without which it would be lifeless, solitary, and alone." In its absoluteness, the absolute requires the throne as the height in which it is sedent but not abased.

The parousia of the absolute takes place as phenomenology. Experience is being, and in accordance with it the absolute wills to be with us. Since the presentation that essentially belongs to experience has nothing else to present but phenomenology in the sense of the parousia, already at the end of the first paragraph at the beginning there is named that in which the work ends: parousia. It is true that this parousia – the fact that the absolute is already in and for itself with us and wills this – is mentioned only inconspicuously in a subordinate clause. At the culmination of the work, the subordinate clause is turned into a single main clause. The "with us" has unveiled itself as "not without us."

In the "with us" at the beginning of the piece, the essence of "us" is still unthought. In the "not without us" at the end of the work, the essence of "us" has been determined. We are the ones who are attentive, skeptically, to the being of beings specifically, and in this way genuinely attend to it.

The circle closes. The last words of the work, like an echo, lose themselves in the beginning. The sixteen paragraphs of the piece, usually called the "Introduction to *The Phenomenology of Spirit*," are already the genuine beginning of phenomenology.

The heading "Introduction" is not found in the original edition of 1807. Only in the "Table of Contents," which was added later, is the piece that follows the "Preface" given the title "Introduction," perhaps out of embarrassment at having no name for it. For the fact of the matter is that the piece is really not an introduction, which may well be why it was not until the work was finished that the much more extensive "Preface" was drafted as a preparative to the work. The sixteen paragraphs of the piece do not constitute an introduction, because they cannot constitute any such thing. They cannot be an introduction because there is no introduction to phenomenology. There is no introduction to phenomenology because there can be no introduction to phenomenology. The phenomenology of spirit is the parousia of the absolute. Parousia is the being of beings. For men, there is no introduction [*Einleitung*] to the being of beings because the essence of man in the company [*Geleit*] of being is this company itself. Provided that the "to be with us" of the absolute prevails, we are already in the parousia. We can never been escorted from somewhere else into it. Yet how are we in the parousia of the absolute? We are in it according to the habit of natural consciousness. Each thing appears to natural consciousness as though all presences were alongside each other. Even the absolute habitually appears to it as alongside the rest. Even that which is above or over habitually represented beings is over against them, for natural consciousness. It is this "alongside" present in the direction upward that we ourselves are alongside. Following the pull of its representation, natural consciousness lingers among beings and does not turn itself toward being, by which nonetheless it is attracted in advance, and even attracted for that pull toward the being of beings. Nonetheless, when natural consciousness becomes attentive to being, it assures us that being is an abstraction. That by which consciousness is attracted into its own essence is passed off by consciousness as something abstracted. No greater reversal is possible for natural consciousness than this opinion.

The perversities [*Verkehrheiten*] of the circumstances in which natural consciousness roams about pale compared to this reversal [*Verkehrung*]. It tries to eliminate one perversity through the organization of another, but without being mindful of the real reversal. This is the reason for the enduring necessity that consciousness turns around from its non-self-turning to the being of beings and turns itself toward the appearance of phenomena. Natural consciousness cannot be led into where it already is. However, in turning around neither must it abandon its stay in the midst of beings. It must be prepared to accept its residence specifically in its truth.

We could take, literarily, the sixteen paragraphs to be the exegesis of the title which then was dropped. However, if our thinking is based on the subject matter, then the book's title does not matter; the work itself does.

Or we might even say: not even the work matters, but rather that which it presents – experience, phenomenology, as what is essential in the parousia of the absolute. And then again, the reason it matters is not that we take note of it, but rather that we ourselves are in the experience which our being also *is*. That is what matters in the old, traditional sense of being: to be a presence among . . . the presences.

The sixteen paragraphs of the piece direct natural consciousness back into the appropriation of its stay. This redirection occurs by turning consciousness around; through that turn consciousness arrives into the experience as which the parousia of the absolute truly happens. Natural consciousness can only be retrieved from its habitual representation and directed into experience if we start from the representations which natural consciousness makes (at once and in its own way) out of that which encounters it with the claim to be absolute knowledge. To start from the opinions of natural consciousness marks the style and coherence of the paragraphs of the piece.

This piece, the beginning of the actual body of the work, is the beginning of the skepsis that prevails through thoroughgoing skepticism. To begin the skepsis means: to perform the having-seen all the way into the absoluteness of the absolute and to keep to it there. The text is the ineluctable opportunity to induce natural consciousness to release within itself the knowledge in which it already is through being its own concept. Only when the reversal of consciousness has been carried out in which the appearance of spirit has turned to us do the phenomena come to presence as phenomena "for us." "For us" means precisely not "relative to us," representing as we ordinarily do. "For us" means: "in itself," i.e., appearing out of the absoluteness of the absolute into the pure site of its appearance.

It is only when this text has induced us to turn around, actually to begin the presentation, that the presentation of the experience of consciousness can begin. The presentation begins absolutely with the absoluteness of the absolute. It begins with the extreme force of the will of the parousia. It begins with the extreme self-externalization of the absolute in its appearance. In order to be able to look ahead into this appearance, we must take the phenomena as they appear and keep them free from our opinions and thought about them. Yet this letting the encounter happen, this letting go, is an activity which takes its certainty and endurance only from our contribution of the reversal. Our reversal is that we go skeptically, i.e., with open eyes, to encounter the appearance of phenomenal consciousness, which has already come to us in the parousia, in order to be on the route in which experience is the phenomenology of the absolute.

The presentation begins by letting "sense-certainty" appear absolutely:

> The knowledge, which is at the start or immediately our object, can be nothing else than just that which is immediate knowledge, knowledge of the immediate, of what *is*. We have, in dealing with it, to proceed, too, in an immediate way, to accept what is given, not altering anything in it as it is presented before us, and keeping mere apprehension free from conceptual comprehension.

Once the presentation of the appearance of sense-certainty has been carried out, then there arises a new object, which is the being of what that presentation takes to be true beings, namely the truth of certainty, a certainty which is self-consciousness that knows itself. The presentation of the appearance of "The Truth Which Conscious Certainty of Self Realizes" begins with the following sentences:

> In the kinds of certainty hitherto considered, the truth for consciousness is something other than consciousness itself. The conception, however, of this truth vanishes in the course of our experience of it. What the object immediately was *in itself* – whether mere being in sense-certainty, a concrete thing in perception, or the power in the case of understanding – it turns out, in truth, not to be this really; but instead, this in-itself proves to be a way in which it is for an other. The concept of the object gives way before the actual concrete object, or the first immediate idea is cancelled in the course of experience. Mere certainty vanished in favor of the truth.

Nietzsche's Word: "God Is Dead"

The following commentary is an attempt to point in the direction where, perhaps, the question about the essence of nihilism can one day be posed. The commentary derives from a thinking that is beginning to win an initial clarity about Nietzsche's fundamental place within the history of Western metaphysics. To point in this direction clarifies a stage of Western metaphysics that is in all likelihood its final stage, since metaphysics, through Nietzsche, has deprived itself of its own essential possibility in certain respects, and therefore to that extent other possibilities of metaphysics can no longer become apparent. After the metaphysical reversal carried out by Nietzsche, all that is left to metaphysics is to be inverted into the dire state of its non-essence. The supersensory has become an unenduring product of the sensory. But by so disparaging [*Herabsetzung*] its antithesis, the sensory denies its own essence. The dismissal [*Absetzung*] of the supersensory also eliminates the purely sensory and with it the difference between the two. The dismissal of the supersensory ends in a "neither-nor" regarding the distinction between sensory (αἰσθητόν) and non-sensory (νοητόν). It ends in the senseless. However, it remains the unthinking and insuperable assumption behind blind attempts to evade the senseless through a sheer fiat of sense.

Throughout the following, metaphysics is thought as the truth of beings as such in their entirety, not as the doctrine of a thinker. In each instance, a thinker has his fundamental philosophical position within a metaphysics. For that reason, a metaphysics can be named after a thinker. In accordance with the essence of metaphysics as it is thought here, this in no way implies that a particular metaphysics is the achievement and possession of a thinker as a personality acting within the public setting of cultural affairs. The destiny of being makes its way over beings in abrupt epochs of truth;

in each phase of metaphysics, a particular piece of that way becomes apparent. Nietzsche himself interprets the course of Western history metaphysically, namely as the advent and development of nihilism. To think through Nietzsche's metaphysics becomes a matter of reflecting on the situation and place of contemporary men, whose destiny with respect to truth is still little experienced. Every such reflection, however, if it is to do more than idly repeat information, goes beyond that at which reflection is directed. To go beyond is not, without further ado, to raise higher or even to exceed, nor is it to overcome at once. To reflect on Nietzsche's metaphysics does not mean that besides his ethics and his epistemology and his aesthetics, we also, and above all, deal with a metaphysics; rather it means: that we try to take Nietzsche seriously as a thinker. However, even for Nietzsche thinking means: to represent beings as beings. All metaphysical thinking is onto-logy or it is nothing at all.

For the reflection that is attempted here, it is a matter of preparing for a simple and inconspicuous step forward in thought. It is the concern of preparatory thinking to clear a free scope within which being itself[a] would again be able to take man with regard to his essence into an initial relationship.[b] To be preparatory is the essence of such thinking.

This essential thinking, essential and therefore everywhere and in every respect only preparatory, proceeds in inconspicuousness. Here, all fellow thinking, however clumsy and groping, is an essential help. To share in thinking is the unobtrusive sowing of sowers: the sowing is not made good by acknowledgment or profit, and the sowers may never see blade or fruit and not know a harvest. They serve the sowing, and even more willingly they serve the preparation for sowing.

Before sowing comes plowing. It is essential to reclaim the field that had to remain in obscurity while the land of metaphysics was inescapably dominant. It is essential first of all to sense, to intuit, this field; then to find it; and then to cultivate it. It is essential to go out to this field for the first time. Many are the paths still unknown. Yet each thinker is allotted only one way, his own, in the tracks of which he must go back and forth, time and again, in order at last to keep to it as his own, though it is never his, and say what he came to know on this one path.

Perhaps the title *Being and Time* is the signpost of such a way. In keeping with the essential involvement of metaphysics (an involvement that

[a] First edition, 1950: the Event.

[b] First edition, 1950: custom.

metaphysics itself demands and seeks anew time and again) with the sciences, themselves the offspring of metaphysics, preparatory thinking must also move now and then in the area of the sciences because in many different shapes they are claiming still to predetermine the fundamental form of knowledge and the knowable, either knowingly or through the nature of their validity and effectiveness. The more plainly the sciences are carried along by their predetermined technological essence and its characteristic form, the more definitely the question is resolved about the epistemological possibility claimed in technology, about the nature, limits, and rights of this possibility for knowledge.

To think preparatorily and to fulfill such thinking involves an education in thinking in the midst of the sciences. For this, the difficult thing is to find an appropriate form so that this education in thinking is not liable to be confused with research and erudition. This goal is in danger above all when thinking must, simultaneously and perpetually, first of all find its own place to stay. To think in the midst of the sciences means: to go past them without despising them.

We do not know what possibilities the destiny of Western history still has in store for our people and the West. Nor is the external organization and arrangement of these possibilities what is necessary in the first instance. What is important is only that learners in thinking are fellow learners – fellow learners who in their own way stay on the path and are present at the right moment.

The following commentary, in its intention and consequence, keeps to the area of the one experience out of which *Being and Time* is thought. This thinking has been concerned constantly with one occurrence: that in the history of Western thinking, right from the beginning, beings have been thought in regard to being, but the truth of being has remained unthought. Indeed, not only has the truth of being been denied to thinking as a possible experience, but Western thinking itself (precisely in the form of metaphysics) has specifically, though unknowingly, masked the occurrence of this denial.[a]

Preparatory thinking therefore necessarily keeps to the realm of historical reflection. For this thinking, history is not the sequence of historical periods but a unique proximity of what is the same, which concerns thinking in the incalculable ways of destiny and with variable degrees of immediacy.

[a] First edition, 1950: denial and withholding.

Our reflection is now to be aimed at Nietzsche's metaphysics. His thinking sees itself under the sign of nihilism. That is the name for a historical movement, discerned by Nietzsche, which after dominating the preceding centuries has determined the current one. The interpretation of this movement Nietzsche concentrated into the brief statement: "God is dead."

One might suppose that "God is dead" expresses the belief of Nietzsche the atheist and hence that it is only a personal opinion and therefore biased, and thus also easily refuted by pointing out that everywhere today many people attend churches and endure hardships out of their Christian trust in God. Yet the question remains whether the word of Nietzsche which we quoted is only an extravagant view of a thinker whom it is easy to characterize correctly: he went mad in the end. It must still be asked whether Nietzsche, if anything, is not rather expressing [*ausspricht*] here the word that has always been implicitly [*unausgesprochen*] spoken within the metaphysically determined history of the West. Before reaching any position too hastily, we must first of all try to think "God is dead" in the way that it is intended. Hence we will do well to distance ourselves from the rash opinions that obtrude themselves at once at this terrible statement.

The following considerations are an attempt to comment on Nietzsche's word in a few essential respects. Let it again be stressed: Nietzsche's word gives the destiny of two millennia of Western history. And we, unprepared as all of us are together, we must not think that we will alter this destiny by a lecture about Nietzsche's statement or even learn to know it only adequately. Nonetheless, this one thing is now necessary: that out of reflection we are receptive to instruction and that on the way to instruction we learn to reflect.

Not only must any commentary gather the substance from the text, it must also, imperceptibly and without being too insistent, add something of its own to it, from its substance. This supplement is what the layman, regarding what he takes to be the content of the text, always feels as an interpolation; it is what he, with the right he arrogates to himself, criticizes as arbitrary. A proper commentary, however, never understands the text better than its author understood it, though it certainly understands it differently. Only this difference in understanding must be such that it encounters the same thing which the explicated text is meditating.

The first time Nietzsche pronounced "God is dead" was in the third book of *La Gaya Scienza*, published in 1882. This work was the beginning of Nietzsche's path toward developing his fundamental metaphysical position. It is between this work and the fruitless toil that went into shaping his planned masterwork that *Thus Spoke Zarathustra* was published. The planned masterwork was never completed. Provisionally it was to be entitled *The Will to Power* and subtitled "Attempt at a Revaluation of All Values."

As a young man Nietzsche was already familiar with the disturbing thought of the death of a God and the mortality of the gods. In a note that dates from the time he was drafting his first work *The Birth of Tragedy*, Nietzsche wrote (in 1870): "I believe in the ancient German saying: all gods must die." At the end of his treatise *Faith and Knowledge* (1802), the young Hegel identifies the "feeling on which the religion of the modern age rests – the feeling that God Himself is dead . . . "[1] Hegel's word thinks something different from what Nietzsche thinks in his. Nonetheless, between the two there is an essential connection that conceals itself in the essence of all metaphysics. Plutarch's remark, cited by Pascal – "Le grand Pan est mort" (*Pensées*, 695) – belongs, though for contrary reasons, in the same domain.

Let us, first of all, listen to the complete text of section 125 of *La Gaya Scienza*. The section is entitled "The madman" and runs:

The madman. – Haven't you heard of that madman who lit a lamp in the bright morning, ran to the market, and cried out ceaselessly: "I'm looking for God! I'm looking for God!" – As there were a number of people standing about just then who did not believe in God, he aroused a good deal of laughter. "So did he get lost?," someone said. "Has he lost his way, like a child?," another asked. "Or maybe he's in hiding?" "Is he afraid of us?" "Gone to sea?" "Emigrated?" – so were they shouting and laughing riotously. The madman jumped into the midst of them and his eyes transfixed them: "Where did God go?," he cried, "I'll tell you where. *We've killed him* – you and I. We are all his murderers. But how have we done this? How were we able to drink the sea dry? Who gave us the sponge to wipe the entire horizon away? What did we do when we unchained this earth from its sun? Where is it moving to now? Where are we moving to? Away from all the suns? Is there no end to our plummeting? Backwards, sidewards, forwards, in every direction? Is there still an up and a down? Aren't we astray as in an endless nothing? It's the empty space, isn't it, we feel breathing on us? It has become colder, hasn't it? Isn't it always nightfall and more night? Don't lamps need to be lit in the morning? Do we not yet hear any of the noise of the gravediggers who are burying God? Do we not yet smell anything of the divine putrefaction? – even gods become putrid. God is dead! God remains dead! And we killed him. How are we to find consolation, we the murderers of all murderers? The holiest and mightiest that the world has hitherto possessed has bled to death under our knives. What water can cleanse us? What ceremonies of expiation, what sacred games, will we have to invent? Isn't the greatness of this deed too great for us? Don't we have to become gods ourselves in order merely to appear worthy of it? There has never been a greater deed – and whoever will be born after us will partake, for this deed's sake, of a history higher than all history in times past!" – Here the madman fell silent and looked again at his audience; they too were silent and looked at him and were taken aback. At last he threw his lamp to the ground, so that it broke into pieces and went out. "I come too early," he said, then, "the time is not yet mine. The enormous event is still on the way, itinerant – it hasn't got as far as the ears of men. Thunder and lightning take time, the light from stars takes time, deeds take time even after they have been done, to be seen and heard. This deed is still farther from them than the farthest stars – *and yet they have done it themselves!*" It is told that on the same day the madman forced his way into different churches and started to sing his *Requiem aeternam deo* in them. Led out and questioned, he would only reply: "What else are these churches, then, if not the crypts and tombs of God?"

To the four books of *La Gaya Scienza*, Nietzsche appended a fifth in 1886, four years later; he gave it the title "We the Fearless." The first section of this book (aphorism no. 343) is headed: "*What Cheerfulness Is All About*." It begins: "The greatest modern event – that 'God is dead,' that faith in the Christian God has become untenable – is already beginning to throw its first shadows across Europe."

It is clear from this sentence that Nietzsche, in speaking about the death of God, means the Christian God. But it is no less certain and no less to be kept in mind beforehand that Nietzsche uses the names "God" and "Christian God" to indicate the supersensory world in general. God is the name for the realm of ideas and the ideal. Since Plato, or more accurately, since the late Greek and the Christian interpretations of the Platonic philosophy, this realm of the supersensory has been considered the true and actually real world. In contrast to it, the sensory world is only the unreal this-worldly world, the changeable and therefore the merely apparent world. The this-worldly world is the vale of tears in contrast to the mountain of eternal bliss of the other side. If, as is still the case in Kant, we call the sensory world the physical world in the broadest sense, then the supersensory world is the metaphysical world.

"God is dead" means: the supersensory world has no effective power. It does not bestow life. Metaphysics, which for Nietzsche is Western philosophy understood as Platonism, is at an end. Nietzsche understands his own philosophy as the countermovement against metaphysics, i.e., for him, against Platonism.

As a mere countermovement, however, it necessarily remains trapped, like everything anti-, in the essence of what it is challenging. Since all it does is turn metaphysics upside down, Nietzsche's countermovement against metaphysics remains embroiled in it and has no way out; in fact it is embroiled in it to such a degree that it is sealed off from its essence and, as metaphysics, is unable ever to think its own essence. This is the reason that, for and through metaphysics, there remains hidden what actually happens in and as metaphysics itself.

If God – as the supersensory ground and as the goal of everything that is real – is dead, if the supersensory world of ideas is bereft of its binding and above all its inspiring and constructive power, then there is nothing left which man can rely on and by which he can orient himself. That is why in the passage we quoted, the question is asked, "Aren't we astray in an endless nothing?" The statement "God is dead" contains the realization that this nothing is spreading. Nothing means here: absence of a supersensory, binding world. Nihilism, "the eeriest of all guests,"[2] is standing at the door.

The attempt to comment on Nietzsche's word "God is dead" is synonymous with the task of explaining what Nietzsche understands by nihilism and therefore of describing how Nietzsche stands in relation to nihilism. However, since this name is so often used only as a tabloid slogan and not infrequently even as a damning invective, it is necessary to know what it means. Not everyone who adverts to the Christian faith or to some metaphysical conviction thereby stands outside nihilism. Conversely, to ponder about nothing and its essence does not necessarily make one a nihilist.

That name is popularly used in a tone insinuating that the word "nihilist" is itself sufficient – without thinking any further with it – to prove that reflecting on the nothing leads to a descent into the nothing and implies that a dictatorship of the nothing is to be established.

In general the question is whether the name "nihilism," thought rigorously in the sense of Nietzsche's philosophy, has only a nihilistic (i.e., negative) meaning that pursues its course into void nothing. Since the title of nihilism has been used vaguely and arbitrarily, it is necessary, before a more exact discussion of what Nietzsche himself says about nihilism, to win the proper perspective from which we may ask the very first questions about nihilism.

Nihilism is a historical movement, not just any view or doctrine held by just anyone. Nihilism moves history in the way of a scarcely recognized fundamental process in the destiny of the Western peoples. Hence nihilism is not just one historical phenomenon among others, not just one spiritual-intellectual current that occurs within Western history after others have occurred, after Christianity, after humanism, and after the Enlightenment.

Nihilism, thought in its essence, is on the contrary the fundamental movement of the history of the West. Its roots are so deep that its development can entail only world catastrophes. Nihilism is the world-historical movement of the peoples of the earth who have been drawn into modernity's arena of power. That is why it is not only a phenomenon of the present age, nor even a product originally of the nineteenth century, when admittedly a keen eye for nihilism awoke and its name became common. Nor is nihilism a product of particular nations whose thinkers and writers speak specifically of nihilism. Those who imagine themselves free of it are perhaps the ones advancing its development most fundamentally. Part of the eeriness of this eeriest guest is that it cannot name its own origin.

Nihilism does not prevail only when the Christian God has been denied, or when Christianity is embattled, or when a freethinking cheap atheism is still all that is preached. As long as we look exclusively at this unbelief which has abandoned Christianity and at its manifestations, our attention will be fixed externally on the meager façades of nihilism. The speech of the madman says specifically that the word "God is dead" has nothing in common with the opinions of those standing about and talking confusedly, of those who "do not believe in God." To those merely lacking faith in this way, nihilism as the destiny of their own history has not yet penetrated at all.

As long as we grasp "God is dead" only as the formula of unbelief, we are thinking in terms of theological apologetics and are eschewing what matters to Nietzsche, namely reflection that thinks about what has already happened with the truth of the supersensory world and with its relation to man's essence.

Nor, therefore, does nihilism in Nietzsche's sense in any way coincide with the state (conceived in a purely negative way) of no longer being able to believe in the Christian God of the biblical revelation, since by "Christianity" Nietzsche does not mean the Christian life that existed once for a short time before the Gospels were set down in writing and before Paul disseminated his missionary propaganda. For Nietzsche, Christianity is the historical, secular-political phenomenon of the Church and its claim to power within the formation of Western humanity and its modern culture. Christianity in this sense and the Christian life of the New Testament faith are not the same. Even a non-Christian life can affirm Christianity and make use of it for the sake of power; conversely, a Christian life is not necessarily in need of Christianity. Therefore, a confrontation with Christianity is by no means an absolute battle against what is Christian, no more than a critique of theology is a critique of the faith for which theology is supposed to be the interpretation. For as long as we fail to pay due attention to these essential differences, we do not move past the lowlands of the conflicts among world views.

In "God is dead" the name "God," thought essentially, stands for the supersensory world of ideals that contain the goal that exists beyond the earthly life for this life; they determine it thus from above and so in certain respects from without. But when the pure faith in God as defined by the Church fades, when theology in particular, the doctrine of the faith, finds itself curbed and forced to one side in serving its role as the normative explanation of beings in their entirety, then in no way does that fundamental structure break down in accordance with which the goal set on the scale of the supersensory has dominated the earthly life of the senses.

The place of God's vanished authority and the Church's profession of teaching has been taken by the authority of conscience and, forcibly, by the authority of reason. The social instinct has risen up against these. Historical progress has replaced the withdrawal from the world into the supersensory. The goal of eternal bliss in the hereafter has been transformed into the earthly happiness of the greatest number. The diligent care that was the *cultus* of religion has been replaced by enthusiasm for creating a culture or for spreading civilization. Creation, once the prerogative of the biblical God, has become the mark of human activity, whose creative work becomes in the end business transactions.

Whatever is thus going to be put in the place of the supersensory world will be variations of the Christian-ecclesiastical and theological interpretation of the world, an interpretation which adopted its schema of the *ordo*, the hierarchical order of beings, from the Hellenistic-Judaic world and whose fundamental structure was established through Plato at the outset of Western metaphysics.

The realm for the essence and event of nihilism is metaphysics itself, always assuming that by "metaphysics" we are not thinking of a doctrine or only of a specialized discipline of philosophy but of the fundamental structure of beings in their entirety, so far as this entirety is differentiated into a sensory and a supersensory world, the former of which is supported and determined by the latter. Metaphysics is the space of history in which it becomes destiny for the supersensory world, ideas, God, moral law, the authority of reason, progress, the happiness of the greatest number, culture, and civilization to forfeit their constructive power and to become void. We are calling this essential ruin [*Wesenszerfall*] of supersensory its putrefaction [*Verwesung*]. Unbelief in the sense of apostasy from the Christian doctrine of faith is therefore never the essence or the ground of nihilism; rather, it is always only a consequence of nihilism: for it could be that Christianity itself represents a consequence and a form of nihilism.

From this point we now recognize the final misstep, to which we are still liable, in grasping and supposedly battling against nihilism. Since we do not experience nihilism as a historical movement which is already of long duration and whose essential ground lies in metaphysics itself, we fall victim to the pernicious desire to take the phenomena, which are in fact only the consequences of nihilism, for nihilism itself, or to represent consequences and effects as the cause of nihilism. In thoughtlessly accommodating ourselves to this manner of representation, we have for decades been used to adducing the dominance of technology or the revolt of the masses as the causes of the historical condition of our age; we tirelessly analyze the spiritual situation of the time in these respects. Yet every analysis, however knowledgeable and clever, of man and his position among beings remains thoughtless and produces only the semblance of reflection, so long as it refrains from thinking about a settlement for man's essence and from experiencing that place in the truth of being.

As long as the mere phenomena of nihilism are taken for nihilism itself, any opinion about it will remain superficial. And it does not help in the least when out of discontentment at the condition of the world, or from a half-avowed despair, or from moralistic outrage, or from devout and self-righteous superiority, opinions take on a degree of frantic resistance.

In contrast to this, it is above all essential that we reflect. That is why we will now ask Nietzsche himself what he understands by nihilism; to begin with, we will leave it an open question whether with this understanding Nietzsche has already caught the essence of nihilism or whether he can catch it.

In a note from 1887, Nietzsche poses the question (*The Will to Power*, aphorism no. 2): "What does nihilism mean?" He gives the answer: "*That the highest values devalue themselves.*"

This answer is emphasized and a supplementary explanation is provided: "The goal is missing; the answer to 'why?' is missing."

Nietzsche, accordingly, comprehends nihilism as a historical process. He interprets this process as the devaluation of the hitherto highest values. God, the supersensory world as the world that truly is and that determines everything, ideals and ideas, the goals and grounds that determine and support all beings and human life in particular: all these are represented here in the meaning of the "highest values." According to a view current even now, what one understands by that term is truth, goodness, and beauty: truth, i.e., that which truly is; goodness, i.e., what everything is everywhere dependent upon; beauty, i.e., the order and unity of beings in their entirety. The highest values, however, have already devalued themselves now by coming to understand that the ideal world is not, and not ever, going to be realized within the real world. The compulsory nature of the highest values begins to falter. The question is raised: what is the purpose of these highest values if they do not also secure the guarantee for, as well as the ways and means of, realizing the goals they set?

If, however, it were now our intention to understand Nietzsche's definition of the essence of nihilism according to its wording (that the highest values are in the process of becoming valueless), an interpretation of the essence of nihilism would ensue which has meanwhile become current and whose currency is sustained by the label "nihilism": that the devaluing of the highest values obviously means decadence. Yet in no way for Nietzsche is nihilism only a phenomenon of decadence; rather, nihilism, as the fundamental process of Western history, is also and above all the intrinsic law of this history. For that reason, even in his observations about nihilism, Nietzsche cares rather little about describing the course of the process of devaluation historically and at the end deriving from it the decline of the West; instead, he thinks nihilism as the "inner logic" of Western history.

In this way Nietzsche recognizes that, even with the devaluation of the hitherto highest values for the world, the world itself remains; and above all that the world grown value-less is inevitably impelled toward a new dispensation of value.[a] After the hitherto highest values have lost their validity, the new dispensation of value is changed, in regard to the former values, into a "revaluation of all values." The no to the former values is derived from the yes to the new dispensation of value. Since (in Nietzsche's view) this yes neither negotiates nor compromises with the previous values, an absolute no is part of this yes to the new dispensation of value. In order to secure the absolute character of the new yes against a regression to the former values, i.e., in order to ground the new dispensation of value as a countermovement, Nietzsche calls even the new dispensation of value "nihilism," namely, a nihilism which, through devaluation, completes itself in a new and exclusively normative dispensation of value. This normative phase of nihilism Nietzsche calls "fulfilled," i.e., classic nihilism. By nihilism, Nietzsche understands the devaluation of the hitherto highest values. Yet at the same time Nietzsche finds himself affirming nihilism in the sense of a "revaluation of the highest values." The name "nihilism" is therefore ambiguous;

[a] First edition, 1950. Under what assumption? That "world" means beings in their entirety, the will to power in the eternal return of the same.

seen in relation to its extremes, it always has two meanings from the start, in that it designates the pure devaluation of the former highest values, but at the same time it also means the absolute countermovement to devaluation. Pessimism, which Nietzsche takes as the early form of nihilism, has the same double meaning. According to Schopenhauer, pessimism is the belief that in this the worst of worlds, life is not worth being lived and affirmed. According to this doctrine life, which means at the same time beings as such in their entirety, is to be negated. This pessimism, according to Nietzsche, is the "pessimism of weakness." Everywhere it sees only gloom, finds the reason that everything will end in failure, and claims to know (in the sense of universal failure) how everything will come out. In contrast, the pessimism of strength, and as strength, is in no way deceived, sees the dangers, wants no glossing over or dissimulation. It sees through to the disastrousness of merely lying in wait for the hitherto to return. It penetrates into phenomena analytically and demands awareness of the conditions and powers which, in spite of everything, secure the mastery of our historical situation.

A more essential reflection would be able to show in what Nietzsche calls the "pessimism of strength" how the uprising of modern humanity into the absolute domination of subjectivity within the subjectity of beings is fulfilled. Through pessimism in its twofold form, the extremes come to light. Extremes, as such, preserve their preponderance. So a condition is produced that is an absolute intensification into an either-or. An "intermediate" situation begins to show in which it is clear that, on the one hand, the former highest values are not being realized. The world appears value-less. On the other hand, through being made conscious of this fact, attention is directed to the source of the new dispensation of value, without the world thereby recovering its value.

It is true that, in face of the faltering domination of the former values, something else can be tried. That is, even if God in the sense of the Christian God has vanished from his place in the supersensory world, still the place itself is preserved, although it has become empty. One can still hold fast to the evacuated realm of the supersensory and ideal world. The empty place even invites its own re-occupation and calls for the God who disappeared from it to be replaced by another. New ideals are being erected. As Nietzsche represents it (*The Will to Power*, no. 1021, from 1887), this is happening through the doctrines of world happiness and through socialism, and likewise through Wagner's music, i.e., everywhere that "dogmatic Christianity" "has gone bankrupt." Thus "incomplete nihilism" arises, about which Nietzsche writes (*The Will to Power*, no. 28, from 1887): "*Incomplete* nihilism, its forms: we live right in their midst. The attempts to escape nihilism *without* revaluing the former values: they produce the opposite, make the problem more acute."

We can grasp Nietzsche's thoughts about incomplete nihilism more clearly and acutely by saying: incomplete nihilism indeed replaces the former values by others, but it always puts them in the old place, which is, as it were, preserved as the ideal region of the supersensory. Complete nihilism, however, must eliminate even the place of value itself, the supersensory as a realm; and it must accordingly alter and revalue values differently.

It is clear, then, that the "revaluation of all values" is indeed part of the complete, fulfilled, and consequently classic nihilism, but the revaluation does not merely replace old values by new ones. The revaluing becomes a reversal of the nature and manner of valuing. The dispensation of value requires a new principle, i.e., something that provides it with a point of departure and the place to maintain itself. The dispensation of value requires another realm. No longer can the principle be the world of the supersensory, now grown dead. Therefore, nihilism aiming at revaluation (understood in this way) will seek out what is most alive. So nihilism itself turns into the "ideal of the most abundant life" (*The Will to Power*, no. 14, from 1887). In this new highest value is concealed another estimation of life, i.e., of the basis of the determining essence of all living things. So let us now ask what Nietzsche understands by life.

The allusion to different stages and forms of nihilism demonstrates that in Nietzsche's interpretation nihilism is always a history dealing with values: dispensing values, dispensing with values, revaluing values; with dispensing values anew; and ultimately, actually with the differently valuing establishment of the principle behind every dispensation of values. The highest goals, the grounds and principles of beings, ideals and the supersensory, God and the gods – they are all conceived in advance as value. Therefore, we will not grasp Nietzsche's concept of nihilism adequately until we know what he understands by value. Only then will we understand "God is dead" as it is thought. A sufficiently clear elucidation of what Nietzsche thinks with the word "value" is the key to understanding his metaphysics.

In the nineteenth century, talk of values became frequent, and it became customary to think in values. However, it was only as a consequence of the broadcasting of Nietzsche's writings that talk of values has become popular. People speak of life-values, of cultural values, of eternal values, of the hierarchy of values, of spiritual values which, for example, are believed to be found in antiquity. With scholarly activity in philosophy and with the recasting of neo-Kantianism, we arrive at value philosophy. Systems of values are constructed; in ethics, values are subdivided. Even in Christian theology God is defined as the highest value: the *summum ens qua summum bonum*. The sciences are taken to be value-free, and value judgments are consigned to world views. Value and what is valuable are turned into a positivistic substitute for the metaphysical. That talk about value is so frequent accords with the indeterminacy of the concept. The indeterminacy, for its part, accords with the obscurity of the essential origin of value from being. For assuming that value, so often invoked in these guises, is not nothing, it will have its essence in being.

What does Nietzsche understand by value? In what is the essence of value grounded? Why is Nietzsche's metaphysics the metaphysics of values?

In a note (1887/88) Nietzsche states what he understands by value (*The Will to Power*, no. 715): "The viewpoint of 'value' is the viewpoint of the *conditions for preservation-increase* in regard[a] to the complex structures, relatively enduring, of life in the midst of becoming."

The essence of value is based on its being a viewpoint. Value means that which one has in mind [*ins Auge gefasst*]. Value is the point of sight for a seeing that has its eye on something, or, as we say, that counts on [*auf etwas rechnet*] something and thereby has to deal with [*mit anderem rechnen*] something else. Value stands in an inner relation to a this-much, to quantity and number. Values are therefore (*The Will to Power*, no. 710, from 1888) related to a "scale of number and measure." The question still remains: on what is the scale of increase and diminishment, for its part, grounded?

In characterizing value as a viewpoint, the one essential thing for Nietzsche's concept of value follows: as a viewpoint, value is always posited by a seeing and for a seeing. This seeing is of such a kind that it sees in that it has seen, and that it has seen by re-presenting to itself as a particular thing that which was sighted, thereby positing it. It is only through this setting within representation that the point which is necessary for keeping an eye on something and which therefore directs the visual course of this seeing becomes a point of sight, that is, becomes what matters in seeing and in all activity directed by vision. Before this, therefore, values are not something in themselves, so that they could be taken when necessary as points of sight.

Value is value provided it is valid. It is valid provided it is posited as what matters. It is so posited by aiming and keeping one's sight on what must be counted. The point of sight, the regard, the field of view are here

[a] First edition, 1950: perpective, horizon.

synonymous with sight [*Gesicht*] and seeing [*Sehen*] in the sense identified by the Greeks, but which has gone through the transformation of "idea" from εἶδος to *perceptio*. To see is to represent; since Leibniz, this representation has been grasped more explicitly in its fundamental character of striving (*appetitus*). All beings are representing beings to the extent that *nisus* is part of the being of beings: *nisus*, the urge to make an appearance, the urge that enjoins a thing to arise [*Aufkommen*] (appear) and so determines its occurrence [*Vorkommen*]. The *nisus*-like essence of all beings takes and posits for itself in this way a point of sight. The point of sight provides the perspective which it is essential to follow. The point of sight is value.

With values as points of view, the "*conditions for preservation-increase*" are posited, according to Nietzsche. By the very way he writes this – in omitting the "and" and substituting a hyphen for it – Nietzsche intends to make it clear that values as viewpoints are, in their essence and therefore constantly, simultaneously conditions of preservation *and* increase. When values are posited, both kinds of conditions must be constantly contemplated in such a way that they remain in a unified relation to each other. Why? Obviously simply because the representing-striving beings themselves in their essence are such that they require these twofold points of sight. For what do values as viewpoints serve as conditions, if they must be conditions simultaneously for both preservation and increase?

Preservation and increase mark the fundamental traits of life; these traits intrinsically belong together. The desire to grow, increase, is part of the essence of life. To preserve life is to serve the increase of life. Any life that is restricted to mere preservation is already in decline. For living creatures, it is never the goal, for example, to secure lebensraum; rather it is the means to an increase of life. Conversely, life that has been increased intensifies in its turn the prior need for enlarging one's space. Increase, however, is only possible where a durable resource has already been preserved as something made secure and therefore only then capable of increase. Hence living things are linked by the two fundamental traits of increase and preservation, i.e., they are "complex structures of life." As points of view, values guide seeing in "regard to complex structures." Seeing is always a seeing by the glance of life, a glance which governs all living things. By setting the points of sight for living things, life in its essence proves to be that which sets values (cf. *The Will to Power*, no. 556, from 1885/6).

The "complex structures of life" are dependent on the conditions of a preservation and of a stability [*Beständigung*], yet the dependence is such that stability [*das Beständige*] endures [*besteht*] only in order to become – through an increase – unstable [*ein Unbeständiges*]. The duration of these complex structures is based on the interrelation of increase and preservation. Hence it is a comparative duration. The duration of living things, i.e., of life, is "relatively enduring."

According to Nietzsche, value is "the viewpoint of the conditions for preservation-increase in regard to the complex structures, relatively enduring, of life in the midst of becoming." Here, and generally in the conceptual language of Nietzsche's metaphysics, the stark indefinite word "becoming" does not signify just any flux of all things, nor the mere alteration of states, and not just any development or vague evolution. Becoming means the transition from something to something, that movement and being moved which Leibniz in the *Monadology* (§ 11) calls *changements naturels*, which govern the *ens qua ens*, i.e., the *ens percipiens et appetens*. Nietzsche takes this governance as the fundamental trait of all reality, i.e., he takes it in the very broad sense of beings. He understands that which thus determines beings in their *essentia* as the "will to power."

When Nietzsche concludes his characterization of the essence of value with the word "becoming," that final word points to the essential realm where values and the dispensation of value generally and uniquely belong. "To become" – that, for Nietzsche, is "the will to power." So the "will to power" is the fundamental trait of "life," which Nietzsche also often uses in a broad sense, by which it has been equated within metaphysics (cf. Hegel) to "becoming." Will to power, becoming, life, and being in the broadest sense have the same meaning in Nietzsche's language (*The Will to Power*, no. 582, from 1885/6 and no. 689 from 1888). Inside of becoming, life, i.e., the living, takes shape as centers of the will to power that are active at particular times. These centers are therefore structures of ruling power. It is as such that Nietzsche understands art, the state, religion, science, society. That is why he can also say (*The Will to Power*, no. 715) "'Value' is essentially the viewpoint for the gain and loss of these centers of ruling power" (namely, with regard to their ruling character).

So long as Nietzsche, in his delineation of the essence of value cited above, grasps value as the viewpointed condition of the preservation and increase of life, but sees life as grounded in becoming and becoming as the will to power, the will to power reveals itself as that which sets those viewpoints. The will to power is that which, on the basis of its "inner principle" (Leibniz) as the *nisus* in the *esse* of the *ens*, esteems according to values. The will to power is the ground for the necessity of dispensing values and the origin of the possibility of value-estimation. Hence Nietzsche says (*The Will to*

Power, no. 14, from 1887): "*Values and their alteration* stand in relation to the *growth in power of the one that sets values.*"

With this it becomes clear: values are the conditions, posited by the will to power itself, of the will to power itself. It is not until the will to power comes to light as the fundamental trait of all that is real, i.e., only when it becomes true and is accordingly conceived as the reality of all that is real, that we see where values originate from and by what means all value-estimation is supported and directed. The principle of dispensing values has now been discerned. The dispensation of values can be accomplished in the future "in principle," i.e., on the basis of being as the ground of beings.

This is why the will to power, as this principle that has been discerned and therefore willed, is at the same time the principle of a new dispensation of value – new because it is now achieved for the first time knowingly, in the knowledge of its principle. The dispensation of value is new because it itself makes its principle secure and at the same time holds fast to this securement as a value established on the basis of its principle. As the principle of the new dispensation of value, however, the will to power is also (in relation to the former values) the principle of the revaluation of all former values. Yet because the hitherto highest values ruled the sensory from the height of the supersensory, and because metaphysics is what structured that rule, to establish the new principle of the revaluation of all values is to bring about the reversal of all metaphysics. Nietzsche takes this reversal as the overcoming of metaphysics.[a] However, every reversal of this kind will only be a self-blinding entanglement in what is the same though become unrecognizable.

However, so long as Nietzsche grasps nihilism as the intrinsic law operating in the history of the devaluation of the hitherto highest values, but takes devaluation in the sense of the revaluation of all values, nihilism in his interpretation derives from the rule and breakdown of values and so from the possibility in general to posit values. This possibility is itself based on the will to power. This is why Nietzsche's concept of nihilism and his statement "God is dead" can only be adequately understood on the basis of the essence of the will to power. Let us therefore take the last step in shedding light on that remark by explaining what Nietzsche is thinking with the title he coined, "The Will to Power."

The name "The Will to Power" is taken to be so obvious that it is incomprehensible why someone would still take pains to explain this word

[a] First edition, 1950: i.e., for Nietzsche: of Platonism.

combination in particular. What "will" means, after all, anyone can know by experience at any time. To will is to strive after something. The meaning of power, as everyone knows today from daily experience, is the exercise of mastery and force. Clearly, then, the will "to" power is the striving to come to power.

The title "The Will to Power," according to this view, presupposes two different elements that were subsequently put together to form a relationship: willing on one side and power on the other. When we finally come to ask about the ground of the will to power, not just to rephrase it but also to clarify it, what emerges is the sense that because it is a striving for something that is not yet a possession, it originates from a feeling of lack. Striving, the exercise of mastery, and the feeling of lack are states (mental faculties) and representational modes that we grasp through psychological knowledge. For this reason, an explanation of the essence of the will to power belongs to psychology.

What we have just set forth about the will to power and the possibility of knowing it is indeed clear, but in every respect such thinking misses what Nietzsche thinks with the phrase "will to power" and how he thinks it. The title "Will to Power" provides a fundamental word of Nietzsche's ultimate philosophy, which can therefore be fairly described as the metaphysics of the will to power. What the will to power means in Nietzsche's sense, we will never understand by means of popular ideas about will and power, but rather only by way of a reflection on metaphysical thinking, and that means also reflecting on the entirety of the history of Western metaphysics.

The following commentary on the essence of the will to power thinks in terms of these contexts. Although adhering to Nietzsche's own explanations, it must also put them more clearly than Nietzsche himself could say directly. Yet what has become clearer to us is only what has already grown more meaningful to us. Something is meaningful if in its essence it grows closer to us. What has preceded and what follows, throughout, is thought from out of the essence of metaphysics, not only from one of its phases.

It is in the second part of *Thus Spoke Zarathustra* (written during 1883, the year after *La Gaya Scienza* was published) that Nietzsche first places the "will to power" in the context in which it must be understood: "Where I found the living, there I found the will to power; and even in the will of the one who serves I found the will to be master."

To will is to will to be master. Will thus understood is found even in the will of him who serves. Not, it is true, in the sense that a servant might strive to emerge from the role of vassal to become a master himself. Rather, the vassal as vassal, the servant as servant, always has the will to have something else under him, over which he has command in the course of his service and whose service he makes use of. Therefore, as a vassal he is still a master. Even to be a vassal is to want to be master.

The will is not a desire and not a simple striving for something; rather, will is in itself command (cf. *Thus Spoke Zarathustra*, parts I and II; in addition, *The Will to Power*, no. 668, from 1888). Command has its essence in that fact that the commanding master is conscious that he has at his disposal the possibilities of effective action. What is commanded in the command is the realization of this disposal. In the command, the one giving the command (and not just the one carrying it out) is obedient to this disposal and to the condition of having at his disposal: this is how he obeys himself. In this way, by continuing to risk himself, the one giving the command is superior to himself. To command, which is to be carefully distinguished from merely ordering others about, is to overcome oneself and is more difficult than obeying. Will is gathering oneself together for the task at hand. Only he who cannot obey himself must continue to be specifically subject to command. Will strives for what it wills not just as for something that it does not yet have. Will already has what it wills. For will wills its willing. Its will is what it has willed. Will wills itself. It exceeds itself. In this way will as will wills above and beyond itself, and therefore at the same time it must bring itself beneath and behind itself. This is why Nietzsche can say (*The Will to Power*, no. 675, from 1887/8): "*To will* at all amounts to the will to become *stronger*, the will to grow. . ." Here "stronger" indicates "more power," and that means: only power. For the essence of power is to be master over the level of power attained at a particular time. Power is power only when and only for as long as it is an increase in power and commands for itself "more power." To halt the increase of power only for a moment, merely to stand still at one level of power, is already the beginning of a decline in power. Part of the essence of power is the overpowering of itself. This overpowering belongs to and springs from power itself, since power is command and as command it empowers itself to overpower the level of power it has at any time. So power is indeed constantly on the way to power itself, but not as a will available for itself somewhere, not as a will which is trying (in the sense of striving) to come to power. Nor does power empower itself to overpower its level of power merely for the sake of the next level, but rather for this one reason alone: in order to seize hold [*bemächtigen*] of itself in the absolute character of its essence. To will, according to this definition of its essence, is much less a striving than striving is the residual or incipient form of will.

In the expression "Will to Power" the word "power" gives the essence of the mode in which will wills itself to the extent that it is command. As command, will joins itself to itself, i.e., to what it has willed. This self-gathering is the empowering of power. Will exists for itself no more than power for itself. Will and power, therefore, are not subsequently linked by the will to power; rather, will, as the will to will, exists as the will to power in the sense of the empowerment of power. Power, however, has its essence in the fact that it stands in relation to will as the will that is inside the will. The will to power is the essence of power. It indicates the absolute essence of will which wills itself as sheer will.

Hence the will to power cannot be dropped in favor of a will to something else, e.g., the "will to nothing"; for this will too is still the will to will – that is what enables Nietzsche to say (*On the Genealogy of Morals*, Third Treatise, § 1, from 1887): "it [the will] will will *nothing* rather than *not* will."

To "will nothing" in no way means to will the sheer absence of all reality, but rather precisely to will reality but to will it as a nullity everywhere and at every time and only in this way to will annihilation. In such willing, power is still securing for itself the possibility of command and the ability to be master.

As the essence of will, the essence of the will to power is the fundamental trait of all reality. Nietzsche writes (*The Will to Power*, no. 693, from 1888): The will to power is "the inmost essence of being." Here "being" is used in accordance with the language of metaphysics: beings in general. As the fundamental character of beings, therefore, the essence of the will to power and the will to power itself are not to be ascertained through psychological observation; rather, it is the other way round: psychology itself gets its essence, i.e., the ability to set and to recognize its object, only through the will to power. Hence Nietzsche does not understand the will to power psychologically, but rather the opposite: he gives psychology a new definition as the "morphology and *doctrine of the development of the will to power*" (*Beyond Good and Evil*, § 23). Morphology is the ontology of the ὄν, whose μορφή (which too was changed when εἶδος was changed into *perceptio*) appears as the will to power in the *appetitus* of the *perceptio*. Since antiquity, metaphysics has thought beings as ὑποκείμενον, *subiectum*, in regard to being; that metaphysics has turned into psychology as defined by Nietzsche attests (though only as a derivative phenomenon) to the essential event which consists in a change of the beingness of beings. The οὐσία (beingness) of the *subiectum* becomes the subjectity of self-consciousness,[3] which now brings its essence to light as the will to will. As the will to power, will is the command to more-power. In order for will, in the overpowering of itself, to be able to overcome the level it has reached at a given time, this level must already have been attained, secured, and retained. To secure a given level of power is the condition necessary for intensifying power. However, this necessary condition is not sufficient to ensure that the will is able to will itself, i.e., that a will to be stronger *is*, that an increase of power *is*. Will must look into the field of sight, must first open this field, in order that the possibilities from there (possibilities that indicate the way for an increase in power) show themselves in the first place. Will must set such a condition of willing-above-and-beyond-itself. Above all, the will to power must set: conditions for the preservation and increase of power. Part of willing is the setting of these conditions which belong together intrinsically.

Will, in general, amounts to the will to become *stronger*, the will to grow – and also to will "the *means to that end*" (*The Will to Power*, no. 675, from 1887/88).

The essential means are the conditions of the will to power itself that are posited by the will to power itself. Nietzsche calls these conditions "values." He writes (*Werke*, vol. XIII, "Nachgelassene Werke," § 395, from 1885): "In all will is an *esteeming estimation*." To esteem means: to constitute and ascertain value. The will to power esteems in that it constitutes the condition of increase and fixes the condition of preservation. In accordance with its essence, the will to power is the will that posits values. Values are the conditions of preservation-increase within the being of beings. The will to power, as soon as it comes to light specifically in its pure essence, is itself the ground and realm for the dispensation of value. The will to power has its ground not in a feeling of lack; rather, it is itself the ground of the most abundant [*überreichsten*] life. Life means here the will to will. "'*Living*': that already means 'to esteem'" (loc. cit.).

Since will is the overpowering of itself, no richness [*Reichtum*] of life will satisfy it. It has its power in overreaching [*im Überreichen*] – namely, in reaching over its own will. Thus it, as the same, is constantly coming back unto itself as the Same. The mode in which beings (whose *essentia* is the will to power) in their entirety exist, their *existentia*, is the "eternal return of the same." The two fundamental terms of Nietzsche's metaphysics, "will to power" and "eternal return of the same," determine beings in their being in accordance with the perspectives which have guided metaphysics since antiquity, the *ens qua ens* in the sense of *essentia* and *existentia*.

The essential relation between the "will to power" and the "eternal return of the same" must be thought in this way; however, we cannot yet represent it here directly because metaphysics has neither considered nor even inquired about the origin of the distinction between *essentia* and *existentia*.

If metaphysics thinks beings in their being as the will to power, then it necessarily thinks them as setting values. It thinks everything in the horizon of values, the validity of values, devaluation, and revaluation. The metaphysics of modernity begins with and has its essence in the fact that modern metaphysics seeks the absolutely undoubtable, what is certain, certainty. According to Descartes' words[4] *firmum et mansurum quid stabilire*, it is essential to bring something firm and lasting to a stand [*zum Stehen*]. As object [*Gegenstand*], this standing [*das Ständige*] satisfies the essence of beings that has prevailed since antiquity: beings are that which are enduringly [*beständige*] present, which are everywhere already available (ὑποκείμενον, *subiectum*). Descartes, too, like Aristotle, inquires into the ὑποκείμενον. Descartes seeks this *subiectum* in the course laid down for metaphysics, and as a result he (thinking truth as certainty) discovers the *ego cogito* as what is constantly [*ständig*] present. So the ego becomes the *subiectum*, i.e., the subject becomes self-consciousness. The subjectity of the subject is determined out of the certainty of this consciousness.

By positing its own preservation, i.e., the securing of its own continued existence, as a necessary value, the will to power simultaneously justifies the necessity of such securing in all beings which, representing in an essential way, therefore also hold things to be true. Securing by holding to be true is called certainty. In Nietzsche's judgment, it is only in the will to power that certainty is truly grounded as the principle of modern metaphysics, assuming of course that truth is a necessary value and that certainty is the modern form of truth. This makes clear the extent to which, in Nietzsche's doctrine of the will to power as the "essence" of all reality, the modern metaphysics of subjectity is completed.

This is the reason Nietzsche writes: "The question of value is *more fundamental* than the question of certainty: the latter becomes serious only under the assumption that the question of value has already been settled" (*The Will to Power*, no. 588, from 1887/88).

However, once the will to power has been recognized as the principle of the dispensation of value, inquiry into value must at once reflect on the identity of the highest value that necessarily follows from this principle and accords with it. In that the essence of value manifests itself as the condition of preservation-increase posited in the will to power, a perspective has been opened for characterizing the normative structure of value.

To preserve the levels of power which the will has attained at particular times requires that the will surround itself with that which it can reliably and at any time fall back on and from which its security is to be guaranteed. These surroundings enclose the enduring existence [*Bestand*], at the immediate disposal of the will, of that which presences (οὐσία in the ordinary meaning of this word among the Greeks). This enduringness [*Beständige*] is however turned into a permanence [*Ständige*], i.e., into that which is [*steht*] constantly [*stets*] at one's disposal, only by its being brought to stand [*Stand*] by having set it in place. This placing [*Stellen*] has the nature of a production [*Herstellens*] that re-presents [*vor-stellenden*]. That which continues to endure [*Beständige*] in such a mode is that which remains. True to the essence of being (being = lasting presence) that has prevailed in the history of metaphysics, Nietzsche gives to these enduring things [*Beständige*] the name "beings." Often he gives them the name "being," again true to the manner of speaking used by metaphysical thinking. Since the beginning of Western thinking, beings have been considered as the true and as truth, while in the meantime the sense of "beings" and "true" have transformed themselves in many ways. When Nietzsche gives just the simple name "being" or "beings" or "truth" to what is fixed in the will to power for the preservation of that will, he remains in the unbroken line of the traditions of metaphysics, despite all its reversals and revaluations. Accordingly, truth is a condition set in the essence of the will to power, namely, the condition of the preservation of power. Truth, as this condition, is a value. However, because the will can will only on the basis of having something enduring at its disposal, truth is the value necessary for the will to power and originating from the essence of the will to power. The name of "truth" signifies now neither the unconcealment of beings nor the agreement of knowledge and object of knowledge, nor certainty as the delivering and securing [*Zu- und Sicherstellen*] of what has been represented [*Vorgestellten*]. Truth – to be precise, truth that has its essential-historical origin in the modes of its essence indicated above – is now that securing which makes durables endure [*die beständigende Bestandsicherung*] and which secures the surroundings out of which the will to power itself wills.

For securing the level of power attained at a given time, truth is the necessary value. But it is not enough to attain a level of power; for what is enduring, taken in itself, is powerless to give what the will needs before all else in order to go above and beyond itself, i.e., what it must have in order to go into the possibilities of command. These possibilities are given only by a penetrating preview that is of the essence of the will to power; for as the will to more-power, the will to power is in itself perspectival toward possibilities. Making such possibilities open and available constitutes the condition, characterized as follows, for the essence of the will to power: that as the condition which is antecedent in the literal sense of going before, it exceeds the condition originally mentioned. That is why Nietzsche writes (*The Will to Power*, no. 853, from 1887/88): "But truth is not to be taken as the highest value, and even less as the highest power."

The creation of the possibilities for the will, possibilities which enable the will to power to free itself for itself in the first place, is for Nietzsche the essence of art. In accordance with the metaphysical concept of art, Nietzsche does not, under the rubric "art," think exclusively or even primarily of the aesthetic realm of artists. Art is the essence of the willing that opens perspectives and takes possession of them. "The artwork, where it appears *without* an artist, e.g., as body, as organization (Prussian officer corps, Jesuit order). To what extent the artist is only a preliminary stage. The world as an artwork that gives birth to itself" (*The Will to Power*, no. 851, from 1888).

The essence of art, grasped on the basis of the will to power, is the fact that art excites the will to power toward the will in the first place and spurs it to willing above and beyond itself. Because Nietzsche, in a faded echo of the ζωή and φύσις of the early Greek thinkers, often refers to the "will to power" (understood as the reality of what is real) as "life," he is able to say that art is "the great stimulant of life" (*The Will to Power*, no. 851, from 1888).

Art is the condition, set in the essence of the will to power, that enables the will, as the will that it is, to climb to power and to heighten power. Because it sets such a condition, art is a value. As that condition which takes precedence in the hierarchy of the conditions for securing durables and which therefore precedes all conditions, art is the value which first opens all the heights to be climbed. Art is the highest value. In comparison with the value of truth, it is the higher value. One summons the other, each in its different way. Both values determine in their value-relationship the unitary essence of this will to power that intrinsically sets values. This will is the reality of what is real, or, taking the word further than Nietzsche usually cares to employ it: it is the being of beings. If metaphysics is obliged to speak beings in respect to being and thereby and in accordance with its nature to specify the ground of beings, then the ground-thesis of the metaphysics of the will to power must state that ground. The thesis declares which values are set essentially and in which hierarchy of values they are posited within the essence [*Wesen*] of the value-setting will to power as the "essentia [*Essenz*]" of beings. The thesis runs: "Art is *worth more* than truth" (*The Will to Power*, no. 853, from 1887/88).

The ground-thesis of the metaphysics of the will to power is a thesis of value.

From the highest thesis of value it becomes clear that the setting of value as such is essentially twofold. In the dispensation of value there is set, whether explicitly or not, one necessary and one sufficient value; both, however, are set on the basis of the prevailing relationship of the two toward each other. This doubleness of the dispensation of value corresponds to its principle. The will to power is where the dispensation of value as such is sustained and directed from. Out of the unity of its essence, it both desires [*verlangt*] and suffices for [*langt*] the conditions for its own increase and preservation. A look at the twofold essence of the dispensation of value brings thinking expressly before the question about the essential unity of the will to power. Since the will to power is the "essentia" of beings as such, and since saying this is the metaphysically true, we will be asking about the truth of the true whenever we think about the essential unity of the will to power. With this question we arrive [*gelangen*] at the highest point of this and every metaphysics. Yet what do we mean here by the highest point? Let us explain what is meant in connection with the essence of the will to power in order to remain within the bounds set for the current examination.

The essential unity of the will to power can be nothing but this will itself. Its unity is the mode by which the will to power as will brings itself before itself. The unity places the will itself into the will's own examination. Moreover, it places the will before itself in such a way that it is not until the will is subject to this examination that it purely represents itself and therefore represents [*repräsentiert*] itself in its highest form. Here, however, representation [*Repräsentation*] is in no way a supplement to presentation [*Darstellung*]; rather, the presence [*Präsenz*] that is determined on the basis of representation is the mode in which and as which the will to power *is*.

Yet this mode, in which the will to power is, is at the same time the manner in which it places itself into the unconcealment of itself. Its truth lies in this unconcealment. The question about the essential unity of the will to power is the question about the nature of this truth in which the will is as the being of beings. At the same time, however, this truth is the truth of beings as such; metaphysics is as this truth. Accordingly, the truth now in question is not the truth which the will to power sets as the necessary condition of beings as particular beings, but rather the truth in which the condition-setting will to power essences as such a will. This oneness in which it essences, its essential unity, concerns the will to power itself.

Of what nature is this truth of the being of beings? It can be determined only from that of which it is the truth. But within modern metaphysics the being of beings has been determined as will and thereby as self-willing; however, self-willing is intrinsically already self-knowing-itself; therefore, beings, the ὑποκείμενον, the *subiectum*, are essentially in the mode of self-knowing-itself. Beings (*subiectum*) present [*präsentiert*] themselves, in fact they present themselves to themselves, in the mode of the *ego cogito*. This self-presenting, the re-presenting [*Re-präsentation*] (representation [*Vor-stellung*]), is the being of beings qua *subiectum*. Self-knowing-itself becomes the quintessential subject. In self-knowing-itself all knowledge and all that knowledge can know is gathered. It is a gathering of knowledge, like the mountain range [*Gebirge*] is a gathering of mountains [*Berge*]. The subjectivity of the subject, as a gathering of this sort, is the *co-agitatio* (*cogitatio*), the *conscientia*, *Ge-wissen*, *conscience*.[5] The *co-agitatio*, however, is *intrinsically* already *velle*, to will. With the subjectity of the subject, will comes to light as the essence of that subjectity. Modern metaphysics, as the metaphysics of subjectivity, thinks the being of beings in the sense of will.

As the primary determination of its essence, subjectity requires that the representing subject assures itself of itself, which means that it also constantly assures itself of what it has represented as a particular something. In keeping with that assurance, the truth of beings as certainty [*Gewissheit*] has the character of security [*Sicherheit*] (*certitudo*). Self-knowing-itself (the place of certainty as such) is for its part a variant of the former essence of truth, namely the correctness (*rectitudo*) of representation. However, what is correct now no longer consists of an adequation to what presences unthought in its presence. Correctness now consists in adjusting all that is to be represented to the standard that is set in the knowledge-claim of the *res cogitans sive mens*. This claim appeals to the security that consists in the fact that representation and everything to be represented are driven together and gathered into the clarity and distinctness of the mathematical *idea*. The *ens* is the *ens co-agitatum perceptionis*. Representation, now, is correct if it does justice to this claim to security. Demonstrated as correct [*richtig*] in this way, representation, as made right [*recht gefertigt*] and at our disposal, is justified [*gerecht-fertigt*]. As security (*certitudo*), the truth of beings in the sense of the self-certainty of subjectity is fundamentally the justification [*Recht-fertigen*] of representation and what it represents before the brightness proper to representation. Justification [*iustificatio*] is the achievement of *iustitia* and is therefore justice [*Gerechtigkeit*] itself. By being always a subject, the subject makes itself certain of its securing. It justifies itself before the claim to justice that it has itself set.

At the beginning of modernity, the question dawned anew how man amidst the entirety of beings, which means before the beingmost ground of all beings (God), can become and be certain of his own continuing duration, i.e., of his own salvation. This question of the certainty of salvation is the question of justification, i.e., of justice (*iustitia*).

Within modern metaphysics, it is Leibniz who first thinks the *subiectum* as the *ens percipiens et appetens*. It is Leibniz, thinking on the *vis* which characterizes the *ens*, who for the first time clearly thinks the willing essence of the being of beings. In his twenty-four theses about metaphysics, Leibniz writes (Thesis 20): *iustitia nihil aliud est quam ordo seu perfectio circa mentes*. The *mentes*, i.e., the *res cogitantes*, are (Thesis 22) the *primariae Mundi unitates*.[6] Truth as certainty is the securing of security, is order (*ordo*) and a universal ascertainment [*Fest-stellung*], i.e., a thorough and complete making [*Durch- und Ver-fertigung*] (*per-fectio*). Making secure characterizes the primary and actual beings in their being; this character is *iustitia* (justice).

In his critical groundwork of metaphysics, Kant thinks the final self-securing of transcendental subjectivity as the *quaestio iuris* of transcendental deduction. This is the legal question [*Rechtsfrage*] of the justification [*Rechtfertigung*] of and by the representing subject, which has fixed for itself its essence in the self-rightedness of its "I think."

In the essence of truth as certainty (certainty thought as the truth of subjectity and subjectity as the being of beings), justice is hidden, experienced on the basis of the justification by security. Although this justice prevails as the essence of the truth of subjectity, it is not, however, thought within the metaphysics of subjectity as the truth of beings. And yet justice must come into the thinking of modern metaphysics as the being of beings that knows itself, just as soon as the being of beings appears as the will to power. The will to power knows itself as that which essentially sets values, that which secures itself in the positing of values, and that which thereby constantly does justice to itself and in such doing is justice. It is in and as this justice that the proper essence of the will to power must represent, which means, thought in the terms of modern metaphysics: must be. In Nietzsche's metaphysics, the thought of value is more fundamental than the fundamental thought of certainty in Descartes' metaphysics, since certainty can only count as right if it also counts as the highest value. Similarly, in the age that has witnessed the completion of Western metaphysics in Nietzsche, the lucid self-certainty of subjectity has proved to be the justification by the will to power in accordance with the justice that prevails in the being of beings.

Nietzsche, in an early and more widely known piece (the second untimely observation, "On the Use and Disadvantage of History for Life"), already replaced the objectivity of historical knowledge with "justice" (section 6). But otherwise he was silent on the topic. Not until the decisive years 1884–85, when the "will to power" stood before his thoughtful eye as the fundamental trait of beings, did he write down two thoughts about "justice," without publishing them.

The first note (1884) is entitled "The Ways of Freedom." It runs: "*Justice* as the manner of thinking which builds, eliminates, annihilates out of value-estimation; *the highest representative of life itself*" (*Werke*, vol. XIII, "Nachgelassene Werke," § 98).

The second note (1885) states: "*Justice*, as the function of a power that sees far and wide, that sees past the narrow perspectives of good and evil, therefore has a wider horizon of *interest*: the intention to preserve something that is *more* than this or that person" (*Werke*, vol. XIII, "Nachgelassene Werke," § 158).

A meticulous explication of these thoughts would exceed the bounds of the reflection attempted here. Here let it suffice to point to the essential area where justice, as thought by Nietzsche, belongs. To prepare to understand the justice that Nietzsche has in mind, we must exclude all the ideas about justice that come from Christian, humanist, Enlightenment, bourgeois, and socialist morality. For Nietzsche does not at all understand morality as something determined in the first place within the ethical and juridical realms. Rather, he thinks morality on the basis of the being of beings in their entirety, i.e., on the basis of the will to power. What is just [*das Gerechte*] is in accordance with what is *right* [*dem Rechten*]. However, what is right is determined on the basis of that which is in being as a being. That is why Nietzsche says (*Werke*, vol. XIII, "Nachgelassene Werke," § 462, from 1883): "Right = the will to make a momentary power relation obtain eternally. To be satisfied with that power relation is the pre-condition. Everything venerable is called in to let what is right appear to be eternal."

Parallel to this is a note from the following year: "The problem of *justice*. The first and most powerful thing is precisely the will and strength to overpower. The ruler establishes "justice" only afterward, which means, he measures things in accordance with his own measure. If he is *very powerful*, he can go very far in recognizing and letting alone the individual *who is trying* (*Werke*, vol. XIII, "Nachgelassene Werke," § 181). Although it may well be expected that Nietzsche's metaphysical concept of justice will still disconcert conventional ideas, he nonetheless hits on the essence of the justice which was already historically true at the beginning of the completion of the modern age, in the struggle for mastery over the earth, and which therefore determines all human transactions in this age, explicitly or not, hiddenly or openly.

Justice thought by Nietzsche is the truth of the beings that are in the mode of the will to power. However, even Nietzsche failed to think justice explicitly as the essence of the truth of beings; nor, out of such thought, did he bring up the metaphysics of completed subjectity. Justice, however, is the truth of beings that is determined by being itself. As this truth, justice is metaphysics itself in its modern completion. In metaphysics itself is hidden the reason why Nietzsche is indeed able to experience nihilism metaphysically but nonetheless is not able to think the essence of nihilism.

We do not know what hidden form, enjoined out of the essence of justice as the truth of justice, has been obtaining for the metaphysics of the will to power. The first ground-thesis of this metaphysics has scarcely been expressed and not even in the form of a thesis. Certainly, within this metaphysics the thesis-character of this thesis is *sui generis*. Certainly, the first thesis of value is not the major premise in a deductive system of theses. Even if we understand the rubric "ground-thesis of metaphysics" in the conservative sense that it identifies the essential ground of beings as such, i.e., it identifies them in the unity of their essence, it is still sufficiently broad and complex to determine, in accordance with the nature of a given metaphysics, the mode in which that metaphysics speaks of this ground.

Nietzsche expressed the first value-thesis of the metaphysics of the will to power in yet another form (*The Will to Power*, no. 822, from 1888): "We possess *art* so that we do *not perish of the truth*."

This thesis about the metaphysical relation in essence (which means here the metaphysical relation in value) between art and truth is admittedly not something to be grasped according to our ordinary ideas about truth and art. If this happens, everything becomes banal and we lose – and this is now very dire – the possibility of seeking an essential confrontation with the hidden position of modern metaphysics that is bringing itself to completion, a confrontation that would free us from the obfuscation of histories and world views.

In the formula just given for the ground-thesis of the metaphysics of the will to power, art and truth are thought as the fundamental structures of mastery for the will to power in relation to man. How the essential relation of the truth of beings as such to the man's essence is in fact to be thought within metaphysics and in accordance with the essence of metaphysics still remains hidden from our thinking. The question is hardly asked, and because of the predominance of philosophical anthropology, it is utterly confused. In any case, however, it would be a mistake should someone take this formula of a value-thesis as evidence that Nietzsche philosophized "existentially." That he never did. But he did think metaphysically. We are not yet ready for the rigor of a thought like the following, which Nietzsche wrote around the time he was thinking about the masterpiece he had planned, *The Will to Power*:

> Around the hero, everything becomes a tragedy; around the demi-god, everything turns into a satyr play; and around God, everything becomes – what? maybe the "world" –
>
> (*Beyond Good and Evil*, § 150 [1886])

Though it is bound to show a different face if taken from the point of view of histories and rubrics, Nietzsche's thinking, as we must now learn to realize, is no less rigorously substantial than the thinking of Aristotle, who in the fourth book of the *Metaphysics* thinks the principle of contradiction as the first truth about the being of beings. It has become the customary practice (though not less problematic for being customary) to juxtapose Nietzsche and Kierkegaard, but this juxtaposition fails to recognize the essence of Nietzsche's thinking; it therefore fails to see that Nietzsche as a metaphysical thinker preserves a proximity to Aristotle. Although he cites Aristotle more often, Kierkegaard is essentially distant from him. For Kierkegaard is not a thinker but a religious writer, and not just one religious writer among others but the only one who accords with the destiny of his age. His greatness lies in this fact – unless talking in this way is already a misunderstanding.

In the ground-thesis of Nietzsche's metaphysics, the essential unity of the will to power is identified along with the essential relation of the values art and truth. It is from this essential unity of beings as such that the metaphysical essence of value is determined. Value is the twofold condition of the will to power itself, a condition set in the will to power for the will to power.

Because Nietzsche experiences the being of beings as the will to power, his thinking must think outward to values. That is why it is essential to pose the question of value everywhere and before anything else. This question is experienced as a historical question.

What is happening with the hitherto highest values? What is the significance of the devaluation of these values in regard to the revaluation of all values? Because thinking in terms of values is grounded in the metaphysics of the will to power, Nietzsche's interpretation of nihilism, as the process of devaluing the highest values and revaluing all values, is a metaphysical interpretation; it is metaphysical, in fact, in the sense of the metaphysics of the will to power. However, in that Nietzsche grasps his own thinking (the doctrine of the will to power as the "principle of the new dispensation of value") in the sense of the actual completion of nihilism, he no longer understands nihilism only negatively as the devaluation of the highest values, but rather also positively, as the overcoming of nihilism; for the reality of what is real as that reality is now explicitly experienced, the will to power, has become the origin and measure of a new dispensation of values. The values of this dispensation of values directly determine human representation and likewise fuel human transactions. Being human is raised into a different dimension of occurring.

In the excerpt we read, § 125 from *La Gaya Scienza*, the madman has this to say about the action by men through which God was killed, i.e., through which the supersensory world was devalued: "There has never been a greater deed – and any who will be born after us will partake, for this deed's sake, of a history higher than all history in time past!"

With the consciousness that "God is dead" a consciousness begins to form of a radical revaluation of the hitherto highest values. After such consciousness, man himself moves into another history that is higher because in it the principle of all dispensation of value, the will to power, is specifically experienced and undertaken *as* the reality of what is real, as the being of beings. Self-consciousness, in which modern humanity has its essence, thereby takes the final step. It wills itself as the enforcer of the absolute will to power. The decline of normative values is at an end. Nihilism – "that the highest values devalue themselves" – is overcome. The humanity that wills its own being-human as the will to power and finds this being-human to be at home in the reality determined in its entirety by the will to power is determined by a form of human essence that goes beyond erstwhile man.

The name for this form of humanity's essence that goes beyond the previous race is "the overman." By that term Nietzsche does not understand some isolated human specimen in whom the capacities and intentions of the men we see every day have been gigantically magnified and intensified. Nor is "the overman" the sort of man who only comes into being by way of applying Nietzsche's philosophy to life. The name "overman" refers to the essence of the humanity that, as modern humanity, begins to enter into the completion of the essence of its age. "The overman" is the man which man *is* on the basis of the reality determined by the will to power and for this reality.

The man whose essence is the essence that is willing and willed out of the will to power is the overman. The willing of the essence that is willing and willed in this way must correspond to the will to power as the being of beings. Along with the thinking that thinks the will to power, therefore, the question necessarily arises: in what shape must the human essence, willed and willing out of the being of beings, place itself and develop so that it will satisfy the will to power and thus be able to undertake mastery over beings? Unexpectedly [*unversehens*] and above all unprepared [*unversehen*], man finds himself placed, on the basis of the being of beings, before the task of undertaking mastery of the earth. Did erstwhile man sufficiently consider in what mode the being of beings appears in the meantime? Did erstwhile man make certain of whether his essence has the maturity and strength to redeem the claim of this being? Or has erstwhile man been helped along only with makeshifts and by detours that have continually driven him away from experiencing that which is? Erstwhile man would like to remain erstwhile man; at the same time, he is already the being that is willed and willing among beings, the being of which beings is beginning to appear as the will to power. Erstwhile man in his essence is not yet prepared at all for the being that meanwhile prevails over beings. In it prevails the necessity that man go beyond erstwhile man, not from mere desire and not merely arbitrarily, but solely for being's sake.

Nietzsche's thought that thinks the overman originates from a thinking that thinks being ontologically as beings and so submits to the essence of metaphysics without, however, being able to experience this essence within metaphysics. That is why, for Nietzsche just as in all metaphysics before him, it remains hidden in what way the essence of man is determined on the basis of the essence of being. That is why, in Nietzsche's metaphysics, the ground of the essential connection between the will to power and the overman is necessarily obscured. Yet in every obscuration an appearing is already prevailing at the same time. The *existentia* that is part of the *essentia* of beings, i.e., of the will to power, is the eternal return of the same. Being, thought in that return, contains the relation to the essence of the overman. However, this relation necessarily remains unthought in its essence that is related to being [*seinsmäßigen*]. That is why, even for Nietzsche himself, the connection is obscure between the thinking that thinks the overman in the shape of Zarathustra and the essence of metaphysics. That is why the character of the work *Thus Spoke Zarathustra* as a work remains hidden. Only when future thinking has been brought into a position to think this *Book for Everyone and No One* along with Schelling's *Philosophical Inquiries into the Nature of Human Freedom* (1809), which means along with Hegel's work *The Phenomenology of Spirit* (1807) too, and also along with the *Monadology* (1714) of Leibniz; and only when this future thinking has been brought to think them not only metaphysically, but also on the basis of the essence of metaphysics; only then are the right and duty to confront this work, as well as the ground and horizon for a confrontation, established.

It is easy but irresponsible to be outraged by the idea and the figure of the overman, which was designed to be misunderstood; it is easy but irresponsible to pretend that one's outrage is a refutation. It is difficult but for future thinking unavoidable to attain the high responsibility out of which Nietzsche reflected on the essence of that humanity destined (in the destiny of being as the will to power) to undertake mastery over the earth. The essence of the overman is not a warrant for a fit of capricious frenzy. It is the law, grounded in being itself, of a long chain of the highest self-overcomings, which alone will make man ripe for beings which as beings are part of being. This being as the will to power brings to light its essence as the will to power and through this disclosure is epoch making, that is, it makes the last epoch of metaphysics.

According to Nietzsche's metaphysics, erstwhile man is called erstwhile because although his essence is determined by the will to power as the fundamental trait of all beings, he nonetheless has not experienced and taken over the will to power as this fundamental trait. The man moving beyond erstwhile man receives the will to power (as the fundamental trait of all beings) into his own willing and thus wills himself in the sense of the will to power. All beings *are* as beings set in this will. What, in the mode of goal and norm, used to condition and determine man's essence has forfeited its unconditional and immediate – and above all its ubiquitously infallibly effective [*wirksame*] – power to effect [*Wirkungsmacht*]. No longer does that supersensory world of goals and norms inspire and sustain life. That world has itself grown lifeless: dead. The Christian faith will still exist here and there. However, the love that prevails in such a world is not the effecting-effective [*wirkend-wirksame*] principle of that which is taking place now. Thought as the effective reality [*wirksame Wirklichkeit*] of everything real [*Wirklichen*], the supersensory ground of the supersensory world has grown unreal [*unwirklich*]. This is the metaphysical sense of the metaphysically thought word "God is dead."

Are we going to continue to close our eyes before the truth of this word that is to be thought in this way? Even if this is our intention, Nietzsche's word will not lose its truth through this unaccountable blindness. God ceases to be a living God if in our continuing attempts to master the real we fail to take his reality seriously beforehand and question it, if we fail to reflect whether man has so matured toward the essence into which he is forced from out of being that he withstands this destiny that sends him out of his essence, and does so without the false relief of mere expedients.

The attempt to experience the truth of that statement of God's death without illusions is something different from a confession of faith in Nietzsche's philosophy. Had that been our intention, then thinking would not be served by such assent. We attend to a thinker only by thinking. This requires that we think everything essential that is thought in his thought.

If God and the gods are dead in the sense of the metaphysical experience described above, and if the will to power is consciously willed as the principle behind every setting of conditions on beings, i.e., as the principle of the dispensation of value, then mastery over beings as such in the shape of mastery over the earth passes over to the new human willing, determined by the will to power. Nietzsche closes the first part of *Thus Spoke Zarathustra* (written in 1883, a year after *La Gaya Scienza*) with the sentence: "*All the gods are dead: it is now our will that the overman live!*"

It is possible, thinking crudely, to believe that Nietzsche's word says that mastery over beings passes from God to man, or, even more crudely, that Nietzsche sets man in the place of God. Those who take it in that way, however, are not thinking very divinely about the essence of the divinity. Man can never be set in God's place because the essence of man never attains the essential realm of God. On the contrary, compared with that impossibility, something far eerier happens, the essence of which we have scarcely begun to reflect upon. The place which, metaphysically thought, is proper to God is the region of causal effectivity and the preservation of beings as created beings. This region for God can remain empty. In its place, another (i.e., a place that corresponds to it metaphysically) can open up that is identical neither to the essential realm of God nor to the essential realm of man, who, however, is again entering into a distinctive relationship with this other place. The overman does not, and not ever, step into the place of God; rather the place for the overman's will is another realm of another grounding of beings in their other being. This other being of beings has meanwhile (and this marks the beginning of modern metaphysics) become subjectity.

All that is is now either what is real [*das Wirkliche*] as an object, or what is effective [*das Wirkende*] as the objectifying within which the objectivity of objects is formed. Objectifying delivers up [*stellt zu*] the object to the *ego cogito* by representing it [*vor-stellend*]. In this delivery, the ego proves itself to be that which lies at the basis of its own activity, its own representing delivery [*vor-stellenden Zu-stellen*]: the *subiectum*. The subject is subject for itself. The essence of consciousness is self-consciousness. All beings, for that reason, are either the object of the subject or the subject of the subject. Everywhere the being of beings is based on posing a self before itself [*Sich-vor-sich-selbst-stellen*] and thus in imposing a self [*Sich-auf-stellen*]. Man rises up within the subjectity of beings into the subjectivity of his essence. Man enters into the uprising. World becomes object. In this insurgent objectification of all beings, that which must previously have been brought into the disposal of representation and production [*Vor- und Her-stellens*] – earth – moves into the center of human setting and confronting. Earth itself can show itself now only as the object of the attack arranged in the willing of man as absolute objectifying. Because it is willed out of the essence of being, nature appears everywhere as the object of technology.

From this period 1881/82, when the "madman" piece was written, comes this note of Nietzsche's: "The time is coming when the battle for the mastery of the earth will be fought – and fought in the name of *fundamental philosophical doctrines*" (*Werke*, vol. XII, "Nachgelassene Werke," § 441).

This is not to say that the battle to exploit the earth without limit as the domain of raw materials, and to employ "human resources" soberly and without illusion in the service of the absolute empowering of the will to power into its essence, explicitly makes use of an appeal to a philosophy. We should suppose the contrary: philosophy as the doctrine and as the structure of culture is disappearing and in its current form can disappear, since it has already (so far as it has been genuine) brought the reality of the real into words and so has already brought beings as such into the history of their being. The "fundamental philosophical doctrines" do not mean academic doctrines but rather the language of the truth of beings as such, a truth that is metaphysics itself in the shape of the metaphysics of the unconditional subjectity of the will to power.

In its historical essence, the battle for the mastery over the earth is in fact the consequence of the fact that beings as such appear in the mode of the will to power, without, however, being recognized or at all understood as this will. At any rate, the concomitant doctrines of action and the ideologies of representation never say what is and therefore happens. With the beginnings of the battle for mastery of the earth, the age of subjectity presses to its completion. Its completion means that beings, which are in the sense of the will to power, are becoming certain [*gewiss*] and therefore also conscious [*bewusst*] of their own truth about themselves, each in its way in every respect. To make something conscious is a necessary instrument of the will that wills out of the will to power. It occurs, as regards the objectifying, in the form of planning. It occurs in the region of man's uprising into self-willing through the continuing analysis of the historical situation. Thought metaphysically, the situation is always the station for the action of the subject. Whether it knows it or not, each analysis of the situation is grounded on the metaphysics of subjectity.

"The great noontide"[7] is the time of the brightest brightness: namely, the consciousness that has become unconditionally and in every respect conscious of itself as that knowledge which consists of knowingly willing the will to power as the being of beings; and, as such will, rebelliously to withstand each necessary phase of the objectification of the world, and in this way to secure the enduring duration [*beständigen Bestand*] of beings for a willing as uniform and regular as possible. In the willing of this will, however, the necessity comes upon man to will along with the conditions of such willing. This means: to set values and esteem everything according to values. In this manner, value determines all beings in their being. Which brings us to the question:

What *is* now, in the age when the unconditional mastery of the will to power is manifestly dawning and when this manifestness and its public character are themselves becoming a function of this will? What is? We are not asking about incidents and facts; in the realm of the will to power, testimonies for any fact or incident are produced or dismissed at any time, as required.

What is? We are not asking about this or that being but about the being of beings. Or rather: we are asking, what is going on with being itself? And we are not asking this idly but in regard to the truth of beings as such, a truth that is articulated verbally in the shape of the metaphysics of the will to power. What is going on with being in the age when mastery begins to be exercised by the unconditional will to power?

Being has become value. To make the duration of durables endure [*Beständigung der Beständigkeit des Bestandes*] is a condition that is set by the will to power itself and that is necessary for securing the will to power.

After all, how can being be more highly esteemed than through its express elevation into value? And yet, by being appreciated as a value, being is deprecated as a mere condition set by the will to power itself. For ages now, through having been esteemed at all and so appreciated, being has been robbed of the worth of its essence. When the being of beings is stamped as value and its essence is thereby sealed, then within this metaphysics (i.e., constantly within the truth of beings as such during this age) every path toward the experience of being itself is obliterated. In this manner of speaking, perhaps we are presuming what we must by no means presume: that such a path toward being ever existed and that a thinking about being has ever thought being as being.

Oblivious of being and of its own truth, Western thinking since its beginning has constantly thought beings as such. During that time, it has thought being only in the kind of truth that verbalizes the name "being" rather awkwardly and also ambiguously, since the multiplicity of its meaning is not known by experience. This thinking that has remained oblivious of being itself is the simple and all-bearing (and for that reason enigmatic and unexperienced) event of Western history, which meanwhile is about to expand itself into world-history. In the end, being has sunk down to a value in metaphysics. This shows that being is not permitted as being. What does that mean?

What is going on with being? With being nothing is going on. And what if it is only in that nothing that the formerly disguised essence of nihilism announces itself? Would thinking in values then be pure nihilism? But yet Nietzsche grasps the metaphysics of the will to power precisely as the overcoming of nihilism. And indeed, the metaphysics of the will to power is an overcoming of nihilism – provided that nihilism is understood only as the devaluation of the highest values and the will to power as the principle of the revaluation of all values on the basis of a new dispensation of values. However, in this overcoming of nihilism, value-thinking is elevated into a principle.

If, however, value does not let being be being,[a] be that which it is as being itself, then what was supposed to be the overcoming is but the completion of nihilism. For metaphysics now not only fails to think being itself, but this failure is veiled under the guise of appearing to think being in the most worthy way, by esteeming it as value, with the result that all questions about being become and remain superfluous. If, however, the thinking that thinks

[a] First edition, 1950. What does "being" mean here?

everything according to values is nihilism when thought in relation to being itself, then even Nietzsche's experience of nihilism as the devaluation of the highest values is still nihilistic. The interpretation of the supersensory world, the interpretation of God as the highest value is not thought on the basis of being itself. The final blow against God and against the supersensory world consists in reducing God, the beingness of beings [*das Seiende des Seienden*], to the highest value. The harshest blow against God is not that God is held to be unknowable, nor that God's existence is proved to be unprovable, but rather that the God who is taken for real is elevated to the highest value. This blow is the harshest precisely because it does not come from unbelievers standing about, but from the faithful and their theologians, who talk of the beingmost of all beings without ever letting it occur to them to think about being itself and thereby become aware that this thinking and that talking, from the perspective of the faith, is absolute blasphemy when it is mixed into the theology of the faith.

Only now has even a faint light come into the darkness of the question that we had wanted to put to Nietzsche when we were listening to the passage about the madman: how can it really happen that men are capable of ever killing God? Obviously, however, this is exactly what Nietzsche thinks. For in the entire passage only two sentences are specifically emphasized by italics. The first reads: "*We killed him*," that is, God. The other: "*and yet they have done it themselves*," that is, men did commit the act of the killing of God, although they had not yet heard anything about it to that day.

The two emphasized sentences give the interpretation for the word "God is dead." It does not mean (as it would if spoken from denial and a low hatred): there is no God. The word means something more dire: God has been killed. It is only in this way that the critical thought comes to light. However, understanding it has become even more difficult. For the word "God is dead" would be far more readily understood if it announced: of his own will God himself removed himself from living presence. But that God is supposed to be killed by others, and by men at that, is unthinkable. Nietzsche himself is surprised by this thought. That is why, immediately after the critical declaration "*We've killed him* – you and I. We are all his murderers!", he has the madman ask: "But how have we done this?" Nietzsche clarifies the question by repeating it in three images: "How were we able to drink the sea dry? Who gave us the sponge to wipe the entire horizon away? What did we do when we unchained this earth from its sun?"

We could offer this answer to the last question: what men did when they unchained the earth from its sun is told by the European history of the last three and a half centuries. But what has happened, in the ground of this history, with beings? When he cites the relationship between earth and sun, Nietzsche is not just thinking of the Copernican revolution in the modern conception of science. The word "sun" will also remind us of Plato's parable. According to the parable, the sun and the realm of its light are the surroundings in which beings appear in accordance with their appearance, in accordance with their visible aspect (in accordance with the ideas). The sun forms and delimits the field of vision in which beings show themselves as beings. The "horizon" means the supersensory world as the one that truly is. This is at the same time the entirety that embraces and includes everything in itself like the sea. The earth as the residence of man is unchained from its sun. The realm of the supersensory which has its being in itself [*an sich seienden*] is no longer the normative light above man. The whole field of vision has been wiped away. The entirety of beings as such, the sea, has been drunk dry by men. For man has risen up into the I-hood of the *ego cogito*. With this uprising all beings become objects. As what is objective, beings are swallowed up into the immanence of subjectivity. The horizon no longer illuminates of itself. It is now only the viewpoint set in the dispensation of value of the will to power.

With the help of these three images, "sun, horizon, sea" (which, for our thinking, are probably something quite other than images), the three questions explain what is meant by the event in which God is killed. This killing means the elimination, through man, of the supersensory world that has its being in itself. This killing identifies the process in which beings as such are not absolutely annihilated, but rather become otherwise in their being. However, in this process, man too, and above all, becomes otherwise. He becomes the one who eliminates beings in the sense of beings in themselves [*des an sich Seienden*]. The human uprising into subjectivity makes beings into objects. However, what is objective is that which, through representation, has been brought to a stand. The elimination of beings in themselves, the killing of God, is accomplished in the securing of duration [*Bestandsicherung*] through which man secures bodily, material, spiritual, and intellectual durables [*Bestände*]; however, these are secured for the sake of man's own security, which wills the mastery over beings (as potentially objective), in order to conform to the being of beings, the will to power.

Securement, as the obtaining of security, is grounding in the dispensation of value. Setting, dispensing, values has killed beneath itself all beings in themselves, thereby doing away with them as beings for themselves. This final blow in the murder of God is struck by metaphysics, which as the metaphysics of the will to power accomplishes thinking in the sense of value-thinking. Yet this final blow, through which being is struck down to a mere value, is no longer recognized by Nietzsche himself for what that blow is when it is thought in relation to being itself. But does not Nietzsche himself say: "We are all his murderers – you and I"? Of course; Nietzsche, accordingly, still conceives even the metaphysics of the will to power as nihilism. To be sure; but for Nietzsche that only means that as the countermovement in the sense of the revaluation of all former values, this metaphysics accomplishes the antecedent "devaluation of the former highest values" most intensely because it does so with finality.

Yet it is precisely this new dispensation of value, based on the principle of all dispensations of value, that Nietzsche must no longer think as a killing and a nihilism. In the field of vision of the will to power that wills itself, i.e., in the perspective of value and the dispensation of value, it is no longer a devaluation.

But what goes on with value-setting itself, when it is thought in regard to beings as such, i.e., at the same time on the basis of the regard to being? Then, to think in values is to kill radically. It not only strikes down beings as such in their being-in-themselves [*An-sich-sein*], but it also puts being entirely aside. Being, when it is still needed, is taken to be value only. The value-thinking of the metaphysics of the will to power is deadly in an extreme sense because it does not permit being itself to come into the dawning, i.e., the vitality, of its essence. To think in accordance with values forestalls being itself from coming to essential presence in its truth.

But is this killing at the roots primarily or exclusively the nature of the metaphysics of the will to power? Is it merely the interpretation of being as value that does not let being itself be the being that it is? If this were the case, then the metaphysics of pre-Nietzschean epochs would have to have experienced and thought being itself in its truth or at least have asked about it. *But nowhere do we find such experience of being itself.* Nowhere do we meet a thinking that thinks the truth of being itself and thereby truth itself as being. This is not thought even where pre-Platonic thinking, as the beginning of Western thinking, prepares for the unfolding of metaphysics by Plato and Aristotle. The ἔστιν (ἐὸν) γὰρ εἶναι[8] does indeed name being itself. But to think of presencing as presencing out of the truth of presencing is precisely what it does not do. The history of being begins – necessarily begins – *with the forgottenness of being.* So it is not the fault of metaphysics as the metaphysics of the will to power that being itself remains unthought in its truth. This strange staying-absent of being is then the sole responsibility of metaphysics as metaphysics. Yet what is metaphysics? Do we know its essence? Is it itself able to know this essence? When it comprehends its essence, it grasps it metaphysically. But the metaphysical concept of metaphysics continually lags behind its essence. The same is true of every logic, assuming that logic is still in fact able to think what λόγος is. Every metaphysics of metaphysics and every logic of philosophy that attempt in whatever way to clamber past metaphysics most certainly fall down beneath it, without coming to know in the process where they have fallen to.

In the meantime, however, at least one trait of the essence of nihilism has become clearer in our thought. The essence of nihilism is rooted in history; accordingly, there is nothing in the appearance of beings as such in their entirety that is going on with being itself and its truth; indeed, as a result, the truth of beings as such is taken as being, since the truth of being stays absent. Nietzsche indeed came to know, in the age in which nihilism was beginning to be completed, some of the traits of nihilism, but at the same time he interpreted them nihilistically, thereby completely burying their essence. Nietzsche never recognized the *essence* of nihilism, like every other metaphysics before him.

However, if the essence of nihilism is rooted in the history that in the appearance of beings as such in their entirety the truth of beings stays absent, and if accordingly there is nothing going on with being itself and the truth of being, then metaphysics, as the history of the truth of beings as such in their essence, is nothing. If in the end metaphysics is the historical ground of the world history that is being determined by the West and by Europe, then it is nihilistic in quite another sense.

Thought in terms of the destiny of being, the *nihil* of nihilism means that there is nothing going on with being. Being does not come to the light of its own essence. In the appearance of beings as such, being itself stays away. The truth of being escapes us. It remains forgotten.

So nihilism then would be in its essence a history that happens with being itself. It would lie then in the essence of being itself that being remains unthought because it removes itself. Being itself removes itself into its truth. It saves [*birgt*] itself in its truth and conceals [*verbirgt*] itself in such shelter [*Bergen*].

In looking at the self-concealing shelter [*das sich verbergende Bergen*] of its own essence, perhaps we catch a glimpse of the essence of the mystery in which the truth of being essences.

Accordingly, metaphysics itself would not be simply overlooking a question about being that is still to be reflected upon. In the end it would not be an error. Metaphysics, as the history of the truth of beings as such, would be what came to be out of the destiny of being itself. In its essence metaphysics would be the unthought – because withheld – mystery of being itself. Were it otherwise, a thinking that diligently holds to what must be thought, to being, could not ceaselessly ask: What is metaphysics?

Metaphysics is an[a] epoch of the history of being itself. In its essence, however, metaphysics is nihilism. The essence of nihilism is part of the history in which, as which, being itself essences. If the nothing, wherever else it points, also points to being, then it may well be more likely that the being-historical determination of nihilism shows the region, at least, within which the essence of nihilism is able to be experienced, in order to become something that is thought [*etwas Gedachtes*], something that concerns our remembrance [*Andenken*]. We are very much accustomed to hear a discordant note in the name nihilism. However, as soon as we reflect on the being-historical essence of nihilism, then something discomfiting is added to our merely hearing a discordant note. The name nihilism says that the *nihil* (the nothing) is, and is in an essential way, in what it names. Nihilism means: with everything in every respect, the nothing is going on. Everything: beings in their entirety. Moreover, a particular being [*das Seiende*], when it is experienced as a particular being, stands in each of its respects. Nihilism means, then, that the nothing is going on with beings as such in their entirety. But beings are what they are and how they are on the basis of being. Provided that every "is" is the responsibility of being, then the essence of nihilism consists in the fact that there is nothing going on with being itself. Being *itself* is being in its *truth*, which truth belongs to being.

If we hear in the name nihilism that other note, in which there sounds the essence of what it names, then we also hear differently into the language of the metaphysical thinking that has experienced something of nihilism but without being able to think its essence. Perhaps with that other note in our ear, we will one day think differently than we have so far about the age in which nihilism was beginning to be completed. Perhaps we will then recognize that neither sociological, nor technological, nor scientific, nor even metaphysical and religious perspectives are enough to think what is happening in this age. What there is for thinking to think is not some deeply hidden deeper meaning, but rather something lying close by: something that is lying most closely, which we, because that is all it is, have therefore

[a] First edition, 1950: the?

continually already passed over. By passing it over, we continually accomplish (without attending to it) that killing of the being of beings.

In order to attend to it and to hear how to attend to it, it must already suffice for us to think for once about what the madman says of the death of God and how he says it. Perhaps we will now no longer overlook in a rush what is said at the beginning of the passage we discussed – that the madman "cried out ceaselessly: I'm looking for God! I'm looking for God!"

In what way is this man mad? He is de-ranged [*Ver-rückt*]. He is moved out [*ausgerückt*] of the level of erstwhile man on which the ideals, now grown unreal, of the supersensory world are passed off as real while the opposite ideals are being realized. This de-ranged man is moved out [*hinausgerückt*] beyond erstwhile man. In moving out, nonetheless, he has only fully moved into [*eingerückt*] the predetermined essence of erstwhile man, to be the *animal rationale*. The man de-ranged in this way has, then, nothing in common with the sort of men standing about in public, "who do not believe in God." For these are not unbelievers because for them God, as God, has become unworthy of belief, but because they themselves have abandoned the possibility of faith since they are no longer able to seek God. They can seek no longer because they can no longer think. Those standing about in public have abolished thinking and replaced it with gossip that smells nihilism everywhere it fears its opinions are threatened. The self-delusion, which is perpetually gaining the upper hand against genuine nihilism, is trying in this way to talk away its dread at thinking. This dread, however, is dread at dread.

It is clear from the first sentences and even clearer for those who can hear from the last sentences of the passage that the madman, in contrast, is seeking God by crying out after God. Perhaps a thinking man has here really cried out *de profundis*? And the ear of our thinking? Does it not still hear the cry? It will not hear the cry so long as it does not begin to think. Thinking does not begin until we have come to know that the reason that has been extolled for centuries is the most stubborn adversary of thinking.

Why Poets?

"... and why poets in a desolate time?" Hölderlin asks in the elegy "Bread and Wine." Today we hardly understand the question. How are we ever going to grasp the answer that Hölderlin gives?

"... and why poets in a desolate time?" The word "time" here means the age to which we ourselves still belong. The appearance and sacrificial death of Christ, for the historical experience of Hölderlin, mean that the end to the days of divinity has set in. Evening is falling. Since the "united three,"[1] Herakles, Dionysus, and Christ, forsook the world, the evening of the world-era has been drawing to its night. The world's night disseminates its darkness. The age is determined by God's keeping himself afar, by "God's default."[2] However, the default of God which Hölderlin experienced does not contradict the fact that a Christian relationship to God continues among individuals and in the churches, and it certainly does not disparage this relationship to God. The default of God means that a God no longer gathers men and things to himself visibly and unmistakably and from this gathering ordains world-history and man's stay within it. However, in the default of God notice is given of something even worse. Not only have the gods and God fled, but the radiance of divinity is extinguished in world-history. The time of the world's night is the desolate time because the desolation grows continually greater. The time has already become so desolate that it is no longer able to see the default of God as a default.

With this default, the ground for the world ceases to be grounding. Abyss [*Abgrund*] originally means the soil and ground toward which, as the lowest level, something hangs down a declivity. In what follows, however, let us understand the "*Ab-*" as the total absence of ground. Ground is the soil for taking root and standing. The age for which the ground fails to appear hangs in the abyss. Assuming that a turning point in any way still awaits this desolate time, it can only come one day if the world turns radically around, which now plainly means if it turns away from the abyss. In the age of the world's night, the abyss of the world must be experienced and must be endured. However, for this it is necessary that there are those who reach into the abyss.

The turning of an age does not occur at just any time by the eruption of a new God or by the new eruption of an old God from an ambush. Where is he supposed to turn to, upon his return, if men have not already prepared for him his residence? How could there ever be for God a residence fit for God unless the radiance of divinity had already begun to appear in all that is?

The gods who "once were here" "return" only "at the proper time"[3] – namely, when there is a turn among men in the right place in the right way. That is why Hölderlin says in the unfinished hymn "Mnemosyne"[4] (written shortly after the elegy "Bread and Wine"):

> All things are not
> Within the power of heavenly ones. That is,
> Mortals first reach into the abyss. For so it turns
> with them. The time is
> Long, but what is true
> Comes to pass.
>
> Nicht vermögen
> Die Himmlischen alles. Nemlich es reichen
> Die Sterblichen eh' in den Abgrund. Also wendet es sich
> Mit diesen. Lang ist
> Die Zeit, es ereignet sich aber
> Das Wahre.

Long is the desolate time of the world's night. It reaches [*gelangen*] its midpoint only at length [*lang*]. In the midnight of this night, the desolation of the time is the greatest. The destitute time is then no longer able even to experience its distress. This incapacity, by which even the distress of desolation sinks into darkness, is the very desolation of the time. The distress is fully eclipsed because it now appears only as a need to be satisfied. Nonetheless, the world's night is to be thought as a destiny that takes place this side of pessimism and optimism. Perhaps the world's night is now approaching its midpoint. Perhaps the time of the world is now fully becoming a desolate time. Perhaps not, however, not yet, still not yet, despite the immeasurable hardship, despite all the sufferings, despite the indescribable sorrow, despite the incessant rampant disquiet, despite the mounting confusion. The time is long because even terror, treated in itself as a ground for a turn, can do nothing as long as there is no turn among mortals. It turns, however, only when mortals come into their own essence. Their essence is based on the fact that they are the ones who reach into the abyss, rather than the gods. Mortals keep closer to absence (if we think of their essence) because they are concerned by presence, the name of being since antiquity. But since presence simultaneously conceals [*verbirgt*] itself, it is itself already absence. The abyss, therefore, saves [*birgt*] and observes [*merkt*] everything. In his hymn "The Titans," Hölderlin calls the abyss "all-observing."[5] The mortal who is to reach into the abyss rather than or differently from others experiences the marks [*Merkmale*] that the abyss observes [*vermerkt*]. These, for the poet, are the tracks of the fugitive gods.[6] This track, in Hölderlin's experience, is what Dionysus, the wine-god, brings down for the God-less during the darkness of their world's night. For the god of the vine preserves in it and in its fruit the essential mutuality of earth and sky as the site of the nuptials of men and gods.[7] Only within this site, if anywhere, can the tracks of the fugitive gods yet abide for God-less men.

. . . and why poets in a desolate time?

. . . und wozu Dichter in dürftiger Zeit?

Hölderlin answers shyly through the mouth of his friend, the poet Heinze, to whom the question was addressed:

> They are, you say, like the wine-god's sacred priests,
> Who roamed from land to land during the sacred night.
>
> Aber sie sind, sagst du, wie des Weingotts heilige Priester,
> Welche von Lande zu Land zogen in heilige Nacht.

Poets are the mortals who gravely sing the wine-god and sense [*spüren*] the track [*Spur*] of the fugitive gods; they stay on the gods' track, and so they blaze [*spuren*] a path for their mortal relations, a path toward the turning point. However, the aether, in which alone gods are gods, is their godhead. The element of this aether, that in which the godhead itself still essences, is the sacred. The element of the aether for the advent of the fugitive gods, the sacred, is the track of the fugitive gods. Yet who is capable of tracing such tracks? Tracks are often inconspicuous, and they are always the legacy of instruction scarcely divined. To be a poet in a desolate time means: singing, to attend to the track of the fugitive gods. This is why the poet, at the time of the world's night, utters the sacred. This is the reason that the world's night, in Hölderlin's language, is the sacred night.

It is in the essence of poets who are truly poets at such a world-era that from out of the desolation of the time, the condition and vocation of the poet have first become poetic questions for them. That is why "poets in a desolate time" must specifically speak the essence of poetry in their poems. Where this happens we may infer that the condition of the poet accords [*s. schickt*] with the destiny [*Geschick*] of the age. The rest of us must learn to listen to what *these* poets say – which assumes that we are not deceiving ourselves about the time that conceals [*verbirgt*] being by saving [*birgt*] it; deceiving ourselves, that is, into calculating the time only on the basis of beings, by dissecting them.

The closer it comes to the midnight of the world's night, the more exclusively desolation reigns in such a way that it withdraws its essence. It is not only that the sacred is vanishing as the track to the godhead, but that even the tracks to this lost track are almost erased. The more the tracks are effaced, the less an individual mortal who reaches into the abyss can still attend there to a hint or instruction. Then it is true all the more that each person gets farthest if he is able to go as far as he can along the way granted to him. The third strophe of the same elegy that asks "and why poets in a desolate time?" pronounces the law which governs its poets:

> One thing is certain; whether at noon or late,
> Toward the middle of the night, a measure endures,
> Common to all, though each also is granted his own,
> Where we come and where we go to, as we can.
>
> Fest bleibt Eins; es sei um Mittag oder es gehe
> Bis in die Mitternacht, immer besteht ein Maas,
> Allen gemein, doch jeglichem auch ist eignes beschieden,
> Dahin gehet und kommt jeder, wohin er es kann.

In his letter to Boehlendorf on December 2, 1802, Hölderlin writes: "and the philosophical light around my window is now my joy; may I preserve the memory of how I have come thus far."

The poet thinks into the place that is determined from that illumination of being which has been stamped as the realm in which Western metaphysics is fulfilled. Hölderlin's thinking poetry has also stamped this realm of the poetic thinking. His poetry dwells in this place more intimately than any other poetry of his time. The place into which Hölderlin came is one where being is manifest, a manifestness which itself belongs in the destiny of being; out of this destiny, the manifestness is intended for the poet.

Perhaps, however, this manifestness of being within the fulfillment of metaphysics is simultaneously the extreme oblivion of being. What if this oblivion were the concealed essence of the desolation of the desolateness of the time? Then there would certainly be no time for an aesthetic flight to Hölderlin's poetry. Then it would not be the moment to fabricate a myth out of the figure of the poet. There would be no chance then to mistreat his poem as a rich storehouse for a philosophy. However, there would be and there is the single necessity: by thinking soberly in what is said in his poetry, to experience what is unsaid. This is the course of the history of being. If we enter upon this course, it brings thinking and poetry together in a dialogue engaged with the history of being. Researchers in literary history will inevitably see the dialogue as an unscholarly violation of what they take to be the facts. Philosophers will see it as a baffled descent into mysticism [*ein Abweg der Ratlosigkeit in die Schwärmerei*]. However, destiny pursues its course untroubled by all that.

Does a poet of today encounter us of today on this course? Does that very poet encounter us, a poet who today is often and hastily dragged into the vicinity of thinking and plastered over with a good deal of half-thought-out philosophy? Yet let us ask this question more clearly with the stringency appropriate to it.

Is Rainer Maria Rilke a poet in a desolate time? How does his poetry bear on the desolateness of the time? How far does it reach into the abyss? Where is it that he comes to, assuming he goes to where he can?

Rilke's valid poems stretch across two slim volumes, patiently collected: the *Duino Elegies* and the *Sonnets to Orpheus*. The long path to these poems is itself a path of poetic questioning. En route Rilke experiences the desolateness of the age more clearly. The age is desolate not only because God is dead but also because mortals scarcely know or are capable even of their own mortality. Mortals are still not in the possession of their essence. Death withdraws into the enigmatic. The mystery of suffering is covered over. No one is learning to love. But mortals are. They are so long as there is language. Song still lingers over their desolate land. The singer's words stay on the track of the sacred. A song from the *Sonnets to Orpheus* says it (I, 19):

> What though the world changes swiftly
> like shapes of the clouds,
> all that is finished falls home
> to the primeval.

Above the passage and change,
more wide and more free,
your foresong yet endures,
God with the lyre.

Sufferings are not recognized,
no one is learning to love,
and what in death displaces us

is unrevealed.
Over the land only song
sanctifies and celebrates.

Wandelt sich rasch auch die Welt
wie Wolkengestalten,
alles Vollendete fällt
heim zum Uralten.

Über dem Wandel und Gang,
weiter und freier,
währt noch dein Vor-Gesang,
Gott mit der Leier.

Nicht sind die Leiden erkannt,
nicht ist die Liebe gelernt,
und was im Tod uns enfernt

ist nicht entschleiert.
Einzig das Lied überm Land
heiligt und feiert.

Meanwhile even the track of the sacred has become unrecognizable. It is an open question whether we still experience the sacred as the track to the godhead of the divine, or whether what we now encounter is only a track to the sacred. It is not clear what this track to a track could be. It is questionable how such a track would show itself to us.

The time is desolate because it lacks the unhiddenness of the essence of pain, death, and love. This desolation is itself desolate because the essential realm in which pain and death and love belong together is withdrawn. Hiddenness exists so long as the realm where they belong together is the abyss of being. However, song still remains and gives a name to the land. What is song itself? How is a mortal capable of it? Where does song sing from? How far does it reach into the abyss?

In order to judge whether or to what extent Rilke is a poet in a desolate time, in order therefore to know what poets are for, we will try to set a few stakes on the path to the abyss. For stakes we will take a few basic words of

Rilke's valid poetry. They are to be understood only in relation to the realm out of which they are spoken. That realm is the truth of beings as it has developed since the fulfillment of Western metaphysics by Nietzsche. Rilke experienced poetically and bore in his own way the unhiddenness of beings which was stamped by this fulfillment. We will see how beings as such, for Rilke, show themselves in their entirety. In order to bring this realm into view, we will attend to a poem that was written in the vicinity of Rilke's fully accomplished poetry and after it chronologically.

We are not prepared to interpret the elegies and sonnets, for the realm from which they speak has, in its metaphysical condition and oneness, not yet been sufficiently thought from out of the essence of metaphysics. For two reasons this thinking is difficult. First, because Rilke's poetry, in its course within the history of being, remains behind Hölderlin in rank and position. Next, because we scarcely know the essence of metaphysics and are unversed in what being says.

Not only are we not prepared to interpret the elegies and sonnets, but we are not entitled to do so, since the essential realm of the dialogue between poetry and thinking can be reconnoitered, attained, and thought through only slowly. Who today would claim that he is equally at home in the essence of thinking and in the essence of poetry? And even more, that he is powerful enough to bring the essence of both into extreme discord in order to establish their concordance?

Rilke did not himself publish the poem that we will explicate below. It is found on page 118 of the volume of the *Gesammelte Gedichte* that was published in 1934 and on page 90 of the collection *Späte Gedichte* (published in 1935). The poem has no heading. Rilke drafted it in June 1924. In a letter to Clara Rilke on August 15, 1924 from Muzot, the poet writes: "However, I have not been dilatory and remiss in *all* directions, fortunately: Baron Lucius received his fine Malte even *before* my departure in June; his letter of thanks has long been ready to be sent off to you. I also enclose for you the improvised verses which I inscribed for him in the first volume of the handsome leather edition."

The improvised verses which Rilke mentions in this letter (according to a note by the editor of the *Briefe aus Muzot*, on p. 404) constitute the following poem:

As nature gives the creatures over
to the risk of dull desire and shelters
none in particular, in soil or bough,
so we too are not more dear to the utmost depth

of our being; it risks us. Only that we,
still more than plant or animal,
go *with* this risk, will it, sometimes even
risk more (and not from self-interest),
than life itself does, by a breath

risk more . . . This fashions us, outside of all defense,
a safebeing, there where the gravity
of the pure forces takes effect; what saves us at last
is our defenselessness and that seeing it threaten
we turned it into the open

in order, somewhere, in the widest compass,
where law touches us, to say yes to it.

Wie die Natur die Wesen überlässt
dem Wagnis ihrer dumpfen Lust und keins
besonders schützt in Scholle und Geäst,
so sind auch wir dem Urgrund unsres Seins

nicht weiter lieb; es wagt uns. Nur dass wir,
mehr noch als Pflanze oder Tier
mit diesem Wagnis gehn, es wollen, manchmal auch
wagender sind (und nicht aus Eigennutz),
als selbst das Leben ist, um einen Hauch

wagender . . . Dies schafft uns, außerhalb von Schutz,
ein Sichersein, dort, wo die Schwerkraft wirkt
der reinen Kräfte; was uns schließlich birgt,
ist unser Schutzlossein und dass wirs so
ins Offne wandten, da wirs drohen sahen,

um es, im weitsten Umkreis irgendwo,
was das Gesetz uns anrührt, zu bejahen.

Rilke refers to the poem as "improvised verses." However, this unforeseen quality opens up for us a point of view from which we will be able to think Rilke's poetry more clearly. Admittedly, the first thing we must learn at this moment of world history is that making poems is also a matter of thinking. We will take the poem as a practice exercise in poetic reflection.

The structure of the poem is simple. It is clearly articulated in four parts: lines 1–5, lines 5–10, lines 10–12, and lines 12–16. Corresponding to the beginning "As nature . . . " is the "so we too . . . " of lines 4–5. The "Only" of line 5 subsequently refers back to this "we." "Only" has a restrictive force, but in a way that marks a distinctive quality, which is made explicit in lines 5–10. Lines 10–12 state the potential of this distinction. What it really consists of is thought in lines 12–16.

Through the "As . . . so" at the beginning, human being enters as the theme of the poem. Human being is contrasted with creatures. These are the living beings, plant and animal. The beginning of the eighth *Duino Elegy*, making the same comparison,[8] calls living beings by the name of "creature."

A comparison sets different things together as equals, in order to make the difference between them evident. They are equal, these different beings, plant and animal on the one hand, human on the other, provided they agree in what is the same. What is the same is the relationship they have as beings to their ground. The ground of creatures is nature. The ground of men is not merely of the same kind as the ground of plant and animal. In both cases the ground is the same. It is nature as "full Nature" (*Sonnets to Orpheus* II, 13).

We must think Nature here in the wide and essential sense in which Leibniz used the capitalized word "Natura." It means the being of beings. It essences as the *vis primitiva activa*. This is the potential to begin which gathers everything to itself, but in such a way that it releases all beings to their own selves. The being of beings is the will. The will is the self-mustering gathering of each *ens* to itself. All beings are, as beings, in the will. They *are* as things willed. Do not misunderstand: beings are not primarily and only as things willed; rather they are, so long as they are, themselves in the mode of willing. Only as things willed are they what wills in the will, each in its own way.

What Rilke calls Nature is not set off against history. Above all it is not understood as the objective domain of the natural sciences. Nor is Nature opposed to art. It is the ground for history and art and for nature in the narrower sense. In the word Nature as it is used here, the echo still lingers of the earlier word φύσις, which is also equated with ζωή, translated by us as life. In early thought, the essence of life is not represented biologically but rather as φύσις, the emergent, that which arises. In the poem, "Nature" is also called "life" in line 9. Here, Nature, life indicate being in the sense of beings in their entirety. Nietzsche once wrote in a note from 1885–86 (*The Will to Power*, no.582): "being – we have no conception of it other than 'life'. – How then can something dead 'be'?"

Rilke calls Nature, as the ground of the beings which we ourselves are, the utmost source [*Urgrund*]. This indicates that men reach further into the ground of beings than other beings. Since antiquity, the ground of beings has been called being. The relation of being that grounds to beings that are grounded is the same with men on the one hand and with plants and animals on the other. It is a matter in each case of being giving beings over to the risk. Being lets beings loose into the risk. This letting-loose that casts off is the actual risking. The being of beings is the relation of casting-off to beings. The beings that are at a particular time are what is being risked. Being is preeminently the risk. It risks us, human beings. It risks living beings. Beings are so long as they remain what is continually being risked. Beings, however, are still risked into being, that is, into a risk. That is why beings, given over to the risk, themselves run risks. Beings are by going with the risk into which they are let loose. The being of beings is the risk. This risk is based in the will, which, since Leibniz, has shown itself more clearly as the being of beings that is revealed in metaphysics. The will that it is necessary to think here is not the abstract generalization of willing as it is psychologically understood. Rather, human willing, experienced metaphysically, is only the willed counterpart to will as to the being of beings. So long as Rilke represents Nature as the risk, he is thinking of it metaphysically in terms of the essence of the will. This essence still conceals itself, both in the will to power as in the will as the risk. Will essences as the will to will.

The poem does not say anything directly about the ground of beings, that is about being as preeminently the risk. But if being as the risk is the relation of casting-off, and if it therefore retains even what is risked in the casting-off, then the poem tells us something indirectly about the risk by speaking of what is risked.

Nature risks living beings and "shelters none in particular." Likewise, neither are we men, having been risked, "more dear" to the risk that is risking us. In both cases, casting-off into danger is part of the risk. To risk is to play with dangerous stakes. Heraclitus thinks of being as the world-era and the world-era as a child's play (Fragment 52 in Diels, *Fragmente der Vorsokratiker*): Αἰὼν παῖς ἐστι παίζων, πεσσεύων· παιδὸς ἡ βασιληίη. "The age of the world is a child playing a child's game; dominion is a child's." Were what is cast off to remain out of danger, then it would not be risked. Beings would be out of danger, however, if they were sheltered [*geschützt*]. *Schutz* (defense, shelter), *Schütze* (marksman), and *schützen* (to defend, shelter) are related to *schießen* (to shoot) as *Buck* (curvature) and *bücken* (to stoop) are to *biegen* (to bend). *Schießen* (to shoot) means *schieben* (to push): to push [*vorschieben*] a bolt shut. The roof juts out ["shoots out," *schießt vor*] over the wall. In the countryside, we still say: the peasant is "shooting in [*schießt ein*]": she pushes [*schiebt*] molded dough into the oven to bake. Shelter is pushed in advance and in front of. It prevents danger from harming, or even concerning, the one under threat. To be sheltered is to be entrusted to the sheltering. Instead of "entrusted," our older and richer language would say "plighted" or "betrothed": loved, held dear. What is unsheltered on the other hand is not more dear. Plant, animal, and man have this in common: that as beings at all, that is, as being risked, they are not specially sheltered. Yet they are in fact distinguished in their being, and therefore there will also be a difference in their unshelteredness.

Although the unsheltered are risked, they are nevertheless not abandoned. If they were, they would be as little risked as sheltered. Delivered only unto annihilation, they would no longer hang in the balance [*in der Wage*]. In the Middle Ages the word "*Wage* [balance]" still meant something almost like danger. To be in the balance means to be in a situation that can turn out in one way or the other. That is why the instrument that moves [*bewegt*] like this, by dipping one way or the other, is called the balance [*Wage*]. It librates; it plays about the beam and plays itself out. The word "*Wage* [balance]" in the sense of danger and as the name of the instrument is derived from *wägen*, *wegen*, to make a way, that is, to go, to be going. *Be-wägen* means to get something underway, to get it going: *wiegen* (to sway or weigh). Something weighs because it is able to tip the balance one way or the other into the play of motion. What weighs has weight. To risk [*wagen*] is to set the play into motion, to lay something on the balance [*Wage*], to let it loose into danger. Thereby what is risked is indeed unsheltered, but since it lies on the balance, it is retained by the risk. It is sustained. It continues to be saved by its ground in its ground. For beings, to be risked is to be willed; retained in the will, they themselves remain in the mode of willing, and risk themselves. In this way, what is risked is care-less, *sine cura*, *securum*, that is, safe. Only so long as what is risked rests safely in the risk, can it follow the risk, follow it, that is, into the unshelteredness of what is risked. What is risked is unsheltered; but not only does this not exclude a safebeing in its ground, it necessarily implies it. What is risked goes with the risk.

Being, which holds all beings in the balance, therefore constantly attracts beings toward and unto itself, unto itself as the center. Being, as the risk, holds all beings, as risked, in this relation of attraction. However, this center of attractive relation retracts itself from all beings at the same time. In this way the center gives beings over to the risk as which they are risked. In this letting-loose that is a gathering, the metaphysical essence of the will, thought in terms of being, conceals itself. The center of beings that attracts, that mediates everything, the risk, is the faculty that lends a weight, that is, heaviness, to what is risked. The risk is the force of gravity. A late poem, entitled "Gravity," speaks about it (*Späte Gedichte*, p. 156):

Gravity

Center, how you withdraw yourself
from everything, even from those who fly
you recover yourself, center, you, the strongest.

He, standing: as a drink
rushes through thirst, so gravity him.

Yet from the sleeper falls,
as from the low-hanging cloud,
ample rain of heaviness.

Schwerkraft

Mitte, wie du aus allen
dich ziehst, auch noch aus Fliegenden dich
wiedergewinnst, Mitte, du Stärkste.

Stehender: wie ein Trank den Durst
durchstürzt ihn die Schwerkraft.

Doch aus dem Schlafenden fällt,
wie aus lagernder Wolke,
reichlicher Regen der Schwere.

Here what is called gravity is not the same as physical gravitation, which is what we usually hear about; instead, it is the center of beings in their entirety. Rilke calls it therefore "the unheard center" (*Sonnets to Orpheus*, II, 28). The center is the ground, the fellowness, which by mediating holds one thing to another and gathers everything in the game of risking. The unheard center is "the eternal fellow-player"[9] in the worldgame of being. The same poem which speaks poetically of being as the risk calls (lines 11 and 12) the mediating attraction "the gravity of the pure forces." Pure gravity, the unheard center of all risking, the eternal partner in the game of being, is the risk.

By casting off what is risked, the risk simultaneously retains it in the balance. Risk lets what is risked loose, indeed in such a way that it lets loose what is cast off into none other than pull or traction [*Zug*] toward the center. What is risked is vested with this traction toward the center. In this pull, the risk always retrieves what is risked. To retrieve something, to get hold of something from somewhere, to have it come, to attract it, we call "*beziehen*." This is the original meaning of the word "*Bezug*." We still speak of the "*Bezug*" of merchandise, salary, or current. The traction, which as the risk concerns and affects all beings with traction, and retains them in traction toward itself, is attraction [*Bezug*] absolutely. The word "*das Bezug*" is a fundamental word of Rilke's valid poems; to be precise, in the expressions "the pure *Bezug*," "the entire," "the real," "the clearest," and "the other *Bezug*" (i.e., the same attraction in another respect).[10]

We only half understand Rilke's word "*Bezug*," which is to say that we do not understand it at all in such a case when we grasp it only in terms of its current meaning of reference [*Beziehung*], and reference in the sense of relation. We misinterpret the word to an even greater degree if we represent the reference as the human "I" relating an object to itself. This meaning "to relate to oneself" comes later in the history of the language. Rilke's use of the word "*der Bezug*" is indeed also familiar with this meaning, but it does not mean that primarily but only as derived from the original meaning. The phrase "the whole *Bezug*" cannot even be thought if we represent *Bezug* as mere relation. The gravity of the pure forces, the unheard center, the pure *Bezug*, the whole *Bezug*, full Nature, life, the risk are all the same.

All the names just offered name beings as such in their entirety. The conventional idiom of metaphysics offers the name "being" for them as well. According to the poem, Nature is to be thought as the risk. Here the word "risk" simultaneously names the ground that risks and the risked beings in their entirety. This ambiguity is not an accident, and it is not enough to make a note of it. In it the language of metaphysics speaks unambiguously.

Everything that is risked, as a particular kind of being, is admitted into the entirety of beings and rests in the ground of the entirety. The particular being in each case *is* each according to the attracting by which it is retained in the traction of the whole attraction. The kind of attracting within the attraction is the mode of the relationship toward the center as pure gravity. That is why Nature is portrayed when one tells how the thing that is risked is, each time, attracted into the traction toward the center. Accordingly, each time it is then in the midst of beings in their entirety.

The whole attractive relation to which all beings (as beings that are risked) are given over is what Rilke likes to call "the open." This is another fundamental word of his poetry. In Rilke's language, "open" means that which does not impede. It does not impede because it does not bar. It does not bar because it is in itself free of all barriers. The open is the great entirety of all that is unbarred. It lets the creatures that are risked into the pure attraction pull as things pulled, so that they draw onward together in diverse ways without hitting against barriers. Pulling as they are pulled, they open out in the unbarriered, into the infinite. They are not dissolved [*s. auflösen*] into the void nothing, but they redeem [*s. einlösen*] themselves into the whole of the open.

What Rilke is naming with this word "open" is in no way to be defined by openness in the sense of the unhiddenness of beings, an unhiddenness that lets beings as such come to presence. If we were to try to interpret Rilke's "open" in the sense of unhiddenness and the unhidden, then it would be necessary to say: what Rilke experiences as the open is precisely the hidden, the unlit, which draws onward in the unbarriered in such a way that there is no possibility of encountering something unusual or anything at all. Wherever there is an encounter, there a barrier arises. Where there is a barring, what is barred is forced back onto itself and so it is bent back upon itself. Barring twists, cordons off, the relationship to the open and makes this relationship itself into a twisted one. The barring within the unbarriered is constructed [*erstellt*] by human representation [*Vorstellen*]. The athwartness of objects that oppose him [*Das gegenstehender Gegenüber*] does not permit man to be directly in the open. It excludes man from the world, in a certain sense, and places him before the world, where what is meant by "world" is beings in their entirety. In contrast, it is the open itself that has the quality of world; the open as the entirety of unopposingness, unobjectiveness. However, even the term "the open," like the expression "the risk," is ambiguous as a metaphysical term. It signifies both the entirety of the unbarred attractions of the pure attraction and also openness in the sense of the unbarring which prevails everywhere.

The open lets in. Letting in, however, does not mean: granting an entrance and access to what is closed, as though what is hidden were to unconceal itself so that it might appear as unhidden. To let in means: to draw into and fit into the unlit entirety of the tuggings of the pure attraction. To let in is the mode of the open, and it therefore has the character of an attracting inclusion, in the manner of the gravity of the pure forces. The less that admittance into the pure attraction is denied to what is risked, so much the more does what is risked belong in the great entirety of the open. That is why Rilke calls creatures that are directly risked into this whole and are being swayed in it the "great-accustomed things" (*Späte Gedichte*, p. 22).[11] Man is not one of them. The song that sings this different relationship of living beings and of men to the open is the eighth *Duino Elegy*. The difference is based in the different degrees of consciousness. To distinguish beings in this respect is, after Leibniz, familiar to modern metaphysics.

What Rilke is thinking with the word "the open" can be adduced from a letter that he wrote in the last year of his life (February 2, 1926) in response to a Russian reader who had asked him about the eighth elegy. (Cf. M. Betz, *Rilke in Frankreich: Erinnerungen, Briefe, Dokumente*, 1938, p. 289.) "You must grasp the concept of the 'open' that I attempted to put forward in this elegy in *such* a way that the animal's degree of consciousness places it into the world but without the animal placing itself each moment athwart [*gegenüber*] the world (as we are); the animal is *in* the world; we stand *before* it, because of the direction and intensification that our consciousness has characteristically taken." Rilke continues: "Neither is sky, air, and space intended by the 'open'; for the observer and judge, *these* too are 'object [*Gegenstand*]' and therefore 'opaque' and shut. Animals, flowers, I suppose, *are* all that, without having to account to themselves for it; and so they have before and above them that indescribably open freedom which perhaps has (at most momentary) equivalents among us only in the first moments of love when a man sees in someone else, in the beloved, his own expanse, or in his exaltation to God."

Plant and animal are admitted into the open. They are "*in* the world." The "in" means: attracted into the unlit attraction-nexus of the pure attraction. The relationship to the open (if we can still speak of a "to" at all) is the unconscious one of a striving-drawing stride into the entirety of beings. With the intensification of consciousness, the essence of which, for modern metaphysics, is representation, the position [*Stand*] and opposition [*Gegenstehen*] of objects [*Gegenstände*] also intensifies. The higher the consciousness, the greater the degree to which the conscious creature is excluded from the world. That is why, in the words of the letter, man is "before the world." He is not admitted into the open. Man stands athwart the world. He does not live directly in the pull and wind of the whole attraction. The quoted passage facilitates the understanding of the open particularly since Rilke here expressly denies that the open may be thought in the sense of the openness of sky and space. The open in the sense of the essentially more original lightening of being is foreign to Rilke's poetry, which remains moderately in the shadow of a Nietzschean metaphysics.

That which has its proper place unmediatedly in the open is taken up [*eingenommen*] by it into the pull of attracting to the center. Therefore of all the beings that are risked, the ones that belong most in the open are taken away [*benommen*] in accordance with their own essence, so that in the resultant daze [*Benommenheit*] they never aspire to anything that could stand in opposition to them. What so essences is "in dull desire."

> As nature gives the creatures over
> to the risk of dull desire . . .

Dull has here the sense of being muted: not breaking away from the attraction-nexus of an unrestricted drawing onward which is not made unquiet by restless back-and-forth attraction – the state in which conscious representation moves in excessive hurry. Dull means at the same time a dull, muffled tone, which comes from a depth and has found a way of carrying. Dull is not meant in the negative sense of stifling and oppressive. Rilke does not think of dull desire as base and inferior. It testifies that the great-accustomed things of Nature are part of the entirety of the pure attraction. That is why Rilke can say in a late poem: "that for us the being of a flower be great" (*Späte Gedichte*, p. 89; cf. *Sonnets to Orpheus* II, 14). As the passage quoted from the letter thinks of man and living beings with regard to their different relations [*Verhältnis*] of consciousness to the open, so the poem names "creatures" and "us" (men) with regard to their different behavior [*Verhalten*] toward the risk (ll. 5ff.):

> ... Only that we,
> still more than plant or animal,
> go *with* this risk, ...

That man, still more than plant or animal, goes with the risk might at first glance mean that man is admitted into the open with even less hindrance than those creatures. If the "with" were not stressed with italics, the "more" might very well imply exactly that. The stress of the "with" does not indicate that man, with heightened freedom, goes along with the risk; rather it means: for man, to go along with the risk is specifically represented, and represented as something set before him [*das Vorgesetze*] in his intention [*Vorsatz*]. The risk and what it has risked, Nature, beings in their entirety, the world, are set out prominently [*herausgestellt*] before man, from out of the mutedness of unbarred attraction. But that which is set up [*das Gestellte*] – where is it set up [*gestellt*], and by what? Nature is brought before man by human re-presentation [*Vor-stellen*]. Man sets up the world as the entirety of objectiveness before himself and himself before the world. Man delivers [*stellt zu*] the world unto himself and produces [*stellt her*] Nature for himself. We must think of this production [*Her-stellen*] in its wide and diverse essence. Man tills [*bestellt*] Nature when it does not satisfy his representation. Man produces new things when they are lacking to him. Man rearranges [*umstellt*] things when they bother him. Man adjusts [*s. verstellt*] things when they distract him from his plans. Man displays [*ausstellt*] things when he extols them for sale and use. Man displays himself when he emphasizes [*herausstellt*] his accomplishments and advertises his business. In manifold production, the world is brought to a stop [*zum Stehen*] and into position [*in den Stand*]. The open becomes an object and is diverted toward the human creature. It is man who, athwart the world as an object, turns out to be [*s. heraustellt*] and displays himself as the one who deliberately asserts all this production.

To put something before oneself in such a way that what has been put forth (and which has already been represented) determines all the modes of production in every respect is a fundamental trait of the attitude we know as the will. What is called will here is production, or rather production in the sense of the deliberate self-assertion of objectification. Plant and animal do not will since, muted in their desire, they never bring the open before themselves as an object. They cannot go with the risk as with something they had represented. Because they have been admitted into the open, the pure attraction is never the objective other of themselves. Man on the other hand goes "*with*" the risk, because he is the creature who wills in the sense we have given:

> . . . Only that we,
> still more than plant or animal,
> go *with* this risk, will it, . . .

Will, in the sense given here, is the self-assertion whose intention *has already* posited the world as the entirety of objects that can be produced. This will determines the essence of modern man, without his having known anything at first about its far-reaching consequences, and without his being able to know even today the will which, as the being of beings, is the source of this will that is willed. In such willing, modern man turns out to be the one who surges up – in every relation to everything that is and therefore also to himself – as the producer who asserts himself and establishes this insurgency as absolute mastery. The whole inventory of objects, in which guise the world appears, is entrusted to, enjoined upon, the production that asserts itself, and so it is subordinated to the command of production. Will has in itself the nature of command; for deliberate self-assertion is a way in which the situation [*Zuständliche*] of producing and the objectivity [*Gegenständliche*] of the world muster themselves together in an absolute and therefore complete [*vollständige*] oneness. In this self-mustering, the imperative character of the will is announced. With it, in the course of modern metaphysics, there comes to light the long-hidden essence of the will that has long since been essencing as the being of beings.

Accordingly, human willing can also be in the mode of self-assertion only by forcing everything into its realm in advance, even before it surveys anything. For this will, everything, already in advance and therefore in the consequence, is relentlessly turned into the material of self-asserting production. Earth and its atmosphere are turned into raw material. Man becomes a human material that is applied [*angesetzt*] to goals that have been set out before him [*vorgesetzt*]. The absolute self-assertion of the deliberate production of the world is unconditionally established as the condition of human command; this is a process that comes out of the hidden essence of technology. Only in the modern era does this begin to develop as a destiny of the truth of beings in their entirety; in contrast, until recently its scattered appearances and efforts had been incorporated into the comprehensive realm of culture and civilization.

Modern science and the total state, as necessary consequences [*Folgen*] of the essence of technology, are also attendant [*Gefolge*] upon it. The same holds true for the ways and forms that are applied to the organization of global public opinion and the ordinary ideas of people. Not only is life objectified in the techniques of commercial breeding and exploitation, but the attack of atomic physics upon the phenomena of life as such is going full tilt. Fundamentally, the essence of life itself is to be handed over to technical production. That people today in all seriousness find, in the results and the standpoint of atomic physics, possibilities of showing human freedom and setting up a new theory of value, is a sign of the mastery of technological representation. Such mastery has long since evolved far removed from the precinct of individuals' personal views and opinions. The essential force of technology is also shown where people are still trying, in the vicinity as it were, to master technology with the help of the former deployment of values: in these efforts they nonetheless avail themselves of technical means which are by no means only outward forms. For in general the use of machinery and the manufacturing of machines is not technology itself, but rather only one of its appropriate instruments to establish its essence in the objectiveness of its raw material. Even this, the fact that the man has turned into the subject and the world the object, is a consequence of the self-establishing essence of technology, not the reverse.

If Rilke experiences the open as the unobjectiveness of full Nature, by contrast the world of willing men must stand out for him as correspondingly objective. Conversely, to look out for the integral entirety of beings is to take a hint from the phenomena of advancing technology, a hint in the direction of those regions from where, perhaps, an originary, constructive [*bildende*] overcoming of the technical could come.

The amorphous [*bildlosen*] formations [*Gebilde*] of technical production fight their way before the open of the pure attraction. Things which in the past used to grow are rapidly dwindling away. They can no longer show their own across the objectification. In a letter dated November 13, 1925, Rilke writes:

> Even for our grandparents a "house," a "spring," a familiar tower, yes even their clothes, their coat: infinitely more and infinitely more intimate; each thing, almost, a vessel in which they found the human, and preserved and added the human to it. Now, from America, empty indifferent things, sham things, *counterfeit life* are pushing their way across . . . A house, in the American sense, an American apple, or a vine over there, has *nothing* in common with the house, fruit, grape, into which the hope and solicitude of our ancestors had gone . . .
>
> (*Briefe aus Muzot*, pp. 335f.).

However, this Americanness is already only the collected recoil of the willed essence of modern Europe onto a Europe for which, in Nietzsche's fulfillment of metaphysics, there were forethought some areas at least of the essential questionableness of a world in which being has begun to rule as the will to will. It is not America that is the primary threat to us of today; in fact the unexperienced essence of technology had already threatened our ancestors and their things. What is significant in Rilke's reflection is an attempt to rescue still the things of the forefathers. With even greater forethought, we must recognize what it is that is becoming questionable about the thingness of things. For Rilke writes even earlier from Duino on March 1, 1912: "The world withdraws into itself; and things, for their part, behave in the same way, by transferring their existence increasingly into the vibration of money and developing for themselves a kind of spirituality there that even now exceeds their tangible reality. In the period that I am dealing with" – Rilke means the fourteenth century – "money was still gold, still metal, a lovely object, the handiest, the most lucid thing of all" (*Briefe aus den Jahren 1907 bis 1914*, p. 213). A decade earlier still, he published in the "Book of Pilgrimage," the second of the *Book of Hours*, the far-foreseeing verses (*Gesammelte Werke*, vol. II, p. 254):

> The kings of the world are old,
> and they will have no heirs.
> The sons are dying as boys,
> and their pale daughters gave
> all the sickly crowns to force.
> The rabble grinds them into specie;
> the time-serving lord of the world

distends them in the fire; makes them machines
that grumble and serve his will;
but happiness is not among them.
The ore is homesick. Its desire
is to forsake the coins and wheels
that teach it to live small.
And from the factories and from the tills
it will return into the earthly veins;
the adits of the mountains
close behind it on its return.

Die Könige der Welt sind alt
und werden keine Erben haben.
Die Söhne sterben schon als Knaben,
und ihre bleichen Töchter gaben
die kranken Kronen der Gewalt.
Der Pöbel bricht sie klein zu Geld,
der zeitgemäße Herr der Welt
dehnt sie im Feuer zu Maschinen,
die seinem Wollen grollend dienen;
aber das Glück ist nicht mit ihnen.
Das Erz hat Heimweh. Und verlassen
will es die Münzen und die Räder,
die es ein kleines Leben lehren.
Und aus Fabriken und aus Kassen
wird es zurück in das Geäder
der aufgetanen Berge kehren,
die sich verschließen hinter ihm.

The objectiveness of technical domination over the earth is pushing increasingly faster, more recklessly, and more totally into the place where the worldly content of things used to give of itself freely since it used to be safeguarded. The mastery not only sets up all beings as producibles in the process of production, but it also delivers the products of production through the market. What is human about humans and thingly about things is dissolved, within the self-assertion of producing, to the calculation of the market value of a market that is not only a global market spanning the earth but that also, as the will to will, markets in the essence of being and so brings all beings into the business of calculation, which dominates most fiercely precisely where numbers are not needed.

Rilke's poem thinks man as the creature that is risked into a will that, without yet experiencing it, is willed in the will to will. Willing in this way, man can go with the risk in such a way that he thereby sets himself forth in all that he does as the one who asserts himself. Therefore man risks more than plant or animal. Accordingly he is also differently in danger than they are.

None of the creatures (plant and animal) are particularly sheltered even though they are admitted into the open and made secure in it. Man, in contrast, as the one who wills himself, is not merely not particularly sheltered by the entirety of beings, but he is also outside of all defense (v. 13). As the representer and the producer [*Vor- und Herstellende*], he stands before the obstructed [*verstellte*] open. Thereby he himself and his things are exposed [*ausgesetzt*] to the growing danger of becoming mere material, a mere function of objectification. The intention [*Vorsatz*] itself of self-assertion [*Sichdurchsetzen*] expands the realm of the danger that man will lose his own self to absolute producing. The threat which the human essence incurs arises from this essence itself. However, this human essence is located in the attraction of being to it. Therefore, by his self-willing, man in an essential sense is threatened, i.e., in need of defense, but by the nature of his essence, he is at the same time defenseless.

This "our defenselessness" (v. 13) differs from the not-particularly-shelteredness of plants and animals in the same way that their dull desire differs from the self-willing of man. The difference is an infinite difference because there is no transition from dull desire to objectification in self-assertion. However, not only does this put man "outside of all defense," but also to assert the objectification of the world destroys, with increasing decisiveness, even the possibility of defense. By setting up [*aufbaut*] the world technologically as an object, man blocks [*s. verbaut*] willfully and completely the way into the open that was already obstructed in any case. Whether he as an individual knows it or not, wills it or not, self-asserting man is a functionary of technology. He not only stands before the open only from outside it, but through the objectification of the world, he turns specifically away from "the pure attraction." Man cuts himself off [*sich scheidet ab*] from the pure attraction. Man in the age of technology stands, in such a departure [*Ab-schied*], against the open. This departure is not a departure from ... but a departure against ...

Technology is the absolute establishment (posed in man's self-assertion) of the absolute defenselessness which is based on the turning away (which dominates in all objectivity) against the pure attraction, which as the unheard center of beings draws all the pure forces to itself. Technical production is the organization of the departure. The word "departure," in the meaning sketched just now, is another fundamental word of Rilke's valid poetry.

It is not as a particular deadly machine that the much discussed atom bomb is deadly. What has long threatened man with death, indeed with the death of his essence, is the absoluteness of his sheer willing in the sense of his deliberate self-assertion in everything. What threatens man in his essence is the willful opinion that through the peaceful release, transformation, stockpiling, and delivery of natural energies, man could make man's being bearable for all and happy in general. However, the peace of this peacefulness is merely the undisturbed, lasting frenzied restlessness of self-assertion deliberately thrown back on itself. What threatens man in his essence is the opinion that this assertion of production would be risked without danger if only other interests in addition to it, perhaps those of a faith, remain valid – as though the present relationship of our essence to the entirety of beings (a relationship into which the technological mode of willing has shifted us) could still be housed in some separate annex, some residence on the side that would be able to offer more than temporary resorts to self-deception, such as the flight to the Greek gods. What threatens man in his essence is the opinion that technological production would bring the world into order, when it is exactly this ordering that flattens out each *ordo*, that is, each rank, into the uniformity of production and so destroys in advance the realm that is the potential source from which rank and appreciation originate out of being.

It is not only the fact that this willing has become total that is the danger; rather, the danger is willing itself in the form of self-assertion within a world that is allowed to be only will. The willing that is willed in terms of this will has already decided on absolute command. With this decision willing is already delivered into the service of total organization. Above all, however, technology itself precludes any experience of its essence. For while technology is being fully realized, it develops in science a knowledge of a kind that is prevented from ever gaining access to the essential realm of technology, let alone thinking back to its essential source.

The essence of technology is dawning only slowly. This day is the world's night made over as the purely technological day. This day is the shortest day. It raises the threat of a single endless winter. Man now forgoes not only defense, but the unbroken entirety of beings remains in darkness. What is whole [*das Heile*] withdraws. The world is being emptied of what is whole and heals [*heil-los*]. As a result, not only does the holy [*das Heilige*] remain hidden as the track to the godhead, but even what is whole, the track to the holy, appears to be extinguished. Unless there are still mortals capable of seeing what is unwhole and unhealing threaten *as* unwhole and unhealing.

They would have to discern which is the danger that assails man. The danger consists in the menace that bears on the essence of man in his relationship to being itself, but not in accidental perils. This danger is *the* danger. It conceals itself in the abyss in its relation to all beings. In order to see and to expose the danger, there must be such who first reach into the abyss.

> But where the danger lies, there also grows
> that which saves.
> (Hölderlin, *Sämtliche Werke*, vol. IV, p. 190)[12]
>
> Wo aber die Gefahr ist, wächst
> Das Rettende auch.

Perhaps any salvation other than that which comes from *where the* danger lies is still within the unhealing unholiness. For man endangered in his essence, any salvation by any makeshift, however well intended, is still an empty sham for as long as his destiny endures. Salvation must come from where there is a turn among mortals in their essence. Are there mortals who first reach into the abyss of the desolate and desolation of the desolate? These most mortal of mortals would be the most risked. They would risk even more than the self-asserting human essence that already risks more than plant and animal.

Rilke says in lines 5ff.:

> . . . Only that we,
> still more than plant or animal,
> go *with* this risk, will it, . . .

And Rilke continues in the same line:

> . . . sometimes even
> risk more (and not from self-interest),
> than life itself does, by a breath
>
> risk more . . .

Man not only in his essence risks more than plant and animal. Man, at times, even risks more "than life itself does." Life means here: beings in their being: Nature. Man at times risks more than the risk, is more being than the being of beings. However, being is the ground of beings. Who risks more than the ground risks himself to where all ground is lacking, into the abyss. However, if man is the one who, being risked, goes with the risk by willing it, then men who sometimes risk even more must also will even more. But can this willing be intensified beyond the absoluteness of deliberate self-assertion? No. Those, then, who sometimes risk more can only be more willing provided their willing is different in its essence. Then willing would not at once be the same as willing. The ones who will to a greater degree out of the essence of willing stay more in keeping with will as the being of beings. They accord rather with being that shows itself as will. They will more insofar as they are more willing. Who are the more willing ones, who risk more? The poem, apparently, does not have an explicit answer to this question.

Still, lines 8–10 say something about the ones who risk more, by negation and in approximate terms. Those who risk more do not risk themselves from self-interest, for the sake of their own person. They are attempting neither to obtain an advantage nor to indulge in self-seeking. Neither can they, although they risk more, lay claim to an outstanding achievement. For they only risk slightly more: "by a breath risk more." The "more" they risk is as slight as a breath that remains fleeting and imperceptible. From such hints it is not possible to identify who are the ones who risk more.

On the other hand, lines 10–12 say what this risk brings which is risked out beyond the being of beings:

> ... This fashions us, outside of all defense,
> a safebeing, there where the gravity
> of the pure forces takes effect;

We, like all creatures, are beings only by being risked in the risk of being. Yet because we (as creatures who will) go with the risk, we are risked more and so sooner given up to the danger. So long as man is set fast in deliberate self-assertion and establishes himself by the absolute objectification in departure against the open, he himself promotes his own defenselessness.

On the other hand, the risk that risks more fashions us a safebeing. Of course this does not take place by erecting a sheltering defense around the defenseless; for in that case a defense would be set up only in those places where it was absent. For that purpose, production would again be required. This is only possible in objectification, which, however, seals us off against the open. The risk that risks more does not produce a defense. However, it fashions us a safebeing. Safe, *securus*, *sine cura* means: without care. Care has here the nature of deliberate self-assertion along the ways and by the means of absolute production. We are without this care only when we do not set up our essence exclusively in the precinct of production and command, of utilization and defense. We are safe only where we are neither taking the defenseless into account nor counting on a defense erected in the will.

A safebeing exists only outside of the objectified turning away from the open, only "outside of all defense," outside of the departure against the pure attraction. This is the unheard center of all attracting that draws each thing into the unbarriered and attracts each thing for the center. This center is the "there" where the gravity of the pure forces takes effect. The safebeing is the sheltered repose in the attraction-nexus of the whole attraction.

The risk that risks more, which wills more than each self-assertion because it is more willing, "fashions" us a safebeing in the open. Fashion [*schaffen*] means: create or retrieve [*schöpfen*]. To retrieve from a source means to take in what rises up and to bring away what has been received. The more risking risk of the willing will manufactures nothing. It receives and gives what it has received. It brings away by realizing what it has received in its fullness. The more risking risk brings to completion, but it does not produce. Only a risk that risks more so long as it is willing can bring to completion by receiving.

Lines 12–16 encompass that which constitutes the more risking risk, the risk which ventures into the outside of defense and brings us into a safebeing there. In no way does this eliminate the defenselessness that is posed with deliberate self-assertion. So long as the essence of man is engrossed into the objectification of beings, it remains defenseless amidst beings. Undefended in this way, man is of course, in the mode of deprivation, attracted to defense and so inside of defense. Safebeing on the other hand is outside of every relation to defense: "outside of all defense."

Accordingly it appears that safebeing and our attaining safebeing requires a risk that abandons every relation to defense and defenselessness. However, this only appears to be the case. In truth, when we think from the closure of the whole attraction, we come at last to know that which in the end (that is, in advance) relieves us of the care of undefended self-assertion (lines 12f.):

> ... what saves us at last
> is our defenselessness ...

How is defenselessness supposed to bring us to safety [*bergen*] when only the open affords security [*Geborgenheit*] and when defenselessness consists in continuous departure against the open? Defenselessness can only save when the turning away against the open is reversed, so that it is turned toward the open – and turned into it. Therefore, defenselessness in reverse is that which saves us. To bring to safety means here, on the one hand, that it completes the reversal of departure and, on the other, that in a certain way defenselessness itself affords safebeing. What saves:

is our defenselessness and that seeing it threaten
we turned it into the open . . .

The "and" leads into the explanation that tells us how this astonishing thing is possible, that our defenselessness outside of defense sends us a safebeing. Certainly defenselessness never saves anything by our turning it each time that it threatens in a particular case. Defenselessness saves only so far as we have already turned it. Rilke says that "we turned it into the open." In having turned it, there is a notable mode of reversal. In having turned it, defenselessness is turned in advance as a whole in its essence. What is notable about this turning is that we saw defenselessness as that which threatens us. Only such having-seen sees the danger. It sees that defenselessness as such threatens our essence with the loss of belonging in the open. Having-turned must be rooted in this having-seen. Then defenselessness is turned "into the open." Through having seen the danger as a danger to our essence, we must have completed the reversal of the turning away against the open. This implies: the open itself must have inclined itself toward us in a way that we can turn defenselessness toward it:

in order, somewhere, in the widest compass,
where law touches us, to say yes to it.

What is the widest compass? Presumably Rilke is thinking of the open and moreover in a particular respect. The widest compass encircles everything that is. To encompass is to unite around all beings, so that it is indeed, in the union that unites, the being of beings. But what is it to be "being [*seiend*]"? The poet, it is true, calls beings in their entirety by the name "Nature," "life," "the open," "the whole attraction." Following the conventional language of metaphysics, he even calls this round entirety of beings: "being." But still, we do not experience which essence belongs to being. However, is something not said about it when Rilke designates being the risk that risks everything? Certainly. Accordingly we tried to think this designation back into the modern essence of the being of beings, into the will to will. But now this talk of the widest compass has nothing very clear to tell us when we try to think of it as the entirety of beings, and of encompassing as the being of beings.

It is true that, when we think, we remember the fact that originally the being of beings was already thought with regard to the encompassing. Nonetheless, our thinking about this sphericality of being is too facile and will always be superficial unless we have already asked and experienced how the being of beings originally essences. The ἐόν, the being, of the ἐόντα, of beings in their entirety, is called the Ἕν, the One that ones, the union that unites. What, however, is this encircling union, as a fundamental trait of being? What is being? ἐόν, being, means: presencing, that is presencing precisely in the unhidden. In presencing, however, there is hidden the displaying that comes from unhiddenness, which allows what is present to essence as such. But what is actually present is just presencing itself, which is everywhere the same in its own center and, as its own center, is the sphere. The sphericality is not based on a circling which then surrounds, but rather on the unconcealing center that in throwing light saves what is present. The sphericality of the union and the union itself have the character of an unconcealing illumination, within which what is present can presence. That is why Parmenides calls the ἐόν, the presencing of what is present, the εὔκυκλος σφαίρη (Fragment 8, line 43, in Diels, *Fragmente der Vorsokratiker*). This well-rounded globe should be thought as the being of beings in the sense of the unconcealing-illuminating union. This union that unites everywhere in this way permits us to call it the illuminating globe which does not embrace, but rather itself releases illuminatingly into presencing. We must never represent the globe of being and the sphericality of the globe of being objectively. Therefore, non-objectively? No; that would be merely to dodge behind a phrase. The sphericality must be thought in terms of the essence of original being in the sense of unconcealing presencing.

Does Rilke's phrase about the widest compass mean this sphericality of being? Not only do we not have a ground for such an interpretation, but also his characterization of the being of beings as the risk (will) completely goes against it. Nonetheless, Rilke himself at one point speaks of the "globe of being," and he does this in a context that directly bears upon the interpretation of this talk of the widest compass. He writes in a letter on Epiphany [January 6], 1923 (cf. *Insel-Almanach auf das Jahr, 1938*, p. 109): ". . . like the moon, so life surely has a side continually turned away from us, which is not its opposite, but rather its complement toward perfection, toward full measure, toward the real, whole, and full sphere and globe of *being*." Although we must not press the figurative reference to heavenly bodies that are presented objectively, it nonetheless remains clear that Rilke is not thinking of sphericality from the perspective of being in the sense of the illuminating-oneing presencing, but rather from the perspective of beings in the sense of the full measure of all their sides. What Rilke calls here the globe of being (that is, the globe of beings in their entirety) is the open as the closure of the pure forces that overflow into each other without barrier and so act toward each other. The widest compass is the entirety of the whole attraction of attracting. To this widest circle there corresponds the strongest center, "the unheard center" of pure gravity.

To turn defenselessness into the open means: "to say yes" to defenselessness within the widest compass. Such an affirmation is possible only where the entirety of the compass in every respect is not only in full measure but also of equal measure, and so already lies before us and accordingly is the *positum*. Only position and never negation can correspond to it. Even the sides of life that are turned away from us are to be taken positively, provided they are in being. The letter of November 13, 1925, mentioned above, says: "Death is the *side of life* turned away from us, unlit by us" (*Briefe aus Muzot*, p. 332). Death and the kingdom of the dead belong, as the other side, to the entirety of beings. This realm is "the other attraction," that is, the other side of the whole attraction of the open. In the widest compass of the globe of beings, there are such realms and places that, since they are turned away from us, appear to be something negative, but they are nothing of the sort if we think into the widest compass of beings.

Seen from the open, defenselessness too, as the departure against the pure attraction, seems to be something negative. The departing self-assertion of objectification everywhere intends the constancy of produced objects; it lets only this constancy count as a being and as positive. The self-assertion of technological objectification is the constant negation of death. Through this negation, death itself becomes something negative; it becomes the archetype of the inconstant and the void. However, when we turn defenselessness into the open, we turn it into the widest compass of beings, within which we can only affirm defenselessness. Turning into the open is the refusal to read that which is as negative. But what is more being, and therefore, as moderns think it, what is more certain than death? The letter cited above from January 6, 1923, says that it is valid "to read the word 'death' *without* negation."

When we turn defenselessness as such into the open, we then reverse it in its essence (i.e., as the departure against the whole attraction) into an inclining toward the widest compass. It only remains to affirm what has been reversed in this way. Yet this affirmation does not mean turning the no into a yes, but rather to acknowledge the positive as that which already lies before us and presences. This happens when we allow the defenselessness that has been inverted to belong within the widest compass, "where law touches us." Rilke does not say: a law. He therefore does not mean a rule. He is thinking of what "touches us." Who are we? We are the ones who will, who set up, in the mode of deliberate self-assertion, the world as object.

When we are touched from out of the widest compass, then this touching concerns our essence. To touch means: bring into motion. Our essence is brought into motion. In stirring us, our will is shaken, so that only then does the essence of will come to light and become set in motion. Only then it is possible to will willingly.

Yet what is it that touches us directly from out of the widest compass? What is it that, in the ordinary will to objectify the world, is obstructed and withdrawn from us by us ourselves? It is the other attraction: death. It is death that touches mortals in their essence and so places them on the way to the other side of life and so into the entirety of the pure attraction. This is how death gathers into the entirety of what has already been placed, into the *positum* of the whole attraction. As this gathering through placement [*Setzen*], death is the law [*Ge-setz*], just as the mountain range [*Gebirg*] is the gathering of the mountains [*Berge*] into the entirety of their nexus [*Gezüges*]. There where law touches us within the widest compass is the place where we can admit inverted defenselessness positively into the entirety of beings. Defenselessness so turned saves us at last outside of all defense, into the open. Yet how is this turning possible? In what way can the reversal [*Umkehrung*] of turning away [*Abkehr*] that departs against the open take place? Presumably in this way alone: this reversal first inclines us [*zukehrt*] toward the widest compass and lets us in our essence come [*einkehren*] into it. The realm of safebeing must first be shown to us; it must be accessible beforehand as the potential scope for reversal. However, what brings us safebeing, and with it the dimension of certainty in general, is that risk which sometimes risks more than life itself does.

But this risk that risks more does not busy itself here and there about our defenselessness. It does not attempt to adjust this or that way of objectifying the world. On the contrary it turns defenselessness as such. The risk that risks more actually brings defenselessness into its own realm.

What is the essence of defenselessness, if it consists of objectification which is based on deliberate self-assertion? The objectiveness [*Gegenständige*] of the world becomes *constant* [*ständig*] in representational production. This representing makes a presentation. However, what is present is present in a representation that has the nature of calculation. This representing knows nothing of the immediately visible [*Anschauliches*]. What is immediately visible in things, the picture they offer to direct sensible intuition [*Anschauung*], falls away. Calculating production is an "action without image" (*Ninth Elegy*). Facing the immediately visible image [*Bild*], deliberate self-assertion, in its projects, places a scheme based only on calculated constructions [*Gebilde*]. When the world enters into the objectiveness of factitious constructions, it is placed in the insensible, the invisible. This constancy of objectiveness [*das Ständige*] owes its presence to a placement whose activity belongs to the *res cogitans*, that is, to consciousness. The sphere of the objectivity of objects remains within consciousness. The invisibility of objectiveness belongs to the inwardness of the immanence of consciousness.

However, if defenselessness is departure against the open, and if departure nonetheless rests on the objectification that belongs to the invisibility and inwardness of calculating consciousness, then the essential sphere of defenselessness is the invisibility and inwardness of consciousness.

If, however, the inversion of defenselessness into the open concerns the essence of defenselessness in advance, then the reversal of defenselessness is a reversal of consciousness, or more precisely *within* the sphere of consciousness. The sphere of the invisible and the inward determines the essence of defenselessness, but it also determines the nature of the turning of defenselessness into the widest compass. Consequently, it can only be to the most invisible invisibility and the most inward inwardness that the essentially inward and invisible must turn itself in order to find what is actually its own. In modern metaphysics, the sphere of the invisible inward is defined as the realm of the presence of calculated objects. Descartes characterized the sphere as the consciousness of the *ego cogito*.

At about the same time as Descartes, Pascal discovered the logic of the heart in contrast to the logic of calculating reason. The interior and the invisible of the heart's space is not only more inward than the interior of calculating representation, and therefore more invisible, but at the same time it also reaches further than the realm of objects that are merely produced. Only in the invisible innermost of the heart does man tend toward that which is to be loved: ancestors, the dead, childhood, those who are coming. These belong in the widest compass, which proves now to be the sphere of the presence of the whole integral attraction. Admittedly, this presence, like that of the conventional consciousness of calculating production, is a presence of immanence. However, the interior of unwonted consciousness remains the interior space in which everything, for us, is beyond the numbering [*Zahlhafte*] of calculation and, freed from these barriers, can overflow into the unbarred entirety of the open. This overflowing beyond number [*überzählige*] springs up, with regard to its presence, in the inward and invisible of the heart. The last words of the *Ninth Elegy*, which sings of men belonging to the open, run: "Existence beyond number springs up in my heart."

The widest compass of beings becomes present in the inner space of the heart. The entirety of the world attains here a presence in each of its attractions that is essentially equal. Rilke calls this presence, in the language of metaphysics, "existence" [*Dasein*]. The whole presence of the world is "worldly existence" in the largest sense. That is another name for the open; this other name comes from thinking the open itself out from the immanence of the calculating consciousness and into the inner space of the heart, which means that the representing-producing turning away against the open has been reversed. The heartful inner space for worldly existence is therefore also called the "world inner space." "Worldly" means the entirety of beings.

Rilke writes in a letter from Muzot on August 11, 1924:

> As extended as the "outside" is, with all its sidereal dimensions it hardly bears comparison *with the depth dimension of our inwardness* which does not even need the spaciousness of the universe to be in itself almost immeasurable. So if the dead, if the future ones, need a residence, *what* refuge would be more pleasant and more proffered to them than this imaginary space? It increasingly appears to me as though our customary consciousness inhabits the apex of a pyramid whose base in us (and in a certain sense beneath us) extends to so great a breadth that the more competent we find ourselves to descend into it, the more generally we seem involved in the facts of earthly, of *worldly* (in the widest sense) existence, facts independent of time and space.

However, the objectiveness of the world is still to be calculated in representation which treats time and space as quanta for calculation and can know as little of the essence of time as of the essence of space. Even Rilke fails to consider the spatiality of the world's inner space further, nor does he even begin to ask whether world inner space, since after all it provides an abode for worldly presence, is grounded by this presence in a temporality whose essential time together with essential space forms the originary oneness of that time-space by which even being itself essences.

However, what Rilke is trying to do, within the sphericality of modern metaphysics (i.e., within the sphere of subjectivity as the sphere of inward and invisible presence), is to understand the defenselessness posed by the self-asserting essence of man in such a way that the defenselessness itself, reversed, saves us in the innermost and most invisible region of the widest inner space of the world. Defenselessness as such brings us to safety. For as the inward and invisible, it gives to its essence the sign for a reversal of the turning away against the open. The reversal points into the inward of the interior. The reversal of consciousness is therefore a memory of the immanence of the objects of representation, a making inward into presence within the heart's space.

As long as man is exclusively absorbed in deliberate self-assertion, it is not only he himself that is defenseless, but also things since they have become objects. In this, it is true, there is another transformation of things into the inward and invisible. However, this transformation substitutes for the frailty of things the factitious constructions of calculated objects. These objects are produced for consumption. The more quickly they are consumed, the more necessary it becomes to replace them ever more quickly and easily. That which is enduring about the presence of objective things is not their resting-in-themselves in their own world. What is constant about things produced as mere objects of consumption is the substitute [*Ersatz*].

Just as the waning and disappearance of familiar things within the supremacy of objectivity is part of our defenselessness, so the safebeing of our essence demands that things be saved from mere objectivity. The salvation of things consists in their being able to rest in themselves within the widest compass of the whole attraction, that is, to rest unrestrictedly in each other. Perhaps the turning of our defenselessness into worldly existence within world inner space actually has to commence with our turning the frail and therefore provisional quality of objective things from out of the inwardness and invisibility of merely productive consciousness and into the actual interior of the heart's space and our permitting it to rise up there invisibly. Accordingly the letter of November 13, 1925 says (*Briefe aus Muzot*, p. 335):

> . . . our task is this, to imprint this provisional, frail earth so deeply, so sufferingly and passionately that its essence rises up again within us "invisibly." We are the bees of the invisible. Nous butinons éperdument le miel du visible, pour accumuler dans la grande ruche d'or de l'Invisible. [We gather constantly the honey of the visible in order to preserve it in the great golden hive of the Invisible.]

Memory, making inward, inverts our essence that only wills assertively, and its objects, into the innermost invisibility of the heart's space. Here everything is inwardly then: not only does everything remain turned toward this actual interior of consciousness, but also within this interior one thing turns itself for us into another without restriction. The inwardliness of world inner space unbars the open for us. Only what we inwardly keep (*par cœur*) in this manner do we really know by heart. In this inwardliness we are free, outside of the relationship to objects that only appear to protect us and that are placed around us. In the inwardliness of world inner space there is a safebeing outside of all defense.

Yet the question we have been asking all along is how can this memory, this making inward, of the already-immanent objectiveness of consciousness happen in the innermost of the heart? It is a matter of the inward and the invisible. For what is remembered (made inward) as well as where it is remembered (made inward) are of such an essence. Memory, making inward, reverses departure into the arrival into the widest compass of the open. Who among mortals is capable of this reversing memory, this making inward that reverses?

Admittedly, the poem says that a safebeing of our essence would be brought to us by the fact that men "sometimes even risk more . . . than life itself does, by a breath risk more."

What do they risk, those who risk more? The poem, it appears, is silent about the answer. We will therefore try to accommodate the poem thoughtfully and draw on other poems for help.

We ask the question: what else could be risked, what would risk more than life itself, that is, more than the risk itself, that is, risk more than the being of beings? In each case and in every respect what is risked must be of such a kind that it affects all beings because they are beings. Being is of such a kind; that is, it is not one particular kind among others, but the mode of beings as such.

If being is the uniqueness of a being, how is it possible to go beyond being? Only through being itself, only through what is its own, or rather in such a way that it comes specifically into its own. Then being would be the uniqueness that preeminently goes beyond itself (the *transcendens* par excellence). However, this surpassing does not go up and over unto another, but rather it comes over unto itself and back into the essence of its truth. Being itself traverses this passage and is itself its dimension.

Thinking this, we find by experience that within being itself there is a "more" belonging to it and so we find the possibility that there too, where being is thought as the risk, that which risks more than even being itself can prevail, if we are representing being as we usually do, on the basis of beings. Being traverses, as itself, its precinct [*Bezirk*] which is demarcated [*bezirkt*] (τέμνειν, *tempus*) by the fact that it essences in the word. Language is the precinct (*templum*), i.e., the house of being. The essence of language is neither exhausted in reference, nor is it only a matter of signs and ciphers. Since language is the house of being, we therefore arrive at beings by constantly going through this house. If we go to the fountain, if we go through the woods, we are already going through the word "fountain," through the word "wood," even if we are not saying these words aloud or have any thoughts about language. By thinking in terms of the temple of being, we can imagine what it is they risk, the ones who risk more than the being of beings. They risk the precinct of being. They risk language. All beings, the objects of consciousness and the things of the heart, the self-asserting men and the men who risk more, all creatures, each in its own way, are (as beings) in the precinct of language. That is why *only in this precinct*, if anywhere, can the reversal from the region of objects and their representation into the innermost of the heart's space be realized.

For Rilke's poetry, the being of beings is determined metaphysically as worldly presence, a presence which remains attracted to representation in consciousness, whether this has the character of the immanence of calculating representation or that of inwardly turning to the open made accessible by the heart.

The entire sphere of presence is present in saying. The objectiveness of production is found in the expression of calculating propositions and theorems of reason that proceed from proposition to proposition. The realm of self-assertive defenselessness is dominated by reason. Not only has reason set up a special system of rules for its saying, for the λόγος as explanatory predicates, but also the logic of reason itself organizes the domination of deliberate self-assertion within the objective. In the reversal of objective representation, the logic of the heart corresponds to the saying of memory. In both realms, which are metaphysically determined, logic prevails because memory, making inward, is to fashion a safebeing from defenselessness itself and outside of all defense. This bringing to safety concerns man as the creature that has language. Within being that has been stamped metaphysically, this is how man has [*hat*] language: he takes it in advance and only as a possession [*Habe*] and thus as a handle [*Handhabe*] for representation and behavior. That is why the λόγος, saying as organon, is in need of organization by logic. Only within metaphysics is there logic.

Now when, however, at the fashioning of safebeing man is touched by the law of the entire world inner space, he is himself touched in his essence by the fact that he, as the one who wills himself, is the one who is already saying. Nonetheless, in that the fashioning of a safebeing comes from the ones who risk more, they must risk it with language. The ones who risk more are the ones who risk saying. Yet if this precinct of risking, language, belongs to being in the unique way that beyond and outside it nothing else of its nature can exist, where is that which is supposed to be said spoken by those who must say? Their saying concerns the remembering (making inward) reversal of consciousness which turns our defenselessness into the invisibility of world inner space. Because it concerns the reversal, their saying speaks not only from both realms but also from the oneness of both, if the reversal has already taken place as the saving union. For this reason, when the entirety of beings is thought as the open of the pure attraction, the remembering reversal must be a saying that says what it has to say to a creature already secure in the entirety of beings because it has already carried out the transformation of represented visibility into the invisibility of the heart. This creature is included in the pure attraction by both sides of the globe of being. This creature, for whom limits and differences among attractions hardly exist any longer, is the creature who manages the unheard center of the widest compass and lets it appear. This creature, in Rilke's *Duino Elegies*, is the angel. This name is another fundamental word of Rilke's poetry. It, like "the open," "the attraction," "departure," "nature," is a fundamental word because what is said in it thinks the entirety of beings in terms of being. In the letter of November 13, 1925 (*Briefe aus Muzot*, p. 337), Rilke writes:

> The angel of the *Elegies* is that creature in whom the transformation of the visible into the invisible, which we are achieving, is already accomplished . . . The angel of the elegies is that being who affirms the recognition of a higher rank of reality in the invisible.

The extent to which, within the fulfillment of modern metaphysics, the attraction to such a creature is part of the being of beings, the extent to which the essence of the Rilkean angel is *metaphysically the same*, with all their differences in content, as the Nietzschean figure of Zarathustra, can only be shown from a more originary unfolding of the essence of subjectivity.

The poem thinks the being of beings, Nature, as the risk. All beings are risked into the risk. As that which is risked, they lie upon the balance. The balance is the way that being always weighs beings, i.e., holds them in the movement of swaying. Everything that is risked is in danger. The realms of beings are differentiated according to the nature of their relationship to the balance. The essence of the angel must also be clarified with respect to the balance, assuming the angel occupies the higher rank in the entire realm of beings.

Plant and animal, in "the risk of their dull desire," are held free from care in the open. Their physicality does not confuse them. Living beings are lulled into the open by their drives. Indeed, they too are threatened, but not in their essence. Plant and animal lie upon the balance in such a way that the balance always plays out in the calm of a safebeing. The balance into which plant and animal are risked does not yet reach into the realm of the essentially and therefore constantly uncalmed. The balance upon which the angel is risked also remains outside the uncalmed; not, however, because the balance does not yet belong in the realm of the uncalmed, but because it no longer belongs there. In accordance with the angel's incorporeal essence, potential confusion through what is visible to the angel's senses has been transformed into the invisible. The angel essences from the calmed quiet of the equilibrated oneness of both realms within world inner space.

Man, on the other hand, as one who deliberately asserts himself, is risked into defenselessness. The scales of danger are essentially uncalmed in the hand of the man who has been so risked. The self-willing man always calculates with things and people as he does with objects. That with which he has calculated turns into merchandise. Everything is constantly changed into new orderings. Departure against the pure attraction is established in the unquiet of the constantly swaying balance. Departure, in the objectification of the world, against its own intention, pursues the inconstant. Risked into defenselessness in this way, man moves in the medium of businesses and "exchanges." Self-asserting man lives by his will's stakes. He lives essentially in the hazard of his essence within the vibration of money and the validity of values. Man, as this constant exchanger and middleman, is "the merchant." He weighs and evaluates constantly and yet does not know the actual weight of things. Nor does he ever know what, in him, actually has weight and outweighs. This is what Rilke says in one of the *Späte Gedichte* (pp. 21ff.):

> Alas, who knows what weighs the most in him.
> Mildness? Terror? Glances, voices, books?
>
> Ach wer kennt, was in ihm überwiegt.
> Mildheit? Schrecken? Blicke, Stimmen, Bücher?

However, man outside of all defense can at the same time fashion a "safebeing" by turning his defenselessness as such into the open and transforming it into the heart's space of the invisible. Once this happens, the uncalm of defenselessness passes over to where, in the equilibrated oneness of world inner space, the creature appears who brings to light the way in which oneness unites and who in that way represents being. The scales of danger then pass from the realm of the calculating will over to the angel. Four lines are preserved from Rilke's late period which evidently constitute the beginning of a draft of a larger poem. They run (*Gesammelte Werke*, vol. III, p. 438):

> When from the merchant's hand
> the balance passes over
> to that angel who in the heavens
> calms and soothes it with the equilibrium of space . . .
>
> Wenn aus des Kaufmanns Hand
> Die Wage übergeht
> an jenen Engel, der sie in den Himmeln
> stillt und beschwichtigt mit des Raumes Ausgleich . . .

The equilibrating space is the world inner space in that it makes space for the worldly entirety of the open. In this way it grants both to the one and to the other attraction the appearance of their uniting union. This union, as the integral globe of being, encompasses all the pure forces of beings by circulating through all creatures, in-finitely unbarring them. Such things become present when the balance passes over. When does it pass over? Who lets the balance pass from the merchant over to the angel? If such a passing happens at all, then it occurs in the precinct of the balance. The element of the scales is the risk, the being of beings. We have been thinking language specifically as the precinct of being.

The usual life of today's man is the ordinariness of self-assertion in the defenseless market of exchangers. In contrast, to pass the balance over to the angel is unusual. It is even unusual not only because it constitutes the exception within the rule but also because it takes man with regard to his essence into the outside of the rule of defense and defenselessness. This is the reason that passing over happens "sometimes." In no way does that mean here: from time to time or as you like; "sometimes" means rarely and at the right time in each single case in its singular way. Passing the balance over from the merchant to the angel, i.e., the reversal of departure, happens as the remembering (the making inward) into world inner space at the time when there are such men who "sometimes risk more . . . by a breath risk more."

Because those who risk more risk it with being itself and therefore risk themselves into language, the precinct of being, they are the ones who say. But is not man, then, the one who has language by his essence and constantly risks his essence with language? Certainly. Then the one who wills in the usual way also already risks saying in calculating production. Of course. Then, however, those who risk more cannot be those who merely say. The saying [*Sagen*] of those who risk more must specifically risk what is said [*Sage*]. Those who risk more are only who they are when they are the ones who say more.

When, in our representing and producing relationship [*Verhältnis*] to beings, we conduct ourselves [*s. verhalten*] by making statements, then such saying is not what is being willed. Making statements remains a way and a means. In contrast, there is a saying that is specially engaged with what is said without, however, reflecting on language and thereby turning it too into an object. To enter into what is said characterizes a saying that pursues what is to be said solely in order to say it. What is to be said would then be that which, in accordance with its essence, belongs in the precinct of language. That, in metaphysical thinking, would be beings in their entirety. Their entirety is the unbrokenness of the pure attraction, the wholeness of the open, in that it grants man space. This happens in world inner space. This space touches man when, within the reversing inward memory, he turns himself [*s. zuwendet*] to the heart's space. Those who risk more turn [*wenden*] the unwholeness of defenselessness into the wholeness of worldly existence. This is what is to be said. In the saying there is a turn [*s. wendet*] toward men. Those who risk more are the ones who say more in the manner of the singer. Their singing is stolen [*entwenden*] from all deliberate self-assertion. It is not a willing in the sense of coveting. Their song does not solicit [*bewirbt*] something to be produced. In song it is world inner space itself that grants space. The song of this singer is not an advertisement [*Werben*] and not a business [*Gewerbe*].

The saying that says more, by those who risk more, is song. However,

"Song is existence"
"Gesang ist Dasein"

is what the third sonnet says in the first part of the *Sonnets to Orpheus*. The word "existence" is here in the traditional sense of presence and is synonymous with being. To sing, to say specifically worldly existence, to say it from the wholeness of the whole pure attraction and only this, that means: to belong in the precinct of beings themselves. As the essence of language, this precinct is being itself. To sing song, means: to be present in presencing itself; it means: existence.

Yet since only those who risk more are capable of it, the saying that says more is only occasional. For it remains difficult. What is difficult is to accomplish existence. What is difficult is not only the difficulty of making a work of the language, but also to pass from the saying work of the vision still covetous of things, from the work of the visage to the "heart's work."[13] Song is difficult when the singing may no longer be solicitation but must be existence. For the god Orpheus, who abides endlessly in the open, song is easy, but not for man. That is why the second stanza of that sonnet asks:

But when *are* we?
Wann *aber* sind wir?

The stress is on the "are," not on the "we." There is no question that we belong among beings and are present in this respect. However, there is still the question of when we are in such a way that our being is song. And not just song whose singing resounds indiscriminately; but song that is truly a singing, song whose sound is not attached to something to be attained in the end but instead is shattered even in the sounding, so that only the very thing that is sung comes to presence. Thus men say more when they risk more than beings themselves are. Those who risk more, according to the poem, "by a breath risk more." The sonnet we have cited concludes:

To sing in truth is another breath.
A breath for nothing. A blowing in God. A wind.

In Wahrheit singen, ist ein andrer Hauch.
Ein Hauch um nichts. Ein Wehn im Gott. Ein Wind.

Herder writes in his *Reflections on the Philosophy of the History of Mankind* (*Sämtliche Werke*, ed. Suphan, vol. XIII, p. 355):

A breath of our mouth is the picture of the world, the type of our thoughts and feelings in the soul of another. Every human thing that man has ever thought, willed, done, and will do upon earth has depended on the movement of a bit of air; for we would all still be wanderers in the woods if this divine breath had not inspired us and hovered on our lips like a charm.

The breath by which those who risk more risk more does not only or primarily mean the hardly noticeable (because fleeting) measure of a difference; rather, it signifies directly the word and the essence of language. The ones who by a breath risk more risk it with language. They are the saying ones who are saying more. For this one breath by which they risk more is not just saying in general; rather, the one breath is an other breath, a saying other than what human saying usually is. The other breath no longer solicits for this or that objective thing; it is a breath for nothing. The saying of the singer says the integral entirety of worldly existence that grants its space invisibly in the world inner space of the heart. Song does not even pursue first what is to be said. Song is the belonging in the entirety of the pure attraction. To sing is drawn [*gezogen*] from the draft [*Zug*] of the wind of the unheard center of full Nature. Song is itself: "A wind."

So, then, the poem in its poetry does after all unambiguously say who they are who risk more than life itself does. They are the ones who "by a breath risk more." There is a point to the ellipsis that follows in the text of the poem after "by a breath risk more." It says what is silently withheld.

Those who risk more are the poets, but poets whose song turns our defenselessness into the open. Because they reverse the departure against the open and inwardly remember its unwholeness [*Heil-loses*] into the integral [*heile*] whole, these poets sing the integral in disintegration [*im Unheilen das Heile*]. The remembering reversal that is made inward has already overtaken the turning away against the open. It is "ahead of all departure"[14] and surmounts, in the world inner space of the heart, everything objective. The reversing inward remembrance is the risk that is dared out of the essence of man in that he has language and is the one that says.

Modern man, however, is called the one who wills. The ones who risk more are the ones who will more, in that they will in another mode than the deliberative self-assertion of the objectification of the world. Their willing wills nothing of this nature. If will remains only self-assertion, they will nothing. They will nothing in this sense because they are more willing. They comply rather with the will which, as the risk itself, draws all the pure forces unto itself as the pure whole attraction of the open. The willing of those who risk more is the willingness of those who say more, who are resolute [*ent-schlossen*], no longer shut [*verschlossen*] in departure against the will by which being wills beings. The willing essence of those who risk more says more sayingly (in the words of the *Ninth Elegy*):

> Earth, isn't it this your will: invisibly
> to rise within us? – Isn't it your dream
> to be invisible one day? – Earth! invisible!
> What, if not transformation, is your urgent mission?
> Earth, dear one, I will.

> Erde, ist es nicht dies, was du willst: unsichtbar
> in uns erstehn? – Ist es dein Traum nicht,
> einmal unsichtbar zu sein? – Erde! unsichtbar!
> Was, wenn Verwandlung nicht, ist dein drängender Auftrag?
> Erde, du liebe, ich will.

In the invisibility of world inner space, as the unity of which the angel appears, the wholeness of worldly beings becomes evident. Only in the widest compass of the whole is the holy able to appear. Because they experience unwholeness as such, poets of the kind who risk more are underway on the track of the holy. Their song sanctifies over the land. Their song celebrates the unbrokenness of the globe of being.

The unwhole, as the unwhole, traces for us what is whole. What is whole beckons and calls to the holy. The holy binds the divine. The divine brings God closer.

Those who risk more experience defenselessness in unwholeness. They bring mortals the track of the fugitive gods in the darkness of the world's night. Those who risk more, as singers of what is whole, are "poets in a desolate time."

The distinctive mark of these poets consists in the fact that for them the essence of poetry has become worth questioning, since they are poetically on the track of that which, for them, is to be said. On the track to what is whole, Rilke arrives at the poetical question: when may song be that sings essentially? This question does not stand at the beginning of the poetic path, but rather at the point where Rilke's saying arrives at the poetic vocation of the poetry that answers to the coming world-era. This era is neither decay nor decline. As destiny it lies in being and lays claim to man.

Hölderlin is the forerunner of the poets in a desolate time. That is why no poet of this era can overtake him. The forerunner, however, does not go away into a future, rather he arrives from it in such a way that in the advent [*Ankunft*] of his words alone the future [*Zukunft*] presences. The more purely the advent takes place, the more essentially, the more essenced, it remains. The more what is coming is secretly conserved in the foretelling, the purer the arrival. That is why it would be erroneous to say that Hölderlin's time would come only when "everyone" understands his poetry. It will never come in such a deformed way. Its own desolation is what puts at the disposal of the era the forces by which, knowing not what it is doing, the era prevents Hölderlin's poetry from becoming timely.

The forerunner [*Vorgänger*] can as little be overtaken as he can pass away [*vergänglich ist*], for his poetry remains as something that has been in an essential way [*Ge-wesenes*]. What essences [*das Wesende*] in the advent gathers itself back into destiny. What does not fall into the course of passing away [*Vergehen*] overcomes at the start all that is transient [*Vergänglichkeit*]. What has merely passed away is already, in advance of its passing away, without destiny. What has been in an essential way, by contrast, is the destining. In what we suppose is eternity, something merely transitory [*Vergängliches*] has been concealed, put away into the void of a now without duration.

If Rilke is a "poet in a desolate time," then only his poetry will answer the question why he is a poet, what it is his song is underway to, where the poet belongs in the destiny of the world's night. This destiny will decide the question of what within his poetry remains destining.

Anaximander's Saying

It is considered to be the oldest saying of Western thinking. Anaximander is said to have lived on the island of Samos from the end of the seventh century until the middle of the sixth.

According to the generally accepted text the fragment reads:

ἐξ ὧν δὲ ἡ γένεσίς ἐστι τοῖς οὖσι καὶ τὴν φθορὰν εἰς ταῦτα γίνεσθαι κατὰ τὸ χρεών· διδόναι γὰρ αὐτὰ δίκην καὶ τίσιν ἀλλήλοις τῆς ἀδικίας κατὰ τὴν τοῦ χρόνου τάξιν.

Whence things have their coming into being there they must also perish according to necessity; for they must pay a penalty and be judged for their injustice, according to the ordinance of time.

Thus the youthful Nietzsche's translation in his treatise of 1873 entitled "Philosophy in the Tragic Age of the Greeks." This treatise was first published posthumously in 1903, thirty years after its composition. It is based on a lecture course Nietzsche had given several times in Basle in the early 1870s under the title "The Pre-Platonic Philosophers with Interpretation of Selected Fragments."

In the same year, 1903, in which Nietzsche's treatise first became publicly available, Hermann Diels' *Pre-Socratic Fragments* [*Fragmente der Vorsokratiker*] appeared. It contained texts critically established according to the methods of modern classical philology, together with a translation. The work is dedicated to Wilhelm Dilthey. Diels translates Anaximander's saying as follows:

But where things derive their coming into being, there their passing away also occurs according to necessity; for they pay each other punishment and penalty for their dastardliness according to firmly established time.

The translations of Nietzsche and Diels arise from different impulses and intentions. Nonetheless they are hardly distinguishable. Diels' translation is in many respects the more literal. But if a translation is merely literal it cannot be assumed to be faithful. It only becomes faithful when its words are words that speak out of the language of the matter.

More important than the general agreement of the two translations is the conception of Anaximander which underlies them. Nietzsche takes him to belong to the pre-Platonics, Diels to the pre-Socratics. Both designations say the same. The implicit standard for explicating and judging the early thinkers is the philosophy of Plato and Aristotle. Both are taken as the philosophers of the Greeks who set the standard both before and after themselves. This perception, *via* Christian theology, has established itself as a general conviction that, to this very day, remains unshaken. Even where, in the meantime, philological and historical research has occupied itself more thoroughly with the philosophers before Plato and Aristotle, their interpretation is still guided by modern versions of Platonic and Aristotelian representations and concepts. This is even the case where one seeks to discover the archaic in early thinking by looking for parallels in classical archeology and literary history. It remains within classical and classicistic representations. One speaks of archaic logic heedless of the fact that such a thing as logic exists for the first time within the Platonic and Aristotelian curriculum.

Merely ignoring later representations leads nowhere unless we, first of all, look to how it stands with the matter which, in the translation from one language to another, is to be translated. The matter here, however, is the matter of thought. Granted that in translation we must take every care to attend to the philologically clarified language, first and foremost, nonetheless, we must think about the matter itself. Hence only the thinkers can help us in the attempt to translate the saying of this early thinker. When, however, we cast about for such help we search in vain.

The young Nietzsche does indeed, in his own way, establish a lively relationship to the personality of the pre-Platonic philosophers, but his interpretation of the texts are thoroughly commonplace, even quite superficial. The only Western thinker who has thoughtfully experienced the history of thought is Hegel. Yet even he has nothing to say about Anaximander's saying. Moreover, Hegel, too, shares the prevalent conviction concerning the classical character of Platonic and Aristotelian philosophy. He endorses the view which classifies the early thinkers as the "pre-Platonics" and "pre-Socratics" precisely through grasping them as the "pre-Aristotelians."

In his lectures on the history of Greek philosophy, at the point where he comes to speak about the sources for our knowledge of the oldest epoch of philosophy, Hegel says the following:

Aristotle is the richest source. He made a thorough study of, in particular, the oldest philosophers. At the beginning of his *Metaphysics* (but in many other places too) he speaks of them in a systematically historical way. He is as philosophical as he is scholarly; we can rely on him. For Greek philosophy we can do nothing better than get to work on the first book of his *Metaphysics*.

(*Werke*, vol. XIII, p. 189)

What Hegel recommends, here, to his listeners in the first decades of the nineteenth century was practiced, in Aristotle's own time, by Theophrastus, his pupil and immediate successor as leader of the Peripatetics. Theophrastus died in 286 BC. He composed a text with the title Φυσικῶν δόξαι, "The Opinions of Those Who Speak of φύσει ὄντα." Aristotle also calls them the φυσιολόγοι, meaning the early thinkers who discuss the things of nature. Φύσις means sky and earth, plants and animals, and in a certain sense, human beings as well. The word designates a special region of beings which, in Aristotle and in the School of Plato in general, is separated from ἦθος and λόγος. For them Φύσις no longer has the wider meaning of the totality of beings. From the beginning of Aristotle's thematic observations in the *Physics*, the kind of being called φύσει ὄντα is contrasted with that of τέχνῃ ὄντα. The former is that which brings itself forth by arising out of itself, the latter is that which is brought forth through human planning and production.

Hegel's remark that Aristotle is as philosophical as he is scholarly means the following: that Aristotle sees the early thinkers from the historical perspective of his *Physics*. For us this means that Hegel understood the pre-Platonic and pre-Socratic philosophers as the pre-Aristotelians. After Hegel, two positions within the general view of philosophy before Aristotle and Plato became firmly established. (1) In their search for the first origins of beings the early thinkers, first and foremost, took nature alone as the object of their reflections. (2) Their pronouncements on nature are inadequate approximations compared with the knowledge of nature which later unfolded in the Platonic and Aristotelian schools, and with the Stoics and in the schools of medicine.

The Φυσικῶν δόξαι of Theophrastus became the chief source for textbooks on the history of philosophy during the age of Hellenism. These textbooks determined the interpretation of those of the early thinkers' original texts that still survived. Out of them, too, grew the subsequent doxographical tradition in philosophy. Not just the content but also the style of this tradition formed the relationship of later thinkers to the history of thought – up to Hegel and beyond.

In about AD 510, the neo-Platonist, Simplicius, wrote a comprehensive commentary on Aristotle's *Physics*. In it he reproduces the text of Anaximander's saying, thereby preserving it for the West. He took it over from Theophrastus' Φυσικῶν δόξαι. From the time that Anaximander uttered his saying – we do not know where, or how, or to whom – until the time Simplicius inscribed it in his commentary, more than a thousand years had elapsed. Between the time of his inscription and the present lies another millennium and a half.

Can the saying of Anaximander, from the historical distance, chronologically reckoned, of two and a half thousand years still speak to us? From what authority should it speak? Only the authority of being the oldest? In themselves, the ancient and the antiquarian carry no weight. Besides, though the saying is indeed the oldest preserved in our tradition, we do not know whether it is the earliest saying of its kind in Western thought. We may surmise this provided we first think the essence of the West from out of that of which the early saying speaks.

But by what right does the early address us, presumably the latest of the latecomers to philosophy? Are we the latecomers of a history that now speeds toward its end, an end in which everything terminates in an ever more desolate ordering of uniformity? Or is there, concealed in the chronological remoteness of the saying, a historical proximity to the unspoken, an unspoken that will speak out in that which is coming?

Do we stand in the very twilight of the most monstrous transformation of the whole earth and of the time of the historical space in which it is suspended? Do we stand before the evening of the night of another dawn? Are we setting forth on a journey into the historical land of the earth's evening? Is the Land of the Evening[1] only now emerging? Will this Evening-Land, rising above Occident and Orient and transcending the European, become the place of the coming, more primordially destined, history? Are we men of today already "Western" in a sense that first arises out of our passage into the world's night? What are merely historiographically constructed philosophies of history supposed to tell us about history if they only dazzle us with a review of the material they adduce, if they explain history without ever thinking the foundations of the principles of explanation out of the essence of history, and this from out of being itself? *Are* we the latecomers who we are? Yet are we also the forerunners of the dawn of an altogether different age which has left behind today's historiographical representations of history?

Nietzsche (from whose philosophy, all too crudely understood, Spengler calculated the demise of the West in the sense of the historical world) wrote in his *The Wanderer and His Shadow*, which appeared in 1880:

> An exalted condition of humanity is possible, one in which the Europe of nations will be lost in dark forgetfulness, but in which Europe will *live on* in thirty very old, but never antiquated, books.
>
> (Aphorism 125)

All historiography calculates what is to come from its images of the past, images which are determined by the present. Historiography is the continual destruction of the future and our historical relation to the advent of destiny. Historicism today has not only not been overcome, but is entering only now the stage of its expansion and establishment. The technical organization of the public image of the world by radio and the press (which is already struggling to keep up) is the authentic form of the dominion of historicism.

Can we, however, represent and portray the dawn of an epoch in ways other than those of historiography? Perhaps it is for us the indispensable method of bringing the historical into the present. That in no way means, however, that historiography, taken in itself, enables us to form a relation that is adequate to reach to the historical within our history.

The antiquity which conditions Anaximander's saying belongs to the dawn of the dawn of the Land of the Evening. What if, however, that very first dawn overtook the latest, overtook it, indeed, by the greatest distance? The "once" of the dawn of destiny would then come as the "once" of the latest (ἔσχατον), that is, as the departure of the long-concealed destiny of being. The being of beings gathers itself (λέγεσθαι, λόγος) in the ultimacy of its destiny. The hitherto prevailing essence of being[a] disappears into its still concealed truth.[b] The history of being gathers itself in this departure. The gathering in this departure, as the gathering (λόγος) of the utmost (ἔσχατον) of its hitherto prevailing essence, is the eschatology of being. As destining, being itself is inherently eschatological.

[a] First edition, 1950. Presence – the allowing of presence: the essencing-to-presence [*das An-wesende*].

[b] First edition, 1950. Clearing [*Lichtung*] of the self-concealing.

We do not, however, understand the word "eschatology" in the phrase "eschatology of being" as the title of a theological or philosophical discipline. We think of the eschatology of being in the sense in which the phenomenology of Spirit is to be thought, i.e., from within the history of being. This phenomenology itself represents a phase in the eschatology of being in as much as being gathers itself, in the extremity of its hitherto – metaphysically determined – essence, as the absolute subjectivity of the will to will.

If we are to think from out of the eschatology of being we must one day await the "once" of the dawn in the "once" of what is approaching and must today learn to ponder this "once" from out of this approach.

If we can manage, just once, to hear the saying it will speak to us no longer as a historically remote opinion. If that happened, then we would not be misled into the vain attempt to reckon historically, that is, psycho-philologically, what was really present in the past, in the man called Anaximander of Miletus, as the condition of his representation of the world. What, however, presuming we have for once heard what is said in the saying, binds us in our attempt to translate it? How do we arrive at what is said in the saying so that it will preserve our translation from arbitrariness?

We are bound to the language of the saying and we are bound to our own native language. In both respects we are essentially bound to language and to the experience of its essence. This bond is stronger and further-reaching, although less conspicuous, than the standard provided by all the philological and historical facts – which only derive their factuality from it. As long as we fail to experience this bond, every translation of the saying must come to light as something completely arbitrary. Yet even when we are bound through that which is said in the saying, not just the translation but the bond, too, retains the appearance of violence. It is as if that which is to be heard is compelled to suffer violence.

Only through a dialogue between thought and what this thoughtful saying says can it be translated. The thinking is, however, poeticizing – though not in the sense of poesy or song. The thinking of being is the primordial form of poeticizing in which, before everything else, language first becomes language, enters, that is to say, its essence. Thinking says what the truth of being dictates.[a] Thinking is the ur-poetry which precedes all poesy. But it

[a] First Edition, 1950. That is to say, thinking is saying which releases [*Ent-sagen*], the saying of the Event.

precedes, too, the poetic in art insofar as art's becoming an artwork happens within the realm of language. All poeticizing, in both this broader and narrower sense of the poetic is, at bottom, thinking. The poeticizing essence of thought preserves the sway of the truth of being. Because it poeticizes thoughtfully, the translation which wishes to allow the oldest saying of thinking to speak necessarily appears violent.

We shall try to translate Anaximander's saying. This requires that we bring hither [*herübersetzen*] into our German language what is said in the Greek. To this end it is necessary that, before the translating, our thinking is translated [*übersetzt*] into what is said in Greek. To make this thoughtful translation to what comes to language in the saying is to leap over a gulf. This by no means consists merely in the chronological-historical distance of two and a half millennia. The gulf is wider and deeper. To leap over it is hard, above all because we stand right on its edge. We are so close to the gulf that we do not have a run up that is adequate for the take off and for the breadth of the leap. It is easy, therefore, to fall short – if, indeed, that lack of a sufficiently solid basis allows any take off at all.

What comes to language in the saying? The question is still ambiguous and therefore imprecise. It might ask for that about which the saying says something. It might also mean that which is said itself.

More literally translated, the saying runs:

> But that from which things have their arising also gives rise to their passing away according to necessity; they give justice and pay penalty to each other for the injustice according to the ordinance of time.

The usual view is that the sentence speaks about the arising and decay of things. It specifies the nature of this process. Arising and decay return to the place from where they came. Things develop and then they decay, exhibiting thereby a kind of barter system in nature's unchanging economy. The exchange between the constructive and destructive processes is, admittedly, established only roughly as a general characteristic of nature. The motions in which resides the mutability of all things are not yet represented in their precise measure. At this point an appropriate formula for a law of motion is still lacking. The judgment of later, more progressive times, is indulgent enough not to ridicule this beginner's attempt at scientific research. It even finds it to be perfectly in order that a first attempt at the observation of nature should describe processes in things in terms of those familiar from the human sphere. This is why Anaximander's saying speaks of justice and injustice, punishment and penalty, sin and recompense in relation to things. Moral and legal concepts infiltrate the picture of nature. Thus Theophrastus criticizes Anaximander for ποιητικωτέροις οὕτως ὀνόμασιν αὐτὰ λέγων, for speaking more poetically than is necessary. Theophrastus has in mind the words δίκη, τίσις, ἀδικία, διδόναι δίκην...

First and foremost, what we must do is to determine what the subject matter of the saying is. Only then will we be able to tell what it says about it.

From a grammatical point of view the saying consists of two sentences. The first begins: ἐξ ὧν δὲ ἡ γένεσίς ἐστι τοῖς οὖσι... The topic of discussion is the ὄντα. Literally translated, τὰ ὄντα means "the being." The neuter plural names τὰ πολλά, "the many," in the sense of the multiplicity of beings. But τὰ ὄντα does not mean an arbitrary or boundless multiplicity: rather, τὰ πάντα, the totality of beings. Hence τὰ ὄντα designates the multiplicity of beings as a whole. The second sentence begins: διδόναι γὰρ αὐτά... The αὐτά refers back to the τοῖς οὖσι of the first sentence.

The saying speaks about the manifold being. Not only things, however, belong among beings. In the fullest sense, things are not just natural things. Human beings, the things they produce, and the situations and circumstances effected and realized by human actions and omissions belong, too, among beings. And so do daemonic and divine things. All these things are not merely "also" beings, they are even more in being than mere things. The Aristotelian-Theophrastean presupposition that τὰ ὄντα are the φύσει ὄντα, natural things in the narrower sense, is completely groundless. It is, for our translation, untenable. But even the translation of τὰ ὄντα as "the things" does not suit the matter which comes to language in the saying.

If, however, the presupposition that the saying is concerned to say something about natural things fails, then so does all support for the assertion that what, strictly speaking, should be represented in the language of natural science is still interpreted in moral and legal terms. With the collapse of the presupposition that the saying strives for knowledge about the specifically demarcated realm of nature another assumption becomes invalid, namely, that at this time the ethical [*sittliche*] and the just were thought in terms of academic disciplines called "ethics" and "jurisprudence." The denial of such boundaries between disciplines does not at all mean that those early times recognized no law or ethics. If, however, our usual way of thinking within a range of disciplines (physics, ethics, philosophy of law, biology, psychology) has, here, no place, then, where boundaries between disciplines are absent, there is no possibility of boundary transgression, no possibility of the illegitimate transfer of representations from one area to another. The absence of boundaries between disciplines does not necessarily mean, however, the boundlessness of indeterminacy and flux. On the contrary, it can well be that purely thought – free of over-simple categorization – the actual structure of the matter comes to language.

The words δίκη, ἀδικία, τίσις have a broad signification which cannot be enclosed within particular disciplines. "Broad," here, does not mean extensive in the sense of flattened or thinned out, but rather far-reaching, rich, and containing much that has been thought out. For this reason it follows that precisely these and only these words are capable of bringing to language the manifold totality in the essence of its authentic unity. For that to happen the unified totality of the manifold, with its own characteristics, must, of course, be thought purely as it is in itself.

This way of letting the manifold being come, in its unity, to essential view is anything but a kind of primitive and anthropomorphic representation.

In order to trans-late ourselves into that which comes to language in the saying we must, prior to all translating, consciously set aside all inappropriate preconceptions. For example, that the saying deals with the philosophy of nature in a way such that inappropriate notions from morality and the law are mixed into the discussion. Or that sharply separated representations taken from the specialized areas of nature, ethics, and jurisprudence are relevant to the discussion. Or, finally, that a primitive outlook still prevails in the saying which interprets the world uncritically and anthropomorphically, and therefore takes refuge in poetic expressions.

However, even this casting aside of presuppositions wherever we find them inappropriate is insufficient so long as we fail to allow ourselves to be drawn into and to listen for that which comes to language in the saying. Only from out of such listening will one succeed in having a dialogue with early Greek thinking. It belongs to such a dialogue that the conversation speaks of the same thing, indeed out of a participation in the same. According to its wording, the saying speaks of the ὄντα. It expresses what and how it is with them. Beings are spoken of in such a way that their being is expressed. Being comes to language as the being of beings.

At the summit of the completion of Western philosophy the following words are said: "To stamp becoming with the character of being – that is the *highest will to power*." Thus wrote Nietzsche in a note entitled "Recapitulation." Going by the character of the handwriting we must locate the note in the year 1885, the time at which, having completed *Zarathustra*, he planned his great work of systematic metaphysics. "Being," as Nietzsche thinks it here, is "the eternal return of the same." It is the mode of permanence in which the will to power wills itself and secures its own presencing as the being of becoming. This is how the being of beings is expressed in the final stage of the completion of metaphysics.

Although the early aphorism of early thinking and the late aphorism of recent thinking bring to language the same, what they say is not the same. Nonetheless, if we can speak of the same being addressed from out of the different, then the fundamental condition for a thoughtful dialogue between the late and the early is automatically fulfilled.

Or does that merely seem to be the case? Does there lie concealed beneath this appearance the gulf between the language of our thinking and the language of Greek philosophy? Only if we take τὰ ὄντα to mean "the being" and εἶναι to mean nothing other than "to be" do we cross whatever gulfs there may be and – in spite of all the differences between the ages – place ourselves together with the ancient thinkers in the region of the same. This same validates for us the translation of τὰ ὄντα and εἶναι as "the being" and "to be." Or to demonstrate the unimpeachable correctness of this translation do we need first to produce as evidence a broad selection of texts from Greek philosophy? All interpretations of Greek philosophy are based already on this translation. Every dictionary gives us the fullest information to the effect that εἶναι means "to be," ἔστιν "is," ὄν "being," and τὰ ὄντα "the being."

This is how things stand. We have no intention of casting doubt on any of it. We do not question the translation of ὄν as "being," nor that of εἶναι as "to be." We ask, merely, whether in these correct translations correct thinking is occurring. We ask, merely, whether, in these most commonplace of all translations, anything at all is thought.

Let us put it to the test. Let us examine ourselves and others. Here something manifests itself: that in these correct translations everything evaporates into fluctuating and imprecise meanings. It becomes clear that the always hasty approximations of the familiar translations are not seen as an inadequacy nor do they disturb, in the slightest, scholarly research and presentation. Greater efforts are perhaps made to bring out what the Greeks may have really represented to themselves with words like θεός, ψυχή, ζωή, τύχη, χάρις, λόγος, φύσις and ἰδέα, τέχνη and ἐνέργεια. But what we fail to notice is that these and similar efforts get nowhere and fail to refer to any realm, so long as that realm of all realms, the ὄν and the εἶναι, is insufficiently clarified in its Greek essence. Scarcely, however, have we named εἶναι a "realm" than its character as a realm is represented as universal and all-embracing *via* the logical explication of γένος and κοινόν. This grasping-together [*concipere*] in the manner of the representational concept is supposed, in advance, to be the only possible way in which to think being as such. It is still taken to be applicable when one takes refuge in the dialectic of concepts [*Begriffe*] or in the un-graspability (*Un-Begriffliche*) of magic signs. It remains completely forgotten that the supremacy of the concept and the interpretation of thinking as conceptually grasping is based solely on the unthought – because unexperienced – essence of the ὄν and εἶναι.

In the main we thoughtlessly attribute to the words ὄν and εἶναι that which we mean by the corresponding (but unthought) words of our own language: beings and being. To be precise, we attribute to the Greek words no significance at all. We adopt them directly from whatever vague comprehensibility is lent to them by the ordinary understanding of our own language. We support the Greek words with nothing but the accommodating negligence of hasty opinion. This may do at a pinch when we read, for example, εἶναι and ἔστιν in the historical works of Thucydides or ἦν and ἔσται in Sophocles.

How is it, however, when τὰ ὄντα, ὄν and εἶναι come to sound in language as the fundamental words of thinking; not just some particular way of thinking, but rather as the key words for all Western thinking? Then an examination of the use of language in the translation reveals the following state of affairs:

It is neither clear nor firmly established what we ourselves think with the words "being" and "to be";

nor is it clear or firmly established whether what we variously mean corresponds to what the Greeks talk about with the words ὄν and εἶναι.

It is neither clear nor firmly established what ὄν and εἶναι, thought in the Greek manner, say;

nor, given this situation, can we ever conduct an examination of whether, and to what extent, our thinking corresponds to that of the Greeks.

Thus, simple relations are thoroughly confused and unthought. Within them, however, and hovering above them, a boundless chatter about being has spread itself far and wide. In conjunction with the formal correctness of the translation of ὄν and εἶναι as "being" and "to be," this continually covers over the confused state of affairs. But it is not only we of today who wander about in this confusion. All representations and presentations left to us by the philosophy of the Greeks remain in it, too, captivated for millennia. The confusion stems neither from mere philological negligence nor from an imprecision in historical research. It arises, rather, out of the abyss of the relationship in which being[a] has appropriated the essence of Western humanity. Thus the confusion cannot be removed by creating, *via* some kind of a definition, a more precise meaning of the words ὄν and εἶναι, "being" and "to be." On the contrary, the attempt to be aware of the confusion and to bring its dogged power to a resolution may well prove to be the occasion which releases another destiny of being. The preparation of such an occasion would be reason enough to set in motion, within the abiding confusion, a dialogue with early thinking.

If we stubbornly insist on thinking Greek thought in a Greek manner, this is by no means because we intend to produce a portrait of the Greeks as a past humanity intended to be, in numerous respects, more accurate. We seek what is Greek neither for the sake of the Greeks nor for the advancement of science. We seek a clearer dialogue not for its own sake but solely for the sake of that which wishes to come to language in such a dialogue, provided it comes of its own accord. This is that same which, in different ways, is destined to concern both the Greeks and us. It is that which brings the dawn of thinking into the destiny of the West. It is as a consequence of this destiny that the Greeks first became, in the historical sense, the Greeks.

As we use the word, "Greek" designates neither an ethnic nor national, neither a cultural nor an anthropological characteristic. What is Greek is that dawn of destiny as which being itself[b] lights itself up in beings and lays claim[c] to an essence of humanity, a humanity which, as destined, receives its historical path, a path sometimes preserved in, sometimes released from, but never separated from being.

The Greek, the Christian, the modern, the global, and, in the already indicated sense, the Evening-land, we think out of a fundamental trait of being which, as the Ἀλήθεια in the Λήθη, is more concealed than revealed. But this concealing of its essence and essential origin is the trait in which being's primordial self-illumination occurs, occurs, indeed, so that thinking can precisely *not* pursue it. The being itself does not step into the light of being. The unconcealment of the being, the brightness granted it, darkens the light of being.

By revealing itself in the being, being withdraws.

[a] First edition, 1950. *As* appropriating [***als*** *er-eignen*].

[b] First edition, 1950. The Event.

[c] First edition, 1950. Custom-uniting [*Brauch-Vereignung*].

In this way, in its illuminating, being invests the being with errancy. The being happens in errancy in which it strays from being and so – to speak in the manner of princes and poets – founds error. This is the essential space of history. In it the historically essential strays past what is like being. This is why what happens historically is necessarily misinterpreted. Throughout this misinterpretation destiny waits for what will become of its seed. It brings those whom it concerns into the possibility of the destined and the un-destined. Destiny tries out its destiny. The inability of human beings to see themselves corresponds to the self-concealment of the lighting of being.

Without errancy there would be no connection from destiny to destiny, no history. Chronological distance and causal sequence belong to historiography, but not to history. When we are historical we are at neither a large nor a small distance from the Greek. But we are in errancy toward them.

By revealing itself in the being, being withdraws.

In this way being, with its truth, keeps to itself. This keeping to itself is the way it discloses itself early on. Its early sign is the 'Α-λήθεια. By bringing the being's unconcealment, it founds, for the first time, the concealment of being. Concealment remains, however, the characteristic of the refusal that keeps to itself.

This illuminating, keeping to itself with the truth of its essence, we may call the ἐποχή of being. Here, however, this word which is taken from the language of the Stoics does not mean, as it does for Husserl, the methodological setting aside of the act of thetic consciousness in objectification. The *epoche* of being belongs to being itself. We think it out of the oblivion of being.

Out of the *epoche* of being comes the epochal essence of its destining in which authentic world-history lies. Each time that being keeps to itself in its destiny, suddenly and unexpectedly, world happens. Every epoch of world-history is an epoch of errancy. The epochal essence of being belongs to the concealed temporal character of being and indicates the essence of "time"[a] thought from within being. What one may otherwise represent by this term is only the vacuity of the appearance of time derived from beings thought of as objects.

For us, however, the correlate of the epochal character of being we can experience most immediately is the ecstatic [*ekstatische*] character of *Da-sein* [being-there]. The epochal essence of being appropriates the

[a] First edition, 1950. The space of temporal play [*Zeit-Spiel-Raum*] as the illumination of the self-concealing concealing.

ecstatic essence of *Da-sein*. Man's ek-sistence [*Ek-sistenz*] sustains the ecstatic thereby preserving what is epochal in being, to whose essence the *Da* [there],[a] and therefore *Da-sein*, belongs.

Epochally thought, the beginning of the epoch of being lies in what we call "the Greek." This beginning, which is itself to be thought epochally, is the dawn of the destiny in being from out of being.

Little depends on what we represent and present to ourselves from the past; but a great deal depends on the manner in which we are mindful of the destined. Can this ever happen without thinking? If it happens, however, then we abandon the claims of shortsighted opinion and open ourselves to the claim of destiny. Does this claim speak in the early saying of Anaximander?

We are not certain whether its claim speaks to our essence. It remains open to question whether the glance – and this means the lightning (Heraclitus, Fragment 64 in Diels, *Fragmente der Vorsokratiker*) – strikes into our relation to the truth of being; or whether only the weak glimmer of a storm long past casts the pallid light of its brightness into our knowledge of what has been.

Does the saying speak to us of the ὄντα in their being? Do we apprehend what it says, the εἶναι of the being? Does a lightning-glance penetrate through the confusion of errancy from what ὄντα and εἶναι say in Greek? Only in the brilliance of this glance can we trans-late ourselves into what is said in the saying so as then, in a thoughtful dialogue, to make the translation. Perhaps the confusion which permeates the use of the words ὄντα and εἶναι, the being and being, comes not so much from the fact that the language cannot say everything adequately but rather from the fact that we do not think the matter with sufficient clarity. Lessing once said: "language can express everything we think clearly." So it is up to us to watch out for the right opportunity which allows us clearly to think the matter which the saying brings to language.

We are inclined to discover the opportunity we are looking for in the saying of Anaximander. But in this case we still fail to pay attention to what the way of translation requires.

For what is necessary before interpreting the saying is to trans-late ourselves – at first without the help of the saying – to the place from which what is said in the saying comes; to, that is to say, τὰ ὄντα. This word names that of which the saying speaks, not only what it expresses. That of which it

[a] First edition, 1950. In the sense of the illumination of the self-concealing.

speaks is already, before its expression, what is spoken about by the Greek language in both its everyday and its elevated use. For this reason we must seek the opportunity which allows us to trans-late ourselves outside the saying itself, in order to discover what τὰ ὄντα, thought in the Greek way, says. Furthermore, we must at first remain outside the saying because we have not yet delineated its terms. This delineation is ultimately (first of all in the matter, that is) governed by the knowledge of what in early times was thought and thinkable in such terms – as distinct from the prevailing representations of later times.

The text quoted and translated above from Simplicius' commentary on the *Physics* has traditionally been accepted as the saying of Anaximander. However, the quotation in the commentary is not clear enough for it to be possible to say with certainty where Anaximander's saying begins and where it ends. Even today there are leading authorities on the Greek language who accept the text of the saying in the form in which it was introduced at the beginning of our reflections.

In fact, however, John Burnet, the distinguished and important scholar of Greek philosophy to whom we are indebted for the edition of Plato, already expresses doubts, in his *Early Greek Philosophy*, as to whether the Simplicius quotation begins where it is usually said to begin. In criticism of Diels, Burnet says

> Diels ... begins the actual quotation with the words ἐξ ὧν δὲ ἡ γένεσις ... The Greek practice of weaving quotation into the text speaks against this. It is very rare for a Greek writer to begin immediately with a literal quotation. It is, moreover, safer not to ascribe the terms γένεσις and φθορά, in the technical sense they have in Plato, to Anaximander.
>
> (Second edition, 1908. German translation, 1913, p. 43, footnote 4)

On the basis of these considerations Burnet has Anaximander's saying beginning only with κατὰ τὸ χρεών. What Burnet says about Greek quotation in general speaks in favour of excluding what precedes these words. On the other hand his remarks based on the terminological use of the words γένεσις and φθορά cannot be accepted as they stand. That γένεσις and φθορά are firmly established conceptual terms in Plato and Aristotle, and therefore become academic terms, is correct. But γένεσις and φθορά are old words, already known to Homer. Anaximander would not have used them as conceptual terms. He cannot have used them in this way since conceptual language is something necessarily foreign to him. For this first became possible with the interpretation of being as ἰδέα, after which it indeed becomes inevitable.

Nevertheless, the whole of the sentence that precedes κατὰ τὸ χρεών is, in terms of construction and sound, far more Aristotelian than archaic. The same later character is betrayed by the κατὰ τὴν τοῦ χρόνου τάξιν at the end of the customarily accepted text. Whoever is persuaded to strike out the part of the text found dubious by Burnet cannot retain the usually accepted closing part either. What would therefore remain as the original saying of Anaximander is only this:

... κατὰ τὸ χρεών· διδόναι γὰρ αὐτὰ δίκην καὶ τίσιν ἀλλήλοις τῆς ἀδικίας.

... according to necessity; for they pay one another punishment and penalty for their injustice.

These are precisely the words in reference to which Theophrastus notes that Anaximander speaks in a more poetic way. Since the whole issue – one which often comes up in my lectures – is one I thought through a few years ago, I am inclined to take only these words as the immediately genuine words of Anaximander, albeit with the proviso that the preceding part of the text is not simply abandoned but is rather retained, on the basis of the strength and eloquence of its thought, as secondary testimony concerning Anaximander's thought. This requires that we understand, in particular, the words γένεσις and φθορά as they were thought in Greek, whether they be pre-conceptual words or Platonic-Aristotelian conceptual terms.

Accordingly, γένεσις in no way means the genetic in the sense of the developmental as conceived in modern times; φθορά does not mean the counter-phenomenon to development, as though it involved some kind of regression, shriveling, or wasting away. Rather, they are to be thought out of and within φύσις: as ways of self-illuminating rising and decline. Certainly one can translate γένεσις as emergence; but we must think this emergence as an escape which allows every emergent thing to rise out of concealment and come forth into unconcealment. Certainly we can translate φθορά as "passing away"; but in doing so we must think passing away as a movement which again originates in the unconcealed and departs and withdraws into concealment.

Presumably Anaximander spoke of γένεσις and φθορά. Whether he did so in the form of the traditional statement remains questionable. Nonetheless word-conjunctions as paradoxical as γένεσις ἔστιν (as I would like to read it) and φθορὰ γίνεται – "coming into being *is*" and "passing away comes to be" – again suggest an ancient language. The γένεσις is the coming forth and arriving in unconcealment. The φθορά means: the departure and descent into concealment of that which has arrived there out of unconcealment. The "coming forward into ..." and the "going away to ..." presence within unconcealment between the concealed and the unconcealed. They concern the arrival and departure of what has arrived.

Anaximander must have spoken of that which is named in γένεσις and φθορά. Whether he actually named τὰ ὄντα must remain open, though nothing speaks against it. The αὐτά in the second clause, in the breadth with which it speaks and as a consequence of its reference back to the κατὰ τὸ χρεών, can name nothing other than beings as a whole, experienced in a pre-conceptual way: τὰ πολλά, τὰ πάντα, "the being." We are still speaking this way with respect to τὰ ὄντα, without having clarified what ὄν and εἶναι, thought in the Greek manner, name. Yet we have in the meanwhile achieved a more open field in which to attempt this clarification.

We began with the customarily accepted text of the saying. In the preliminary review of that text we have excluded the usual presuppositions which determine its interpretation. In doing so we have received a hint as to what comes to language from γένεσις and φθορά. The saying speaks of that which, in coming forth, arrives in unconcealment and, having arrived there, withdrawing, departs.

What, however, has its essential nature in such arrival and departure we would prefer to call the coming and the going rather than the being; for we have, for a long time, been accustomed to opposing becoming and being, as if becoming were nothing, not belonging within being, which has for a long time been understood as mere perdurance. If, however, becoming *is*, then we must think being in so essential a manner that it embraces becoming not in an emptily conceptual way but rather so that being bears and molds the essence of becoming (γένεσις – φθορά) in an essential way.

Hence, whether, and with what right, we represent becoming as the transitory does not, here, require discussion. What does, rather, need to be discussed is the question of what essence of being the Greeks think when, in the realm of the ὄντα, they experience coming forth and going away as the fundamental trait of arrival.

What is it that finds expression in their language when the Greeks say τὰ ὄντα? Where is there, apart from Anaximander's saying, a guideline that would trans-late us there? Since the word in question, together with its variations ἔστιν, ἦν, ἔσται, εἶναι, speaks everywhere throughout the entire language – before, indeed, thinking specifically takes this word as its fundamental term – we must become cognizant of an opportunity which, in terms of subject matter, time, and the realm to which it belongs, lies outside philosophy and, in every respect, precedes what thinking has to say.

We find this opportunity in Homer. In him, we possess a passage where the word comes to the fore in a more than merely lexical way. It is a passage, rather, in which what ὄντα names is brought to language poetically. Because all λέξις of the lexicographical sort presupposes the thought of the λεγόμενον, we will refrain from the futile assembly of parallel passages, a practice which, all too often, only goes to show that none of the texts have been thought through. With the help of this much-favored method it is supposed that, by shoving an unclarified passage together with other equally unclarified passages, clarity will suddenly emerge.

The passage we seek to explicate comes from the beginning of the first book of the *Iliad*, lines 68–72. It gives us an opportunity to transport ourselves over into what the Greeks name with the word ὄντα, provided we allow the poet to carry us over to the distant shore of what is being said.

Some preliminary remarks concerning the history of language are necessary with respect to what follows. These observations cannot claim to present the philological problem on which they touch adequately, still less to solve it. In Plato and Aristotle, ὄν and ὄντα confront us as conceptual words. The later terms "ontic" and "ontological" are formed from them. Linguistically, however, ὄν and ὄντα are presumably forms of the original words ἐόν and ἐόντα which have somehow become abbreviated. Only in the original words is the sound still preserved with which we say ἐόν and ἐόντα. The epsilon in ἐόν and ἐόντα is the ἐ in the root of ἐσ, in ἔστιν, *est*, *esse*, and "is." In contrast, ὄν and ὄντα look like rootless participial endings, as though, by themselves, they specifically designate what we must think in those word forms called by grammarians μετοχή, *participium*; in other words, those word forms which participate in the verbal and nominal sense of a word.

Thus ὄν says "being" in the sense of *to be* a being; but ὄν also names a *being* which is. In the duality of the participial signification of ὄν there lies concealed the distinction between "being [*seiend*]" and "a being [*Seiendem*]." Thus represented, what is here set forth looks at first sight like a grammatical splitting of hairs. In truth, however, it is the enigma of being. The participle ὄν is the word for that which, in metaphysics, appears as the transcendental and the transcendent transcendence.

Archaic Greek, and so, too, Parmenides and Heraclitus, use ἐόν and ἐόντα all the time.

But ἐόν, "being [*seiend*]," is not only the singular of the participle ἐόντα, "the being [*Seiendes*]," but also names the singular as such, which, as one in its singleness, is uniquely the uniquely unifying One that precedes all number.

We might say – in an exaggerated way which nevertheless touches on the truth – that the destiny of the West rests on the translation of the word ἐόν, given that the translation [*Übersetzung*] is a crossing over [*Übersetzung*] to the truth of what comes to language in the ἐόν.

What does Homer tell us about this word? We know the situation of the Achaeans before Troy at the beginning of the *Iliad*. For nine days the plague sent by Apollo has raged in the Greek camp. At the assembly of the warriors Achilles commands Kalchas, the seer, to interpret the wrath of the god:

> . . . τοῖσι δ' ἀνέστη
> Κάλχας Θεστορίδης οἰωνοπόλων ὄχ' ἄριστος
> ὃς ᾔδη τά τ' ἐόντα τά τ' ἐσσόμενα πρό τ' ἐόντα
> καὶ νήεσσ' ἡγήσατ' Ἀχαιῶν Ἴλιον εἴσω
> ἣν διὰ μαντοσύνην, τήν οἱ πόρε Φοῖβος Ἀπόλλων·

According to Voss' translation:

> . . . again stood up
> Calchas, Thestor's son, the wisest bird-interpreter
> Who knew what is, what will be or what once was,
> Who guided here before Troy the ships of the Acheans,
> Through the prophetic spirit granted him by Phoebus Apollo.

Before Homer allows Kalchas to speak, he designates him the seer. Someone who belongs to the realm of seers is one ὃς ᾔδη . . . , "who knew. . . ". ᾔδη is the pluperfect of the perfect οἶδεν, he has seen. Only he who has seen genuinely sees. To see is to have seen. What is seen has arrived and remains for him in sight. A seer has always seen already. Having seen already he sees in advance. He sees the future tense out of the perfect. When the poet speaks of the seer's seeing as a having-seen he must say what the seer saw in the pluperfect: ᾔδη, he had seen. What is it that has come to the seer's sight in advance? Obviously it can only be that which is present in the light that illuminates his sight. What is seen in such a seeing can only be that which, through unconcealment, comes to presence. But what comes to presence? The poet names something threefold: τά τ' ἐόντα, the being, τά τ' ἐσσόμενα, the being-becoming, πρό τ' ἐόντα, the being that once was.

The first thing we gather from the poetic word is that τὰ ἐόντα is distinguished from both τὰ ἐσσόμενα and πρὸ ἐόντα. Accordingly, τὰ ἐόντα designates the being in the sense of the present. When we latecomers speak of "the present" either we mean what is "now" – representing this as something that is within time, the "now" counting as a phase within the flow of time – or we bring "present [*gegenwärtig*]" into relation to the objective [*Gegenständigen*]. As something objective [*das Objective*] this is related to a representing subject. If, however, we want to use "present" for a more accurate comprehension of ἐόντα, then we must understand "present" from out of the essence of ἐόντα and not vice versa. But ἐόντα embraces, too, what is past and what is in the future. Both constitute a way of being a present being, namely, being an unpresently [*ungegenwärtig*] present being. Clarifying matters, the Greeks called the presently present τά παρεόντα; παρά means "alongside," that is, having arrived alongside in unconcealment. The "*gegen* [against]" in "*gegenwärtig* [present]" does not mean standing over against a subject, but rather the open region [*Gegend*] of unconcealment into and within which that which has arrived lingers [*verweilt*]. Accordingly, "present," as a trait of the ἐόντα is equivalent to: having arrived for a while within the region of unconcealment. Spoken first, and thereby emphasized, ἐόντα, which is expressly distinguished from both προεόντα and ἐσσόμενα, names, for the Greeks, that which is present insofar as, in the explicated sense, it has arrived in the while within the region of unconcealment. This coming hither is the authentic arrival, the presencing of what is authentically present. What is past and future are also present, present, that is to say, outside the region of unconcealment. The unpresently present is the absent. As such, it remains essentially related to the presently present, insofar as it either comes forth into the region of unconcealment or withdraws from it. The absent is also present and, *as* absent from it, presences in unconcealment. Both what is past and what is to come are ἐόντα. Accordingly, ἐόν means: presencing in unconcealment.

This clarification of ἐόντα reveals that within Greek experience, too, that which is present remains ambiguous, indeed necessarily so. τὰ ἐόντα means on the one hand the presently present, on the other, however, both the presently and unpresently present. However, that which is present in the broader sense must never be represented as the general concept of presence (as opposed to a particular, presently present presence), though this is the usual procedure of conceptual thinking. For, in fact, it is precisely the presently present and the unconcealment that prevails in it, which pervades the essence of the absent as that which is unpresently present.

The seer stands in the sight of what is present in its unconcealment, which at the same time has illuminated the concealment of the absent as the absent. The seer sees inasmuch as he has seen everything as something present; καί, and only on that account, νήεσσ' ἡγήσατ', was he able to guide the Achaean ships on to Troy. He was able to do this through the God-given μαντοσύνη. The seer, ὁ μάντις, is the μαινόμενος, the madman. But what is it that constitutes the essence of this madness? The madman is beside, outside, himself. He is away. We ask: away to where? And from where? Away from the mere crush of what lies before us, of the merely presently present, and away to the absent; away to, at the same time, the presently absent, inasmuch as this is always only the arrival of something that departs. The seer is outside himself in the single breadth of the presence of that which is in every way present. Therefore, within this breadth, he is able to find his way back from the "away," back to what is present here and now, namely, the raging plague. The madness of the seer's being-away does not consist in raving, rolling the eyes or contorting the limbs. The madness of seeing is compatible with the unprepossessing quietness of bodily composure.

For the seer, everything present and absent is gathered and preserved [*gewahrt*] in *one* presencing. The old German word "*war* [was]" means preservation. It is still known to us in "*wahrnehmen* [to perceive]," that is, to take into preservation; in "*gewahren* [to become aware of]" and "*verwahren* [to keep or preserve]." We must think of *wahren* as an illuminating-gathering sheltering. Presencing preserves [*wahrt*] that which presences in unconcealment, both what is present now and what is not. The seer speaks from out of the preservation [*Wahr*] of presencing. He is the sooth-sayer [*Wahr-sager*].

Here, we think the preservation in the sense of illuminating-sheltering gathering; what shows itself here is a fundamental trait of presencing – that is, of being – that has been long concealed. One day we will learn to think our exhausted word "truth [*Wahrheit*]" from out of the protection [*Wahr*] and learn that truth is the preservation [*Wahrnis*] of being, and that being, as presence, belongs to it. Preservation as the protection of being belongs to the shepherd; a shepherd who has so little to do with bucolic idylls and nature mysticism that he can become the shepherd of being only if he remains the place-holder for the Nothing. Both are the same. Man can do both only within the dis-closedness [*Ent-schlossenheit*] of *Da-sein* [being-there].

The seer is he who has already seen the totality of what presences in its presencing. In Latin *vidit*, in German "*er steht im Wissen* [he stands in knowledge]." Having seen is the essence of knowledge. In this having seen there is always something more in play than the completion of an optical process. In the having seen, the relationship to what presences has gone behind every kind of sensory and non-sensory apprehension. What follows is that the having seen is related to the self-illuminating presencing. The seeing is determined, not by the eye but by the lighting of being. Standing within this lighting is the structure of all human senses. The essence of seeing, as having seen, is knowledge. This retains sight. It remains mindful of presencing. Knowledge is the remembrance of being. This is why Μνημοσύνη is the mother of the muses. Knowledge is not science in the modern sense. Knowledge is the thoughtful awareness of the preservation of being.

Whither have Homer's words trans-lated [*über-gesetzt*] us? To the ἐόντα. The Greeks experience the being as that which is present (whether presently so or not), present in unconcealment. Our use of "being" to translate ὄν is no longer obtuse; "to be" as the translation of εἶναι and the Greek word itself are no longer hastily employed codewords for arbitrary and vague representations of indeterminate generality.

At the same time it transpires that being, as the presencing of what is present, is already in itself truth, given that we think the essence of truth as the illuminating-sheltering gathering; that we steer clear of the later prejudice of metaphysics (these days regarded as something self-evident) that truth is a characteristic of the being or of being. Being (the word now thoughtfully spoken), εἶναι as presencing, is, in a concealed way, a characteristic of truth, though not, certainly, truth as a characteristic of divine or human knowledge, and not as a characteristic in the sense of quality. Furthermore, it has become clear that τὰ ἐόντα ambiguously names both the presently and unpresently present, the latter, understood with reference to the former, constituting the absent. The presently present, however, is not something that lies, like a severed slice, sandwiched between two absences. When that which is present stands, in advance, in seeing, everything presences together; one thing brings the others with it, another allows the other to go. That which stands presently in unconcealment stays [*weilt*] in it as the open region. That which presently stays (whiles) [*Weilende (Weilige)*] in that region comes forth into it, into unconcealment, from out of concealment. But the arrival which stays *is* what is present insofar as it is already on its way from unconcealment into concealment. The presently present stays awhile. It lingers [*verweilt*] in coming forth and going away. The stay is the transition from coming to going. What is present is what, in each case, lingers awhile. Lingering awhile, it lingers still in arrival and lingers already in departure.

What is for the time being present, the presently present, presences out of absence. This must be said precisely of whatever is truly present, which our usual mode of representation would like to segregate from all that is absent.

Τὰ ἐόντα names the unified multiplicity of whatever stays awhile. To the extent it is present in unconcealment, everything presences, in its own way, to everything else.

Finally, we gather something else from the passage in Homer: τὰ ἐόντα, the so-called being, in no way means natural things. In the present case, the poet uses ἐόντα to refer to the situation of the Achaeans before Troy: the anger of the god, the raging of the plague, the funeral pyres, the perplexity of the princes, and so on. Τὰ ἐόντα, in the language of Homer, is not a philosophical concept-word but rather a word that is thought and thoughtfully uttered. It does not name merely the things of nature, and does not name at all objects which are nothing but objects of human representing. Man, too, belongs to ἐόντα: he is that present being which, lighting-apprehending and so gathering, allows that which presences to presence as such in unconcealment. If, in the poetic characterization of Kalchas, what is present is thought in relation to the seeing of the seer, this means that, thought in the Greek manner, the seer, as one who has seen, is a present being who in an exceptional sense belongs to the totality of what presences. This does not, however, mean that what presences is, or is only, an object dependent on the subjectivity of the seer.

Τὰ ἐόντα, the presently and unpresently present, is the inconspicuous name of that which comes expressly to language in Anaximander's saying. The word names that which, as the still unspoken – unspoken in thinking – addresses all thought. The word names that which, whether spoken or not, henceforth lays claim to all Western thinking.

But only several decades after Anaximander, through Parmenides, did ἐόν (presencing) and εἶναι (to presence) expressly become the fundamental words of Western thinking. This, admittedly, did not happen – as the popular misconception has it – because Parmenides interprets the being "logically," proceeding from the proposition and its copula. Within Greek thinking, not even Aristotle goes that far when he thinks the being's being in terms of the κατηγορία. Aristotle took the being as something already lying before any proposition, as, that is to say, the unconcealment of what presences for a while. For Aristotle, it was not necessary to explicate ὑποκείμενον, substance, in terms of the subject of the proposition since the essence of the substance, οὐσία in the sense of παρουσία, was already manifest. And neither did he think the presence of what is present in terms of the objectivity of the propositional object. Rather, he thought it as ἐνέργεια which, however, is separated by an abyss from the *actualitas* of the *actus purus* of medieval scholasticism.

In any case, Parmenides' ἔστιν does not mean the "is" which is the copula of the sentence. It names ἐόν, the presencing of what is present. The ἔστιν corresponds to the pure claim of being before the division into first and second οὐσία, into *existentia* and *essentia*. But in this way ἐόν is thought out of the concealed and hidden richness of the unconcealment of the ἐόντα, which was familiar to the early Greeks, without it being possible or necessary for them to experience this essential richness in all its aspects.

It is from out of the thoughtful experience of the ἐόν of the ἐόντα, non-conceptually spoken, that the fundamental words of the early thinking are said: Φύσις and Λόγος, Μοῖρα and Ἔρις, Ἀλήθεια and Ἕν. Only by means of Ἕν, which is to be thought back into the realm of the fundamental words, do ἐόν and εἶναι become the explicit words for what is present. Only from out of the destiny of being, the destiny of the Ἕν, does the modern age, after essential upheavals, enter the epoch of the monadology of substance, which completes itself in the phenomenology of Spirit.

It was not Parmenides who provided the logical interpretation of being. On the contrary, it was logic – sprung from metaphysics but at the same time dominating it – which led to a state of affairs in which the essential richness of being contained in the early fundamental words, remained buried. This is what made it possible for being to assume the fatal status of being the emptiest and most universal concept.

Yet since the dawn of thinking "being" names the presencing of what is present in the sense of the lighting-sheltering gathering which is how the Λόγος is thought and named. The Λόγος (λέγειν, to gather or collect) is experienced out of Ἀλήθεια, the sheltering which discloses. In the conflicted essence of Ἀλήθεια is concealed the thoughtful essence of Ἔρις and Μοῖρα, in terms of which Φύσις is at the same time named.

It is within the language of these fundamental words, words which are thought from out of the experience of presencing, that the words of Anaximander's saying speak: δίκη, τίσις, and ἀδικία.

The claim of being which speaks in these words determines the essence of philosophy. Philosophy does not arise from myth. It comes into being only out of, and in, thinking. But this thinking is the thinking of being. Thinking does not come into being. It is insofar as being presences. But the collapse[a] of thought into the sciences and into faith is the baleful[b] destiny of being.

At the dawn of being's destiny, the being, τὰ ἐόντα, comes to language. What, from out of the measured abundance of what in this way arrives, does Anaximander's saying bring to utterance?

According to what looks to be the genuine text, the saying reads

... κατὰ τὸ χρεών· διδόναι γὰρ αὐτὰ δίκην καὶ τίσιν ἀλλήλοις τῆς ἀδικίας.

In the standard translation:

... according to necessity; for they pay one another punishment and penalty for their injustice.

The saying still consists of two clauses; of the first only the final words are preserved. We begin with the explication of the second clause.

The αὐτά refers to what is named in the previous clause. What is meant can only be τὰ ὄντα, what presences in its totality, presently and unpresently present in unconcealment. Whether or not this is expressly named by the word may, on account of the uncertainty surrounding the text, be left open. The αὐτά names everything that is present, everything that presences in the manner of staying: gods and men, temples and cities, sea and land, eagle and snake, tree and shrub, wind and light, stone and sand, day and night. The things that presence belong together in the unity of presencing in as much as each presences to the others within its duration. This multiplicity (πολλά) is not an assembly of separate objects behind which something stands, embracing them as a whole. Rather, in presencing as such there prevails the staying-with-one-another of a concealed gathering. This is why Heraclitus, catching sight of this collecting-unifying and disclosing essence within presencing, calls the Ἕν (the being's being) the Λόγος.

But first of all, how does Anaximander experience the totality of the things that presence: their having arrived to stay awhile with one another in unconcealment? What is it, basically, that runs everywhere through what is present? The last word of the saying gives the answer. It is with it that we must begin the translation. The word names the fundamental trait of what is present: ἡ ἀδικία, literally translated, injustice. But is the literal translation

[a] First edition, 1950. Collapse into beings through the oblivion of being; compare *Being and Time*.

[b] First edition, 1950. But not "bad."

faithful to the word? In other words, does the word's literal translation pay heed to what in the saying comes to language? Does the αὔτα, the totality of what is present staying awhile in unconcealment, stand before our eyes?

How is it that what presences, staying, stands in injustice? What is unjust about the thing that presences? Does it not have the right to stay awhile, from time to time, and so fulfill its presencing?

The word ἀ-δικία says, first of all, that δίκη is absent. One is accustomed to translate δίκη as "right." The translations even use "penalty." If we steer clear of our judicial-moral representations, if we stick to what comes to language, then ἀδικία says that where it prevails, all is not right with things. That means, something is out of joint. But what is being referred to? The things that are present, staying. But where, in what is present, are the joints? Without joints, how can what presences be without jointure, ἄδικον, that is, out of joint?

The saying says, unambiguously, that what presences is in the ἀδικία, that is, out of joint. That, however, cannot mean that it is no longer present. But neither does it merely say that what is present is just occasionally, or perhaps with respect to some of its characteristics, out of joint. The saying says, of what is present, that, as what is present, it is out of joint. The jointure must belong to presencing as such together with the possibility of being out of joint. What presences is what stays awhile. The while presences as the transitional arrival in departure. It presences between coming hither and going away. Between this twofold absence presences the presencing of all that stays. In this "between" what stays awhile is jointed. This "between" is the jointure according to which, from arrival here to going away from here, that which stays is jointed. The presencing of what stays obtrudes in the "here" of "arrival here" and in the "away" of "going away." Presencing is, in both directions, enjoined toward absence. Presencing occurs in this jointure. What is present emerges in the coming forth and passes away in the going away; indeed, because it stays, it does both at the same time. The while happens in the jointure.

But then that which stays awhile is precisely in the jointure of its presencing and not at all, as we can now say, in the dis-jointure, not in ἀδικία. But the saying says it is. It speaks from the essential experience of ἀδικία as the fundamental trait of ἐόντα.

That which stays awhile presences as staying in the jointure which enjoins presence toward a twofold absence. Yet, as what presences, that which stays awhile – it and it alone – stays the length of its while. What has arrived may even insist on its while, solely to remain more present, in the sense of enduring. That which stays persists in its presencing. In this way it takes itself out of its transitory while. It extends itself in a stubborn pose of persistence. It concerns itself no longer with the other things that are present. As though this were the way to stay, it becomes concerned with the permanence of its continued existence.

Presencing in the jointure of the while, that which presences, staying awhile, is disjointed. Everything that stays awhile stands in this dis-jointure [*in der Un-Fuge*]. To the presence of what presences, to the ἐόν of ἐόντα, ἀδικία belongs. Thus standing in the dis-jointure would be the essence of everything that presences. And so what would come to the fore in this saying of early thinking would be the pessimism – not to say nihilism – of the Greek experience of being.

But does the saying actually say that the essence of what presences consists in the dis-jointure? Yes and no. The saying indeed identifies the dis-jointure as the fundamental trait of what presences, yet only to say

διδόναι γὰρ αὐτὰ δίκην . . . τῆς ἀδικίας.

"They must pay penalty or damages [*Buße*]," as Nietzsche translates – "They must pay the penalty or fine [*Strafe*]" according to Diels – "for their injustice." But the saying says nothing of payment, penalty, or damages. Nor does it say that something is punishable or must be avenged (according to the opinion of those who equate vengeance with justice).

In the meantime, the thoughtlessly uttered "injustice of things" has been clarified by our thinking the essence of that which presences and stays awhile as the dis-jointure in the while. The dis-jointure consists in the fact that what stays awhile tries to have its while understood only as continuation. Thought from out of the jointure of the while, staying as persistence is insurrection on behalf of sheer endurance. In presencing as such – presencing which lets everything that presences stay in the region of unconcealment – continuance asserts itself. In this rebellious whiling, that which stays awhile insists on sheer continuation. It presences, therefore, without and against the jointure of the while. The saying does not say that everything that presences loses itself in the dis-jointure. It says, rather, that that which stays awhile with a view to dis-jointure, διδόναι δίκην, gives jointure.

What does "to give" mean here? How should that which stays awhile, presences in dis-jointure, give jointure? Can it give what it does not have? If it gives anything, does it not immediately give jointure away? Whither and how does that which presences awhile give jointure? We must ask our question more clearly, that is to say, from out of the matter itself.

How should that which presences as such give the jointure of its presencing? The giving in question can consist only in the manner of presencing. Giving is not only giving away. More primordial, is giving in the sense of conceding. Giving of this kind lets belong to another what properly belongs to him. What belongs to what presences is the jointure of the while which it enjoins in its arrival and departure. In the jointure, that which stays awhile keeps to its while. It does not strain to get away into the dis-jointure of sheer persistence. The jointure belongs to what stays awhile which, in turn, belongs in the jointure. The jointure [*Fuge*] is order [*Fug*].

Δίκη, thought out of being as presencing, is the ordering, jointure-giving order. Ἀδικία, dis-jointure, is Dis-order. It is necessary that we think this word we have writ large in a large way – from out of its full linguistic power.

That which stays awhile presences in that it lingers; all the while emerging and passing away, all the while the jointure of the transition from arrival to departure continues. This lingering persistence of the transition is the jointed continuance of what presences. It precisely does not insist on sheer persistence. It does not fall victim to dis-jointure. It overcomes dis-order. Lingering, its while allows what stays awhile to belong to its essence as to the presencing of order. The διδόναι names this "letting-belong-to."

The presencing of that which presences awhile does not consist in ἀδικία as such, not, that is, in disorder. Rather, in διδόναι δίκην . . . τῆς ἀδικίας, in the fact that in each case what presences lets order belong. The presently present is not a slice that is cut off and shoved between the unpresently present; it is present insofar as it allows itself to belong to the unpresent:

διδόναι . . . αὐτὰ δίκην . . . τῆς ἀδικίας,

they, these same beings (in surmounting it) let the order of disorder belong. The experience of the being in its being which here comes to language is neither pessimistic nor nihilistic. Nor is it optimistic. It remains tragic. But that is a presumptuous word. It is likely that we will be on the track of the essence of the tragic if, rather than trying to explain it psychologically or aesthetically, we think its essential mode of being, the being's being, by thinking the διδόναι δίκην . . . τῆς ἀδικίας.

That which presences awhile, τὰ ἐόντα, presences insofar as it lets the enjoining order belong. To whom does the order of the jointure belong and where does it belong? When and in what way does what stays awhile in presence give order? The saying has nothing direct to say about this, not, at least, to the extent we have so far considered it. If we attend, however, to the still untranslated portion it seems to say quite unambiguously to whom or what it is directed:

διδόναι γὰρ αὐτὰ δίκην καὶ τίσιν ἀλλήλοις.

The things which stay awhile let order belong ἀλλήλοις, to one another. So we are generally accustomed to read the text. We relate the ἀλλήλοις to the δίκην and τίσιν, if we represent matters clearly and explicitly as Diels does (though Nietzsche's translation skips over the whole issue). It seems to me, however, that relating the ἀλλήλοις directly to the διδόναι δίκην καὶ τίσιν is neither linguistically demanded nor, more importantly, justified by the matter itself. Hence it is from the matter itself that we must ask whether ἀλλήλοις immediately relates to δίκην, or whether it does not rather relate only to the τίσιν that immediately precedes it. The discussion here partially depends on how we translate the καί that stands between δίκην and τίσιν. But this depends on what τίσις says here.

One is accustomed to translate τίσις as "penalty [*Buße*]." This leads us to give διδόναι the meaning of "pay." Whatever stays awhile pays penalty: it makes this payment as punishment (δίκη). The court of justice is complete: not even injustice is missing, though admittedly no one is properly able to say in what it consists.

τίσις can indeed mean "penalty." It must, however, not do so since this does not name the essential and original meaning of the word. For τίσις is "esteem." To esteem something means to pay heed to it and therefore find satisfaction in what is estimable in it. The essential process of esteem, the finding of satisfaction, can occur in what is good as the bestowing of favour. But with respect to what is bad it can occur as penalty. This mere explanation of the word, however, does not bring us to its matter in the saying unless we are already, as with ἀδικία and δίκη, thinking out of the matter which comes to language in the saying.

According to the saying, αὐτά (τὰ ἐόντα), the things that stay awhile in presence, stand in dis-order. As they while they tarry. They hang on. For in the transition from arrival to departure they pass, hesitantly, through their while. They hang on: they cling to themselves. When the things that stay awhile hang on, they stubbornly follow the inclination to persist in such hanging on, indeed to insist on it. They are concerned with permanent continuance and no longer look to the δίκη, the order of the while.

But in this way everything that tarries pushes itself forward in opposition to everything else. None heeds the lingering essence of the others. The things that stay awhile are without consideration toward each other: each is dominated by the craving for persistence in the lingering presence itself, which gives rise to the craving. For this reason things that stay awhile do not just drift into sheer inconsiderateness. Inconsiderateness itself pushes them into persistence in order that they may still presence as that which presences. The totality of what presences does not disintegrate into merely inconsiderate individuals, does not dissipate itself in discontinuity. Rather, as the saying now says,

διδόναι . . . τίσιν ἀλλήλοις:

they, things which stay awhile, let one thing belong to another: consideration toward each other. The translation of τίσις as consideration better captures the essential meaning of paying heed and esteeming. It is thought out of the presencing of that which stays awhile. For us, however, the word "consideration" applies too directly to human existence. τίσις, on the other hand, because it is said more essentially, applies neutrally to everything that is present: αὐτά (τὰ ἐόντα). Our word "consideration" lacks not merely the necessary breadth but, above all, the gravity to serve as the translation of τίσις as it occurs in the saying, and as the word corresponding to δίκη, order.

Now our language possesses an old word which, interestingly enough, we moderns know only in its negative form and as a term of disparagement, as with the word *Unfug* [disorder]. This usually means for us something like inappropriate and vulgar behaviour, something perpetrated in a crude manner.

In a similar fashion we still use the word "*ruchlos* [reckless[2]]," meaning by it depraved and shameful: without *Ruch* [reck]. We no longer know what *Ruch* means. The Middle High German "*ruoche*" means "solicitude," "care." Care concerns itself with another so that it may remain in its essence. This concerning-itself, when thought of as what stays awhile in relation to presencing, is τίσις, *Ruch* [reck]. Our word "*geruhen* [to deign]" belongs to *Ruch* and has nothing to do with *Ruhe* [rest]. "*Geruhen*" means: to esteem something, to let or allow it to be itself. What we observed with respect to "consideration," that it applies to human relationships, is true of "*ruoche*" too. But we shall take advantage of the obsolescence of the word to adopt it anew in an essential breadth and to speak of τίσις, which corresponds to δίκη as order, as *Ruch* [reck].

Insofar as things which stay awhile are not entirely abandoned to the boundless fixation on aggrandizing themselves into sheerly persisting continuants – a craving which leads them to seek to expel one another from what is presently present – they let order belong, διδόναι δίκην.

Insofar as things which stay awhile give order they thereby allow, in their relationship to each other, reck to belong, in every case, each allowing it to belong to the other, διδόναι . . . καὶ τίσιν ἀλλήλοις. Only when we have thought τὰ ἐόντα as what presences, and this as the totality of what presences awhile, does ἀλλήλοις receive the significance it has in the saying: within the open region of unconcealment each tarrying thing becomes present to all the others. As long as we fail to think the τὰ ἐόντα, ἀλλήλοις remains the name of some indeterminate reciprocity within a blurred multiplicity. The more strictly we think, in ἀλλήλοις, the multiplicity of that which stays awhile, the clearer becomes the necessary relationship of ἀλλήλοις to τίσιν. The more unambiguously this relation emerges, the more clearly we recognize that the διδόναι . . . τίσιν ἀλλήλοις, each giving reck to the other, is the manner in which things which stay awhile in presence occupy the while; that is to say, διδόναι δίκην, giving order. The καί between δίκην and τίσιν is not the vacuous conjunction "and." It signifies, rather, the essential consequence. When the things that presence give order they do it by, as things that stay awhile, according each other reck. The surmounting of dis-order properly occurs through the letting-belong of reck. This means that in the ἀδικία, as the essential consequence of dis-order, lies the non-reck [*Un-Ruch*], the reckless:

διδόναι . . . αὐτὰ δίκην καὶ τίσιν ἀλλήλοις τῆς ἀδικίας

– they let order belong and thereby also reck, one for another (in surmounting) the dis-order.

Letting-belong, as the καί says, is something twofold. For the essence of the ἐόντα is doubly determined. The things which stay awhile come to presence from out of the jointure between approach and withdrawal. They presence in the "between" of a twofold absence. They presence in each time of their while. They presence as the presently present. With a view to their while they grant reck, and even a while, to the others. But to whom do the things that presence allow the order of the jointure to belong?

The now-explicated second clause of the saying does not answer this question. But it gives us a hint. For there remains a word we have overlooked:

διδόναι γὰρ αὐτά . . . , "belonging, namely, they allow . . ." The γὰρ, "for" or "namely," introduces a grounding. In any case, the second clause explains how what is said in the previous clause behaves as it is said.

What does the translated second clause of the saying say? Of the ἐόντα, of that which is present, it says that, as that which stays awhile, it is released into the reckless dis-order; and it tells how, as so present, it surmounts the dis-order inasmuch as it allows order and reck to belong one to another. This letting-belong is the way in which what stays awhile stays, and so presences as what is present. The second clause of the saying names what presences in the manner of its presencing. The saying speaks of the presencing of what is present. It places this in the brilliance of thought. The second clause provides the explication of the presencing of what is present.

It follows that the first clause must name presencing itself, name it, indeed, insofar as it determines that which is present as such. For only to the extent that it does this can the second clause, in its reference back to the first, explicate presence *via* that which presences. Presencing, in relation to that which is present, is always that according to which the latter presences. The first clause names that presencing "according to which . . ." Only its last three words are preserved:

. . . κατὰ τὸ χρεών·

This is translated: "according to necessity." To start with we shall leave τὸ χρεών untranslated. Yet given the explication of the second clause and the nature of its reference back to the first, two reflections are in order. First, that it names the presencing of what is present; second, that if χρεών thinks the presencing of what is present, then, somehow, the relation of presencing to what is present is thought; or it may prove otherwise, that the relation of being to the being, can only come from being, can only rest in the essence of being.

The word κατά precedes τὸ χρεών. It means "down from above" or "from over there." It refers back to something from which something lower comes to presence, as from something higher, and as its consequent. That in reference to which the κατά is said, contains within itself an incline [*Gefälle*] along which other things have fallen out in this or that way.

But in which inclination [*Gefälle*] and in consequence of what can what presences be present as such, if not as a consequence and inclination of presencing? Things that stay awhile stay κατὰ τὸ χρεών. However we are to think the τὸ χρεών, the word is the earliest name for what is thought as the ἐόν of ἐόντα; τὸ χρεών is the oldest name in which thinking brings the being of beings to language.

That which stays awhile in presence presences by surmounting reckless dis-order, the ἀδικία, which itself prevails in the while as an essential possibility. The presencing of what presences *is* such a surmounting. This is accomplished when the things that stay awhile allow order to belong and thereby reck, one to another. The answer to the question of to whom the order belongs has been given. It belongs to that within which presencing, and that means surmounting, presences. Order is κατὰ τὸ χρεών. At this point the essence of the χρεών begins to shine, albeit at first from a great distance. If, as the essence of presencing, τὸ χρεών is essentially related to what is present then it must be implicit in this relation that τὸ χρεών disposes order and with it reck. The χρεών disposes matters so that, within it, that which is present lets order and reck belong. The χρεών lets such disposing reach to that which is present and so grants it the manner of its arrival, the while of its staying awhile.

That which is present presences by surmounting the dis- of disorder, the ἀ of ἀδικία. This ἀπό in ἀδικία corresponds to the κατά of χρεών. The transitional γάρ in the second clause arches over from the one to the other.

So far, we have attempted to think the meaning of τὸ χρεών only *via* the reference of the saying's second clause back to it, without asking about the word itself. What does τὸ χρεών mean? The first word of the saying's text we elucidate last because, according to the matter, it is the first. According to which matter? The matter of the presence of what presences. But to be the being *of* beings[a] is the matter[b] of being.

The grammatical form of the enigmatically ambiguous genitive names a genesis, an origin[c] of what is present from out of presencing. Yet, along with the essence of each of these, the essence of this origin remains hidden. Not only that, but even the relation between presence and what presences is still unthought. From earliest times it has seemed as though presence and what is present are each something for themselves. Unintentionally, presence itself became something present. Represented in terms of something present it became that which is above everything else that is present and so

[a] First edition, 1950. Reference to the ontological difference.

[b] First edition, 1950. Destiny.

[c] First edition, 1950. In the radiance of presencing, that which presences appears, *comes forth*. The radiance itself never appears!

the highest of beings that are present. As soon as presence is named, it is already represented as a present being. Fundamentally, presence as such is not distinguished from what is present. It is taken to be only the most universal and highest of present beings and hence as one of them. The essence of presence together with the difference[a] between presence and what is present remains forgotten. *The oblivion of being is oblivion to the difference between being and the being.*

But oblivion to the difference is by no means the result of a forgetfulness of thinking. Oblivion of being belongs to that essence of being which it itself conceals. It belongs so essentially to the destiny of being that the dawn of this destiny begins as the unveiling of what presences in its presence. This means: the destiny of being begins with oblivion of being so that being, together with its essence, its difference from the being, keeps to itself. The difference collapses. It remains forgotten. Though the two elements of the difference, that which is present and presencing, disclose themselves, they do not do so *as* different. Rather, even the early traces of the difference are extinguished through presencing, appearing as something present and emerging as the highest of beings that are present.

Oblivion to the difference with which the destiny of being begins – so as to complete itself in such destiny – is not a deficiency. Rather, it is the richest and broadest event in which the world-history of the West achieves its resolution. It is the event of metaphysics. What now *is* stands in the shadow of the destiny of oblivion of being that has already preceded it.

The difference between being and the being, however, can be experienced as something forgotten only if it is unveiled along with the presencing of what is present; only if it has left a trace, which remains preserved in the language, to which being comes. Thinking along these lines, we may surmise that the difference has shown up more in the earlier than in the later word of being – though never having been named as such. Illumination of the difference, therefore, cannot mean that the difference appears as the difference. On the contrary, it may be that the relation to what is present announces itself in presencing as such, in such a way, indeed, that presencing comes to speak *as this relation*.

The early word of being, τὸ χρεών, names such a relation. But we would be deceiving ourselves were we to think that we could locate the difference

[a] First edition, 1950. The dif-ference [*Unter-Schied*] is infinitely different from all being, which remains being *of* the being. It is therefore inappropriate any longer to designate the difference with "*Sein* [being]" whether it is written with an "i" or with a "y."

and gain access to its essence merely by persisting with etymological dissection of the word χρεών for long enough. Only when we experience historically what has not been thought – oblivion of being – as that which is to be thought, and only when we have pondered at length what has been long experienced, may the early word perhaps speak in later recollection.

χρεών is generally translated as "necessity." By that one understands the compelling, the inescapable "it must be." But it is a mistake to focus exclusively on this secondary meaning. χρεών is derived from χράω, χράομαι. This suggests ἡ χείρ, the hand. χράω means: I handle something, reach for it, extend my hand to it. Thus, at the same time, χράω means: to place in someone's hands, to hand over and deliver, to let something belong to someone. Such a delivery is, however, of a kind which keeps the transfer in hand, and with it what is transferred.

Originally, therefore, the participial contains nothing of compulsion or "must." Just a little, however, does the word χρεών – originally or ever – denote ratification or ordering.

If we attend fully to the fact that the word must be thought from within Anaximander's saying, then it can only name what is essential in the presencing *of* what is present, together with the relation which is announced – darkly enough – in the genitive. Τὸ χρεών is thus the handing over of presencing, a handing over which hands out presencing to what is present, and therefore keeps in hand, in other words, preserves in presencing, what is present as such.

The relation to what is present that prevails in the essence of presencing is unique. It is comparable with no other relation. It belongs to the uniqueness of being itself. In order to name the essence of being, therefore, language would have to find something unique, the unique word. From this one can gather how daring is every thoughtful word that is addressed to being. Such daring is, nonetheless, not impossible since, in the most diverse ways, being speaks everywhere and always, in every language. The difficulty lies less in the discovery, in thought, of being's word than in preserving the purity of the discovered word in authentic thinking.

Anaximander says: τὸ χρεών. We venture a translation which sounds strange and can easily be misunderstood: τὸ χρεών usage [*Brauch*].

In this translation we attribute to the Greek word a meaning that is neither foreign to the word itself nor contrary to the matter discussed in the saying. Nonetheless, the translation makes strenuous demands. Even if we bear in mind that all translation in the field of thought makes such demands, it does not hide this character.

To what extent is τὸ χρεών usage? The strangeness of the translation is ameliorated by thinking our word more clearly. Generally, we understand "to use" to mean to utilize and need within the area of that to the use of which we enjoy a right. As the translation of τὸ χρεών, "usage" is not to be understood in these customary but secondary meanings. Rather, we attend to the root meaning: to use is *bruchen* [to brook[3]], in Latin *frui*, in German *fruchten*, *Frucht* [to bear fruit, fruit]. We translate this freely as "to enjoy [*geniessen*]" which, in its original form [*niessen*], means to take joy in something and so to have it in use. Only in its secondary meaning does "to enjoy" come to mean to consume and gobble up. We encounter what we have called the root meaning of "to use" as *frui* when Augustine says "*Quid enim est aliud quod dicimus frui, nisi praesto habere, quod diligis?*"[4] (*De moribus ecclesiae*, lib. I c. 3; cf. *De doctrina christiana*, lib. I, c. 2–4). *Frui* contains: *praesto habere. Praesto, praesitum* means in Greek ὑποκείμενον, that which already lies before us in unconcealment, the οὐσία, that which presences awhile. Accordingly, "to use" says: to let something that is present come to presence as such. *Frui, bruchen* [to brook], to use, usage, means: to hand something over to its own essence and, as so present, to keep it in the protecting hand.

In the translation of τὸ χρεών, usage is thought of as essential presencing in being itself. *Bruchen* [to brook], *frui*, is now no longer predicated of enjoyment as human behavior; nor is it said in relation to any being whatever, even the highest (*fruitio Dei* as the *beatitudo hominis*). Rather, "usage" now designates the way in which being itself presences as the relationship to what is present which is concerned and handles it as what is present: τὸ χρεών.

Usage hands over what is present to its presencing; to, that is, its while. Usage imparts to it the portion of its while. The while, apportioned in each case to what stays, rests in the jointure which disposes what presences in the passage between the two absences (arrival and departure). The jointure of the while confines and bounds what presences as such a thing. That which presences awhile, τὰ ἐόντα, presences within its boundary (πέρας).

As the apportioning of participation in the jointure, usage is the destining decree: the disposal of order and thereby reck. Use hands out order and reck by, in advance, reserving to itself what is handed out, gathering it into itself, and sheltering it as what is present in presencing.

Usage, however, disposing order and so containing that which presences, hands out boundaries. As τὸ χρεών, therefore, it is at the same time τὸ ἄπειρον, that which is without boundaries since its essence consists in sending the boundary of the while to that which presences awhile.

According to the tradition reported in Simplicius' commentary on Aristotle's *Physics*, Anaximander is supposed to have said that that which presences has its essential origin in that which presences without bounds: ἀρχὴ τῶν ὄντων τὸ ἄπειρον. What is without bounds is not disposed by order and reck. It is not one of the things that are present but rather τὸ χρεών.

Disposing order and reck, usage releases the present being and delivers each to its while. By doing so, however, it places it in permanent danger that its tarrying in the while will petrify into mere persistence. Thus, at the same time, usage hands presencing over into dis-order. Usage conjoins the "dis-."

For this reason what stays awhile in presence can come to presence only insofar as it allows order and reck to belong: to usage. What presences always presences κατὰ τὸ χρεών, within the lines of usage. Usage is the disposing and preserving gathering of what presences always into its tarrying presence.

The translation of τὸ χρεών as "usage" is not based on etymological or lexical considerations. The choice of the word is based, rather, on a prior *translation* of thought which tries to think the difference within the essence of being, in the destining beginning of oblivion of being. "Usage" is dictated to thinking in the experience of oblivion of being. A trace of what properly remains to be thought in the word "usage" is presumably to be found in τὸ χρεών. This trace quickly vanishes in the destining of being which unfolds in world-history as Western metaphysics.

Thinking what presences in its presence, Anaximander's saying explicates that which is named by τὸ χρεών. What is thought as χρεών in the saying is the first and highest thoughtful interpretation of what the Greeks experienced under the designation Μοῖρα, as the allotment of lots. Both gods and men are subordinate to Μοῖρα. Τὸ χρεών, usage, is the handing in and handing over of everything that presences, each to its while in unconcealment.

Τὸ χρεών harbours within it the still-hidden essence of the lighting-sheltering gathering. Usage is gathering: ὁ Λόγος. Out of the essence of the Λόγος, thought in this way, the essence of being is determined as the unifying One: Ἕν. Parmenides thinks this same Ἕν. He thinks the unity of this unifying One explicitly as Μοῖρα (Fragment 8 in Diels, *Fragmente der Vorsokratiker*). Thought out of the essential experience of being, Μοῖρα corresponds to the Λόγος of Heraclitus. The essence of Μοῖρα and Λόγος is thoughtfully prefigured in Anaximander's Χρεών.

To hunt for dependencies and influences between thinkers is a misunderstanding of thought. What every thinker is dependent on is the address of being. The extent of this dependence determines the freedom from irrelevant influences. The broader the dependence the more capacious the freedom of thought; and therefore the danger that it will wander past what was once thought only, perhaps, to think the same.

We latecomers, admittedly, must, in recollection, first have thought Anaximander's saying in order to meditate on the thought of Parmenides and Heraclitus. If we have done so, then the view that the philosophy of the one is a doctrine of being, the other a doctrine of becoming is exposed as a misunderstanding.

But to think Anaximander's saying we must first of all – but then again and again – take the simple step by means of which we cross over to what that always unspoken word ἐόν, ἐόντα, εἶναι says. It says: presencing in unconcealment. Still concealed in the word is this: *presencing itself brings unconcealment with it.* Unconcealment itself is presencing. They are the same, though not identical.

What is present is that which, presently and unpresently, presences in unconcealment. Along with Ἀλήθεια, which belongs to the essence of being, the Λήθη remains completely unthought and, as a consequence, "presently" and "un-presently" as well; that is to say, the area of the open region within which every being that presences arrives and in which the presencing-to-one-another of beings that stay is unfolded and delimited.

Since the being is that which, having arrived in unconcealment, presences in the manner of staying awhile, it can – lingering there – appear. Appearance is an essential consequence of presencing and of its nature. Only what appears – thinking this always from within presencing – shows visage and aspect. Only thinking which, from the beginning, has thought being in the sense of presencing in unconcealment can think the presencing of what presences as ἰδέα. Yet what stays awhile in presences stays at the same time as that which is brought forth into unconcealment. It is so brought forth when, arising out of itself, it brings itself forth. Or it is so brought forth when it is pro-duced by man. In both cases what comes forth into unconcealment is, in a certain sense, an ἔργον, thought in the Greek manner: something brought forth. The presencing of what presences, its ἔργον character thought in the light of presence, can be experienced as that which presences in brought-forth-ness. This is the presencing of what presences. The being of the being is ἐνέργεια.

This ἐνέργεια which Aristotle thinks as the fundamental character of presencing, of ἐόν, the ἰδέα which Plato thinks as the fundamental character of presencing, the Λόγος which Heraclitus thinks as the fundamental character of presencing, the Μοῖρα which Parmenides thinks as the fundamental character of presencing, the Χρέων which Anaximander thinks as what is essential in presencing, all name the same. In the concealed richness of the same lies the unity of the unifying One, the Ἕν which, in his own way, is thought by every thinker.

Meanwhile, an epoch of being soon arrives in which ἐνέργεια is translated into *actualitas*. The Greek is shut away and appears, right up to our own times, only in its Roman guise. *Actualitas* becomes reality. Reality becomes objectivity. But even this, in order to remain in its essence as objectivity, requires the character of presencing. It is the "presence" in the representation of representing. The decisive turn [*Wende*] in the destiny of being as ἐνέργεια is the transition to *actualitas*.

Could a mere translation have caused all this? But perhaps we have learned to consider what can happen in translation. The truly destining encounter of historical languages is a silent event. But in it the destining of being speaks. Into what language is the land of the evening *translated*?

We will now try to translate Anaximander's saying:

. . . κατὰ τὸ χρεών· διδόναι γὰρ αὐτὰ δίκην καὶ τίσιν ἀλλήλοις τῆς ἀδικίας.

. . . along the line of usage; for they let order and reck belong to one another (in the surmounting) of dis-order.

This translation cannot be scientifically established: nor should we have faith in it on the basis of some kind of authority. Scientific proof will not take us far enough. Faith has no place in thought. We can only reflect on the translation by thinking through the saying. Thinking, however, is the poeticizing of the truth of being in the historical dialogue between those who think.

For this reason the saying will never speak to us so long as we explain it in a merely historical and philological manner. Strangely enough, the saying first speaks to us when we lay aside the claims of our usual mode of representing, as we ask ourselves in what the confusion of today's world-destiny consists.

Man is about to hurl himself upon the entire earth and its atmosphere, to arrogate to himself the hidden working of nature in the form of energy, and to subordinate the course of history to the plans and orderings of a world government. This same defiant man is incapable of saying simply what *is*; of saying *what* this *is*, that a thing *is*.

The totality of beings is the single object of a singular will to conquer. The simplicity of being is buried under a singular oblivion.

What mortal can fathom the abyss of this confusion? In the face of this abyss one can try to shut one's eyes. One can erect one illusion after another. The abyss does not retreat.

Theories of nature, doctrines about history, do not remove the confusion. They further confuse things until they are unrecognizable, since they themselves are nourished by the confusion which surrounds the difference between beings and being.

Is there any rescue? It comes first and only when the danger *is*. The danger *is* when being itself reaches its extremity and when the oblivion which issues from being itself turns about.[a]

But what if being, in its essence, *needs to use* [*braucht*] the essence of man? What if the essence of man rests in thinking the truth of being?

Then thinking must poeticize on the enigma of being. It brings the dawn of thought into proximity to that which is to be thought.

[a] First edition, 1950. The set-up [*das Gestell*] as the utmost oblivion and, at the same time, an intimation of the Event.

Notes

The Origin of the Work of Art

1 A car manufactured by the (now defunct) Adler company.
2 Conrad Ferdinand Meyer (1825–98), Swiss poet.
3 "Conflict is for all the creator that causes to emerge but for all the dominant preserver. For it makes some to appear as gods, others as men; and it creates some as slaves, others as freemen."
4 *Ent-schlossenheit*. Heidegger's hyphenated version of this normally unhyphenated word emphasizes its literal meaning: un-closedness. Compare *Being and Time*, trans. J. Macquarie and E. Robinson (Oxford: Blackwell, 1962), p. 346, footnote 3.
5 Pp. 323–36.
6 See "The Question Concerning Technology" in *The Question Concerning Technology and Other Essays*, trans. W. Lovitt (New York: Harper and Row, 1977), pp. 3–35. Lovitt translates *Ge-stell* as "Enframing."

The Age of the World Picture

1 Heidegger's appendices to this essay begin on p. 73 below.
2 "Argument from the things" in place of "argument from the [authoritative] word."
3 "For thought and being are the same thing."
4 Heidegger is mistaken here. The poem actually continues through several more stanzas.
5 The reference is to Ernst Jünger's "Die totale Mobilmachung" in *Blätter und Steine* (Hamburg: Hanseatische Verlaganstalt, 1934).

Hegel's Concept of Experience

1 The translation of Hegel is based on J. B. Baillie's translation (1910) of *The Phenomenology of Mind*. It has been lightly revised here, mainly to be made more literal in those instances where greater literalness is important in Heidegger's analysis.
2 See also, e.g., Hegel, *Vorlesungen*, ed. Pierre Garniron and Walter Jaeschke (Hamburg: F. Meiner, 1986), vol. IX, p. 88.

3 Hegel, *Werke*, ed. Eva Moldenhauer and Karl Markus Michel (Frankfurt, 1970), vol. II: *Jenaer Schriften, 1801–1807*, p. 558.
4 "The Mind's Journey into God" is the title of a work by St. Bonaventure.
5 To know, *wissen*, developed from an Indo-European root meaning "to see," the past participle of which acquired the sense of "to know" in German. Greek offers an analogous formation: οἶδα (perfect used as present tense "I know") derived from *εἴδω ("I see").

Nietzsche's Word: "God Is Dead"

1 Cf. Hegel, *Faith and Knowledge*, trans. Walter Cerf and H. S. Harris (Albany, NY: SUNY Press, 1977), p. 190.
2 From the opening of *The Will to Power*: "Nihilism is standing at the door. But where did this eeriest of all guests come from?"
3 "Self-consciousness" translates *Selbstbewusstsein*, which means both self-consciousness and self-assertion.
4 From the first sentence of the first of Descartes' *Meditationes de prima philosophia*.
5 The Latin word *cogitatio*, "thinking," "reflections," "thought," Heidegger derives from *co-agitatio*, "driving or movement [along with]"; it shares its prefix with the Latin word *conscientia*, "consciousness," which we are implicitly invited to see as "knowing [along with]." Because of its prefix, we have been prepared to read the German word *Gewissen*, "conscience," as "a gathering of knowledge." The French word *conscience* means "consciousness."
6 *Iustitia nihil aliud*...: "Justice is nothing but order or perfection in respect to minds." *Primariae Mundi unitates*: "the primary unities of the world." See *Philosophische Schriften*, ed. C. I. Gerhardt (Berlin: 1890), vol. VII, pp. 290–91.
7 A term that appears half a dozen times in *Thus Spoke Zarathustra*. It occurs first at the end of Part I, immediately following the sentence Heidegger quotes above (p. 190): "'*All the gods are dead: it is now our will that the overman live!*' – may this be our last wish on the great noontide."
8 Parmenides, "for there is being (a being)," discussed by Heidegger in, e.g., the "Letter on 'Humanism'" (1946).

Why Poets?

1 "The Wanderer," line 99.
2 "The Vocation of the Poet," line 64.
3 "Bread and Wine," lines 139–40.
4 "Mnemosyne," lines 14–19. Heidegger refers to Hellingrath's edition (*Sämtliche Werke*, Berlin: Propylaen, 1923). Subsequent editors, in establishing the precise text of this poem, and in particular that of the first strophe, sometimes differ from Hellingrath. Some editions print a manuscript variant giving an explicit subject (*das Echo*) to the verb "turns." Most subsequent editors print "reichen ... an" rather than "reichen ... in" (that is, "reach toward" rather than "reach into" the abyss).

5 Line 74.
6 "Bread and Wine," line 147.
7 "The Rhine," line 180 "Then men and gods celebrate their nuptials."
8 "With all its eyes the creature sees the open."
9 From Rilke's poem beginning "Solang du Selbstgeworfenes fängst" ["As long as you catch what you yourself have thrown"].
10 The pure *Bezug*: *Sonnets to Orpheus* II, 13, line 6; the whole *Bezug*: "To some it is like wine" ["Manchen ist sie wie Wein"], lines 17–18; the real *Bezug*: *Sonnets to Orpheus* I, 12, line 6; the clearest *Bezug*: *Sonnets to Orpheus* I, 6, lines 10-11; the other *Bezug*: *Duino Elegies* IX, lines 21–23.
11 From the poem "Forest pond, tender, withdrawn" ["Waldteich, weicher, in sich gekehrter"].
12 "Patmos [Erste Niederschrift]," lines 3–4.
13 An allusion to Rilke's poem "Turning," lines 46–47: "The work of the visage is done, do heart-work now."
14 *Sonnets to Orpheus* II, 13, line 1: "Be ahead of all parting . . . "

Anaximander's Saying

1 *Land des Abends*. In German, "*Abendland*," literally, "Land of the Evening," means "the West."
2 An old meaning of "reck" is "care, heed, consideration, regard."
3 In an old usage, "to brook" means "to enjoy the use of, to profit by, to hold."
4 "For what else do we mean when we say *frui* if not to have at hand something especially prized?"

List of sources

"The Origin of the Work of Art." The first version represents the contents of a lecture delivered on the November 13, 1935 to the Art-Historical Society of Freiburg in Breisgau, and repeated in January 1936 in Zürich, at the invitation of the student body of the University. The present version consists of three lectures delivered on November 17, November 24, and December 4, 1936 in the Freies Deutsches Hochstift of Frankfurt on the Main. The Epilogue was written some time later. The Appendix was written in 1956 and first appeared in the special edition of the essay that appeared in Reclam's *Universal-Bibliothek* in 1960. The text of the essay presented here has been lightly reworked and, as with the last version of the Reclam edition, has been more extensively divided into paragraphs.

"The Age of the World Picture." The lecture was delivered on June 9, 1938 under the title "The Founding of the Modern World Picture by Metaphysics." It was the last of a series of lectures on the foundations of the world picture of modernity, organized by the art-historical, scientific, and medical societies of Freiburg. The Appendices were written at the same time but not delivered.

"Hegel's Concept of Experience." The contents of the essay were delivered in a form more suited to the classroom in seminars on Hegel's *The Phenomenology of Spirit* and Aristotle's *Metaphysics* (Books IV and IX) during 1942/3, and during the same period presented in two lectures before a smaller audience.

"Nietzsche's Word: 'God Is Dead.' " The main part of this was repeated several times before small audiences in 1943. The contents are based on the Nietzsche lectures delivered over five semesters between 1936 and 1940 at the University of Freiburg. They undertake the task of grasping Nietzsche's thought as the completion of Western metaphysics from out of the history of being. The passages quoted from Nietzsche's works follow the large octavo edition.

"Why Poets?" The lecture was delivered to a small audience to commemorate the twentieth anniversary of the death of R. M. Rilke (he died on December 29, 1926). On the question of the text see the work of Ernst Zinn in *Euphorion*, new series, 37 (1936), pp. 125ff.

"Anaximander's Saying." The piece is taken from an essay written in 1946. For textual criticism see, too, Franz Dirlmeier, "The Statement of Anaximander of Miletus," *Rheinisches Museum für Philologie*, new series, 87 (1938), pp. 376–82. I agree with the delimitation of Anaximander's text, though not with the basis on which it is done.

In the meantime, the essays have been revised several times and, in places, clarified. Their structure and respective levels of reflection have been preserved and with them, the differing uses of language.

Editor's epilogue to the seventh edition of Holzwege

I

For the sixth edition (1980) of *Holzwege*, the improved text from the *Collected Works* (volume V) was used for the first time; however, it dropped the marginalia which Heidegger wrote in his own copies of the text and which were printed in the *Collected Works* as footnotes. The seventh edition presented here now also includes these marginalia; thus in all subsequent printings, this edition will be identical in respect to both word and page number with volume V of the *Collected Works*.

Since the sixth edition, the text of the essay "The Origin of the Artwork" is the version which Heidegger revised for its separate publication in Reclam's *Universal-Bibliothek* in 1960. In comparison with the version printed previously in *Holzwege*, various passages have been lightly reworked, it has been more extensively divided into paragraphs, and it has been enlarged through the addition of an appendix written in 1956.

This edition takes its text from the new edition of *Holzwege* in the *Collected Works* and therefore also incorporates a few stylistic and clarifying corrections marked by Heidegger in his own copies of the work. Since they are concerned merely with polishing the style, their character is distinct from that of the marginal comments *about* particular passages. Even the way that Heidegger made use of proof correction marks to distinguish them makes them stand in contrast to the marginal comments. According to Heidegger's instructions, such corrections in the text are not to be explicitly indicated.

For the publication of *Holzwege* in the *Collected Works* a few obvious errors by Heidegger in spelling and punctuation were silently corrected.

II

The printing of the marginalia from Heidegger's own copies requires a few explanations. The small superscript letters introduced in the text refer to the marginalia reproduced in the footnotes. In Heidegger's copies, we find marginal comments either on the margins of the pages or, if it is a copy with blank pages inserted for corrections, also on the pages designed for that purpose. The words in the text to which the editor assigned a small superscript letter were chosen in accordance with the reference marks the author himself set down or, when these were lacking, from the sense of the context.

There is a working copy of the first edition of *Holzwege* (1950). "Messkirch working copy" is written in handwriting on the endpaper. For the essay "The Origin of the Artwork," there is in addition a separate copy from the third edition of *Holzwege* (1957) and two copies of its special publication in Reclam's *Universal-Bibliothek* (1960), of which the one most used had been printed with blank pages interleaved within the text. From that copy the greatest number of marginal comments have been taken. Martin Heidegger had specifically emphasized their importance to the editor.

The compilation of the marginalia was prepared by the editor in accordance with the guidelines given by the author. These obligated him to make a selection of the handwritten remarks that was as concise as possible, aiming only at the essential. Moreover, despite their brevity they had to be clear to readers. A marginal comment is essential and communicable to a reader when it has the character of a substantive note on a passage that is suited to advance the reader's comprehension. In this sense, there are three respects in which marginal notes are essential: first, they can be a clarification of a passage that remains on the same level of reflection as the passage; second, we encounter self-critical remarks that belong to a level of reflection that has altered; third, we meet with entries in which the substantial relation between a key word from a later period and an earlier thought is indicated.

The character of the marginalia and the circumstances in which they were composed prevent the marginal comments from being dated securely and unambiguously. With few exceptions, they were not developed as, for example, appendices or self-contained short texts; rather, they often emerged only as isolated bits in the course of repeated readings and consultations. In most cases it is a matter of chance fragments of thought that were recorded hastily. It is obvious that such notes in the course of reading and re-reading cannot be dated like texts which an author has prepared.

The dates of the editions used as working copies, given in the footnotes before each marginal comment, provide an aid for orienting oneself toward a rough dating. The marginalia selected from the Messkirch copy were written between 1950 and 1976. The marginal comments to the essay "The

Origin of the Artwork" derived from both working copies of the Reclam edition, were composed in the period between 1960 and 1976.

However, there is no point in dating the marginalia if we are occupied with it for its own sake and not, rather, in the interest of thoughtfully mapping out the different stations that Martin Heidegger occupied along the path of this thinking. Those who have read Heidegger's works carefully and repeatedly will know themselves to be in a position to relate the marginal comments, on the basis of their intellectual content and style, to an earlier or later stage of Heidegger's path.

Because the marginalia were written as notes in the course of reading over a long period of time, beginning with the year of publication of each edition that was used as a working copy and often continuing through later editions, they must not be taken as a whole to constitute the author's final word on his writings. This is especially true with the remarks that belong to a level of reflection of a stage that has already been traversed. However, to say this is not to foster the opinion that only the marginalia from the philosopher's last stage are of interest, as though he abandoned the ones that had led the way. He did not seek out a new stage because the previous one proved to be false, but rather because the same matter for thinking revealed itself to him in a way that had been transformed. Each one of these way stations gives proof of its truth in the fact that it granted a questioning step in asking a question of being. Just as we may not renounce the writing from an earlier stage, so too the marginal comments that stem from an earlier level of reflection retain their own weight.

F.-W. v. Herrmann
Freiburg, September 1, 1994

Glossary

anwesen	to presence, to come to presence, to be present
das Anwesende	that which presences, that which is present
bergen	to shelter, to conceal, to bring to safety
der Bezug	attraction, attractive relation, relation
die Bildung	formation of consciousness
das Ereignis	the Event
die Eröffnung	opening up, disclosing
gewöhnlich	ordinary, familiar, habitual
heil	integral, whole
heimisch	at home, homely
Herrschaft	rule, mastery
die Kehre	reversal, turning
kehren	reverse, turn
die Lichtung	clearing, illumination, lighting
der Riss	design, rift
das Seiende	beings, the being, that which is
das Seiende im Ganzen	beings in their entirety, beings as a whole, beings as a totality
die Stätte	site, place
ungeheuer	extraordinary, awesome
die Unverborgenheit	unhiddenness, unconcealment
die Wende	turning, turning point

wesen	to presence, to come to presence, to essence, to be in an essential way, to be essentially
das Wesen	essence, nature, creature
die Wirklichkeit	reality, actuality, effective reality
das Zeugsein	equipmentality, equipmental being
der Zug	draft, pull, tugging, traction